Proceedings

Eighth Data Communications Symposium

Sea Crest Lodge
North Falmouth, MA
October 3–6, 1983

Association for Computing Machinery Special Interest Group on Data Communications (SIGCOMM)

IEEE Computer Society Technical Committee on Computer Communications

IEEE Communications Society Tech. Committees on Data Communication Systems, Computer Communications

1884 · 1984 A CENTURY OF ELECTRICAL PROGRESS THE INSTITUTE OF ELECTRICAL AND ELECTRONICS ENGINEERS, INC.

IEEE COMPUTER SOCIETY PRESS

ACM ORDER NO. 533831
IEEE CATALOG NO. 83CH1925-7
LIBRARY OF CONGRESS NO. 83-81667
IEEE COMPUTER SOCIETY CATALOG NO. 494
ISBN 0-89791-113-X

Prepaid Price
Members $18.75
Nonmembers $37.50

Library of Congress Number 83-81667

ISBN 0-89791-113-X

Additional copies may be ordered from:

ACM Order Department
P.O. Box 64145, Baltimore, MD 21264
ACM Order No. 533831

IEEE Computer Society
P.O. Box 80452
Worldway Postal Center
Los Angeles, CA 90080
Computer Society Order No. 494

IEEE Service Center
445 Hoes Lane, Piscataway, NJ 08865
IEEE Catalog No. 83CH1925-7

acm Association for Computing Machinery

Message from the General Chair

The Eighth Data Communications Symposium continues the tradition of the previous symposia in both form and function. Our history has been that of technical excellence, and our program, put together by William Lidinsky, has again proven to be of the highest caliber. The attraction of top researchers to the conference has always been the symposium's key to success, and again this year the symposium has provided a forum for top researchers to present their results.

The selection of Cape Cod for our location was made to ensure that the symposium was held in a location that would provide ready access from major metropolitan areas to pleasant surroundings which would enhance the interpersonal relationships that are so important to our symposium.

The emphasis on state-of-the-art results to be presented as papers, combined with informal "birds-of-a-feather" sessions should provide the attendees with a balanced program. The emphasis on timely issues is the key to this year's technical program.

To undertake a symposium the size of the Data Communications Symposium is an incredible amount of work. Each of the committee members made an outstanding effort to insure the success of this year's symposium. Without the continuing support of the sponsoring societies, the symposium could not be held and for this support the committee owes a debt of gratitude. Two committee members, Helen Wood and William Lidinsky, deserve a special thank you for their tremendous efforts in organizing the symposium and its program. When all is said and done, it is the general committee, the speakers and panelists, the session chairpeople, and program committee that make a symposium successful, and I personally wish to thank all of the people who so ably assisted in the preparation of this symposium.

Speaking for all of the volunteers, we wish to take this opportunity to welcome you to the Symposium and we hope that you find the symposium a rewarding experience.

Kenneth J. Thurber

Message from the Program Chair

It has been 16 years since the first of these symposia ushered in data communication as a distinct field of technological activity. In the intervening time the field has matured but interest has not waned. In fact the opposite is true. Advancements in microelectronics and the proliferation of computers and intelligent devices have fueled the need for the transportation of data. This is evidenced by the fact that today a variety of computer communication conferences dot the technological landscape. Further evidence lies in the fact that this symposium like its predecessor experienced a response to the call for papers of well over 100 submissions. Unfortunately the symposium program has space for less than one-third of these and as a result many excellent papers could not be accepted.

This symposium has retained its character as a meeting of practitioners in the field. Sequential non-parallel sessions have been arranged with ample time and facilities available for ad hoc "birds-of-a-feather" meetings. The goal is to foster intensive and in-depth interaction.

This year's symposium is characterized by a mixture of implementation and application issues. There are six implementation sessions: one session on internetworking; one session on exception handling, identification, and OSI/RM implementation; two sessions in protocols covering design, analysis, performance and optimization; one session on network reliability; and one session on interfaces and protocols. Three application oriented sessions include topics on integrated data and video. Multimedia capabilities founded upon intergraded services have become an increasingly important topic. Also included this year for the first time are three scheduled workshop sessions covering topics in network security, multimedia computer mail, and comparisons between bus LANs and digital PBXs. These workshop sessions consist of very short position papers by the scheduled presenters followed by extemporaneous discussion and presentation by members of the audience.

Three tutorials are being presented as part of the program. These are Practical Considerations in Network Protocols by David Clark of MIT, Description of Integrated Services Digital Networks by Warren Gifford of Bell Laboratories, and Local Network Operating Systems by Bill Wood, Don Thompson, and Laurie Rogers of Burroughs. This excellent tutorial program was organized by Bart Struck.

My sincere thanks go to the reviewers, the session chairs, and the program committee for their efforts in bringing together what I feel is a superb program. In addition I owe a debt of gratitude to Joan Maroscia who helped organize the program and who handled so many of the details necessary to making this symposium a success.

William P. Lidinsky

Conference Committee

General Chairman

Kenneth J. Thurber
Architecture Technology Corporation
P.O. Box 24344
Edina, MN 55424
(612) 935-2035

Vice Chairman

Helen M. Wood
National Bureau of Standards
Building 225/Room A255
Washington, D.C. 20234
(301) 921-3553

Program Chairman

William Lidinski
Bell Telephone Laboratories
Naperville-Wheaton Road
Naperville, IL 60566
(312) 979-6246

Treasurer

Alan K. Nunokawa
Hawaiian Telephone Company
P.O. Box 2200
Honolulu, HI 96841
(808) 546-7890

Registration

Andres C. Salazar
Bell Laboratories, Room 4F535
Crawfords Corner Road
Holmdel, NJ 07733
(201) 949-5504

Publicity Committee

George Kraft
Department of Electrical Engineering
Illinois Institute of Technology
Chicago, IL 60616
(312) 567-3238

Ronald A. Frank
Joe English Road
Mount Vernon, NH 03057
(603) 673-8431

Local Arrangements Committee

Dave Oran
Digital Equipment Corporation
1925 Andover Street
Tewksbury, MA 01876
(617) 851-5071 x2861

Steering Committee

Mischa Schwartz
Department of Electrical Engineering
Columbia University
New York, NY 10027
(212) 280-3125 or 3104

Wushow Chou
Computer Studies Program
N.C. State University
Raleigh, NC 27650
(919) 737-2654

Liaison

ACM SIGCOMM Liaison

David Wood
MITRE Corporation
1820 Dolly Madison Blvd.—MS W430
McLean, VA 22102
(703) 827-6394

IEEE Computer Society

J. Scott Haugdahl
Architecture Technology Corp.
P.O. Box 24344
Minneapolis, MN 55424
(612) 941-2952

IEEE Communications Society

Dr. N.H. Le
Bell Northern Research—Dept. 3G83
P.O. Box 3511, Station C
Ottawa, Canada K14 4H7
(613) 727-6571

Robert R. Boorstyn
Polytechnic Institute of New York
333 Jay Street
Brooklyn, NY 11201
(212) 643-4485

Program Committee

Casteret Cheung
Satellite Business Systems
8283 Greenboro Drive
McLean, VA 22101
(703) 442-6189

Dr. Phillip Enslow
School of Information & Computer Science
Georgia Institute of Technology
Atlanta, GA 30332
(404) 894-3187

Frank Ferrante
Mail Stop W438
Washington C^3I Operation
MITRE Corporation
1820 Dolly Madison Blvd.
McLean, VA 22102
(703) 827-7077

Dr. James Field
Dept. of Electrical Engineering
University of Waterloo CCNG
Waterloo, Ontario N2L 3G1
(519) 885-3127

Bill Lidinsky
6H-541
Bell Laboratories
Naperville-Wheaton Road
Naperville, IL 60566
(312) 979-6246

Bart Stuck
2D-228
Bell Laboratories
600 Mountain Avenue
Murray Hill, NJ 07974
(201) 582-6954

Joan Maroscia
6B-330
Bell Laboratories
Naperville-Wheaton Road
Naperville, IL 60566
(312) 979-6817

Referees

William Bartels
David Biran
Bernard Bleazard
Flaminio Borgonovo
Robert T. Braden
J. B. Brenner
Edward Burke
Edward Cain
Tony Carlson
William L. Cook
Ronald D. Coop
Michael Corrigan
David Crocker
Andre Danthaine
John Day
Raymond Feldman
Michael Ferguson
James Field
Leonard Fishler
G. David Forney
Paul J. Fox
Alexander Fraser
Luigi Fratta
R. G. Gallager
Nicolas Georganas
William D. Glenn
James Gray
Paul Green
John G. Gruber
Harvey Hershkowitz
John B. Holmblad
Ron Horn
Ingemar Ingermarsson
Stephen T. Kent
Ian Kerr
Peter T. Kirstein
George Kraft
Chet Lanctot
Michael Ming-Tsan Liu
James J. Mansell
J. F. Mollenauer
Warren Montgomery
Louis S. Nidus
Donald L. Nielson
Christos Nikolaou
A. A. Nilsson
Raj N. Pandya
Jon Postel
Wyn Price
Gaylord Richards
Paul Santos
Mischa Schwartz
B. M. Segal
Adrian Segall
Robert F. Steen
Carl Sunshine
Virgil W. Wallentine
David C. Wood
Herbert Zimmerman

Table of Contents

Interfaces and Protocol (Chair, N. Tobol)

Internetworking

Chairman

R. Perlman

INTERNETTING BETWEEN VAX AND APOLLO RING NETWORK

by N. N. Y. Chu

Bell Telephone Laboratories, Incorporated
Naperville-Wheaton Road
Naperville, Illinois 60566

Abstract

Specifications for a network design to connect the Apollo DOMAIN network with the VAX system are discussed in this paper. Three networking approaches were considered which represent three distinct chronological stages in the evolution of computer communications. Based on a comparison of data transfer rate and the installation cost among these three alternatives, the LAN, represented by the Ethernet, was recommended as the connecting hardware.

The OSI Reference Model was used as a starting basis to discuss protocol issues to be built for the chosen LAN. Of particular interest are the transport, presentation, and application layers. The transport layer was designed to perform functions of the network and session layers in the OSI model. The presentation layer incorporated a text mapping algorithm to convert incompatible characters in filenames created on the VAX versus those on the Apollo. The application layer was designed with the capability to send and receive files between these two systems.

1. Introduction

This paper discusses the first step in developing a Distributed Software Development Environment (DSDE). The motivation for a DSDE is based on the assumption that if the computer were near the programmer, the user could expect rapid system responses to on-going software tasks. The essence of a DSDE is the synergistic integration of tools on hardware of the 1990's to provide strong and close support for future software development.

The first step was to provide a distributed network where fast responsive support could be given to programmers having intelligent work stations[1]. Via the network, the intelligent work stations would distribute the computation power directly to the programmer's desk.

The experiment was geared towards problems associated with programming in-the-large. It was necessary to have a convenient way of pursuing through long listings of program files in this environment. Thus, building an on-line listing capability was proposed as the first step to examine the problems. This paper addresses a network design experiment for the on-line listing and file transfer.

In order to carry out this experiment, Apollo intelligent work stations were used in the test-bed because they provided high-resolution and high-bandwidth displays, and overlaying windows manipulated by keyboard inputs or a touch pad. The prototype consists of the following configuration (see Figure 1):

1. A VAX 11/780 that has 300 megabytes total disk space. A postulated source listing file would need to be processed and expanded into a 300-megabyte object code.

2. The expanded object code has to be transported to three Apollo computers, forming a ring called a DOMAIN network, which is located half a mile away. Each Appollo has a 156-megabyte Winchester disk.

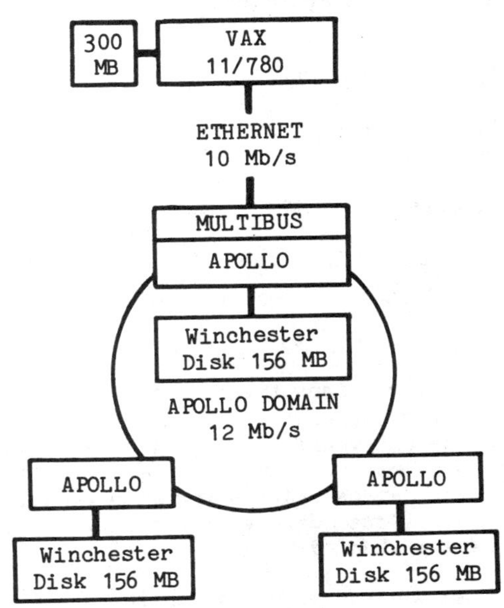

Figure 1. VAX - Apollo Network

The experiment required that the VAX and the Apollo be interconnected. Filename characteristics of the VAX and the Apollo were different. The VAX distinguished upper and lower cases in filenames. Each name contained up to 14 characters. Characters such as "\", "~" are allowed in composing a filename, but not "$".

The Apollo naming convention was quite different and often just the opposite. Upper and lower case letters were treated the same. Character "$" would be allowed, but "\" and "~" would not be allowed. Maximum 32 characters were allowed in a filename.

The hardware of this network needed to be identified, and a design of layering protocol for communications was proposed for implementation.

2. Networking Issues

In this section, the hardware of this network is identified.

When connecting the VAX and the Appollo systems, three areas needed to be considered to allow applications such as file transfer capabilities on the network:

1. Communications Network - Among many available networking options, which one should be selected and why?

2. Protocol - Higher layer protocols must be provided to coordinate sending and receiving files between the systems.

3. Mapping - A mapping algorithm should be implemented to do text conversion. How does the mapping function work and what would cause mapping algorithms to be incorrect?

These issues are discussed separately in sections below.

2.1 Communications Network

Three internetting approaches were considered:

1. a manual operation,

2. extremely high-speed electronic connections, and

3. LAN.

These mechanisms typify three distinct stages in the evolution of computer communications in recent years. Except for the first approach, a commercially available product was chosen as a representative for each of these approaches. Consequently, the following hardware media were evaluated:

1. transporting by tapes for the manual operation,

2. NSC Hyperchannel for the extremely high-speed electronic communication, and

3. Ethernet[2] for the LAN.

The transmission data rate and the installation cost of each option were examined since these two factors were considered the most dominant in decision making. A few assumptions were made to simplify the comparison. First, all hardware media were assumed to perform at about the same error rate. Second, the protocol overhead was treated as needing a similar amount of processing in all cases. Therefore, the time of transferring 300 megabyte files under each approach was based on the hardware transmission speed across the bridging network involved. A summary of the results is listed in Table I.

Table I: Comparison of Networking Hardware

	NSC Hyperchannel	Tapes	Ethernet
Data Rate	50 Mb/s	4 Mb/s	10 Mb/s per 150 MB tape
Time to Transfer 300 MB	48 sec.	10 min.	4 min.
Manual Transportation	-	15 min. + shuttle delay	-
Total Cost (1+2+3 below)	$55K per 4 connections	>$16K	$8K
1. Basic Hardware	$50K per 4 connections	$16K	$2K
2. Interface Cost	$5K	-	$6K
3. Manual Delivery	-	?	-

2.1.1 Transporting Tapes

The first hardware option was a primitive approach using the conventional tapes with manual delivery between locations.

Time: In this case, the data transfer rate becomes a composite of the disk-to-tape transfer rate and the manual delivery rate. For a 300-megabyte file, it was estimated to take 25 minutes to copy from the disk to the tape, plus the interlocation transportation time for a person to deliver the tapes.

Cost: From the cost viewpoint, adding an Apollo tape drive would require $16,000. Furthermore, tape administration and handling would introduce additional complex costs to this process. As a result, the traditional way of using tapes did not seem attractive.

2.1.2 NSC Hyperchannel The NSC Hyperchannel represents one of the extremely high-speed communication mechanisms.

Time: The NSC offers a 50-Mb/s data transmission rate over a short distance (normally much less than a half mile). The 300 megabyte files can be transferred in 48 seconds. However, the feasibility of using the NSC to connect computers located a half mile apart while maintaining the same high data throughput remains to be seen. The Hyperchannel is sold in groups only, each group provides four connections regardless of whether they are in full use. The extra connections would allow all three Apollos to directly tie in with the VAX. With a properly-managed simultaneous file transfer, it is conceivable that three consecutive parts of the 300 megabyte files could be shipped in parallel to the DOMAIN in approximately one-third of the time quoted above, namely 16 seconds. Obviously this estimate represents an optimistic situation since the Winchester disk imposes an access bottleneck, and the DOMAIN network operates at 12 Mb/s. These aspects require further investigation.

Cost: The Hyperchannel is quite expensive due to its military grade. A cost of $55,000 was estimated for four connections, including a Hyperchannel box, and the Apollo and VAX interfaces.

2.1.3 LAN The last option was a LAN. The Ethernet was chosen as an example for evaluation because of its well published specifications.

Time: The Ethernet would provide a 10-Mb/s data transfer rate which would take 4 minutes to transfer 300 megabytes.

Cost: The Ethernet would be relatively economical to implement. The cost was estimated at $8,000.

2.2 Conclusion of Hardware Choice

A tradeoff between the cost and the file transfer speed based on the above analysis led to the recommendation of the Ethernet for interconnecting the VAX and Apollos. A proposed network topology is shown in Figure 1. The Ethernet would provide the physical layer and the data link layer protocol for communications from the VAX to the gateway Apollo. The storage of 300 megabyte files across the DOMAIN network would be controlled by the gateway Apollo. This design reflects an interesting environment where a token passing ring network, the DOMAIN, connects to the Ethernet, a baseband contention bus network. Further study is suggested for detailed internetting scenarios.

3. Protocol

In this section, a high-level design of layering protocol for communications is proposed for implementation.

The International Organization of Standardization (IOS) has proposed the Open System Interconnection (OSI) Reference Model for computer communications[3]. The protocol design addressed by this paper started with the seven layers of the OSI Reference Model. It was assumed that the Ethernet handles the physical and link layer protocols.

Since the file transfer function was to be point-to-point (from the VAX to the Apollo, or vice versa), the network layer did not need to implement the routing function. This left congestion control as the major function to be resolved by the network layer. The probability of creating a congestion condition within the simple configuration of the prototype was viewed as very small. It was suggested that a point-to-point flow control could be incorporated into the transport layer. Furthermore, the transport layer would also handle the Ethernet interface and frame retransmission. In essence, the transport layer merged functions that would normally be performed by the network layer. Because of this merging, the network layer became a null layer. The packet overhead imposed by the network layer was therefore eliminated. This expansion of the transport layer greatly simplified our design.

The session layer is normally responsible for session address assignment, authenticity checking, and guaranty of file integrity in the case of a broken transport connection. Because the prototype consisted of a dedicated point-to-point connection between the VAX and the gateway Apollo, the session addresses would always be known. Also, the transport address would be the same as the session address. Authenticity checking in this friendly, simple prototype environment was not viewed as essential. In this experiment, the only session that would be established was related to the file transfer. File integrity with respect to the file transfer application was assumed to be taken care of by the transport layer. All that was wanted in this design was a raw communication service, thus the session and transport layers were merged into a single layer. Like the network layer discussed above, the session layer was absent or null.

The presentation layer, as defined by the OSI Reference Model, would process text conversion of filenames. Since the conversion only needed to be done in one machine, the VAX was chosen because it had excessive processing memory. After the presentation layer converted filenames into recognizable forms, the application layer would interface with the user to execute the file transfer function.

The communicating process for our prototype was revised from the OSI 7-layer model to a 5-layer model consisting of the Ethernet physical and link layers, and the transport, the presentation, and the application layers. Detailed design for the transport, presentation, and application layers is described in the sections below.

3.1 Transport Layer Protocol

The transport layer became the focal point of the design since it literally carried out functions designated for three layers of the OSI Reference Model. After close examination, transport functions were grouped into two major responsibilities:

1. interfacing to the Ethernet from both the VAX and the Appollo and

2. handling frame retransmission for error recovery.

Tables II and III summarize design details of the interface and the retransmission characteristics. These responsibilities were translated into a Transmit Frame and a Receive Frame function.

Table II: Ethernet Interface and Frame Retransmission

Interface to Ethernet: both VAX and Apollo

1. Transmit Frame function
   Transmit status
   a. transmitOK
   b. excessive Collision Error

2. Receive Frame function
   Receive status
   a. receiveOK
   b. frame Check Error
   c. Alignment Error

Table III: Error Retransmission Strategy

On transmit:
  For excessive Collision Error
  -> resend frame

On receive:
  For frame Check Error or
  Alignment Error
  -> send resend request

3.1.1 Transmit Frame Function The status of:

1. transmitOK and

2. excessive Collision Error would be detected and reported.

The first acknowledgment dealt with intact packets, while the second status would control buffer spaces on each machine. The second status was also reserved for later growth of the prototype where an Ethernet contention environment might arise and press for a contention resolution.

3.1.2 Receive Frame Function The status of:

1. receiveOK,

2. frame Check Error, and

3. Alignment Error would be detected and reported.

These status further strengthened the transport layer in recovering losses due to data link errors or a session breakage.

3.1.3 Retransmission The frame retransmission strategy could have been determined by an excessive Collision Error status within the Transmit Frame function. However, it was likely that retransmission would occur during the execution of the Receive Frame function rather than that of the Transmit Frame. Therefore, retransmission would take place when the frame status of Check Error or Alignment Error were detected in the Receive Frame function. The retransmission procedure would be carried out by a resend request to the transmitting machine.

The above protocol design of the transport layer was believed to be adequate for the prototype although specifics of the interface for the transport layer with the Ethernet layer remain to be investigated.

3.2 Presentation Layer Mapping

The presentation layer would perform text conversion for the two machines. In the LAN plan, only the filenames would need to be converted since the file content would have been processed into machine independent object code. An algorithm was designed to map VAX 11/780 filenames to Apollo filenames as shown in Table IV.

Basically, on the VAX, every lower case letter would be doubled for the Apollo; every capital letter would be converted to its lower case preceded by a "$". For example, "a" would be converted to "aa", "B" would be converted to "$b", etc. The special characters "\" and "~", would be converted to "a$" and "b$", respectively, for the Apollo. This mapping represented one of the possible conversion algorithms and when it was checked out, it did not have any conflicts. Table IV summarizes this algorithm.

Table IV: Mapping Algorithm
(Implemented in the Presentation Layer)

Note: Mapping is for filenames only.

VAX 11/780		Apollo
a	->	aa
b	->	bb
.		.
.		.
.		.
z	->	zz
A	->	$a
B	->	$b
.		.
.		.
.		.
Z	->	$z
\	->	a$
~	->	b$

Table V: Incorrect Algorithm

Mapping:

VAX 11/780		Apollo
a	->	a
b	->	b
.		.
.		.
.		.
A	->	$a
B	->	$b
\	->	$$
~	->	a$

Confusion caused when:

a\a	->	a$$a
~A	->	a$$a

An incorrect mapping algorithm was also identified to demonstrate possible confusion and to indicate the need of choosing double characters for the text conversion. This incorrect algorithm would keep lower case letters the same and convert capital letters to their corresponding lower case preceded by a special character, e.g., "$". Special characters "\" and "~" would be mapped into "$$" and "a$", respectively. If this algorithm is used, a filename on the VAX containing "a\a" would appear the same as that containing "~A", since both would appear as "a$$a" on the Apollo after the conversion. Thus, confusion would arise whenever two names were searched on the VAX where one consisted of two identical lower case letters separated by a "\" and the other consisted of "~" followed by the matching capital letter. Table V summarizes the incorrect algorithm.

3.3 Application Layer Function

The file transfer function proposed for the application layer would provide 2-way communications from the VAX to the Apollo for the file sending function and from the Apollo to the VAX for the file receiving function. Capabilities for the sending and receiving functions were symmetric between VAX and Apollo. The request command would specify the filename and block space needed. Positive and negative acknowledgments would be issued and error conditions would be flagged for the user. Handshaking between the two machines would be done twice to assure a valid file transfer request and to set up the machines in a ready state for either a sending or a receiving mode. If the environment became hostile, capabilities of authenticity checking and file protection could be easily added for the application layer. With the present design, files would be transmitted one Ethernet frame at a time until the end-of-file character was received. Tables VI and VII detail these functions.

Table VI: File Transfer
Function

File Send From VAX to Apollo

VAX ----->	Issue file request giving: 1) Filename (VAX representation). 2) Space needed in blocks.
APOLLO -->	Issue acknowledgment: 1) ACK - good request. 2) NACK - cannot service.
VAX ----->	On receipt of acknowledgment: 1) For ACK - send file, one Ethernet frame at a time. After last frame, send end-of-file indicator. 2) For NACK - inform user.
APOLLO -->	Receiving data frames piece incoming frames into a file. On receipt of end-of-file indicator, file is complete and may be distributed in the DOMAIN Local Area Network.

Table VII: File Transfer Function

File Receive From Apollo to VAX

```
VAX -----> Issue file request:
           1) Filename
              (VAX representation).

APOLLO --> Issue acknowledgment:
           1) GOOD - Good request,
              include number of blocks.
           2) BAD  - Cannot service.

VAX -----> On receipt of acknowledgment:
           1) For GOOD - Send either:
                    ACK - Go ahead and
                          send file.
                   NACK - Do not send
                          file.
           2) For BAD  - Inform user.

APOLLO -->
           1) Receive ACK - Send file,
              one Ethernet frame at a
              time, with end-of-file
              frame at end.
           2) Receive NACK - Ignore
              request.
```

The VAX user interface was specified as shown in Table VIII. Commands "tx -r <filename>" and "tx -s <filename>" would be used for receiving and sending files, respectively. A file transfer daemon process was required to queue requests from all users and to process requests one at a time.

Table VIII

VAX User Interface

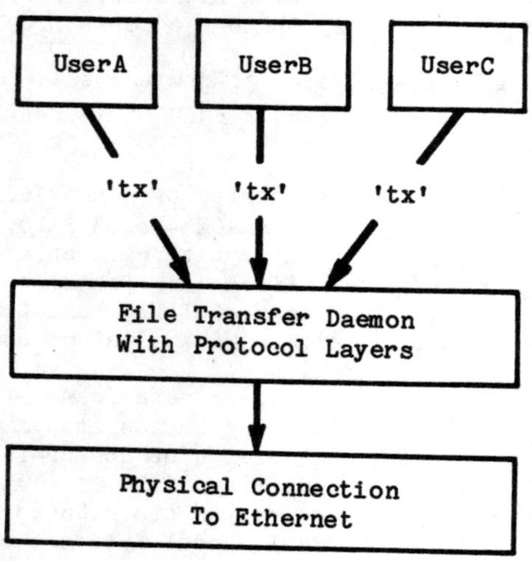

To receive file: tx -r <filename>
To send file: tx -s <filename>

4. Summary

A high-level design plan for communications between the VAX and the Apollo network was specified as having five layers: the Ethernet physical and link layers, and the transport, the presentation and the application layers. Since Ethernet interfaces could be purchased for both machines, the networking design needed only to emphasize the higher layers of protocol: the transport layer would handle the Ethernet interfaces and frame retransmission; the presentation layer would map incompatible character representations in filenames; and the application layer would execute file transfers of 300 megabytes.

5. Acknowledgment

The author appreciates the effort of Messrs. T. H. Butler, D. R. Cornwell, and D. C. Easley of Bell Laboratories who contributed numerous information on the network design which started the writing of this paper.

References

[1] Apollo Computer, Inc., 19 Alpha Road, Chemsford, Massachusetts, 01824, (617)256-6600.

[2] The Ethernet - A Local Area Network, Data Link Layer and Physical Layer Specifications, AA-K759A-TK, by DEC, Intel, and Xerox, Version 1.0, September 30, 1980.

[3] A. S. Tanenbaum, Computer Networks, Prentice-Hall Inc., Englewood Cliffs, N.J., 1981.

Local Networking and Internetworking in the V-System

David R. Cheriton

Computer Science Department
Stanford University

Abstract

Local networking can be treated as a subset of internetworking for remote terminal access and file transfer. However, a distributed operating system, such as the V-System uses a local network more as an *extended backplane* than a fast, minature long-haul network.

This paper describes the use of server-based "intelligent gateways" to provide internetworking using standard protocols in conjunction with an efficient light-weight protocol for V IPC on a local network. Besides providing good local network performance, this design allows a gateway to act as an access control mechanism, addressing some reliability and security issues that arise with local networks.

Introduction

A local network can be viewed as an *extended backplane* when it interconnects a *cluster* of the workstations and server machines managed by a distributed operating system. The cluster operates as a multi-user system with the distributed operating system providing services analogous to a conventional multi-user machine and operating system.

The V-System[1](pronounced "Vee") is a distributed operating system developed at Stanford that uses Ethernet[2] as such an extended backplane to connect a collection of diskless SUN workstations[3] and server machines. A distributed kernel provides uniform, transparent message-based interprocess communication on a single workstation and between processes on different workstations. Dedicated server processes, often running on dedicated server machines, provide file access, printing, internetwork access and other services. Application processes access system services using *stub* routines that format, send and receive messages to interact with the required servers.

We have developed a specialized *light-weight local network protocol* for interkernel communication between different workstations. We developed this protocol rather than using an existing protocol for two reasons. As part of our research, we are investigating specialized protocols to improve network IPC performance, which has been a major problem with previous attempts to realize the basic system design of V. (The V design is similar to many message-based and distributed operating systems.) Also, there is no established standard interprocess communication protocol that suits the V interprocess communication. Nevertheless, we have a strong need and desire to support and use standard internetwork protocols, in particular, being part of the ARPA Internet community, the IP/TCP family of protocols.

Normally, use of internetwork protocols on a local network is not a problem. Most local networks are used for *Remote Terminal Access and File Transfer (RTA/FT)*, similar to long-haul networks. For RTA/FT users accustomed to long-haul network performance, local network performance is more than adequate even though internetwork protocols may impose a significant overhead and end-to-end data rates may not be comparable to the underlying local network speed.

However, our use of a local network as an extended backplane means that local network performance must be compared to intra-machine communication performance, not long-haul network performance. Using this comparison, we argue that using internetwork protocols on a local network for IPC communication leads to minimal benefits and significant costs.

This paper describes the use of server-based "intelligent gateways" to provide internetworking using standard protocols in conjunction with an efficient light-weight protocol for V IPC on a local network. Besides providing good local network performance, this design allows the gateways to efficiently implement access control mechanisms, addressing reliability and security issues that arise with local networks.

The next section describes local networks, particularly the problems they pose for computer communication. The following section explores the issues in using internetwork protocols, in particular ARPA Internet protocols, as a basis for local network IPC. We then describe the V-System interprocess communication and its performance on a local network. Subsequent sections describe our internetworking techniques.

Local Networks

By *local network*, we mean a multi-megabit, low delay, low error rate communication facility connecting up to a few hundred computer nodes over a few kilometers at relatively low cost. The Cambridge ring[4], MIT ring[5] and Xerox Ethernet[2] are a few examples.

The advantages of local networks need no repeating here. Suffice it to say that they provide sufficiently high bit transfer rates between nodes to makes peripheral sharing (e.g. disk storage) and truly distributed computation practical. There are, however, several problems to solve before realizing this potential.

Efficiency

It is difficult to achieve data transfer rates anywhere close to the bit transfer rate of most local networks with current protocols and interfaces. For instance, the maximum data transfer rate of a Telnet connection between two VAX/UNIX systems over the 3 megabit Ethernet at Stanford is about 56000 bits per second, about 2 percent of the raw network speed.

This work was sponsored in part by the Defense Advanced Research Projects Agency under contracts MDA903-80-C-0102 and N00039-83-K-0431.

In measurements of data transfer time between two SUN workstations[3], Motorola 68000-based workstations running at 8-10 MHz, using no protocol[1], the time to transfer 512 bytes between 8-MHz workstations connected by 3 megabit Ethernet is 3.65 milliseconds, almost three times the 1.39 milliseconds expected from the bit transfer rate of the network. Performance is worse relative to physical bit rate using a faster network (such as the 10 megabit Ethernet) and adding the necessary protocol processing for reliable data transport.

These measurements clearly indicate that, unlike long-haul networks where physical communication capacity is usually the critical resource, processing and interface overhead is critical in local network performance. Therefore, local network protocols should be designed to minimize processing overhead, presumably exploiting the low error rate and low delay of local networks. Similarly, network interfaces should offload the processor in some cost-effective fashion. While DMA is the obvious approach to fast network interfaces, without some type of scatter-gather capability as part of the interface the processor is generally forced to do an extra copy of each packet.

Several studies have shown that the choice of protocol and its implementation must be carefully tuned to local network characteristics to achieve performance commensurate with local network speeds. Speedups by factors of up to 30 have been reported as a result of stripping away layers, honing the protocols and tuning the implementations[6, 7]. In most cases, processor time used by a protocol is the crucial issue in performance, not the network bandwidth. This is certainly the case with the V interkernel protocol[1].

Reliability

The speed of a local network presents a reliability problem for all connected machines because one machine can flood one or more others with packets faster than the packets can be discarded. For instance, a workstation that fails in a tight loop sending erroneous packets to a network file server can easily generate packets faster than the file server can discard them. This will dramatically degrade, if not disable, the file server for properly behaved clients.

Another similar failure is what might be called *broadblasting*, where a node sends out broadcast packets very rapidly. If, as is typical on the Ethernet, every node receives all broadcast packets, packets are handled at the kernel interrupt level, and broadcast packets are generated faster than they can be processed, every machine on the network is effectively disabled.

Over the past 2 years, the author has observed several such failures on the Stanford 3 megabit Ethernet which currently connects about 100 machines. These failures are notable in both the number of machines affected and the amount of difficulty in tracking down the problem, with machines in obscure locations behind locked doors. Besides total failure, we have also observed unexplained load and significant response degradation that were subsequently traced to a high level of strange network activity.

This problem is not unique to the Ethernet but could be expected on any local network not explicitly (and expensively) engineered to prevent it.

In contrast, dealing with bad packets is not such a problem in long-haul networks because of their low speed and restricted user-level access to the network. Established techniques for authentication, error checking and access control suffice to protect each host.

Security

Most local network technologies are based on a common shared channel so all host-network connections "see" all the data. When data is sent unencrypted, it is generally possible for each host to read all data that is transmitted. Encryption adds a significant overhead, not only for the actual encryption process but also for the extra communication required for distribution of encryption keys and authentication[8].

A more subtle problem arises from the use of broadcast to locate a server. An impostor can respond and play havoc with the requesting client. We have experienced this problem at Stanford, not from malicious intent, but from someone bringing up their own version of a name server which responded incorrectly. The name server ran on a lightly loaded machine, invariably responded first and effectively disabled the name service by responding incorrectly. This problem might also be considered an aspect of the reliability problem when it arises from failure as opposed to malicious intent.

Summary

These three problems can be addressed by hardware (or hardware-supported) mechanisms in every node. For instance, a large host can feasibly have a front-end communications processor to insulate it from the broadblasting and packet flooding problems. However, the V-System, as with many distributed operating systems, is designed for modest-sized workstations and server machines. In our design, the protection and security mechanism is concentrated in the gateway, thus amortizing the cost over multiple workstations. Local communication avoids extra overhead for reliability and security by relying on the gateway. Misbehavior on the local network can be detected by networking monitoring programs that take advantage of the "shared channel" structure of most networks, e.g. promiscuous mode on the Ethernet.

In the next section, we argue that internetwork protocols do not provide the best basis for solving these problems.

Internetwork Protocols

Standard internetwork protocols can be used on local networks, treating each local network as just another network in an internetwork. For example, the ARPA Internet protocols[9] provide a uniform base of internetwork packets (IP)[10] across both long-haul and local networks independent of network technology. A transport-level protocol, TCP[11] provides bi-directional byte streams for internetwork RTA/FT. When a local network is used primarily for RTA/FT, this is a simple and effective approach. For instance, the Stanford Ethernet-based campus network has run in this mode for several years using the ARPA Internet and PUP family[12] of protocols.

However, internetwork protocols do not provide a communication model well-suited to distributed systems. A distributed system requires a transport-level facility for inter-program and possibly intra-program communication that works transparently within a single machine as well as across the network between machines. Because of the predominant use of procedure call-like communication within systems (even message-based systems) the appropriate model is some form of request-response transaction-style communication, where a transaction typically consists of requesting a service and getting a response back. With appropriate language processor support, this can take the form of a transparent *remote procedure call (RPC)* as an extension of the procedure call mechanism of the programming language system, as was done for Mesa[6].

The Internet protocols present two options for implementing this communication: TCP byte streams or IP datagrams.

TCP Byte Streams

TCP, the transport-level of the Internet protocol family, provides a bi-directional byte stream. This is precisely the right choice for internetworking because it supports RTA/FT well and allows efficient implementation over long-haul networks using standard techniques like sliding window flow control and piggy-backed acknowledgements. However, for distributed system communication on local networks, byte streams provide little benefit to RPC-like communication and impose significant overhead to implement. Consider, for instance, a file write operation across the network.

In general, a network datagram can hold file parameters plus a file page or block. Using a low-level specialized protocol, a network file write consists of sending a packet containing data and parameters to the file server and receiving a reply packet back, with reliable transport implemented relying on network CRC checks and retransmissions until a valid reply packet is received. For added efficiency, the specialized protocol can rely on the idempotency of the write operation and not bother to filter out duplicate packets arising from retransmissions or to save reply packets for retransmission.

Using a byte stream, a copy of the data is made on transmission to allow for retransmission even though the process will typically wait for a reply message. Similarly, a copy is made of the reply even though the operation may have been idempotent. Furthermore, a byte stream-level acknowledge is sent for the request data in addition to the IPC-level reply that is set to provide return values for the operation. The IPC mechanism must also impose a message structure, similar to the datagram structure, on top of the byte streams, thus contributing to further overhead. Also, the IP and TCP headers add 60 bytes to every packet. Finally, the byte-stream model imposes a cost for connection setup and tear-down, which becomes significant if a separate connection is established for each message transaction and otherwise requires a sophisticated connection management mechanism.

According to our measurements, a V kernel communication mechanism implemented using TCP would be slower by more than a factor of 2 and significantly complicate and enlarge the kernel code. The slowdown is primarily due to the extra processing overhead because roughly the same number of packets are sent in both cases.

With the natural realization of request-response communication using datagrams, an alternative is to implement a specialized request-response transport-level protocol using IP, the internetwork packet protocol or UDP, the user datagram protocol, as a basis. While we do not preclude this approach in our work, (in fact there is an IP-based version of the V kernel), there are costs associated with this approach and fewer benefits than one might expect, as described below.

Internet Datagrams

Encapsulating all packets in IP packets introduces overhead to:

1. Construct and prepend the IP header along with transmitting and receiving the header.
2. Calculate the checksum(s).
3. Determine the internetwork destination address as well as the local network address of the next (and usually only) hop.

Using UDP, one may incur the additional overhead of calculating a checksum for the data portion of the packet. Note that we are only considering the case of the packet going to a destination on the same local network so fragmentation and reassembly are not an issue.

Using an IP-based version of the V kernel using no checksums and no packet routing or reassembly (i.e. only constructing and prepending the IP header), we measured a slow-down of 20 percent for 32-byte data messages (the common size used in our system). While larger messages such as those for transporting file pages incur less percentage overhead, the addition of IP and UDP checksums, internetwork routing and reassembly would increase the overhead. The significant cost in space for code and data for packet reassembly and addressing should also be considered.

Note that it is important not to overestimate the cost of general protocols. Clark[13, 14] has shown that the overhead can be minimized by careful design, choice of algorithms and optimization for the common case. Even reassembly can be done in roughly 400 instructions of code with an overhead of one or two tests in the normal case of one-fragment packets.

However, there are other costs to encapsulating local communication in IP packets. For one, broadcast and multicast IP packets present problems. We are exploring the use of multicast for efficient communication in a distributed computation. We use a publishing paradigm in which information is distributed by a *publisher* to multiple *subscribers* using multicast packets. IP does not define behavior for broadcast and multicast packets. In fact, because it is not feasible or necessarily desireable to support multicast across an internetwork, it is unclear how to define this facility without violating the transparent, uniform internetwork behavior of IP.

Using a purely local network protocol, the domain of broadcast or multicast is automatically defined to be a single local network, and the underlying hardware generally supports this facility directly. Moreover, with the local network protocol implemented directly on top of the network interface provided by the hardware, easier access is provided to the multicast filtering implemented by some network interfaces.

Our experiments with an IP-based version of the V kernel pointed out another problem with this approach. We discovered our IP gateway to the ARPAnet goes into a loop retransmitting any broadcast IP packet it sees until the hop count in the packet exceeds the maximum hop count. This gateway was developed outside of Stanford, we cannot remedy the problem ourselves, and we are told that the problem is non-trivial to fix because of the design of the gateway. The net result is that we currently cannot run our IP-based version of the kernel with the IP gateway operational. The problem results in part because IP does not define behavior for broadcast packets. While one might argue that this problem will be eliminated with a fix to the gateway, we contend that it is indicative of the type of problems that occur when internetwork mechanisms are exposed to unusual communication peculiar to local networks.

Another cost of IP encapsulation is the loss of meaning to the packet type field provided by most networks. Local network datagrams typically contain a type field specifying the type of protocol used with each datagram. If a local network protocol is so identified, an IP gateway can discard such packets at the lowest level with minimal overhead. If all communication is encapsulated in IP packets, this type field becomes meaningless and higher-level software is required to demultiplex or discard packets. This leads to a confusion of layers in the IP-based version of the V kernel where the kernel must intercept IP packets containing V interkernel packets but passes other packets, both IP and non-IP, through for access by process-level implementations of other protocols like PUP BSP and TCP.

These overheads need to be compared with the benefits of using IP encapsulation. Superficially, it would appear that IP encapsulation allows one to transparently extend the network IPC across gateways. However, several problems arise. First, IPC messages are addressed to processes, not machines, so process naming must also be extended to multiple networks. The larger and more general name space required as a consequence has a detrimental effect on intra-machine and local network IPC performance.

Second, the timeout periods and maximum retransmission

count that are tuned for local network speed, delay and error rate are unsuitable when additional delay and error is introduced by the gateway. For instance, a kernel may retransmit and timeout before a gateway has managed to transmit the first packet on a slow connected network.

Finally, we have argued earlier from a reliability and security standpoint that a gateway should act as an access control mechanism. However, it is relatively difficult to implement efficient access control in an Internet gateway because it is intended to act as a simple *packet shuffler*, performing only routing and fragmentation/reassembly. This is in fact one of the intentions behind using internetwork datagrams.

In general, IP offers uniform transparent communication across the internetwork in the form of datagrams, as a generalization of the datagrams in a single packet-switched network. Distributed computation seems best supported by a uniform, transparent communication mechanism that is an extended implementation of an intra-machine communication mechanism. The uniformity and transparency of distributed system communication cannot be extended fully to the domain of IP packets simply by encapsulating messages in IP packets. Moreover, the degree to which it does extend is difficult to define or control. In addition, IP introduces a significant performance penalty.

Considering that 95 percent of the communication is local in our system, these arguments show that local network IPC protocols are best separated from internetwork protocols. In many ways, sending local IPC in IP packets seems analogous in overhead and potential security/reliability risk to sending office memos around the office in airmail envelopes. Although our discussion has focused on the IP/TCP protocols, our conclusions appear to apply to other internetwork protocol families such as XNS and the X.25/X.75 family.

Two Fallacies

The author has been exposed to two other arguments against using local network protocols in place of internetwork protocols that are misleading if not incorrect.

Argument 1: If local networks do not use internetwork standard protocols, every local network will use a different set of protocols.

Counter Argument: There can be a standard for local networks that is distinct from internetwork standards (the latter are then used primarily between networks). Consider as an analogy the electrical power distribution system. There are standards for wide-area distribution using voltages of 50,000 Volts and up, well suited to long distance transmission. However, the local standard of 120 Volts is not forced by any link to the wide-area standard but by the economies of standardization, e.g. standard appliances with standard plugs. Gateways can act analogously to the transformers in this analogy, converting between internetwork protocols and local network protocols. Using internetwork protocols locally would be like having a 50,000 Volt service in one's house and consequently require, for instance, a 50,000 Volt toaster.

Argument 2: Protocol translation is impractical because one ends up with N protocols and N x N-1 protocol translators. Moreover, it is never possible to exactly translate from one protocol to another.

Counter Argument: This argument is true if N is large and the protocols are relatively high-level or diverse. However, only one local network transport protocol is required, as with the V-System. It is only necessary to translate between it and usually one internetwork protocol. Because the local network mechanism is used for all inter-program communication and the client-server interface uses this inter-program communication, the translation occurs as part of a client accessing the server and the server implementing the internetwork transport protocol under the control of its client interface. For example, because the local V IPC is used for inter-program communication, any program that implements (for instance) TCP automatically translates between the local IPC to TCP because the local IPC is its "user interface". Thus, there is one protocol translator for each internetwork protocol, namely the implementation of that internetwork protocol. The predominate use of internetwork communication for RTA/FT (including mail) further simplifies the problem. Finally, higher-level internetwork communication can be handled by special programs. For instance, the details of a particular virtual terminal protocol can be buried in a program implementing remote terminal access.

In general, the internetwork environment and internetwork protocols provide a very powerful communication facility. The challenge is to provide access to this without compromising the potential of local network communication. The next sections describe the approach taken in V.

V Local Network Communication

All transport-level local network communication in the V-System uses the message-based interprocess communication facility provided by the distributed V kernel. Interprocess communication is transparent with respect to the processes being on the same host or different hosts.

This facility provides an ideal base for a distributed system because it allows software above the kernel level to be designed and implemented independent of whether the clients it serves and the services it uses are local or distributed. For instance, we are using diskless personal workstations with all file access and program loading via IPC messages to network file servers. Adding a disk and local file server process to a workstation requires no changes to the workstation software other than adding a disk driver to the kernel.

In this use of a local network as an extended backplane, the vast majority of the traffic is local to the network. Consequently, V network IPC is implemented using a specialized local network protocol that takes advantage of transactional communication and the properties of local networks. The following briefly describes the IPC model provided, the protocol and its performance. For further details, the interested reader is referred to a separate in-depth study[1].

The sending and receiving processes are specified by process identifiers, structured as two 16-bit subfields: logical host and local process identifier.

logical host	local process identifier

Fig.1 Process Identifier Subfields

The logical host field is mapped to a particular network address and the local pid is mapped to a process on the machine at that network address.

The basic interprocess communication is in terms of three primitives: Send, Receive and Reply that implement a message transaction or request-response pair of messages, as shown in Fig. 2.

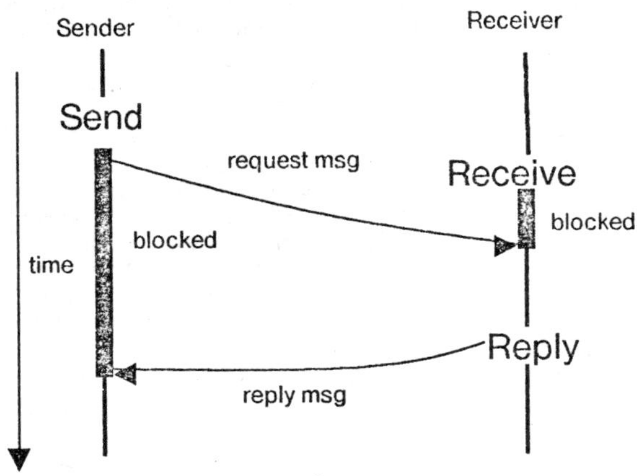

Fig. 2 Send-Receive-Reply Message Transaction

The sender sends a message to the receiver and is blocked until the message is received and it receives a reply message back. The time for a Send-Receive-Reply sequence using 32-byte messages between two processes on separate SUN workstations connected by a 3 megabit Ethernet is 2.56 milliseconds.

Messages are restricted to 32 bytes. Larger data transfers are handled by separate primitives, MoveTo and MoveFrom, which move an arbitrary number of bytes between the sender and the receiver of a message while the sender is still awaiting the reply message. Basically, the recipient of a message can use MoveFrom and MoveTo to read and write the memory space of the message sender up to the point that the reply message is sent.

Using MoveTo for program loading from a network file server into a diskless SUN workstations (assuming the program text is in the file server's memory buffers), a 64 kilobyte program can be loaded in 338 milliseconds on the 3 megabit Ethernet. This performance is within 13 percent of the speed at which a SUN workstation can write packets out to the network with no protocol overhead. It is also a factor of 5 faster than the maximum data rate we can achieve using our TCP implementation over the Ethernet.

Streams can be implemented efficiently on this IPC facility as well. For instance, with a disk delivering a 512 byte page every 15 milliseconds, a file can be read sequentially averaging 17.13 milliseconds per page. This is comparable to the performance of highly tuned special-purpose file access protocols[15]. With this performance, the V IPC facility is also entirely adequate as a transport level for remote terminal access and file transfer.

The efficiency of the interprocess communication is in part due to the use of a request-response model of communication and matching protocol. For instance, the response serves as an acknowledge to the request as well as transporting a reply message. MoveTo and MoveFrom are implemented as multiple packet versions of a request-response interchange. Buffering and flow control are made simple by the synchronous communication regime arising from request-response. Surprisingly, the request-response model still allows considerable concurrency of execution between two communicating nodes despite the synchronism of the client interface. Performance also benefits from use of a minimal network header and direct mapping from process identifier to network address.

The efficiency of the V kernel IPC is essential to the practicality of this approach, yet requires the communication be specialized to local network operation. The following sections describe how we provide internetwork communication with no penalty to local network performance.

Logical Local Networks

A *logical local network* is a collection of two or more physical local networks that logically function as one network from the standpoint of the node networking software. When multiple networks are required because some physical limitation of the networking technology has been exceeded (such as maximum number of nodes or maximum length), one can avoid changing existing networking software by organizing multiple physical networks as one logical network. This requires that the local network addressing be adequate to address all the nodes of the logical network. For instance, the 48-bit Ethernet address is (theoretically) adequate to uniquely address every Ethernet port in the world. Also, if the different physical networks use different technologies, the datalink packets must either be compatible or easily mappable from one form to another. Finally, it requires a connecting node we call a *bridge* that can receive all packets addressed to nodes on other networks and retransmit these packets on the appropriate networks transparently with respect to both the sender and receiver of the packet. Generally, a bridge receives all packets transmitted on the networks they connect but only transfers the appropriately addressed packets to a connecting network.

For example, the Stanford research network includes several Ethernets connected by bridges. The bridge is built from a SUN workstation with Ethernet ports on two or more networks receiving promiscuously. It is basically a software version of the Ethernet repeater except it does not transmit packets destined for a node on the network of origin to the other networks. We measure a 2.7 millisecond delay in transmission through the bridge for a 1024 byte packet. V kernel IPC is regularly used through one and two bridges, although with some degradation in performance. Thus, except for performance, multiple physical Ethernets appear as a single network to the networking software. In addition, "local" traffic on one physical network (except for broadcast) does not load other physical networks.

Using bridges, a single "logical" network could be quite large (into the thousands of nodes) and in fact use different network technologies (up to the limitations mentioned above). However, our experience has been that one soon encounters problems of security and reliability, not to mention addressing, packet format and packet size compatibility problems.

Although hardly a new idea, logical local networks are mentioned here to show that the use of multiple physical networks does not necessarily imply the need for internetworking in the conventional sense. In their limitations, they also point out the need for access control for large-scale networking.

V-System Internetworking

V IPC internetworking is supported by an intelligent gateway that provides local alias processes for remote processes. A *local alias process* is a (pseudo) process created by a V interkernel gateway that represents on the local network a process that executes on a machine connected to another network, which we call a *remote process*. For a process to communicate with a remote process, it must first ask the gateway to create a local alias for the remote process, and then specify this local alias process in all IPC operations. An agent in the gateway takes the necessary action to translate IPC with a local alias process into IPC with the remote process.

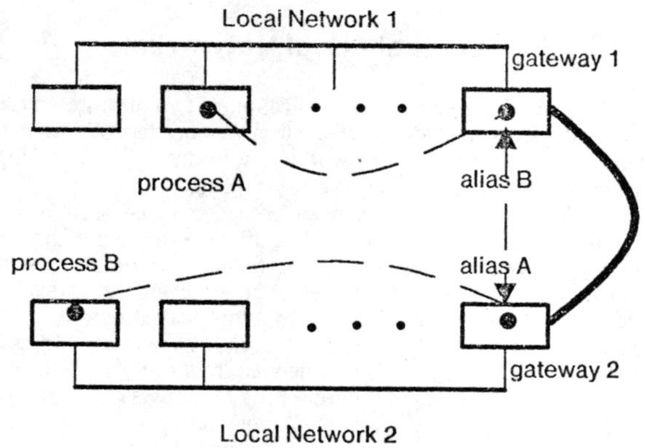

Fig. 3 Remote IPC using Alias Processes

In Fig. 3, process A sends to alias process B (transparently implemented in the local gateway) which communicates with the gateway on process B's network to cause the alias process A to send to process B. The message is sent by A just as though B is local to its network and received by B just as though A is local to its network.

A range of process identifiers are reserved for use as local alias process identifiers (the 16th bit of the process identifier is 1 for an alias process and 0 for a real process). This makes identification of alias processes easy for the kernel and for applications.

The use of local alias processes for internetworking has several advantages.

No Penalty to Local Communication

First, internetworking does not impose any cost on local network communication. Local IPC takes place just as though internetworking had not been considered at all in the design. Packets addressed to alias processes on the gateway machine are simply passed by its kernel to the interkernel gateway software instead of being processed directly by the kernel as done for the local case. This structure has the additional advantage of providing a clean split between the handling of local network communication and internetwork communication.

Internetwork Transparency

Internetwork communication is almost identical to local network communication. A process can communicate with a remote process through a local alias as though they were on the same network, and in fact as though they were on the same machine.

A flaw in transparency arises because the process identifier name space is local to a logical local network, so process identifiers cannot be passed and used transparently between networks. A process identifier on network 1 must be translated into an alias process identifier for network 2 before being passed to a process on network 2. Otherwise, the process identifier would be interpreted incorrectly on network 2. In particular, when the file server responds to an open file request specifying the server process that will handle read and write operations on the file, it must be aware of whether the process is remote and perform the translation of the process identifier to a remote alias if so.

Problems arising from this complication are reduced by several considerations. First, the primary use of this facility is for accessing a remote file server, printer server or other standard server. It is not unreasonable for such servers to be properly programmed to handle the alias translation. Second, in our experience to date, process identifiers are rarely included in messages. Third, for security, accounting and scheduling, it is often desireable for a server to know whether a process is local to the network or not. For example, a printer server may give higher priority to locally submitted print jobs, while still accepting remote submissions. Finally, testing for "remoteness" is efficient because it is indicated by a bit in the process identifier.

Access Control

Control over the creation of local alias processes allows the gateway to control access to a network because, without a local alias process, no communication is possible. Authorization can be sought from a local authentication server or from the designated receiving process. Moreover, local processes can easily identify alias processes, and thus remote processes, by examining the process identifier.

We imagine the gateway by default not allowing messages from outside the network to be sent to arbitrary local hosts. Servers designed to provide services via internetwork access explicitly authorize the gateway to provide this access. Because the required alias processes are created previous to communication occurring and may persist over the lifetime of the associated processes, access control does not impose an overhead on individual IPC operations.

In summary, the use of local alias processes allows internetwork communication to be provided with no local networking penalty, a strong degree of transparency, and a simple mechanism for controlling access to the network. The next section describes the basic gateway design that provides this capability.

Gateway Design

A V interkernel gateway connecting two V-System local networks is structured as two half gateways, with each half-gateway viewed as a protective "front door" for the network to which it is attached. This contrasts with the conventional motivation for half-gateways, namely reducing the amount of different gateway software required (although we plan to benefit from this advantage too). Half-gateways are also appealing because the administration of each network can provide and maintain its respective half. In general, while internetworks are generally drawn as networks connected by gateways, the protection, accounting, security and administration boundary runs through the gateway, as illustrated in Fig. 4.

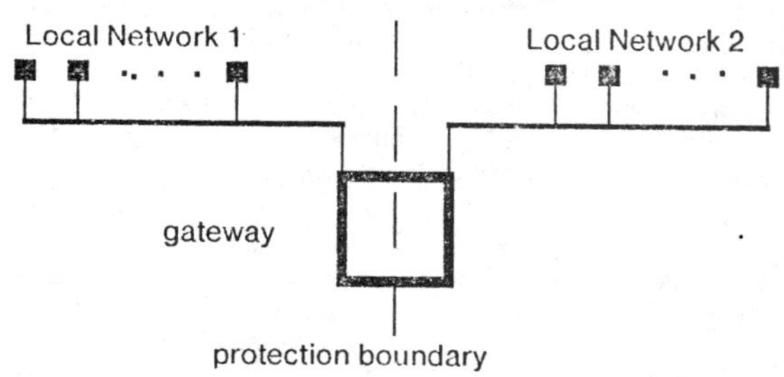

Fig. 4 Internetwork Boundary Splitting a Gateway

Each half gateway runs on a separate processor, communicating with the other half by a large shared memory buffer area, as shown in Fig. 5.

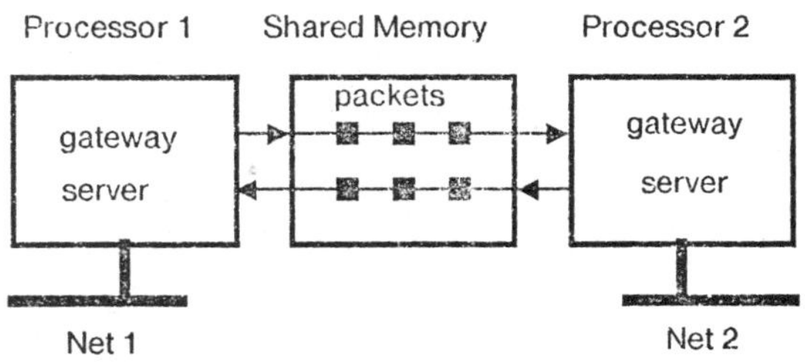

Fig. 5 Dual-Processor Gateway Structure

The use of separate processors and loosely coupled communication between them prevents either network from totally disabling the gateway by bombarding the gateway with packets. The bombarded half may be effectively disabled in handling the packets but the other half can continue to function. In particular, it can take some action in response to the packet flooding from the other half. Using separate processors also has the advantage of insulating the processor requirements of one half of the gateway from the other. Finally, each network can use extra cycles in its half-gateway processor for running additional software, an authentication and name server being one good example. In fact, because the gateway uses a standard version of the V kernel, we can run such a server on the half-gateway transparent to the gateway software, the clients of the server and the server itself.

The gateway software itself is structured very similarly to the kernel software. In fact, the current gateway software is a version of the kernel heavily modified to run as a process and to implement alias processes and the required communication with remote networks. The real kernel simply passes V interkernel packets addressed to alias processes on to the gateway software, rather than handling them itself, as it does for real local processes.

Gateways take an active role in optimizing communication with remote processes across the long-haul connections. For instance, suppose two networks are only connected by a long-haul network that uses TCP. In this case, the two half gateways implementing the alias processes are also separated by an Internet TCP connection. Because TCP provides a reliable transport connection, the retransmissions generated as part of the local IPC transport mechanism can be filtered out and "ack'ed" by the gateway, eliminating unnecessary traffic over the long-haul connection and insulating the time-out for local network operation from the delays of long-haul communication.

As a further optimization the gateway can combine IPC packets as appropriate to make the optimum use of the TCP connection when IPC packet boundaries are not significant. For instance, a MoveTo data transfer consisting of multiple packets can be transformed into a TCP bytes stream with the packet boundaries discarded. The receiving gateway is free to repacketize the byte stream into IPC packets of a size most suited to its network. The lack of significance to packet boundaries in V IPC bulk data transfers gives the gateways flexibility to optimize beyond that possible using internetwork datagrams where packet boundaries must be preserved by gateways.

A TCP module is included in the gateway to allow it to establish connections to remote gateways for communication with remote processes corresponding to the alias processes it implements. This TCP implementation is also made available as a service by the gateway to clients on the local network requiring internetwork RTA/FT. Thus, a program can use TCP connections as though TCP was implemented on their workstation even though it is in fact implemented in the gateway and no IP/TCP is used on the local network. Similar modules could be provided in the gateway for other internetwork protocols.

In summary, our gateway provides a full range of services for internetwork communication ranging from access control to optimization on long-haul communication to implementation of internetworking protocols. This functionality localizes the cost of internetworking to the gateway and protects the autonomy of the local network as an administration, protection and security domain.

Current Status

The V kernel has been in use with diskless workstations at Stanford and elsewhere for more than a year. In the diskless configuration, the kernel and a command interpreter are resident on the workstation. A variety of applications run in this environment, including a VLSI layout editor, interactive debugger, two text editors, illustrators and various standard command facilities. An initial form of remote command execution is in use. File access is currently provided by server programs on our VAX/UNIX systems. A server-based TCP implementation has been in use for one year as well.

Our initial gateway is targeted to connect 3 megabit and 10 megabit Ethernet since we are in the process of switching to 10 megabit Ethernet. At the time of writing, the gateway code for handling the Send-Receive-Reply sequence, creation of alias processes and use of TCP connections is written and passes initial tests, but only in single processor configuration. We hope to have the gateway in production use later this year.

Concluding Remarks

Local networks provide cheap and powerful communication yet pose some hard problems, like performance, reliable operation and security. The distributed V-System achieves high performance on the local network with a transparent network IPC facility based on a simple request-response interkernel protocol. Measurements indicate that this facility gives performance superior to internetwork protocols and the performance is sensitive to additional protocol overhead. In particular, processor time is the critical factor.

Several mechanisms have been described for internetworking, none of which imposes a penalty for local network performance. We argue that the V-System design is a practical, efficient approach that both builds on the current work and standards for internetworking and also provides a possible base for local networks standardization.

The novel aspects of our system are:

- Transparent, message-based interprocess communication for all transport-level local network communication as well as intra-host communication.
- Use of a request-response type of transport protocol for local network communication.
- The local network as a protection, security and reliability domain with the required policies implemented by intelligent gateways structured as two connected half gateways.
- Semi-transparent internetwork operation of the interprocess communication at no penalty to local network performance.

The interprocess communication facility suffices as the single transport-level communication mechanism on the local network as well as for all inter-program communication, whether local or distributed. It is as efficient to use for local network file access, file transfer and terminal access as more specialized protocols.

The use of intelligent gateways that support and control transport-level communication into and out of a local network protects the typically failure-prone and unprotected local network from the internetwork and insulates the local network protocol and its performance from internetwork considerations.

The use of a single transport protocol on the local network

minimizes the the protocol-translation problems for the gateway. The active role of a gateway in protocol translation provides a good basis for imposing access control policies between a local network and the internetwork.

Acknowledgements

Willy Zwaenepoel and Tim Mann are major contributors to the V kernel implementation. Domingo Lampaya has contributed to the refinement of these ideas and the implementation of the V-System gateway. The Internet server providing IP/TCP in the gateway was implemented by Marvin Theimer. These colleagues have also made valuable comments and suggestions on this paper.

References

1. D.R. Cheriton and W. Zwaenpoel, "The Distributed V Kernel and its Performance for Diskless Workstations," *Proceedings of the 9th Symposium on Operating System Principles,* ACM, 1983, .

2. Digital Equipment Corporation, Intel Corporation and Xerox Corporation, "The Ethernet: A Local Area Network - Data Link Layer and Physical Layer Specifications, Version 1.0",

3. A. Bechtolsheim, F. Baskett, V. Pratt, "The SUN Workstation Architecture," Tech. report, Computer Science Department, Stanford University, January 1982.

4. M.V. Wilkes and D.J. Wheeler, "The Cambridge Digital Communication Ring," *Local Area Communication Networks Symposium,* Mitre Corp. and National Bureau of Standards, 1979, .

5. J. Saltzer and K. Pogran, "A Star-shaped Ring Network with High Maintainability," *Proc. Local Area Communication Network Symposium,* May 1979, .

6. B.J. Nelson, *Remote Procedure Call,* PhD dissertation, Carnegie-Mellon U., 1981, published as CMU technical report CMU-CS-81-119

7. A. Spector, "Performing Remote Operations Efficiently on a Local Computer Network," *Comm. ACM,* Vol. 25, No. 4, April 1982, pp. 246-260.

8. A.D. Birrell and B.J. Nelson, "Communication Techniques for Remote Procedure Calls," *Proceedings of the 9th Symposium on Operating System Principles,* ACM, 1983, .

9. J.B. Postel, "Internetwork Protocol Approaches," *IEEE Trans. on Comm.,* April 1980, .

10. DARPA, "DOD Standard Internet Protocol," Tech. report IEN-128, Defence Advanced Research Projects Agency, January 1980.

11. DARPA, "DOD Standard Transmission Control Protocol," Tech. report IEN-129, Defence Advanced Research Projects Agency, January 1980.

12. D.R. Boggs, J.F Shoch, E.A. Taft and R.M Metcalfe, "Pup: An Internetwork Architecture," *IEEE Trans. on Comm.,* April 1980, .

13. D. Clark, "IP Datagram Reassembly Algorithms," Tech. report RFC 815, DARPA, 1982.

14. D. Clark, "Modularity and Efficiency in Protocol Implementation," Tech. report RFC 817, DARPA, 1982.

15. G. Popek, B. Walker, J. Chow, D. Edwards, C. Kline, G.Rudisin, G. Thiel, "LOCUS: A Network Transparent, High Reliability Distributed System," *Proceedings of the 8th Symposium on Operating Systems Principles,* ACM, December 1981, pp. 169-177.

Architecture and Protocols of STELLA: A European Experiment on Satellite Interconnection of Local Area Networks

(*)
N.Celandroni, E.Ferro, L.Lenzini (CNR)
B.M.Segal, K.S.Olofsson (CERN)

CNR - National Research Council - CNUCE, Pisa, Italy
CERN - European Organization For Nuclear Research, Geneva
Switzerland

STELLA (Satellite Transmission Experiment Linking LAboratories) is a European wide-band data transmission experiment. STELLA makes use of the European Orbital Test Satellite (OTS) which provides a 2 Mb/s broadcast data transmission channel. The first phase of the STELLA project (STELLA/I) is summarized. The more important design characteristics of an improved version (STELLA/II) of STELLA/I are emphasized. Collaboration between STELLA/II and UNIVERSE projects in the framework of COST-11Bis is then outlined.

Introduction

The development of the first phase of STELLA (STELLA/I) was the result of the efforts of several persons working at European Physics Laboratories and at Informatics Institutes. STELLA/I was implemented almost on schedule and in accordance with the initial design [1]. The objectives and requirements formulated by the partners were largely met. Previous papers ([1], [2]) have already introduced STELLA, its goals, participants, and major design choices, and it is superfluous to repeat it here. However it is important to report here some information concerning the objectives as well as the drawbacks of the STELLA/I system which led us to a redesign of it (STELLA/II).

STELLA/I

The geographic map of the participants is shown in Figure 1.
The standard STELLA/I configuration consists of (Figure 2):

- The antenna and R.F. systems for transmission and reception at 14 and 11 GHz respectively, with low level interface at 70 MHz.
- The modem/codec between 70 MHz two phase modulated and 1 MHz digital signals, with half-rate coding and Viterbi decoding.
- The Communications Interface Module (CIM) between the above and the Link Driving Computer (LDC). CIM performs CPU-intensive and time-critical functions for the LDC, and also permits the use of disparate LDC types at different sites.
- The LDC with tape unit, operator console and logging system.
- Some measurement facilities for station and environment parameters.
- At some sites, connections to other computers.

Figure 1

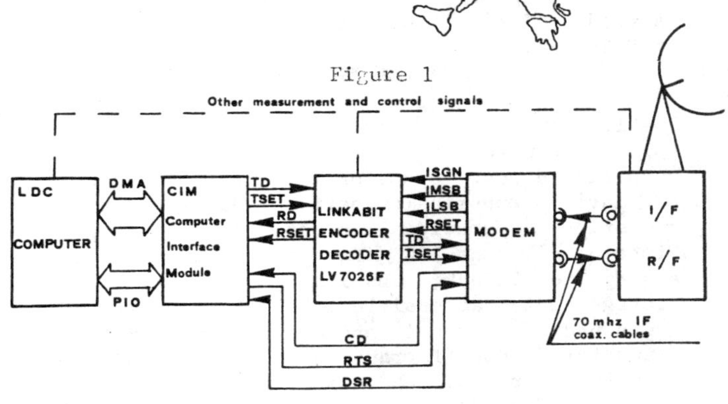

Figure 2
Equipment block diagram

The aims of STELLA/I as designed and now implemented were to try out in practice a potentially

(*) The Italian part of the project was partially supported by INFN.

The aims of STELLA/I as designed and now implemented were to try out in practice a potentially useful application of satellite data transmission using small earth stations, in the simplest and most economical way. The resulting design was limited to the transfer of big files stored on magnetic tapes or disks from a master LDC to a slave LDC. The choice of master station is made before each run; it is not dynamic.

	**	LDC	LDC Software
CERN	operating	GEC 4080	O.K.
CNUCE	operating	PDP 11/70	O.K.
RAL	operating	GEC 4080	O.K.
DESY	operating	AEG 8060	adapted CERN version
DUBLIN	installed	PDP 11/45	have got CNUCE version
GRAZ	operating	PDP 11/44	have got CNUCE version
INFN Frascati	*	PDP 11/34	have got CNUCE version

* The RF/System and Modem/Codec are those used by ESRIN in the framework of the SPINE project.

** Antenna RF/System, Modem/Codec and CIM

Table 1

For accessing the OTS satellite, STELLA/I utilized a fixed-allocation TDMA scheme specifically designed for file transfer. Each station is allocated one fixed transmission window relative to the operating cycle (typically 75 msec.). The master is allocated most of the bandwidth (e.g. 40 msec.); the slave(s) divide the rest. At the physical level, HDLC frames were used, with a restriction to a single frame being transmitted in a single TDMA slot. At the data link level, a simple but appropriate transmission protocol, not conforming to any of the HDLC classes of procedures standardized by ISO is used. Table 1 summarizes the current state of STELLA/I.

STELLA/II aims

The limitation in STELLA/I to data sources/sinks able to be directly mounted on a site's LDC, and requiring direct operator intervention on that LDC during transmission periods, was found to be a serious operational defect in the system. First of all, the LDC often represented a processing bottleneck, and limited the types of storage medium accessible to STELLA/I (e.g. most LDC's had no 6250 bpi tape drives, and many data tapes for STELLA/I transmission were submitted on 6250 bpi reels). LDC disks were mini-computer scale (a few 10's of Megabytes) and could not store large data samples online for later transmission: often data were in fact resident on large batch-processing system disks and not conveniently transportable to the LDC.

It became clear that a solution to all these problems would be found by attaching each LDC to a Local Area Network (LAN) to provide general access to the required data sources/sinks for satellite transmission. At the same time a more autonomous operational system would be obtained, without the need for simultaneous human intervention at each site; also it was decided to provide access not only for bulk data but also for the much more heterogeneous forms of data found as traffic on any LAN, namely independent streams of multiplexed data between multiple remote processes. To achieve these extended aims it was necessary to redesign all the STELLA/I architecture and protocols.
The studies for STELLA/II evolved, therefore, towards a design whose objectives are:

- to design and implement an architecture for the interconnection of satellite, terrestrial and LAN networks according to the "local network independence" principle [8];
- to demonstrate the feasibility of a so-called Remote Control Room; i.e. by extending CERN's existing LAN (CERNET) via a satellite broadcast channel into the remote physics Institutes, to allow physicists there the same access to a CERN physics experiment as they have via CERNET at CERN;
- to measure the performance of the system for the types of traffic generated in the physicists' environment;
- to evaluate the impact of satellite technology on the Open Systems Interconnection/Reference Model both from the services and protocol viewpoints.

The Networks

The components of the STELLA/II communication system are:

- The Local Area Networks;
- The Satellite Network;
- The X.25 Network.

Each of these will be described in turn.

Local Area Networks

In this section a sketch of the various LANs used in STELLA/II is given.

a) CERNET

It is a packet net with 15 switching nodes built up at CERN [3] over the last five years, which allows nearly 100 small and large computers of different makes to intercommunicate at speeds of up to several hundred Kb/s, with very low error rates. File transfer, terminal traffic and process-to-process communication are facilities currently used by physicists to carry out their work. At CNUCE a small-size CERNET is already installed and used routinely by physicists working in the Pisa area.

b) Cambridge Ring

The Cambridge Ring [4] allows a number of users to share a single communications link. The version used in STELLA/II operates at 10 Mb/s, with 40-bit minipackets containing two data bytes, a source and destination data byte, and eight control bits. The intrinsic minipacket error rate is low (2x10-), and a simple parity error check is adequate to protect this data. The empty packet scheme is used for transmitting packets.
There is a monitor station needed during turn-on and to take action after certain types of error.
At CNUCE a 3033N running under VM/370, a PDP11/70 (LDC) running under RSX-11M, and a Zilog Z80 acting as the Name Server will be initially attached to the Cambridge Ring. At CERN a NORD 10/S (LDC) running under SISTRAN III, a PDP 11/45 running under UNIX, a PERQ personal work station and a Z80 Name Server will form the initial Cambridge Ring configuration.

c) INET

It is an X.25 network installed at the Joint Research Center located in Ispra (near Milan) which uses six Solar 16/65 machines as switching nodes as well as hosts [5], connected by 48 kb/s lines. The network uses the EURONET ESP20 protocol for interactive terminal sessions and the 'Blue Book' protocol for file transfer, with the Euronet remote printing protocol.

The Satellite Network

It is made up of the OTS Satellite and of the components shown in Figure 2. The Satellite Network must function simultaneously both as a transit network with attached internetwork gateways and as a network per se supporting directly Applications of differing capabilities and requirements. The Satellite Network was also requested to accomodate packets with a wide range of lengths, allowing a short packet containing a message with a small number of characters to coexist efficiently with a packet containing a long message or perhaps several host-multiplexed messages.
To achieve these extended aims, a new symmetric, dynamic-allocation TDMA channel access scheme was developed for both STELLA/II and UNIVERSE projects [9]. This was implemented primarily by minor CIM hardware modifications and major CIM firmware and LDC software changes with respect to STELLA/I. Essentially all link level protocol is performed by the CIM, with the exception of the actual TDMA allocation algorithm which is implemented in the LDC; all network level protocol is implemented in the LDC.
There are two principal features [10] involved; the dynamic allocation of transmission windows for all stations (mediated by one master station, which also provides reference synchronization as in STELLA/I), and the ability to pack multiple HDLC frames into a single window, with a different address possible on a frame-by-frame basis. The dynamic window allocation is received in the master burst by each station, and is immediately activated in each CIM for the next cycles, until a new allocation arrives. This was implemented easily in the CIM by invoking the programmable timer features already incorporated.
The typical operating cycle of STELLA/II is as shown in Figure 3. A reference burst (transmitted by the master) begins the cycle, containing small and large data window allocations for the succeeding cycle(s). A large data window is allocated dynamically to each station, in which multiple HDLC frames may be put; the reference and small-data windows are by convention limited to a single HDLC frame each. The large data windows are allocated with a minimum size but are large enough to allow the transmission of one internet data unit having the maximum length. Typical values of these entities are 2K bytes for the data length and 20 m sec for the large window, considering the increase due to the HDLC bit stuffing. A wider large data window may be assigned upon request of the station which needs it if there is some space left after the minimum size is assigned to the other users. The remaining time is anyway shared among all the users. An elegant feature of the system encourages system routines to fill transmission windows without regard to overflow (which is hard to estimate in an HDLC environment due to the presence of bit-stuffing) and any truncated block at the end of a data window will be retransmitted by the low level driver as

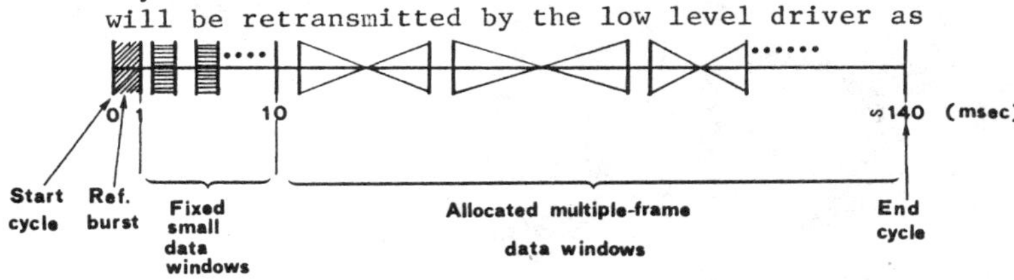

STELLA II Operating cycle

Figure 3

All stations, including the master, set up allocations simultaneously upon (correct) reception of each master burst; in case of a missed or bad master burst, the station is inhibited by the CIM from any transmission in the next cycle, to avoid possible allocation clashes. The frequency of allocation changes is kept low (well below once per operating cycle). In the STELLA/II-UNIVERSE scheme, small amounts of data can be sent in the allocated small-data window, as well as allocation request messages.
At present there is no provision for flow and congestion control between LDCs. It is optimistically assumed that the low error rate on the satellite hop and the amount of buffers in the LDC, together with end-to-end transport level protocol error detection and recovery procedures, will suffice to ensure efficient data communication.

The X.25 Network

In the STELLA/II project the EURONET Packet Switched Network is used to interconnect INET to the Pisa LDC. The INET gateway and the Pisa LDC are connected to the EURONET node in Rome by means of two 9.6 Kb/s leased lines respectively.

STELLA/II Architecture

The STELLA/II architecture has already been specified [6]. It reflects the current understanding of the architectural structure of the Network Layer, as defined in the Reference Model for Open Systems Interconnection (OSI/RM) [7]. The STELLA/II architecture was designed to accomodate a diverse assortment of underlying subnetworks (X.25, Satellite and Local Area Network subnetworks) (Figure 4) according to the "Local Network Independence" principle [8]. In the rest of the paragraph the major design characteristics of STELLA/II are outlined.

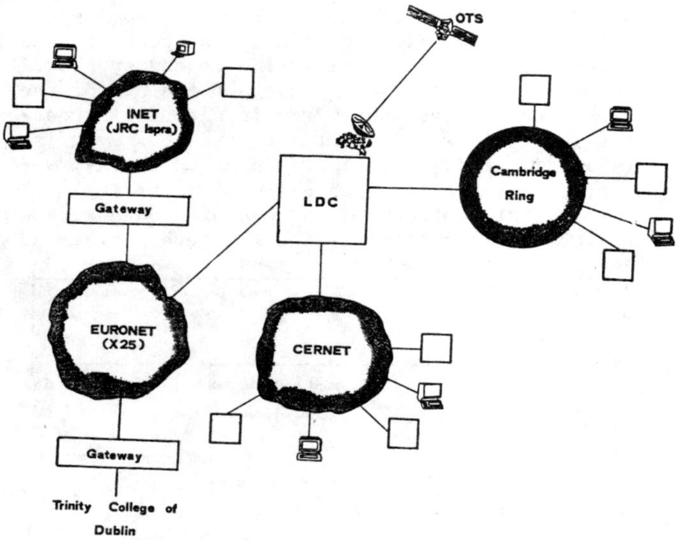

Figure 4

Network Layer Structure and Internet Protocol for STELLA/II

The STELLA/II architecture includes the interconnection of subnetworks via Network Layer relays (also referred to as internet gateways).

Current work within ECMA, NBS, and ISO defines, for the purpose of interconnecting subnetworks, a sublayering within the Network Layer. The STELLA/II architecture includes only the subnetwork interconnection sublayer, which is referred to, within ECMA, as sublayer 3c [11].
Sublayer 3c provides the functions necessary to transmit data-units (see below) from a source to a destination internet-entity over an interconnected system of subnetworks (Global Network). Figure 5 illustrates the layering for communication over two LAN subnetworks. Layers 1, 2 and sublayer 3a are subnetwork specific. Connectionless is the type of service available to sublayer 3c for internetworking. Sublayer 3c provides to the transport layer a connectionless type of service.

The Internetworking (or Internet) Protocol (IP), which is operated by sublayer 3c does not include mechanisms providing data reliability, sequencing and end-to-end flow control which are provided by the transport layer protocols. Reliable data delivery is guaranteed only to the extent that the subnetworks comprising the Global Network provide reliability.

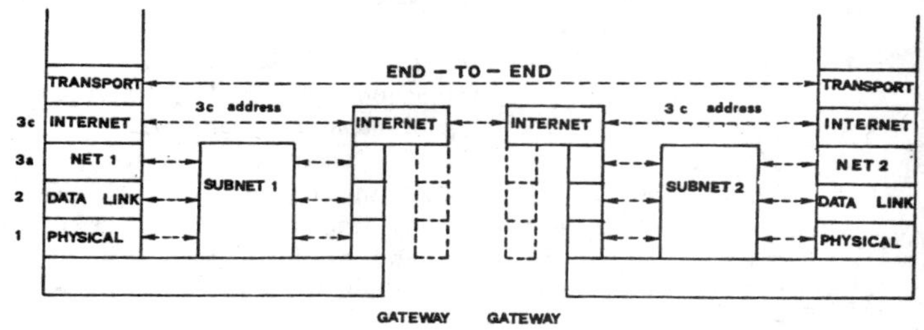

Figure 5

When a gateway discards a data-unit for any reason, the gateway tries to return some information to the source internet-entity which uses this information to modify its transmission strategies (for example to temporarily stop transmission if the data-unit was discarded due to congestion). Higher layer protocols may be notified of the failure.
The STELLA/II IP is adaptable to fit features or special needs not originally foreseen [6]. In the following the foreseen IP features for STELLA/II are described.

- Fragmentation and Reassembly
  Data-units are fragmented at gateways (ING and/or ESG, see below) where necessary, and reassembled by the destination ESG.
- Recording of Route
  Each gateway appends its address to a list of addresses in the data-unit. Thus, when the data-unit arrives at its final destination, the route it has taken is available.
- Internet Timestamp
  This feature allows the source of data-unit to indicate the time that the data-unit was sent. This is very useful for testing and debugging of the Global Network and for determining the speed of one or several paths through the Global Network.
- Error Checking
  An error check is provided to detect errors in the header of data-units. Data-units with errors are discarded.

Gateway Structure

Two types of gateways are distinguished:

- Inter Subnetwork Gateways (ING) which are placed between subnetworks to perform the necessary adaptations;

- End-System Gateways (ESG) which are placed between (End-System) transport entities and subnetwork(s). End-System Gateways mask to the transport entities in End-Systems the existence of the individual subnetwork and Inter Subnetwork Gateways

In STELLA/II each subnetwork can implement its gateway on a fully owned and controlled machine, or even as additional code on an existing End-System. Gateways can be connected together (see Figure 6) via the broadcast satellite channel provided by OTS or by means of an X.25 Virtual Circuit provided by EURONET (see Figure 7). The internal structure of an Inter Subnetwork Gateway (Figure 8) closely resembles that of an End-System Gateway (Figure 9).

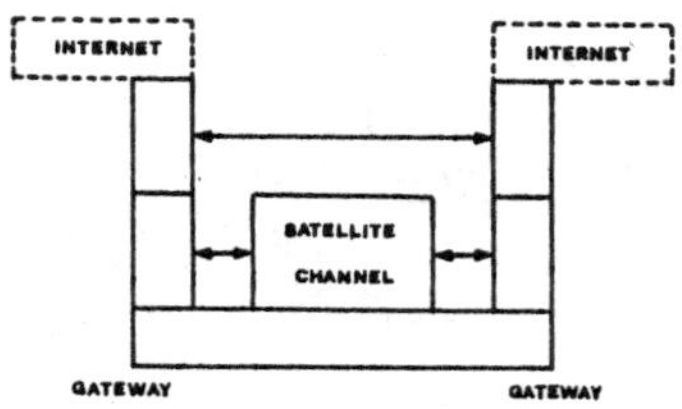

Figure 6

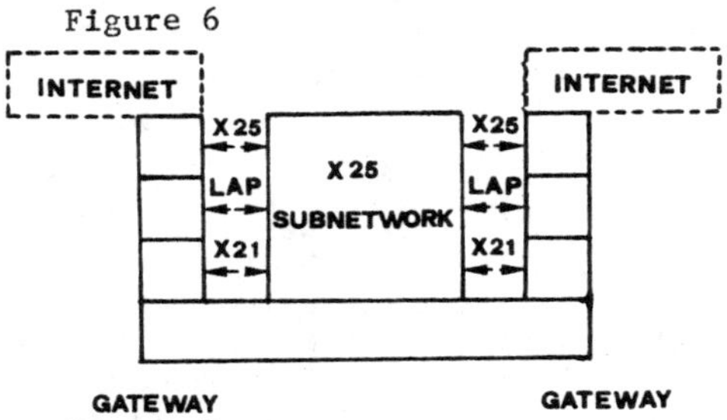

Figure 7

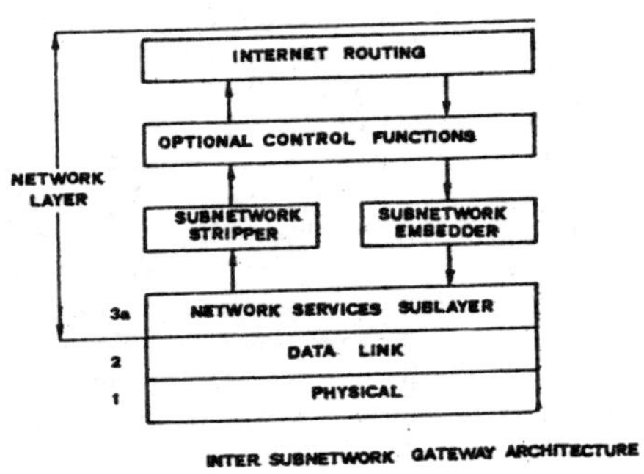

Figure 8

A) Satellite Gateway

As it was shown above, through the use of a Demand Assignment (DA), the satellite acts as a central concentrator.
By permitting continuous real-time reassignment of the satellite capacity to meet the varying LDC needs, a satellite network offers an attractive alternative to traditional point-to-point terrestrial communications systems. The satellite subnetwork can then be regarded as a fully connected subnetwork where each LDC is connected to all the others (physical layer) by means of point-to-point circuits (in general of different capacity) provided by the OTS satellite.

From the OSI/RM the existence of a satellite link is generally invisible to the data link layer. In principle the same data link protocol may then be used regardless of whether a land line or a satellite link is involved. Moreover, the existence of a quarter-of-a-second transmission delay has an important impact on the performance of standard error control techniques. For that reason it was decided not to use conventional stop-and-wait automatic repeat request (ARQ) techniques (such as Reject (RJ) or Selective Reject (SRJ) provided by HDLC) which are obviously inefficient over satellite channels. HDLC framing functions (Flag Generation, Bit Insertion/Deletion, FCS Generation/Checking) are used instead.
Each point-to-point circuit is then managed by a straightforward data link control protocol (data link layer) which does not even take care of error free data transfer (Figure 6). This is justified by the fact that using the Viterbi Forward Error Correction the BER is lower than

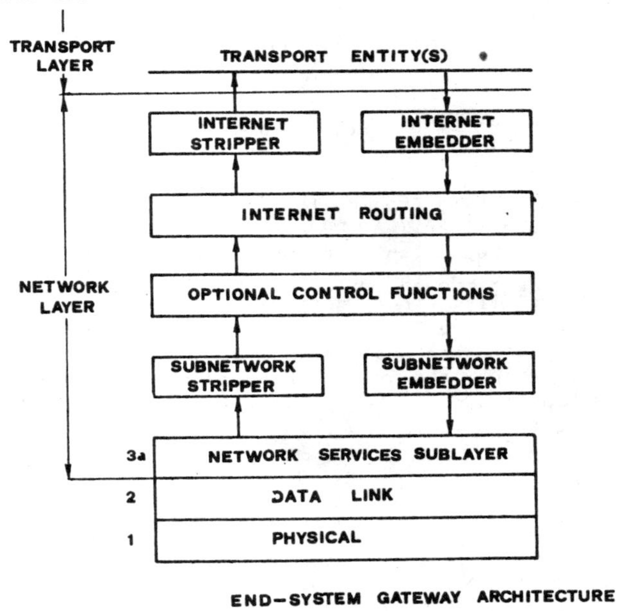

Figure 9

In order to be able to interconnect this subnetwork with X.25, CERNET and the Cambridge Ring subnetwork, they are first de-enhanced and then the subnetwork interconnection sublayer is added on top of them and the satellite subnetwork.

B) INET Gateway

The most straightforward solution [12] to the problem of interconnecting INET to EURONET would be that of multiplexing, on the EURONET gateway, INET virtual circuits on one EURONET virtual circuit as shown in Figure 10. However this approach would require some modifications/additions to the EURONET gateway software in order to perform the above mentioned multiplexing.

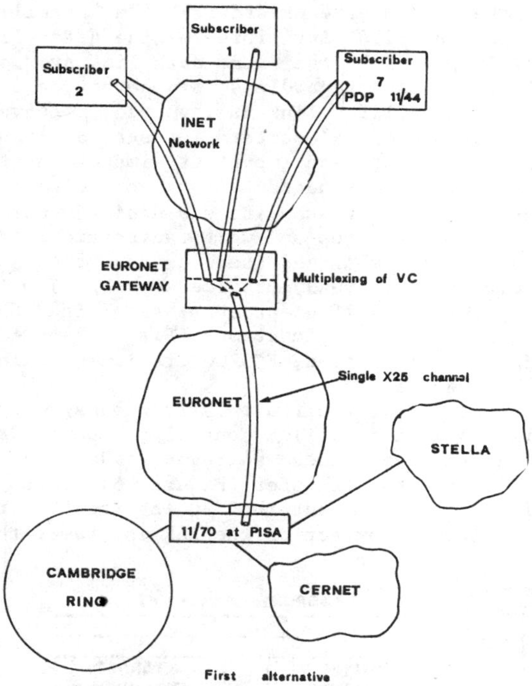

Figure 10

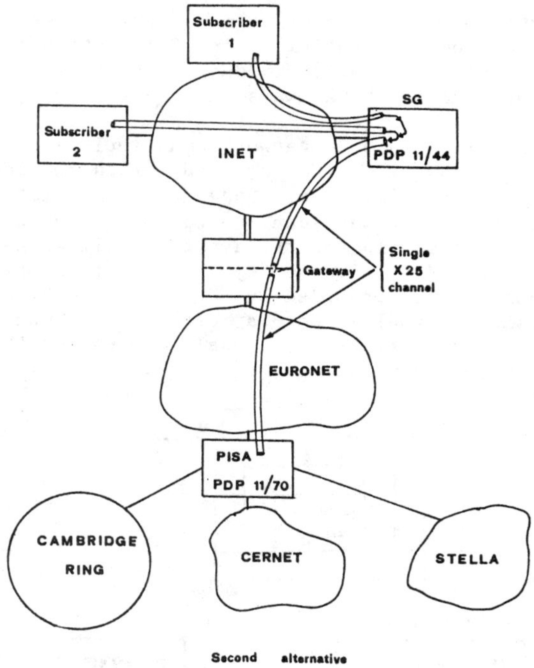

Figure 11

To bypass this problem it was decided to use an INET subscriber, a PDP 11/44, as a "STELLA/II" gateway (SG) with a Permanent Virtual Circuit between SG and the LDC (gateway) located in Pisa (Figure 11). In practice there is a virtual circuit between the SG and the EURONET gateway across INET and another one between the EURONET gateway and the SG across EURONET. The above mentioned process of multiplexing would then be implemented in the SG (Figure 11).

When an INET subscriber wants to communicate with an external one (reachable from Pisa), he must address the local subscriber SG. There will be a local convention inside INET for addressing an external subscriber: the address is composed of the INET address of the SG followed by a number identifying the "remote" subscriber.
The task of internetworking is under the responsibility of SG. This manages the various virtual calls which are addressed to itself, recognizes the destination subscriber (performs an address translation), builds the internet header and sends the packets to the gateway located in Pisa (LDC) through the X.25 channel.
When SG receives internet-data-units coming from the LDC at Pisa, it analyzes the internet header, retrieves the corresponding virtual circuit in INET, strips the internet header and sends the internet-data-unit to the INET subscriber.
At the other end of the X.25 channel, the Pisa LDC plays the same role. Incoming internet-data-units are routed to the destination subnetwork and subscribers according to the contents of the internet header. Outgoing internet-data-units which are destined for an INET subscriber are sent to SG at Ispra thorugh the X.25 channel. According to this approach no changes need be made to the existing INET software.

Protocol Headers, Addressing and Routing

A protocol header structure like that illustrated in Figure 12 is used in STELLA/II. The Subnetwork-Access-Protocol Headers (from now on called Local Headers (LHs)) would be added as the message enters each subnetwork, and stripped off as it leaves. These functions are carried out by the "Subnetwork Embedder" and "Subnetwork Stripper" respectively (Figures 8 and 9). The Internet Protocol Header (IPH) would be added when the message enters the Global Network, and stripped off when it leaves. These functions are carried out by the "Internet Embedder" and "Internet Stripper" respectively (Figure 9) The transport and higher level protocol headers are added at source and stripped off at the ultimate destination, without any intermediate operations. This layered protocol header structure complies fully with the local net independence principle because no changes at all are required in subnetwork addressing and routing strategies. Subnetworks are completely unaware that they are carrying internet traffic. The internet protocol features are managed by the "Optional Control Functions" module (see Figure 8 and 9). The transport protocols envisaged for layer 4 are CERNET [13]; STELLA/I [1] and ISO [14].

SUBNETWORK—ACCESS—PROTOCOL HEADERS (1 2 3a)	INTERNET PROTOCOL (3c)	TRANPORT PROTOCOL (4)	ETC.

LAYERED PROTOCOL HEADER STRUCTURE

The IPH, in STELLA/II, includes a two level internet address of the form <subnet, local address>. These internet addresses are operated on by sublayer 3c functions and are carried "over the top of" each subnetwork involved (see Figure 5).
On each subnetwork, gateways are given addresses consistent with the addressing conventions of the subnetwork they are attached to. Each gateway contains a Routing Table to perform internet routing. Within STELLA/II, routing is provided by fixed table lookup.

STELLA-UNIVERSE Collaboration

In the second half of 1981 the COST-11bis management promoted meetings between the STELLA-UNIVERSE communities and other specialists in the area of satellite data transmission in order to discuss possibilities of a wider European collaboration in some projects in the field of satellite teleinformatics. It was realised that the work on STELLA and on UNIVERSE overlapped considerably, and could produce results of more general value if the two groups worked together with this in mind. The particular topic which looked most suitable was the design of:

a) a common channel access scheme to allow sharing of satellite time. This is already a reality, as shown before;
b) a common Internet Protocol which has already been defined [15].

With a common Internet Protocol, it will be feasible to extend some of the UNIVERSE experiments to CERN and to CNUCE by installing small Cambridge Rings on their sites. This would allow independent comparisons of the Ring and a high speed packet net and of the satellite interconnections in the three laboratories in very different environments. A common Internet Protocol would also allow experimentation with the Remote Control Room Application, conceived for STELLA/II, in the combined STELLA-UNIVERSE environment. It was also seen that the connection of such high speed LANs via X.25 networks should be tested. This is feasible by using the INET interconnection to the CNUCE LDC located in Pisa.
In addition, a theoretical group, made up of STELLA, UNIVERSE and NADIR [16] people as well as other European specialists in the area of satellite data transmission is evaluating the influence of the satellite technology on the OSI/RM.

STELLA/II Status and Operational Planning

As of July 1983 the state of the software/hardware development can be summarized as follows:

- The STELLA/II Global Network, made up of CERNETs, Cambridge Rings and Satellite Network subetworks, works properly. In particular, physicists using mainframes attached to CERNET in each laboratory involved in STELLA/II Network can exchange files through the Satellite Network with physicists using mainframes attached to CERNET at CERN;
- Demonstrations showing the feasibility of the Remote Control Room capability are in preparation;
- The INET interconnection to the Satellite Network through EURONET is well under way and in a few weeks it is expected to be working;
- File transfer and interactive terminal access between mainframes attached to Cambridge Rings belonging to STELLA and the UNIVERSE site at RAL will be tested before the end of the year.

Conclusions

The benefits which the STELLA/II project could produce can be classified as:

- Practical experience: the mixing of different technologies which the experiments require will certainly bring up problems, and hopefully solutions, relevant to future operational systems. Further, the considerable user participation will also show up points not obvious to the network designer, but important for successful public services. The whole field is so new that it would be rash to predict just where interesting problems will arise, but it would be even more rash to assume that there will be none, and that their analysis and proper reporting will not benefit other providers and users of networks.
- Theoretical results could help later designers in their analysis of network interconnections and in the choice of protocols, and could suggest how existing network standards should be modified or extended to cover the very different speeds and other technical parameters of Local Area Networks tomorrow.

The STELLA/UNIVERSE collaboration is an extension of already on-going work, whose results will similarly be enhanced and deepened by the wider range of experiments the project will permit.

Acknowledgements

The STELLA project has necessitated the collaboration of many people. The authors would like to thank everybody involved for their assistance, in particular Dr M.G.N. Hine (CERN), Prof. G. Pierazzini (INFN-Pisa), and Dr J. Burren (RAL), as well as the Directors of the Laboratories concerned, of the European Space Agency, and of the Commission of the European Community who provided resources and much help in setting up the experiment. Particular thanks are to be given to C.J. Adams (RAL) and B.W. Evershed (CERN) for their major contributions respectively in the area of channel access schemes and in that of measurements.

References:

[1] A.B.Bonito, N.Celandroni, E.Ferro, L.Lenzini, E.Perotto, B.M.Segal, K.S.Olofsson, C.J.Adams, STELLA: Status and Trends, Fifteenth Hawaii International Conference on System Sciences 1982 (Volume I), Honolulu, Hawaii, January, 6-8, 1982.

[2] B.N.Celandroni, E.Ferro, L.Lenzini, B.M.Segal, K.S.Olofsson, STELLA-Satellite Interconnection of Local Area Networks: Present State and Future Trends, Proceedings of the Sixth International Conference on Computer Communication, London, 7-10 September 1982.

[3] J.M. Gerard, The development and use of a high speed packet switching network in a high-energy physics laboratories, EURO IFIP Proceedings, 1979, December 1981.

[4] M.V.Wilkes and D.J.Wheeler, The Cambridge Communication Ring, Proceedings of the LACN symposium, May 1979.

[5] J.C. Rey, Le reseau interne du CCR Ispra, IIIA81, Paris, June 1981.

[6] N.Celandroni, E.Ferro and L.Lenzini, Gateway Architecture and Internet Protocol for STELLA, STELLA/CNUCE/82/01, March 1982.

[7] ISO, Information Processing System - Open Systems Interconnection - Basic Reference Model, Draft Proposal ISO/DP 7498, 4 February, 1982.

[8] Carl A.Sunshine, Interconnection of Computer Networks, Computer Networks, 1 (1977).

[9] P.T.Kirstein, J.Burren, R.Daniels, J.W.R.Griffiths, D.King, C.McDowell, R.Needham, The UNIVERSE Project, Proceedings of the sixth International Conference on Computer Communication, London, 7-10 September 1982.

[10] A.G.Waters and C.J.Adams, Satellite Transmission Protocol: implementation protocol, Universe Paper UP/48, November 1981.

[11] ECMA, Network Layer Principles, TR/13, September 1982.

[12] A.Endrizzi, L.Lenzini, J. Loquet and M.Mannocci, INET Interconnection to STELLA, Rapporto Interno C82-7, Gennaio 1982.

[13] C. Adams et al, Network Project Note 16, Version 3, CERN, Geneva, 01/08/80.

[14] ISO, Information Processing Systems - Open Systems Interconnection - Transport Protocol Specification, ISO/TC97/SC16/N1169, Tokyo, June 1982.

[15] N.Celandroni, E.Ferro, L.Lenzini, C.J.Adams, I.Barely, J.Burren, R.Cole and I.Leslie, Internetwork Architecture Proposal for STELLA and UNIVERSE, INDRA Note 1201, Universe paper 74.3, April 1982.

[16] NADIR ou l'utilization informatique des satellites de telecommunication, Agence de l'Informatique, Note d'Information No. 13, Fevrier 1982.

INTERCONNECTION OF BROADBAND LOCAL AREA NETWORKS

by C. Sunshine, D. Kaufman,
G. Ennis, and K. Biba

Sytek, Inc.
Los Angeles Operations
Culver City, CA 90230

ABSTRACT

Interconnection of multiple broadband local area networks to form an integrated packet transport system presents several challenges. To take full advantage of broadband systems, assignment of nodes to channels must be dynamic, leading to the use of a flat address space. Combined with the desire to avoid reliance on a central server or complex routing in packet forwarders, this addressing scheme leads to adoption of a controlled flooding technique to "discover" the best path to a destination node. This discovery procedure sets up a path through internetwork forwarders for use by subsequent packets to the same destination. This paper describes the design and implementation of such a technique in Sytek's LocalNet(TM) systems along with several refinements which increase performance and keep the worst case load for route discovery below a few percent of network capacity.

INTRODUCTION

While interconnection strategies for long-haul networks have been fairly well studied, interconnection of local area networks is in an earlier stage of development. Broadband LANs present a special challenge due to their support for multiple channels on the same physical medium. Unlike baseband systems with their relatively short distance and single channel limitations, broadband systems can support distances of 25 or more kilometers and numerous channels. The individual channels are typically operated as logically separate networks, allowing high total traffic across all channels while limiting contention within each channel.

In addition to different logical networks on the same broadband cable system, networks on different cables may also be interconnected. Each logical network may have its own independent (and possibly different) means for exchanging packets between nodes within that logical network. That is, each network has its own physical and link layer procedures for transmission medium access, packet framing, and contention resolution. Interconnection of logical networks to form a network system is accomplished via packet store-and-forward gateways operating at the network level in the protocol hierarchy.

To take full advantage of broadband systems, assignment of nodes to channels must be dynamic, with network interfaces able to move freely among channels (by tuning of a frequency agile modem). It is also desirable that user nodes have constant addresses by which they can be identified regardless of their current channel assignment. These goals lead to use of a "flat" address space for all nodes in a broadband system, rather than the hierarchical addressing (with explicit network number) often used in long-haul systems. The cost of this approach is greater difficulty in finding nodes (routing). The efficient solution of this problem forms the central topic of this paper.

Sytek's LocalNet(TM) system is the prototypical example of a broadband system of this sort [1,2,3,14]. The basic transmission medium in LocalNet is a standard CATV cable system with two-way transmission capabilities. User nodes (terminals or computers) are attached to the network through Packet Communication Units (PCUs) that implement all protocol layers and provide various interfaces to user nodes (e.g., RS-232 with virtual terminal commands for interactive terminal connection). Packet forwarders called Bridges interconnect different channels; similar units called Links interconnect channels with point-to-point lines to other cables. Bridges and Links are primarily designed to interconnect multiple channels on the same cable system, but otherwise these packet forwarding devices correspond roughly to the "bridges" and "long-distance bridges" discussed in [6]. Figure 1 shows a typical LocalNet configuration.

The purpose of this paper is to describe our goals in interconnecting broadband channels within a LocalNet installation, and the technique developed to meet those goals, called "discovery." We believe that the discovery mechanism is a novel approach representing a previously unexplored and attractive point in the multidimensional space of network interconnection strategies. We first provide some background on previous interconnection strategies, and then explain how our goals determined the general outline of our approach. We then present the details of the discovery mechanism for route establishment and subsequent data transfer. We conclude with some observations on alternatives for future work.

PREVIOUS WORK

Some of the earliest work on network interconnection was done in the Arpanet community. The approach developed in the Transmission Control Protocol [5] and later in the separate Internet Protocol [12] called for hierarchical addresses (network/local) and packet forwarders (called gateways) between networks. To reduce storage requirements (and maintain individual network autonomy), the gateways route incoming packets only on the basis of the network portion of the destination address. For robustness, the gateways continuously exchange information to perform a distributed route optimization function; each arriving packet is routed independently (without regard to virtual circuits). Although this approach has worked well for some time, new demands for mobile or multiply connected hosts and the interconnection of large numbers of independent local networks have revealed some shortcomings [13].

The experimental Ethernet developed by Xerox adopted a very similar strategy with hierarchical addresses and packet forwarders routing only on the network portion of the address [4]. The more recent Ethernet standard specifies an apparently flat address space (over the entire universe of nodes ever manufactured), but Xerox has included an explicit network number within the internet layer protocol of the Xerox Network System [16]. Hence this system, too, functions much as the Arpanet: source nodes must provide the network address of the destination (perhaps by consulting a name server) which the packet forwarders then use to route the packet.

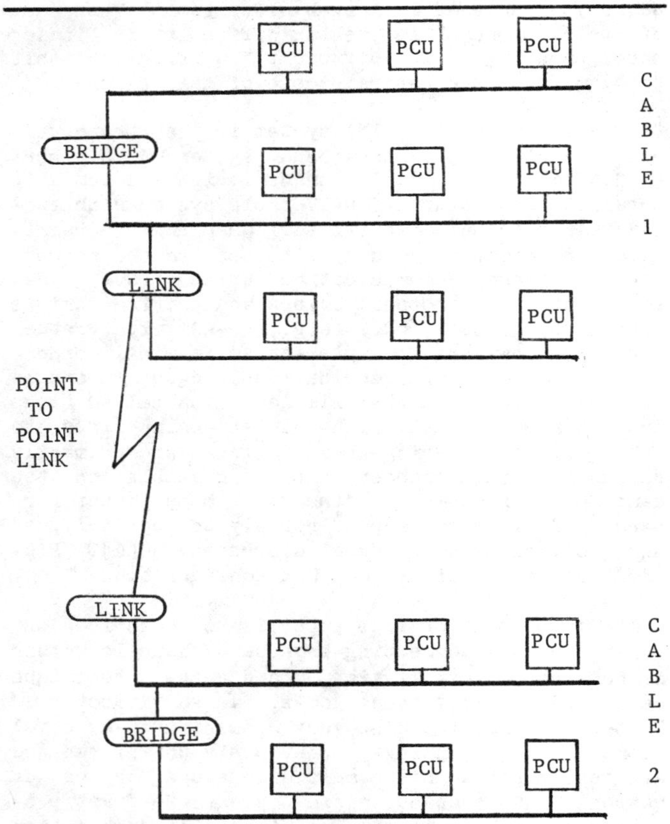

Figure 1. Generalized Architecture of a LocalNet Network.

Both of the above systems treat each packet independently and must make a best route determination for each incoming packet. Another possibility is to introduce the notion of a "path" into the packet forwarders. Paths may be computed in advance, set up by a central authority on demand, or set up by a special message sent from the source. In any case, the routing for that path is recorded in each packet forwarder on the path. Subsequent data packets then carry a path ID so that no new best route decisions need be made, just table lookups to determine the already recorded next link. This approach is used in several public data networks [15] and in IBM's SNA [9].

The benefits of path routing are decreased processing load in the packet forwarders on established paths, maintaining packet sequence (packets cannot get ahead by an alternate route), and decreased packet length (if the path ID is shorter than the destination address as in X.25 networks). The costs are increased table space, less robustness (due to the fixed route), and possibly greater processing load when paths are set up. Path routing is often tied to maintenance of virtual circuits between packet forwarders, but this need not be the case since error recovery, flow control, and sequencing on each link are separate functions from routing.

A final notion relevant to the LocalNet interconnection strategy is distribution of packets to all nodes by flooding or "hot potato" forwarding where an incoming packet is repeated over all links other than the one on which it arrived. Controlling this process to prevent an "avalanche" effect of infinite looping requires short term memory in each packet forwarder of packets recently seen so that duplicates received over a different path will not be resent. A procedure of this sort was developed to distribute routing information among the Arpanet IMPs [11]. While individual LANs often provide full interconnectivity via a broadcast medium, an interconnected system of such nets forms a graph structure much like the Arpanet which is not fully interconnected but does provide multiple paths. In the absence of a spanning tree or shortest path routing tables in the packet forwarders, both of which are difficult to maintain reliably [7], flooding provides a simple way to reach all networks.

GOALS FOR LOCALNET

As noted above, major LocalNet design goals have strongly shaped the development of our interconnection strategy. These goals reflect the unique combination of factors present in large broadband networks used primarily for session-oriented applications such as terminal concentration and terminal switching.

(1) Fixed addresses despite channel mobility. To take full advantage of broadband systems, nodes must be able to change channels easily (e.g., terminals tune to the channel to which the desired server is attached). It is highly desirable for nodes to have constant addresses within the system regardless of their channel tuning, which leads to the adoption of a flat address space with no explicit network or channel component. This allows users of the network layer to see a single integrated system without worrying about details of network topology or node location.

(2) No centralized server required. To maintain robustness and to keep costs low, it should be possible for any node to communicate with any other node in the system without requiring name or route lookup by a centralized server. Directory services are available as an additional option, but direct node-to-node calling capability is the basic service provided.

(3) Very large user population. Because of the relatively large total bandwidth available and long distances spanned on CATV systems, a single LocalNet system is able to support tens of thousands of users. Combined with requirement 1 for a flat address space, this means that unacceptably large databases (and update loads) would be required if the packet forwarders were to maintain knowledge of the location of all nodes. Thus neither a centralized directory (due to requirement 2) nor the Bridges and Links may be relied upon to determine best routes.

(4) Session oriented communication. The vast majority of user communication needs involve prolonged exchanges of information, so that establishment of sessions (or virtual circuits) should be the basic communication service provided. This means that some additional effort at session establishment time is worthwhile to minimize work required for data transfer during a session.

DETAILS OF DISCOVERY

This section presents the detailed operation of the discovery mechanism developed to meet the above goals. We first provide a brief summary of the mechanism, its place in the overall LocalNet protocol architecture, and some addressing issues. The full discovery procedure is then described, followed by some observations on key design elements.

Overview of Discovery

As noted above, the discovery mechanism is intended to establish routes between user nodes in a multi-network system without requiring knowledge of node locations or network topology by centralized servers or packet forwarders. Discovery is employed whenever a user requests a new LocalNet session. The creation of a session requires that a data connection be established between the user's LocalNet access device (PCU) and the requested destination user's PCU. The source and destination PCUs may be located anywhere within the LocalNet installation (i.e., neither their cable nor their current channel affiliation are known prior to the session request).

The first step of the discovery process is for the requesting user's PCU to broadcast a special Discovery packet on the channel to which it is currently "attached" (tuned). Upon receipt of the Discovery packet, each Bridge or Link attached to that channel records the discovery attempt and in turn broadcasts the packet on all other channels/links to which the Bridge/Link is attached. This process is repeated for all Bridges/Links in the LocalNet system and several tentative paths through the system may be built.

Eventually one Discovery packet reaches the destination user's PCU. While other copies of the Discovery packet may subsequently arrive via different paths, the destination PCU then sends a Response packet back along the path followed by the first Discovery packet received. The Response packet establishes that particular route as it returns to the requesting user's PCU. The route is then used for the duration of the session. All other tentative paths will be discarded after not being confirmed by a Response packet within a short time period.

LocalNet Protocol Architecture

Before presenting the detailed discovery procedures, it will be helpful to review the LocalNet protocol architecture [8]. A session layer protocol is used to manage connections between user ports on PCUs. The session layer depends upon the reliable, sequenced, and flow-controlled data transfer service provided by the Reliable Stream Protocol (RSP) at the transport layer. RSP is a connection-oriented protocol and therefore includes packet exchanges to open and to close connections. Each session requires exactly one RSP connection.

RSP utilizes end-to-end acknowledgements and retransmission in order to provide a reliable virtual circuit service. RSP assumes only that the lower layer protocols can (with high probability) deliver a packet to its ultimate destination based upon the destination address. The Packet Transport Protocol (PTP) is LocalNet's network layer protocol and it employs discovery to locate PCUs and subsequently utilizes the paths thereby established. Link protocols provide the basic capability to exchange packets across LocalNet channels or other communication links.

LocalNet Addressing

As mentioned earlier, LocalNet has a flat address space. Each PCU has a single 16-bit node identifier (or address) regardless of the PCU's location or channel affiliation. These node identifiers are the only addresses known to RSP and higher level protocols. Each PCU is also assigned an 8-bit link level address to take advantage of the address detection hardware of the PCU which can only recognize 8 bits. For ideal efficiency, each PCU on a given channel would have a unique link address. However, upon receipt of each packet, PTP checks the node identifier to ensure that it corresponds to the PCU so that even if multiple PCUs on the same channel have the same link address, packets are only delivered if they have the correct node identifier.

Thus in order to send a packet efficiently, the PTP interpreter in the PCU must know what link address to put in the outgoing packet. Similarly, once a path has been established via the discovery mechanism, the Bridges and Links must know which link addresses to use in forwarding packets. A PCU when sending a packet along an established route sends the packet to the specific link address of the Bridge, the Bridge replaces this with the link address of the next Bridge, and so on. If PTP has not yet established a path, then the discovery mechanism is invoked and a link address of 255 is used meaning broadcast. All Bridges, Links, and PCUs will receive broadcast packets and deliver them to their PTP interpreter.

Discovery Procedures

Routing within a LocalNet system is essentially a two phase process. First, whenever a new session (and hence a new connection) is created, a route is established via the discovery procedure. Second, the routing data installed at the source node, the Bridge/Links, and the destination node during discovery is used to route packets while the connection remains open. The paragraphs which follow describe the procedures employed during each of the phases. The packet formats illustrated in Figure 2 indicate the fields used during discovery and subsequent route utilization.

Source Generation of Discovery Packet. The discovery mechanism is initiated any time a user requests a new session. When the session is requested, the RSP interpreter in the user's PCU sends a Connection Open message. The PTP interpreter piggybacks the discovery data on that message (see Figure 2) and broadcasts the resulting Discovery packet. The discovery data consists of the DiscoveryID, the TransactionID, and the Source Link Address together with the Source and Destination NodeIDs which are included in all packets. This data is used by Bridges and Links to detect duplicate Discovery packets and to establish the route as described below. The other trailer fields are set to null values. The TransactionID is unique to this (potential) session on this PCU. The DiscoveryID is set to one (zero is a reserved value).

The PCU saves the TransactionID and the DiscoveryID in a newly created "route table" entry, and awaits a response. If no response is forthcoming, the PCU times out and sends another Discovery packet. This procedure is repeated a fixed number of times; each time the packet transmitted is the same as the original except that the DiscoveryID is incremented. The PCU remembers the last DiscoveryID used. Processing of the response packet is described later.

Bridge Forwarding of Discovery Packet. Upon receipt of a Discovery packet, a Bridge/Link checks to see if the packet is a duplicate. Duplicate packets are discarded while new ones are forwarded on all Bridge/Link channels (except the channel from which the packet was received). A packet is identified by the Bridge/Link as a Discovery packet if the packet was broadcast to the Bridge/Link and if the Destination LogicalID (discussed later) in the packet contains the null value.

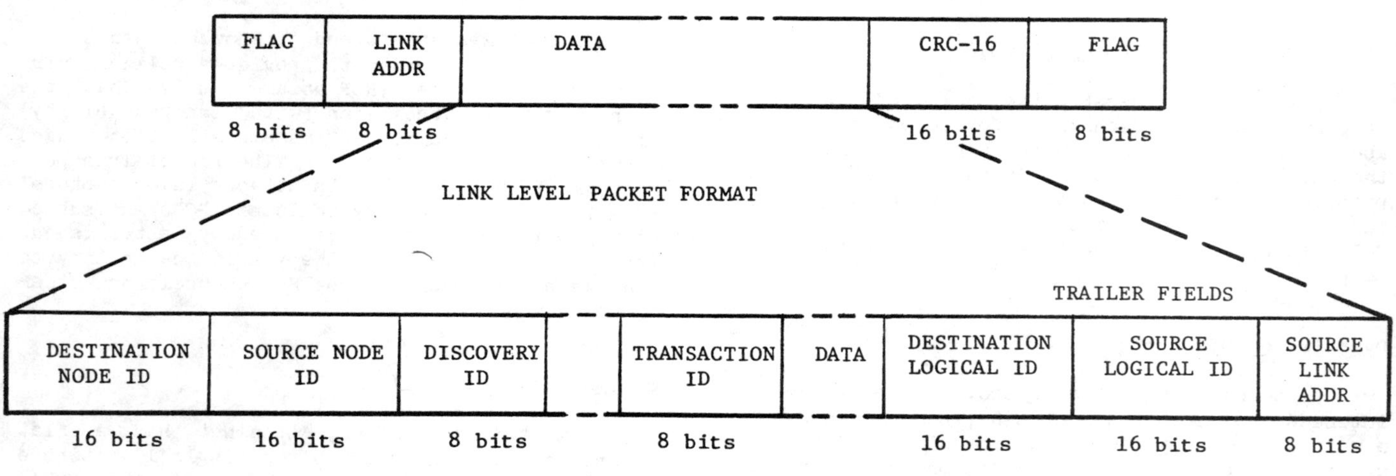

FIGURE 2. LocalNet Packet Formats

Duplicate detection is based on a data structure maintained by the Bridge/Link called the Discovery Pending List (see Figure 3). A Discovery Pending List entry is added each time a new Discovery packet is received by the Bridge/Link. Each entry contains the DiscoveryID, the TransactionID, and the Source NodeID from the packet as well as a timestamp indicating when the packet was received. The three ID fields are used to detect duplicate packets as follows: if the Transaction ID and the Source NodeID of a subsequently received Discovery packet are the same as those in an existing entry, and the DiscoveryID in the packet is less than or equal to that in the entry, the packet is a duplicate and is discarded. The timestamp is used to eliminate list entries after the maximum discovery lifetime has expired.

The Bridge/Link also maintains a second data structure called the Route Table which is used primarily for routing packets in the second phase after a path has been established. The Route Table contains a timestamp and a set of items defining the adjacent nodes (or hops) in each direction along the route (see Figure 3). The Source and Destination LogicalIds included in each Route Table entry are, in effect, pointers to the Route Table entries in the adjacent path nodes. A LogicalID is therefore a route or path identifier which is local to a given Bridge or Link. The timestamp is used to eliminate Route Table entries after "long" periods (i.e., about 15 seconds) of inactivity (because RSP sends a "keep alive" message at least that often on every healthy connection).

A new Route Table entry is created each time a new Discovery packet is received. The timestamp is initialized to indicate the arrival time of the packet; the location data for one of the hops is initialized with the Source NodeID, the Source Link Address, and the Source LogicalID from the Discovery packet as well as an indication of the source channel. That is, the entry now contains the NodeID of the initial source PCU and the location of the previous transmitter (possibly a Bridge/Link) of the packet. Thus the route is built "backwards" with routing information back toward the session initiator filled in from the arriving packet, and the route forward toward the destination left to be completed later.

Prior to forwarding the discovery packet, the Bridge/Link updates the Discovery packet trailer. The Source LogicalID is set to a pointer to the Route Table entry just created. The Source Link Address is set to the Link Address of the Bridge/Link interface used to broadcast the packet; a Bridge/Link may actually have different link addresses for each channel. The packet is broadcast on all channel interfaces.

<u>Destination Processing of Discovery Packet</u>. Upon receipt of a Discovery packet, the destination PCU determines whether the packet is valid. All packets are checked on receipt by all PCUs to insure that the Destination NodeID corresponds to the PCU's ID. Thus Discovery packets searching for other nodes are discarded immediately. Properly received packets are determined to be Discovery packets using the same procedure as the Bridge/Link (i.e., packet must have link address 255 and a trailer with null Destination Logical ID).

Duplicate detection by the receiving PCU also parallels the Bridge/Link: Any Discovery packet containing the same (or lower) DiscoveryID, the same TransactionID, and the same Source NodeID as another recently received packet is discarded.

DISCOVERY PENDING LIST USED TO DETECT DUPLICATE DISCOVERY PACKETS

DISCOVERY ID	TRANSACTION ID	SOURCE NODE ID	TIME
—	—	—	—
—	—	—	—

ROUTE TABLE CONTAINS DATA ON ADJACENT ROUTE HOPS

LOGICAL ID	TIME LAST USED	ADJACENT NODE 1				ADJACENT NODE 2			
		NODE ID	LOGICAL ID	LINK ADDR	CHANNEL	NODE ID	LOGICAL ID	LINK ADDR	CHANNEL
—	—	—	—	—	—	—	—	—	—
—	—	—	—	—	—	—	—	—	—

FIGURE 3. Bridge Data Structures

Note that the destination PCU accepts the first Discovery packet to arrive, thereby selecting the lowest delay route at the time the session is established, and rejecting later duplicate packets that arrive by longer paths.

The receiving PCU must be able to distinguish between attempts to establish a new session (and hence a new route), and repeated discovery attempts for the same session (if the Response packet is lost, the source PCU will try again). Packets with a new TransactionID represent the former, while packets with only a new DiscoveryID represent the latter. Each PCU maintains a set of route entries containing the Source Logical ID and the Source Link Address as well as the Discovery packet identifying fields. A route entry is maintained for each unique TransactionID and Source NodeID combination, also indicating the highest DiscoveryID received. The Source Logical ID and Source Link Address components of the route entry are always updated to reflect the most recently received valid Discovery packet.

The route entry at the destination PCU is used for all packets sent back to the requesting user's PCU. The first packet sent on this route serves as the Response packet and contains a trailer with information needed to complete the Route Table entries in intermediate Bridge/Links. The trailer includes the TransactionID for identification purposes and the Source Link Address. The Source Logical ID from the route entry is placed in the Destination LogicalID field of the trailer and the null value is placed in the Source LogicalID field.

Subsequent packets sent on this route contain trailers only if both PCUs are not on the same channel. While LogicalIDs are required by Bridge/Links to find the correct route table entry, PCUs on the same channel require only each other's Link Address and these values are exchanged in the Discovery and Response packets. The fact that the two PCUs are on the same channel is determined from the Source LogicalID in the Discovery packet. The originating PCU places the null value in this field, while Bridge/Links modify the field to a non-null value.

<u>Bridge Processing of Response Packet</u>. The Response packet appears to Bridge/Links as any other non-discovery packet. The packet contains the Link Address for the Bridge/Link's channel interface and the Destination LogicalID field in the trailer points to a valid entry in the Bridge/Link's Route Table. However, the Route Table entry does not yet contain any data on the source of the Response packet. Recall that the Route Table entry was initialized by the Discovery packet which contained data on its last hop. Naturally the next hop for the route was as yet unknown. Thus the Bridge/Link records in its table the channel on which the Response packet was received as well as the Source Link Address and LogicalID from the Response packet, thereby completing the Route Table entry for the path in both directions.

All non-discovery packets are then forwarded by the Bridge/Link based on the "other" hop data in the Route Table. The Bridge/Link sets the Destination Link Address in the packet header and the Destination LogicalID in the packet trailer in accordance with this data. Also, the packet's Source LogicalID is set to a pointer to the Route Table entry at that Bridge/Link; the Source Link Address is set to the Bridge/Link's Link Address on the channel over which the packet will be transmitted next. A minor optimization is employed on non-response packets. If the next hop is the last (receiver will be the PCU for which the packet is intended), the trailer is suppressed. This action parallels that of the sending PCU as described above.

<u>Source Processing of Response Packet</u>. Upon receipt of the response packet, the source (or originating) PCU completes its route entry. The Source LogicalID and the Source Link Address in the Response packet are recorded. Subsequent packets sent on this route will use the Link Address in the header and the LogicalID as the Destination LogicalID in the trailer. Again, if the LogicalID is null (PCUs on same channel) then trailers are not required.

Once a Response packet has been received, no further Discovery packets need be sent for this session. If the PCU has emitted multiple Discovery packets for this session (i.e., the DiscoveryIDs differ but the TransactionID remains unchanged), it does not affect the acceptance of the Response packet. For each Discovery packet sent by the requesting PCU, the responding PCU will send at most one Response packet (and will update its route at most once).

PERFORMANCE ISSUES

The discovery technique was formulated to satisfy a number of critical design criteria. Several of these, including use of a flat address space, support of node mobility on a per session basis, and independence from a central server have already been discussed. Performance is, of course, also a key concern. The paragraphs which follow briefly review discovery performance with regard to network overhead, switching efficiency, route selection, and network load balancing.

Since the discovery technique employs a flooding mechanism to locate nodes, care must be taken to avoid undue rebroadcasting of Discovery packets. The use of unique identifiers for Discovery packets enables Bridges and Links to detect duplicate discoveries. Thus each Bridge/Link will broadcast a given Discovery packet exactly once. The packet is broadcast once on the requesting PCU's channel and at most once per interfacing Bridge/Link on all other channels.

In order to ensure that duplicate packets are detected, Bridge/Links must retain their Discovery Pending List entries for the lifetime of the Discovery packet. Fortunately, the LocalNet packet lifetime is quite short, typically less than 0.5

seconds. PCUs can therefore use the simple algorithm of incrementing their DiscoveryIDs by one each time the packet is retransmitted and Bridge/Links can easily maintain a safety margin by retaining Discovery Pending List entries for several seconds.

The overhead imposed on the network by discovery traffic is quite modest. This fact can be verified by a simple calculation. For purposes of the calculation, we will assume a Discovery packet lifetime of one second and an average of two broadcasts of each Discovery packet on each channel (i.e., just over two Bridge/Link interfaces per channel). The overhead can be calculated for a single channel; the overhead as a percentage of total network bandwidth will be the same as the percentage overhead on the single channel.

We will assume that during the busiest 15 minutes (e.g., early in the morning, after the lunch hour, or following a power outage) a large number of new sessions are requested and that Poisson arrival can be assumed for the requests during that peak period. It should be noted that LocalNet PCUs employ a rotary call scheme to find an available port on a host supporting a large port pool. This scheme frequently results in multiple calls (i.e., to different PCUs in the same rotary) and hence in multiple discoveries; the average number of calls per session is 2.3 for rotaries at 75% utilization regardless of size. Finally, the calculation below assumes 2500 new sessions during the busy period and that channel utilization is kept below 70% (or 90kbps on the 128kbps channels).

```
avg session requests per sec = 2500/900 sec = 2.78
avg broadcasts per channel per discovery    = 2.0
avg discoveries per session request         = 2.3
=> avg Discovery packets per sec during the
   peak period = 2.78 x 2.0 x 2.3           = 12.79

Since Discovery packets are 168 bits,
  avg discovery load = (12.79 x 168)/90000 = 0.024

Assuming a Poisson distribution for arrival of
Discovery packets,
  avg Discovery packets per sec during the
    peak period (with probability of .9999)   = 29
  peak discovery load = (29 x 168)/90000    = 0.054
```

Therefore, during the busiest anticipated period on a large LocalNet installation, the average load due to discovery is 2.4% and during the peak second is 5.4%.

The LogicalIDs included in packet trailers are integrated into the discovery mechanism in order to improve Bridge/Link switching efficiency. Once the route has been established and a steady-state achieved for the session, the Bridges and Links play the role of packet switches between channels. Each time a Bridge or Link forwards a packet, it must determine the appropriate channel and Link Address to use. The LogicalID which is selected by the Bridge/Link is used as a direct index into the Bridge/Link's Route Table. Since the efficiency of route lookup is a key factor in overall Bridge/Link performance we chose this ID swapping approach to maximize performance at a reasonable cost in Bridge/Link table size [9]. It should also be noted that since RSP guarantees that a packet is sent on every connection on a periodic basis, the Bridge/Link's overhead to manage its Route Table is minimal (unused entries may be timed out quickly).

By its very nature, the discovery technique provides best route selection and traffic load balancing. PCUs always respond to Discovery packets in the order received so the route selected is always the fastest route by which the Discovery packet traversed the network. Typically the route selected will be the fewest hop path between the source and destination PCUs. However, as the load on particular channels and Bridge/Links increases and as their nominal load thresholds are exceeded, the delay on those hops will increase. Therefore, assuming that multiple paths are available between PCUs, the total path delay for Discovery packets will vary with the load and alternate routes will be selected for new sessions.

CONCLUSIONS

The discovery mechanism implemented in Sytek's LocalNet devices provides a powerful and efficient mechanism for establishing routes between user nodes in a large, multiple channel, multiple cable, broadband local network environment where nodes are fully mobile over broadband channels and no central server is required. The discovery mechanism was optimized for a system where session oriented traffic is dominant and substantial effort is justified at session establishment time. The technique automatically provides best route selection and load balancing without requiring any connectivity or delay information to be maintained by packet forwarders, and accomplishes this with modest demands on network resources.

Sytek is also developing interconnection strategies for very large systems (more than 100 channels and 100,000 user nodes) where fully distributed discovery may not be feasible, or where directed tuning of calling nodes to a specific channel is desirable. In such systems a routing server combined with a source routing capability seems attractive, but many of the same path maintenance functions in Bridges and Links can be carried over so that both discovery and directed routing can coexist in the same system.

ACKNOWLEDGEMENTS

The authors wish to acknowledge the participation of Mark Gang, Hemant Kanakia, Steve Butterfield, and Jon More in the development of the broadcast route discovery approach. Additionally, we acknowledge the contributions of Mark Gang and Dave Stevens to the refinement of the discovery technique.

REFERENCES

[1] K. Biba, "LocalNet: A Digital Communications Network for Broadband Coaxial Cable," Proc. COMPCON 81 Spring, IEEE, pp. 59-63.

[2] K. Biba, "Packet Communication networks for Broadband Coaxial Cable," Proc. Local Networks Conf., London, England, May 1981, Online Conferences, Ltd., pp. 611-625.

[3] K. Biba and J. Picazo, "Multiple Channel Data Communication System," U.S.A. Patent No. 4,365,331, December 21, 1982.

[4] D. Boggs et al, "PUP: An Internetwork Architecture," IEEE Trans. on Communications COM-28, 4, April 1980, pp. 612-624.

[5] V. Cerf and R. Kahn, "A Protocol for Packet Network Intercommunication," IEEE Trans. on Communications COM-22, 5, May 1974.

[6] D. Clark, K. Pogran, and D. Reed, "An Introduction to Local Area Networks," Proc. IEEE, November 1978, pp. 1497-1517.

[7] Y. Dalal and R. Metcalfe, "Reverse Path Forwarding of Broadcast Packets," Comm. of the ACM 21, 12, December 1978, pp. 1040-1048.

[8] G. Ennis and P. Filice, "Overview of a Broadband Local Area Network Protocol Architecture," accepted for publication in IEEE Journal on Selected Areas in Communication, November 1983.

[9] R. Jueneman and G. Kerr, "Explicit Path Routing in Communication Networks," Proc. Int. Conf. on Computer Communicaton, Toronto, Canada, August 1976, pp. 340-342.

[10] K. Maruyama and G. Markowsky, "On the Generation of Explicit Routing Tables," Proc. 5th Int. Conf. on Computer Communication, October 1980, Atlanta, Georgia, pp. 90-95.

[11] J. McQuillan, I. Richer, E. Rosen, "The New Routing Algorithm for the ARPANET," IEEE Trans. on Communications COM-28, 5, May 1980, pp. 711-719.

[12] J. Postel, C. Sunshine, and D. Cohen, "The ARPA Internet Protocol," Computer Networks 5, 4, July 1981, pp. 261-271.

[13] C. Sunshine, "Addressing Problems in Multi-Network Systems," Proc. INFOCOM 82, March 1982, Las Vegas, Nevada, IEEE.

[14] Sytek, Inc., "LocalNet 20 Reference Manual and Installation Guide," Doc. No. 2000-RM-382, March 1982.

[15] D. Weir, J. Holmblad, and A. Rothberg, "An X.75 Based Network Architecture," Proc. 5th Int. Conf. on Computer Communication, October 1980, Atlanta, Georgia, pp. 741-750.

[16] Xerox Corp., "Internet Transport Protocols," XS028112, December 1981.

Digital Imaging and Office Information

Chairman

G. Kraft

OFFICE INFORMATION AND TELECOMMUNICATIONS

by Russ Shurig

Information Planning Division, Ontario Hydro
Toronto, Ontario, Canada

Abstract

In order to understand the relationship of office information to office products and to telecommunications, the category of information media must be introduced. Voice, image, text and data information media can be related to one another, to computer and telecommunications technologies and to the needs of different types of workers.

The purpose of business offices, however, is not usually primarily information, computing or telecommunications, but rather knowledge, products and useful work. The information categories including media, transfer, products and work can be related to one another for a better understanding of office information products and telecommunications and in order to predict their future.

Keywords

Telecommunications
Information Media
Worker Archetypes
Products
Prediction

Office Information and Telecommunications

Within an organization, how are we to predict the need for office information, office information tools and information transfer? This problem can be approached by first analyzing the components of a typical business office in terms of the resources used to produce an information product, and then predicting the need for both resources and products. The purpose of the following is to perform this analysis and lay the groundwork for the corresponding synthesis, i.e., information transfer prediction.

After people, information is perhaps the primary resource or component of most business offices. Offices and office staff need to absorb and dispense information. In order to deal with the information resource, the fields of computers and telecommunications are interacting and merging continually: technological advances and new user and office needs in one field are spurring advances and new uses in the other.

Computers are a powerful aid to human information handling capability whereas telecommunications is an extension of human information transfer capability. Basically,

- information:
  is physically embodied by analog or digital electromagnetic signals; sense-data.
- information transfer:
  the movement of information from one point to another, where the points are geographically separated.
- computers:
  are devices used for the manipulation or processing of electromagnetic information.
- telecommunications:
  is the techniques used for electromagnetic information transfer over distances.
- information system:
  an amalgam of people, hardware, software and telecommunications or local communications which achieves a useful purpose or information product.

Computers and telecommunications are the major office information technologies (or vehicles) of our time. But in order to understand the relationship of computers and telecommunications to one another, and to appreciate how they both relate to human and office needs, the category of information media first must be introduced.

Information Media

Just as there are 'mass media' (newspapers, magazines, TV and radio) and 'travel media' (boats, trains, planes), there are also information media. Different information media have different advantages; the most important office information media and their characteristic advantages are:

- mail: a medium for bulk delivery of information, where the latter is usually in the form of paper or film.

- voice: a medium for personal contact; informal, urgent or personal communication or discussion.

- image: a medium for visual display; pictures, pictorial overview or synthesis.

- text: a medium for the preservation of thought; qualitative, contextual or verbal communication or analysis; writing, printing, publications.

- data: a medium for the preservation of measurement; quantitative, numeric, precise information.

The voice, image, text and data information media can be subdivided in several ways, for example:

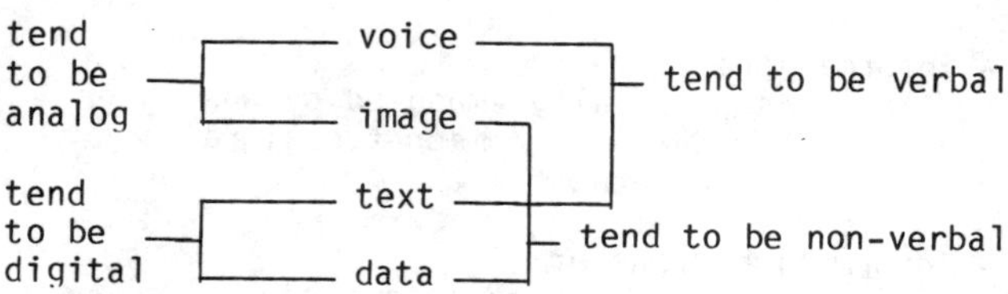

Figure 1: Subdivisions of Information Media

Graphics, colour, computer code and sound can also be considered to be information media; for the sake of brevity, however, they are not included here.

The various information media are often alternatives to one another. Some of the most common interchanges or choices among information media are the following:

data -- graphics (for example business graphics)
voice - text (for example text messaging)
mail -- image (for example document image transfer)

In Figure 2, some of the reasons one might prefer one information medium over another are given.

Traditionally, the main office information media combinations and resulting applications or technologies have been:

- voice/voice: telephone, audio-conferencing
- image/image: facsimile, micrographics, video
- text/text : word processing, electronic mail
- data/data : data processing, database, computation.

With the aid of computers and telecommunications, new information media combinations and applications are being developed continually, for example:

- voice/image: video teleconferencing
- image/text : videotex, photocomposition
- text/data : computer conferencing; word processing & data processing combined; teletext
- voice/data : voice recognition, voice ordering.

Some of the technologies or applications which result from the merging of information media with one another are presented in the chart in Figure 3. Figure 4 is a table of information media and technologies consistent with the response needs of users. The merging and mixing of the different information media in the context of new office products, applications and technologies constitutes the evolution of computing, telecommunications and the office.

	VOICE	IMAGE	TEXT	DATA
Voice	X	people prefer the use of speech rather than text, image or data when message is urgent, informal or personal		
Image	message can not easily be verbalized but can be displayed pictorially	X	message is complex, precise, external in origin or signed	message is intricate or overview is needed or impact is important
Text	message is complex or hard copy record is needed	message is brief and/or verbal in nature	X	message is qualitative and/or non-numeric
Data	the use of data is preferable to the use of voice, image or text when the message is quantitative or precise			X

Figure 2: Comparison of Information Media to Each Other: conditions under which the medium in the row is preferable to the medium in the column.

Worker Archetypes

The need of an office worker for any particular information medium and for information transfer is to a large extent related to the type of worker s/he is. In order that office information

	VOICE	IMAGE	TEXT	DATA
Voice	telephone audio conferencing audio processing	audio graphics videoconferencing picture phone	dictation voice messaging voice annotation display phone text-to-speech	voice recognition voice ordering voice I/O
Image		micrographics image processing facsimile photocopy video	fiche base videotex electronic blackboard photocomposition	graphics computer aided drafting aperture card base optical character recognition
Text			word processing text messaging electronic mail text processing	text base computer conferencing word processing & data processing
Data				data base computation data processing

Figure 3: User needs and application areas by information media combinations.

systems can be designed according to their needs, it is useful to enquire as to the archetypes of workers in business offices. For our purposes, the following archetypes are defined:

1) information worker:
involved primarily in media transcription or conversion; clerks, typists, etc.

2) technical worker:
a technicial or skill worker who puts things together that are supposed to work, or takes them apart; follows prescribed procedures.

3) knowledge worker:
involved primarily in new ideas, relationships and understanding; an analyst or planner involved in design, research, synthesis, etc.

Response Medium	Real-Time	Store-Forward	Interactive
Voice	Telephone Conversation Audioconferencing	Voice Messaging	Voice I/O
Image	Teleconferencing	Image Transfer Facsimile	Graphics Videotex
Text		Text Messaging Text Base	Word Processing Computer Conferencing
Data	Process Control	File Transfer	Transaction Processing Database

Figure 4: Information Applications by Information Media and Type of Response Required.

Medium Archetype	Voice	Image	Text	Data
Information Worker	discussion	retrieval	correspondence	records
Technician Skill Worker	requests queries	design draft	documentation	computation data base
Knowledge Worker	suggestion	synthesis analysis	reports	graphics
Decision Maker	comments commands	signed approvals	decisions policies	decision support

Figure 5: Uses of Information Media by Worker Archetype.

4) decision-maker:
someone responsible for the decisions as to the next move or direction the office, unit or product is to take; policy-maker.

Although we are all one of these types at one time or another, most of us are more one than the other most of the time; also, the ratio of the amount of time we spend in one role as opposed to another does not usually change dramatically from day to day. Figure 5 is a chart of the uses of distinct information media by worker archetype.

Office Information Products

The foregoing has been an analysis of some of the major aspects of office information. An understanding of what is happening in business offices is a preliminary to predicting the future of office telecommunications. Clearly, the purpose of most offices is not, primarily, to absorb and dispense information unless the office happens to be in the information business. An office might be established to:

- produce an information or non-information product
- provide an information or non-information service
- define standards or apply control
- advance our knowledge in a particular field or about a particular subject.

In all of these activities, information is used to accumulate and evaluate knowledge in order to produce products and to enable further action. Information is usually transcribed or converted into records, files, charts and reports of useful information. These records or reports are the basis of knowledge and the origin of the need for information transfer and for telecommunications. Knowledge is important and meaningful information. Importance is conferred onto information to the extent that it meets the needs and intentions of the individual or the office.

Office information products relate directly to Office information media. Examples of these media-product relationships are:

Medium		Product
voice	:	conversations, meetings, voice messages
image	:	illustrations, pictures, copies of documents
text	:	reports, memoranda, text messages
data	:	lists, tables, records of numeric information
data, text	:	computer conference
data, image	:	graphs
image, voice	:	video teleconference

Offices, via human intelligence, initiative, insight, ingenuity, intention and innovativeness transform information into knowledge and knowledge into products or work. The success of the information products metanetwork (depicted in Figure 6) accounts for the success of the office and the usefulness of office information.

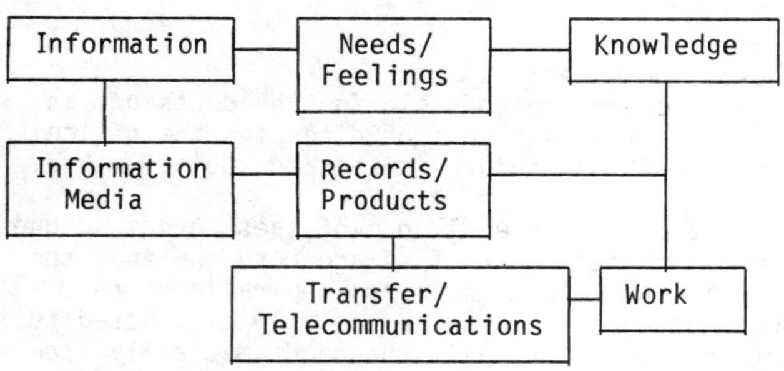

Figure 6: Office Information Products Metanetwork

Telecommunications

The telephone, the computer and television are perhaps the three greatest information tools of the Information Age, (after the typewriter which really belongs to a former age). While uses of the first two are merging via telecommunications (e.g. time sharing), the latter two, in like manner, will have merged (e.g. videotex) before the decade is out.

While, formerly, computer applications formed a large part of the business office budget, we are now seeing a shift to communications applications such as electronic mail, electronic data base, electronic conferencing, electronic document image transfer and resource sharing utilizing telecommunications and/or local area networks.

Telecommunications, or information transfer, has innumerable facets, including:

- communications speeds and protocols;
- interconnect topology and connectivity;
- inter-/intra-office, local/long-haul communications;
- transmission media, switching equipment, wiring;
- voice, image, text and data communications traffic.

The various worker archetypes utilize different telecommunications features for different reasons and applications; but staff, computers and telecommunications must function harmoniously in a successful information system.

Summary

The business office is undergoing increasing scrutiny as to what can be done (or, rather, bought or sold) to make it more effective and more productive. Not surprisingly, machines, or computers, are moved in to take over some work formerly shaped by human labour. These machines (computers) are linked by telecommunications, as people are when they use the telephone, but not necessarily for the same reasons. For example, office telecommunications can be used for bulk information distribution and resource sharing.

The primary resource of most business offices, after people, is information. Since it is the communication of information which is required by most business offices, the notion of information media must be introduced and developed. But most offices do not exist primarily to absorb, produce and communicate information, but rather to generate and use new knowledge. Generally, knowledge is captured in the form of voice, image, text or data records, laying the ground for information systems, information telecommunications, and office information products.

Beyond Videotex: The Library of Congress Pilot Project in Page Image Retrieval and Transmission Digital Optical Disk

W. Nugent and J. Harding

The Library of Congress

This paper arrived late and can be found published in full on pages 257-260 of this Proceedings.

Real-time Packet Video Over Satellite Channels[1]

by

Danny Cohen
USC / ISI
4676 Admiralty Way
Marina del Rey, CA 90292

(A) Abstract

The paper describes major issues and problems in the use of packet satellite channels for real-time video images and suggests some solutions. The DARPA Wide Band Communication Network provides the testbed for this activity.

The main idea in this paper is the automatic online tradeoff between the quality and the dynamics of the communicated images in order to optimally adapt to the changes of the channel performance and of the scene to be communicated.

The paper discusses the problems of real-time packet video, suggests several techniques to cope with them, and describes some new approaches to the encoding of real-time video communication. The paper describes in more detail several encoding schemes based on this approach, using the 2-dimensional Discrete Cosine Transform (DCT).

Section-C describes issues which are arise in the application of packet satellite channels for real-time video communication. Section-D discusses a general approach which addresses these issues. Section-E describes a general methodology for signal coding and compression, and Section-F describes a scheme for the communication of video images using DCT of the raw images in an absolute way, unlike the four differential schemes which are described in Section-G. Section-H describes a scheme which self-corrects the accumulated quantization errors introduced by the encoding and compression. Such errors are totally eliminated for static images.

(B) Introduction

Recent advances in packet communication over satellite links have now made it possible, for the first time, to seriously consider the application of this technology to real-time video transmission. DARPA's Wide Band Network (WBNET) supports up to 3 Mb/s packet communication used for data and real-time voice communication among many computers with which any video communication has to coexist. This network provides a testbed for real-time packet video experiments.

The DARPA Wide Band Packet Satellite system is a domestic satellite network which uses a 3 Mb/s channel of the Westinghouse Westar geosynchronous satellite. The network currently uses four ground stations to share the common wide band channel dynamically on a packet-by-packet basis. The network is based on principles developed and tested in an earlier 64 kb/s Atlantic Packet Satellite system (SATNET) which is still in operation serving DARPA's international experiments in command and control systems technology.

The basic strategy in packet satellite systems developed by DARPA has been to support rapid re-allocation of common (shared) satellite capacity among an arbitrarily large number of ground stations. To achieve this capability to adapt rapidly to varying demand, the system uses a Contention, Priority-Oriented, Demand Allocation (CPODA) technique which allows each ground station to contend for access and use of the channel. All data entering the system is packetized by the computers which act and sources and sinks of traffic. Both "stream" and "datagram" services are supported. ***Datagram*** service accepts a single packet from the source computer and schedules it for transmission

[1]This work was sponsored by the Defense Advanced Research Projects Agency (DARPA) under Contract No. MDA903-81-C-0335. Views and conclusions contained in this report are the author's and should not be interpreted as representing the official opinion or policy of DARPA, the U.S. Government, or any person or agency connected with them.

independently of all other traffic from the source computer. ***Stream*** service permits a source host to request a certain fixed capacity for a given period of time. All packets presented to the ground station marked as associated with that stream are sent during the period reserved by all ground stations for the particular source ground station serving the source host.

The WBNET is a broadcast system; all transmissions are received by all ground stations, including the sending (barring local interference). As a consequence, it is possible for all ground stations to keep track of the demand for satellite capacity and to independently but cooperatively schedule access to the channel according to the requirements posted by each traffic source.

Designed initially to support large numbers of widely dispersed computer systems, the packet satellite technology has also been adapted to the support of point-to-point and conferenced voice traffic. The Wide Band Network is an experiment intended to explore the effectiveness of using packet satellite techniques to support combined and dynamically varying voice and data communication requirements.

The communication of real-time video over the WBNET deals with problems that are caused by several factors: the need to digitize the video signal, the further need to packetize it. compounded with the general characteristics of satellite channels and with the particularities of the WBNET.

Extensive work on digital video has been reported. This paper is not aimed at the issue of digitizing and compression. It uses known and proven video encoding techniques, especially the popular Discrete Cosine Transform.

Packet communication over satellite channels poses several problems for real-time video applications: The data rate required for real-time video applications (above 55 Mb/s) is well above the data capacity on packet satellite channels available to us (up to 3.0 Mb/s). Furthermore, this limited capacity has to be shared dynamically with many other users with unpredictable demands. The packetization of the video bit-stream introduces several problems that are similar to those in packet speech. They deal with the variance in network performance as encountered by each packet, such as the variable delay, ranging from an out-of-order arrival to a total loss of packets.

The delay associated with any use of a geosynchronous satellite (above 230 milliseconds) is large relative to terrestrial delays; the error characteristics vary as a result of many uncontrollable external factors. This delay rules out retransmission of packets for real-time communication, either by timeout or by request (e.g., NACK).

The idiosyncracies of the WBNET, such as protocols and packet size limitations, add to the issues that have to be addressed.

One of the major design goals of our approach to packet image communication is to achieve a low data rate over the channel, while coping with its variable performance[2].

This approach is based on the communication of encoded transforms of the original images, and on performing the inverse operation at the receiver.

Notations used throughout this paper: P is the raw input image of size $x=M$ by $y=N$ by $z=K$ bits; The operation X^{-1} is the inverse (not necessarily in the strict mathematical sense) of the operation X, Y_n is the nth frame of the data Y, and the data Y" is the receiver's estimate of the sender's data Y. I is the identity operator, and operators are usually enclosed in "[ ]".

The term "dynamics" throughout the paper refers only to any changes with respect to time and not to the dynamic range of the images.

(C) Issues in Packet Satellite Communication of Video Images

Packet satellite channels pose some challenges for real-time packet video communication. First and foremost is performance, as measured by data rate (or capacity or throughput), delay, error characteristics, and the great variation of these features.

If the data rate available over the channel is not enough to meet the requirements of the video encoding scheme, then special measures have to be taken to compress the data and to optimize the utility of the available capacity. These measures imply some compromises. In our case, the total capacity of the WBNET packet satellite channel, which has to be shared among all of its users, is only 0.75 to 3.0 Mb/s. Therefore, we cannot use any of the standard digital video communication techniques without using special measures and compromises.

The available data rate depends on the total utilization of the channel which is a function of the total demand of all the simultaneous users. Since computer

---

[2] See "Issues in Packet Satellite Video Communication", by S.L. Casner, D. Cohen and E.R. Cole, ICC'83, pp. 34-38.

applications tend be very bursty and to vary rapidly their communication demands the amount of available data rate may vary suddenly, without any prior warning. The long inherent delay (above 230 milliseconds) due to the high orbit of the geosynchronous satellite reduces the system capability to respond quickly to sudden changes, which are relatively frequent in computer communication. It is more important to respond properly and quickly to a reduction in data rate than to an increase.

The error characteristics of the channel depend on many environmental factors and also may change rapidly. The channel errors fall into two categories, Bit Error Rate (***BER***) and loss of entire packets. For a certain cost (in data rate) data can be protected to achieve a lower ***BER***. It is assumed that the system builder already has protected the headers of packets to minimize packet loss due to damaged headers in general and damaged addresses in particular.

The two major factors which increase the error rate are weather and electromagnetic emissions by other non-cooperative systems, like radars and neighboring microwave systems. Experience shows that these factors do not change very rapidly. Any scheme which monitors the error rate should implement fast response to detected degradations, while possibly responding more slowly to detected improvements.

(D) Approach to Encoding Real-Time Video Images

Our approach to encoding real-time video information is based on:

1. The observation that the required total data rate for this communication is the product of the spatial (***xy***) resolution, the shade/color (***z***) resolution, and the temporal (***t***) resolution,
2. The assumption that the nature/dynamics of the scene varies,
3. The need to cope with sudden changes of channel performance (capacity, delays, ***BER***, etc.), and
4. The assumption that both the sender and the receiver have a certain non-trivial amount of processing power and storage.

Our strategy is both dynamic and adaptive, in the sense that it varies according to conditions observed in real-time, such as the dynamic nature of the scene and of the current load and performance of the channel.

Since the available capacity (up to 3 Mb/s) is less than what is needed for communicating the full ***xy***, ***z***, and ***t*** video resolutions (at least 55 Mb/s), the system must (automatically or manually) decide what to sacrifice. It is well known that for fast motion the spatial and the shade/color resolutions are secondary to the temporal resolution, while the inverse is true for static images. However, any sacrifice must not necessarily be along the ***xy***, ***z*** and ***t*** boundaries but may take other dimensions such as loss of sharpness.

Conventional encoded communication, performed according to a fixed algorithm (such as PCM, CVSD, and LPC) requires the transmission of control information to manage the connection, and of data to convey the signal.

For packet video communication we propose schemes which, in addition to sending connection control and image data, also send "functions" telling the receiver what to do with the data. Therefore the entire encoding algorithm can be dynamically changed if the sender finds it optimal. This includes changes of either entire algorithms or just of parameters like the granularity of coding tables or the block sizes.

It is possible to send successive approximations (or iterations) which lead the receiver to the desired image. If these successive approximations are marked with decreasing priority, then in case of a sudden decrease in channel performance the received images are more likely to suffer from quality degradation only--rather than from total loss of image parts. This happens because of common implementation strategies which automatically drop packets of lower priority when the total demand exceeds the available capacity.

When such successive approximations are used, it is imperative to ensure that hight priority packets are successfully delivered. When such a packet is lost or severely damaged, the entire image has to be discarded.

When fast motion is detected, the data may be sent using a lower spatial and/or shade resolutions but a higher temporal resolution than usual, at the same time instructing the receiver to perform a spatial low-pass filter operation to "smear" the image in the way that human vision and TV cameras do.

The successive approximations may obviously be along any dimension, or a combination of several dimensions. This includes dimensions from the image domain (***xy***, ***z***, and ***t***) or dimensions from any transformation domain, such as logarithmic, or the popular 1- and 2-dimensional Discrete Cosine Transform (DCT).

Consider, for example, the communication of an image of size ***xyz***=512x512x8 bits. One way to send the image is in the ***zxy***-order: sending first all the bits (***z***) for each pixel from the first pixel in the first row, through the second pixel in the first row (***x***), through all the bits of the last pixel in the last row (***y***). This is probably the simplest way of communicating an image.

Another possibility is to use ***xyz***–order, where the most significant bit of every pixel is sent first, then the second most significant bit of every pixel, and so on to the least significant bit of every pixel.

The transmission of all these bits requires the use of many packets. In the latter scheme the priority of the packets should decrease with the significance of the corresponding bits, such that if the channel performance degrades suddenly with no advance warning, some of the least significant packets could be discarded while all the more significant ones would arrive safely.

Similarly, if the error characteristics of the channel are degraded, then more significant packets can be marked for better error protection/correction coding (hence more data intensive) while the less significant ones are left with less protection (or none at all), or may even be sacrificed entirely in order to afford the added data rate needed for the protection of the more significant packets.

If 512x512 bit packets are still too big for reasonable communications they can be divided into smaller packets, either by covering smaller areas, or by having each packet cover the entire 512x512 area but in a lower spatial resolution. The latter is similar to the ways in which smaller memories are organized into bigger ones using various interleaving schemes.

It is best to have the successive approximations converge to the target image not at a uniform rate, but at a rate which starts high and decreases later, such that the first approximations convey "most" of the information and the later ones serve to enhance it. This iterative process may look like focusing a lens, where the entire image is transformed from a low quality image into a high quality image. The above the ***xyz***–order scheme has this property.

The purpose of using such schemes is to be able to react dynamically to performance changes, both in the available data rate and in the error characteristics.

(E) Signal Encoding and Compression

Most digital representations of signals in the time domain do not address the entropy issue and typically require many more bits than other entropy (information) oriented coding schemes.

Let C = S(X) be the encoding of the signal X, and let $Y = S^{-1}(C) = S^{-1}S(X) = H(X)$ be the signal reconstructed from the code C. The distortion caused by the coding is X–H(X) = [I–H](X), which is not as important as the difference between the perception of the 'original signal, ***PER***(X), and the perception of the reconstructed signal, ***PER***(H(X)). Hence the important distortion is ***PER***([I–H](X)). If the operator [I–H] is in the null space of the operator ***PER*** the coding will not cause any perceived distortion.

The degree of freedom exploited by the compression is the deliberate use of the [I–H] distortion if its effect on the perception is small.

The way to achieve optimal coding is by transforming the signal into another space (or domain) whose components have known perceptual significance, and to allocate code bits to each of these dimensions (or features) according to its importance to the perception process.

The number of bits assigned to each feature should also depend on the statistics of the signal (a la Huffman coding).

In many cases, the frequency analysis (temporal or spatial) of the signals suggests the use of block coding. In the case of speech these blocks are usually intervals of about 20 milliseconds, whereas for video images the most interesting blocks are of sizes 8x8, 8x16 and 16x16 pixels. Practical reasons often dictate a compromise which leads to the use of 1–dimensional blocks of size 8 and 16 pixels, this is usually done in order to save logic and memory.

From a pure information–theory point of view, the space of the coded representation cannot be of a lesser dimensionality than the original time domain representation (i.e., the block size) of a general signal without loss of information.

However, two factors make signal compression possible. First, the fact that a certain family of signals (rather than the most general signals) is being coded, and second, the high dimensionality of the null space of ***PER***.

If the signals are restricted to a certain family which can be modeled as the output of some process (or the range of some operator) than the dimensionality of the time domain representation is not as high as the block size but only as the rank of that operator. The inversion of this operator yields parameters which, when given to the process, reproduce the original signal. After simplifying the process to eliminate mapping into the null space of ***PER***, the rank of the process is the dimensionality of the code (i.e., its block size) required to convey the signal.

In image communication, with a fixed block size, increasing the ***x*** resolution of an image usually yields lower spatial frequencies and higher pixel-to-pixel correlation. Similarly higher ***y*** resolution yields higher line-to-line correlation and higher ***t*** resolution yields higher frame-to-frame correlation. The higher these correlations are the better the compression which may be devised. For example, when facsimile machines doubled their resolution from 192 ppi to 384 ppi no increase in the number of bits in the coded representation was required.

High correlations may be exploited either by simple minded differential schemes along the appropriate axis (e.g., run length) or by more complicated transforms into a frequency domain where high spatial correlation concentrates energy in the low spatial frequencies so that very few bits are needed for coding the higher frequencies.

Exploiting high frame-to-frame correlation by block transforms cannot be done without a great amount of storage (to hold several frames) and without additional delay (to wait for more frames) and processing. Therefore the simple minded differential one-step schemes which require the storage of only one frame appear to be a reasonable compromise between compression, delay, processing and memory.

In images with static parts great contribution to the compression can result from special block-oriented codes, like a single code to indicate an all-zero block.

(F) Communication of Absolute Codes

The following is Scheme-(a) for the communication of absolute image codes:

$C_n = T(P_n)$ Perform DCT on the image

$Q_n = S(C_n)$ Encode the DCT

Transmit Q_n

Receive $Q_n'' = G(Q_n)$ May include transmission errors

$C_n'' = S^{-1}(Q_n'')$ Decode it

$P_n'' = T^{-1}(C_n'')$ Invert the DCT

Hence the received image is:

$$\text{(a)}\quad P'' = [T^{-1} S^{-1} G S T](P)$$

The DCT is performed on blocks whose size depends on the general characteristics of the scene.

As mentioned above the key to efficient compression is the choice of the transformation, T, and of the coding, S and S^{-1}. The coding has to be tuned according to the statistics (e.g., distribution) of the $\{C_n\}$ of the images which are expected to be handled by this system.

Both the coding tables and the update rate should be determined dynamically as a function of the channel performance. The choice of coding tables should be done to best match the expected code length to the available data rate over the channel.

In the ideal situation there is no communication noise, $G = I$, and $Q'' = Q$. If the coding is information-lossless such that $S^{-1}S = I$, and if the arithmetic is performed with high enough precision such that $T^{-1}T = I$, then the received image, P", is identical to the input image, P.

Unfortunately, under these conditions it is not possible to achieve a high rate of image compression. Effective compression is achieved by using an encoding operator, S, which discards a great amount of information, which is (due to a clever choice of the transformation, T) perceptually insignificant. The purpose of the DCT is to sort the image information by its perceptual value such that the less perceptually significant information can be ignored.

(G) Differential Image Communication

Scheme-(b) is based on the communication of encoded ***transforms of the differences*** of the image:

$dP_n = P_n - P_{n-1}$ Differentiate the image

$C_n = T(dP_n)$ Perform DCT on difference

$dQ_n = S(dC_n)$ Encode the DCT of difference

Transmit dQ_n

Receive $dQ_n'' = G(dQ_n)$ With transmission errors?

$dC_n'' = S^{-1}(dQ_n'')$ Decode it

$dP_n'' = T^{-1}(dC_n'')$ Invert DCT of difference

$P_n'' = P_{n-1}'' + dP_n''$ Accumulate image difference

The received image is:

$$\text{(b)}\quad P'' = [(I-Z)^{-1} T^{-1} S^{-1} G S T (I-Z)](P)$$

Z is the ***delay*** operator, defined by: $Z(X_n) = X_{n-1}$.

Scheme-(c) is based on the communication of encoded ***differences of the transforms*** of the image:

$C_n = T(P_n)$ Perform DCT on the image

$dC_n = C_n - C_{n-1}$ Differentiate the DCT

$dQ_n = S(dC_n)$ Encode the DCT differences

Transmit dQ_n

Receive $dQ_n'' = G(dQ_n)$ With transmission errors?

$dC_n'' = S^{-1}(dQ_n'')$ Decode it

$C_n'' = C_{n-1}'' + dC_n''$ Accumulate DCT differences

$P_n'' = T^{-1}(C_n'')$ Invert the DCT

The received image is:

$$\text{(c)} \quad P'' = [T^{-1} (I-Z)^{-1} S^{-1} G S (I-Z) T](P)$$

The {dQ} of (b) and (c) are equal because the differentiation operation ($D = [I-Z]$) and the DCT operation (T) commute. Proof:

$$[T D](P_n) = T(P_n - P_{n-1}) = T(P_n) - T(P_{n-1}) =$$

$$= C_n - C_{n-1} = D(C_n) = [D T](P_n) \qquad \text{[QED]}$$

Since the inverse-DCT and the summation also commute there are 2 additional schemes, (d) and (e), which are also feasible.

Figure-(1) shows the 5 schemes mentioned above:

(a) $P'' = [T^{-1} S^{-1} G S T] (P)$

(b) $P'' = [D^{-1} T^{-1} S^{-1} G S T D] (P)$ where $D = I - Z$

(c) $P'' = [T^{-1} D^{-1} S^{-1} G S D T] (P)$

(d) $P'' = [D^{-1} T^{-1} S^{-1} G S D T] (P)$

(e) $P'' = [T^{-1} D^{-1} S^{-1} G S T D] (P)$

Schemes (b) through (e) are mathematically identical, but may have different implementation consequences.

When the dynamics of the scene are limited differential schemes are very efficient.

The occasional transmission of absolute images, as in Scheme-(a), is needed for all the differential schemes in order to protect against loss of packets and against the accumulation of any other errors, like those caused by channel noise. The frequency of the absolute updates has to be determined from the performance of the channel.

The encoding operator, S, used for encoding the $\{Q_n\}$ in the absolute scheme, (a), may be different than the S used for encoding the $\{dQ_n\}$ in the differential schemes, (b) through (e).

The data compression results from the discard of information by the encoding operation, S. The role of the transformation T is to make this discard as perceptually insignificant as possible.

[X] = operation; <Y> = data; (z) = scheme

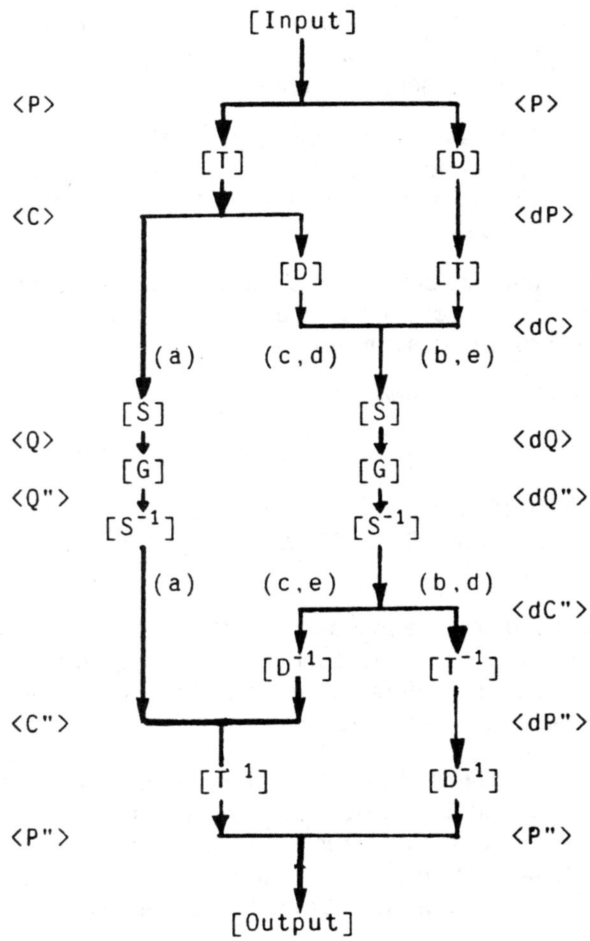

Figure 1: The 5 Communication schemes

(H) Adaptive Differential Scheme

All differential schemes, including (b) through (e) above, suffer from the accumulation/propagation of errors. In these schemes the total distortion of the received image is caused by the errors which are due mainly to the following factors:

1. The DCT precision: $[T^{-1}T] = I$,

2. Quantization, or encoding/decoding errors: $[S^{-1}S] = I$, and

3. Transmission noise: $G = I$.

By using higher precision arithmetic, $[T^{-1}T-I]$ can be made arbitrarily small, and does not have to be a problem.

By using more error protection over the channel, $[G-I]$ may be made arbitrarily small, at the expense of increased data rate which otherwise could be used for improving the picture quality or dynamics. This tradeoff is the subject of another investigation.

A similar tradeoff can reduce $[S^{-1}S-I]$, using more bits for the encoding, given a fixed channel capacity, reduces the error protection or the dynamics of the communication.

The adaptive differential scheme below addresses the problem which arises from the granularity of the coding, but does not result in a higher data rate.

Recall that Scheme-(c) is:

$$P'' = [T^{-1}(I-Z)^{-1}S^{-1}G\,S\,(I-Z)\,T](P)$$

Figure-(2) shows Scheme-(c) with explicit differentiation, $D = [I-Z]$, and integration/summation, $D^{-1} = [I-Z]^{-1}$.

Because the magnitudes of both $[G-I]$ and $[S^{-1}S-I]$ (channel noise and quantization/coding errors) are non-zero, P" differs from P. The following scheme tries to improve the accuracy with which P" tracks P.

If the statistics of the channel noise, $[G-I]$, are known, then S^{-1} should be devised to compensate as much as possible for them. Once this is done, or if the statistics of G are not known, then the receiver should assume that $G = I$ and use dQ" as the best estimate of dQ.

The assumption that $G = I$ yields $dC'' = [S^{-1}S](dC)$, which is known not to be perfect and can cause distortions to C" and to P".

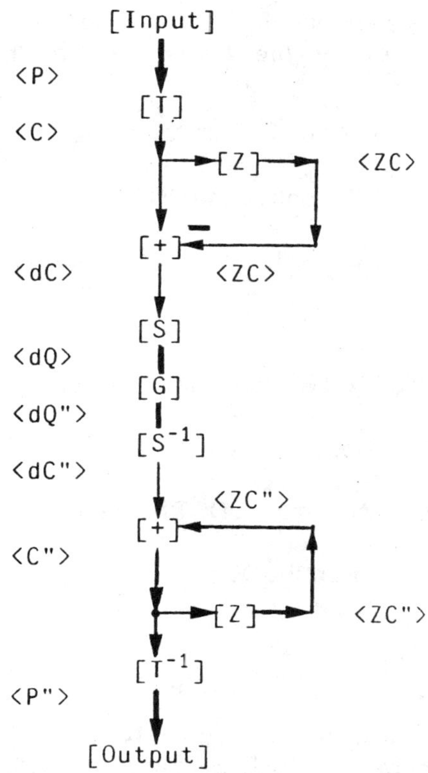

Figure 2: Scheme-(c) with explicit D and D^{-1}

The effect of $[S^{-1}S-I]$ may not be severe by itself, but can be aggravated by the accumulation of quantization errors over time. This can be improved by redefining an adaptive dC, not the previous $dC = [I-Z](C) = C-Z(C)$, but a new $dC = C-Z(C'')$ which is self-correcting such that C" is equal to C modulo the effect of $[S^{-1}S]$, and which does not deteriorate with time.

Unfortunately, C" exists at the receiver and is not available to the sender, who needs it in order to compute the adaptive dC. Sending it from the receiver to the sender results in an excessive data rate, since such transmission would add to the total data rate required over the satellite channel, and also to the end-to-end delay and the processing.

Recall that $C'' = [S^{-1}G\,S](C) = [S^{-1}G_dG_uS](C)$, where S and S^{-1} are the encoding and decoding operators, possibly with a built-in compensation for any known non-zero averages of the channel noise, G, which is the noise on the way up, G_u, combined with the noise on the way down, G_d.

Fortunately, the sender can receive its own transmission. Therefore, it is possible for it to sense the effects of G_u without consuming additional communication resources.

Unfortunately, this includes its own G_d, which is probably different from the G_d at the receiver. Since it can safely be assumed that the G_d is more significant than the G_u there is no point in trying to estimate G dynamically.

Fortunately, the best the sender can do is to ignore this problem and assume that $G = I$.

Therefore, the sender can use C^* to estimate the receiver's C", which is the receiver's estimate of the sender's C. The sender's dC is redefined by $dC = C - Z(C^*)$, where C^* is computed by the summation of $dC^* = [S^{-1}S](dC)$, where $[S^{-1}S](dC)$ is the sender's estimate of dC" which is the receiver's estimate of the sender's dC.

An automatic tradeoff between the ***z*** and ***t*** resolutions will result from the use of coding schemes with fine resolution for small values and coarser resolution for larger values, when coupled with the use of differential schemes. This tradeoff results in the desired effect of blurred images of dynamic objects, but sharper images of static objects.

Scheme–(c*), the modified Scheme–(c), is defined below and shown in Figure–(3).

$C_n = T(P_n)$	Perform DCT the image
$dC_n = C_n - C^*n{-}1$	Differentiate the DCT
$dQ_n = S(dC_n)$	Encode the difference of the DCT
$dC^*n = S^{-1}(dQ_n)$	Estimate dC_n''
$C^*n = C^*n{-}1 + dC^*n$	Estimate C_n''
Transmit dQ_n	
Receive $dQ_n'' = G(dQ_n)$	May include transmission error
$dC_n'' = S^{-1}(dQ_n'')$	Decode it
$C_n'' = C_{n-1}'' + dC_n''$	Accumulate the code differences
$P_n'' = T^{-1}(C_n'')$	Invert the DCT

The adaptive Scheme–(c*) requires that the sender use more processing and storage than the non-adaptive Scheme–(c). The additional processing is very low, a table lookup and an addition per pixel. It seems affordable, unlike schemes which require that the sender performs T^{-1}, the inverse-DCT, for tracking the receiver.

Of the 4 differential schemes, (b) through (e), only (c) can be modified to track the receiver's quantization errors without a severe processing penalty.

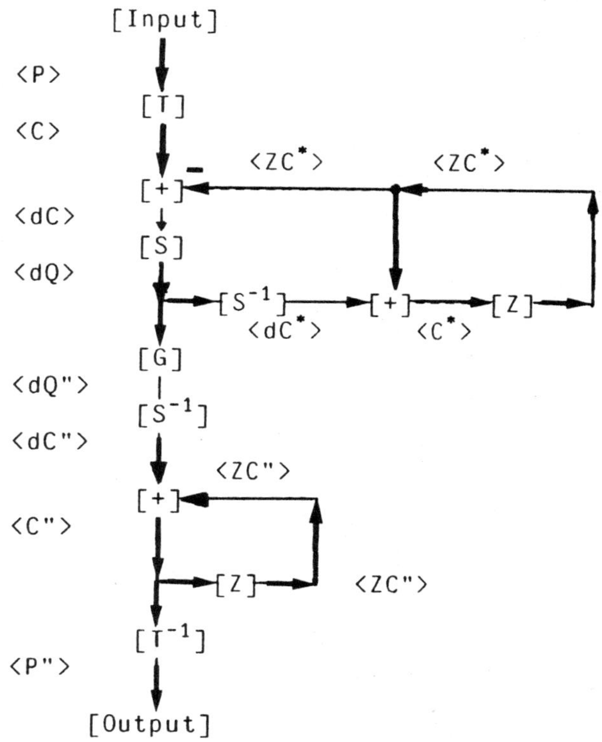

Figure 3: Scheme–(c^*): The adaptive Scheme–(c)

(I) Conclusion

Conventional video compression techniques have to be augmented to cope with the special problems inherent to communication over packet satellite channels. However, with proper attention to the nature of these problems it is possible to support real-time video image communication by adapting dynamically to the variances in the channel performance, such that the system gracefully changes its behavior according to the available resources and to the dynamics of the scene.

It is most important to monitor dynamically the the channel (available data rate, total demand, ***BER***, etc.) in order to optimize its use by performing the proper tradeoffs which depend also on the varying nature of the scene.

(J) Acknowledgements

Randy Cole of ISI and Vint Cerf of MCI provided great help in clarifying these issues through many discussions. Steve Casner and Jon Postel, both of ISI, also provided much needed critique. Anonymous referees contributed several suggestions and Tom Strini converted this paper into readable English.

I wish to thank all of them.

Exception Handling, Identification, and OSI/RM

Chairman

R. Frank

IDENTIFICATION IN COMPUTER NETWORKS*

Zaw-Sing Su
SRI International
Menlo Park, California

ABSTRACT

To communicate across a network system, entities within the system need to be able to identify one another. An identifier usually takes the form of a name or an address. Conventions for the assignment of these identifiers and their resolution affect many aspects of network design. Identification is thus a crucial issue for network architecture and standardization. In this paper, our discussion is first devoted to the semantics of names, addresses, and routes, with emphasis on the relationships among them. We then examine the implications of layered network architecture, syntactic differences of identifiers, and broadcast communication. Finally, we turn our attention to naming and addressing in large dynamic networks.

I. INTRODUCTION

To communicate across a network system, entities within a system need to identify one another. An identifier usually takes the form of a name or an address. Conventions for the assignment of these identifiers and their resolution affect many aspects of network design. Network interconnection, dynamic reconfiguration and large networks have a profound impact on naming and addressing. Identification has become a crucial issue for network architecture [Oppen81, Clark82, Mills81, Su82] and for network standardization [CCITT82, NBS82]. It has been the subject of discussion in many recent works [Cerf78, Shoch78, Sunshine82].

Shoch [Shoch78] has given informal definitions of a name, an address, and a route:

> The name indicates WHAT we seek,
> the address WHERE it is, and
> the route HOW TO GET THERE.

These definitions are useful for differentiating the concepts. However, confusion persists. One of the possible reasons for this confusion appears to be the ambiguity of their semantic relationships. In this paper, we first present the semantics of names, addresses, and routes, with emphasis on the relationships among them. To further elaborate, we examine the implications of layered architecture, syntactic differences of identifiers, and broadcast communication. Finally, we turn our attention to naming and addressing in large dynamic networks.

II. THE SEMANTICS OF NAMES AND ADDRESSES

In networking, names are identifiers used for distinguishing entities from one another. In order to distinguish network entities, it is necessary that names be unique. To help identifying a network entity, a name often incorporates structured information that specifies characterizing attributes of the entity. Such attributes, at the user level for example, may be administrative, geographical, or network topology dependent. However, naming can be accomplished without incorporating any attribute. To illustrate, we borrow the example of U.S. Social Security Number. It is used for resident identification without incorporating characterizing attributes.

*This research was supported, in part, by the Naval Electronic Systems Command under Contract No. N00039-82-C-0399. The views and conclusions contained in this document are those of the author and should not be interpreted as necessarily representing the official policies, either expressed or implied, of the Naval Electronic Systems Command or the U.S. Government.

One class of characterizing attributes useful for identification specifies the location of an entity. Thus, we may conclude that addresses are names which incorporate location attributes, but a name may or may not be an address. A corollary to our observation is that an identifier that does not incorporate any characterizing attribute can only be a name. When a specific reference is necessary, we will refer to a name that is not an address as address-independent, and to one that is an address as address-dependent.

For location specification, the characterizing attributes must be defined with respect to a frame of reference, or a "space". Borrowing from mathematical concepts, one may consider location specification to be necessarily functionally related to a metric defined on that space. An address then specifies the location of a "point" in this space. A postal address, for example, specifies a geographic location. One may consider longitude and latitude to be metrics of the geographic address space. Political jurisdiction can be used for postal addressing because it is functionally related to the geographic space. For computer communications, it may not make much sense to address a host by its geographic location, since its geographic location is not necessarily functionally related to the address space for networking. The address space in this case may be defined by the set of network components and the connection relations among them. An address of a host, for example, should specify "where" in the networking system the host is located.

Paralleling Shoch's definitions for a name, an address, and a route, we may further observe that a route characterizes the location of the destination entity by indicating a path for reaching it. Since a route specifies the location it leads to, we may similarly conclude that a route is an address, while an address may or may not be a route. A source route, for example, can be considered an address.

III. LAYERED NETWORK ARCHITECTURE

For modularity, a layered approach is often adopted for network architecture [ISO82, Cerf82]. Taking such an approach, the network functions are partitioned into protocol layers. Each layer depends upon lower layer functions and provides services to its upper layers. Naming and addressing are crucial components of each protocol layer. The communicating entities within a layer refer to each other by name. The set of communicating entities at a lower layer may form the basis for the address space of the layer above it. The address of an upper layer entity is often defined as the location of an entity within the lower layer with which the upper layer entity is associated. While an address defines the location of a "point" in the address space, a route can be thought of as defining a "line" leading from the originator to the destination in that space.

An identification space, however, need not necessarily coincide with a protocol layer. It is sometimes found advantageous in network design to introduce an extra identification layer. Such an extra layer may provide additional indirection. An indirection is the flexibility in binding between entities belonging to two different spaces. Logical addressing [Rosen81] is an example of an extra identification layer. It provides the advantages of a fixed-length numeric identifier without completing the binding to a network entity.

IV. SYNTACTIC DIFFERENCES OF IDENTIFIERS

Specifying conventions for network entity identification is an important aspect of network system design. An identifier may, for example, be in the form of a character or a numeric string of fixed or variable length. In existing computer networks, an identifier often takes one of two forms: a variable-length character string or a fixed-length numeric string.

A character string offers user-friendliness. Natural language terms meaningful to human users may be readily incorporated in a character string. Variable-length identification offers the possible accommodation of an arbitrary number of different identifiers. It is also useful for accommodating variation in identification. Communication between entities in two different systems can be accommodated, for example, by employing a common and variable-length addressing scheme. The Xerox internet address is 48 bits long, while the DARPA internet address is 32 bits. Without imposing the identification of one system on the other, one possible scheme to accommodate such a difference, at least in theory, is to employ variable-length addressing concatenating the internet address with a prefix for internet indication. Source routing as a form of addressing [Sunshine77] is another example of a situation in which variable-length identification comes in handy For a hierarchical identification scheme, a variable-length address may also allow depth variation in the hierarchy. A proposed convention for DARPA internet domain naming [Su82] is an example of a hierarchical identification scheme allowing depth variation. The disadvantage of variable-length identification is the inefficiency that results from its excessive processing requirements. However, with the continuing increase in processing speed, variable-length identification may become more and more attractive.

Fixed-length identification imposes a finite limit on the number of different identifiers. This limit is a function of the fixed length and the size of the encoding set (e.g., 16-bit identification provides 2^{16}, approximately 64,000, different identifiers). Although the limit is usually large enough for practical purposes, it could be significantly reduced when structured information is incorporated. One advantage of fixed-length identifier is that it can be conveniently embedded in a protocol header to allow efficient processing. The 32-bit DARPA internet addressing [Postel81] offers an example of ingenious incorporation of variable-length identification in a fixed- length format.

The difference between a fixed-length numeric string and a variable-length character string is syntactic, while the difference between a name and an address is semantic. The association of names with variable-length character strings and of addresses with fixed-length numerics often leads to the assumption that such an association is required. However, this is not the case. For example, "mbxA@hostB.netC", a variable-length character string, can semantically be an address specifying the location of a mailbox "mbxA" on host "hostB" that is connected to network "netC"

Name to address resolution is a binding process. When a name is resolved, it is mapped onto one or more specific addresses. The convention for naming affects when this binding takes place. The later the binding the more flexibility there is for the name-to-address mapping relation. Address-independent naming offers the flexibility of an indirection. A change of address can be accommodated by accordingly changing the mapping relation without affecting the identities of the communicating entities. Address-dependent naming offers little indirection. The relocation of a communicating entity from one network address to another may imply a change of its identity. However, the use of address-dependent names for identification allows efficient resolution. Resolution for an address-dependent name may involve only a syntactic translation, e.g., a translation from character strings to numeric ones. In the extreme case, when the same identifier is used for both the name and the address, the resolution process can be avoided all together. A proper choice of naming convention depends largely on the networking environment. It can, however, have a significant impact on the system design.

V. BROADCAST COMMUNICATION

Computer networks initially evolved on the basis of point-to-point communication. This was true at both network and link levels, (e.g, ARPANET). In order to reach a destination in point-to-point communication, the originating entity resolves the destination name into a route, sometimes via an address. The route might be explicitly a source route or implicitly an incremental route. Transmission from an originator proceeds along a single link at a time, propagating toward the destination. Addresses and routes are in particular useful for point-to-point communication.

Broadcasting offers an address-independent mode of communication for computer networking. Broadcast transmission in a local networking environment (e.g., ETHERNET [Metcalfe76]) is an example of broadcast communication at the link level. To broadcast, the originator transmits to all entities attached to the network. Often found in practice is a combination of point-to-point communication at a higher level and broadcasting at a lower level. In order to communicate with a specific destination (i.e., point-to-point at the higher level), the originator incorporates a higher level identifier in the transmission specifying the intended destination. The communication is established with the destination recognizing its identity, i.e., its name not its address.

By the nature of broadcast communication, every transmission from each participant in a communicating community would be received by all others. Without improvements in the technology, the resulting overhead of broadcasting communication may render its application over a large communicating community impractical. However, its address-independent mode of operation potentially provides solutions for the accommodation of multi-homing, multi-casting, and network dynamics [Dalal81].

VI. LARGE DYNAMIC NETWORKS

In this discussion, a large network system refers to a network or an internetwork with a large number of network entities. A critical concern for large networks is to locate the destination. Address-dependent naming can be very useful in that an address-dependent name incorporates at least some hint of where the destination is located. The telephone system is an example of a large network employing address-dependent naming. The telephone number a user of the network uses to identify the destination he is trying to reach is an address-dependent name, or an address. By area code and the prefix for local office, it describes where is the destination within the telephone system.

Networks that are capable of changing dynamically impose challenging requirements for network design. A dynamic networking environment may involve network partitioning, network merging, or mobile network entities [Cerf79]. The principle challenge arises from the fact that the location, and thus the address, of a network entity can change dynamically. In the case of a mobile network entity, its physical movement could cause a change of location with respect to a presumably stationary network environment. This environment constitutes the address space. In the case of network partitioning or merging, the address space itself changes. Such change may in turn affect the "location" of certain network entities relative to the network system.

In a dynamic networking environment, address-dependent naming may not be desirable. Any change of address would imply a change of identity. For connection-oriented communication, such as communication over virtual circuits, the connection established based upon identities of the source and destination could not be maintained. Using address-independent naming requires name resolution or broadcast communication. However, either approach can lead to inefficiency when a large communicating community is involved. Naming and addressing in large dynamic network systems remains an area for further investigation.

VII. SUMMARY

In this paper we discussed the semantics of a name, an address, and a route in computer networks and the relationships among them. An address may be a name, and a route may be an address, but their respective converses are not necessarily true. A rigid association of names with variable-length character strings and of addresses with numerics can lead to unnecessary confusion. The difference between a name and an address is semantic, not syntactic.

We observe that specification of naming and addressing conventions is a crucial aspect of the design of each protocol layer. Extra identification layers may be introduced for additional indirection. We also observed that broadcasting offers an address-independent mode of communication, which can be useful for the accommodation of some advanced communication requirements. Addressing and routing are in particular useful for point-to-point communication.

Finally, we pointed out that the underlying design issue for dynamic network systems is to accommodate the continual change of addresses. Architecture for large dynamic network systems remains a challenging area for further research.

ACKNOWLEDGMENTS

The author would like to thank Donald L. Nielson for his encouragement and support, Jose J. Garcia for our numerous discussions on the subject of naming and addressing, and Jon B. Postel for his review of an earlier version of this paper.

REFERENCES

[CCITT82] CCITT SG VII, "Proposed Draft Recommendation Reference Model of Open Systems Interconnection for CCITT Applications," Special Rapporteur on Layered Models, Melbourne (March 1982).

[Cerf78] Cerf, Vinton G. and Peter T. Kirstein, "Issues in Packet-Network Interconnection," Proceedings of the IEEE, vol.66, No. 11, (November 1978).

[Cerf79] Cerf, Vinton G., "Internet Addressing and Naming in a Tactical Environment," IEN 110, Information Processing Techniques Office, Defense Advanced Research Projects Agency, Arlington, Virginia (August 1979).

[Cerf82] Cerf, Vinton G., and Edward Cain, "The US DOD Internet Architecture Model," presented at NATO Symposium on Interoperability of Automated Data Systems, SHAPE Technical Centre, The Hague, Netherlands (November 8-12, 1982).

[Clark78] Clark, David, "A Proposal for Addressing and Routing in the Internet," IEN 46, Laboratory of Computer Science, Massachusetts Institute of Technology, Cambridge, Massachusetts (June 1978).

[Dalal81] Dalal, Yogen K. and Robert S. Printis, "48-bit Absolute Internet and Ethernet Host Numbers," Proceedings of the 7th Data Communications Symposium, pp.240-245 (October 1981).

[ISO82] International Organization for Standardization, "Reference Model of Open Systems Interconnection," ISO/TC97/SC16, Draft International Standard ISO/DIS/7498 (1982).

[Metcalfe76] Metcalfe, Robert M. and David R. Boggs, "ETHERNET: Distributed Packet Switching for Local Computer Networks," Communications of the Association for Computing Machinery, vol.19, No. 7, pp.395-404 (July 1976).

[Mills81] Mills, David L., "Internet Name Domains," RFC 799, COMSAT Laboratory, Washington, D.C. (September 1981).

[NBS82] National Bureau of Standards, "Naming and Addressing in Computer Based Message Systems," Report No. ICST/CBOS-82-4, (Draft) (August 1982).

[Oppen81] Oppen, Derek C. and Yogen K. Dalal, "The Clearinghouse: A Decentralized Agent for Locating Named Objects in a Distributed Environment," Xerox Office Products Division, Systems Development Department, Palo Alto, California (July 1981).

[Postel81] Postel, Jonathan B., "Address Mappings," RFC 796, Information Sciences Institute, University of Southern California, Marina del Rey, California (September 1981).

[Rosen81] Rosen, Eric C., "Logical Addressing," IEN 183, Bolt Beranek and Newman, Cambridge, Massachusetts (May 1981).

[Shoch78] Shoch, John F., "Inter-Network Naming, Addressing, and Routing," Proceedings of 17th IEEE Computer Society International Conference, pp.72-79 (September 1978).

[Su82] Su, Zaw-Sing and Jonathan B. Postel, "Domain Naming Convention for Internet User Applications," RFC 819, Network Information Center, SRI International, Menlo Park, California, (August 1982).

[Sunshine77] Sunshine, Carl A., "Source Routing in Computer Networks," ACM SIGCOMM Computer Communication Review, vol.7, No. 01, pp.29-33 (January 1977).

[Sunshine82] Sunshine, Carl A., "Addressing Problems in Multi-Network Systems," Proceedings of IEEE INFOCOM 82, Las Vegas, Nevada, pp.311-317 (March-April 1982).

IMPLEMENTING THE ISO-OSI REFERENCE MODEL

by R. Popescu-Zeletin

Bereich Datenverarbeitung und Elektronik
Hahn-Meitner-Institut für Kernforschung Berlin GmbH, Berlin, Germany

Abstract

The ISO-OSI reference model was the design framework for the implementation of a heterogeneous network in a local environment. The HMINET-2 is a network based on standards in data communication. The paper focus on the OSI model feasability and outlines the encountered problems and the adopted solutions in the network design and implementation.

1. Introduction

In the last five years tremendous research and standardization efforts can be witnessed in the data communication field in order to support the requirements of standard communication features in heterogeneous environments.

The fast technological developments in the field of data communication have been materialized in a variety of products which claim to solve the user's requirements for networking. On the other hand, the users have precipitated this invasion by calling for increased connectivity, higher reliability, lower costs in networking and support for interconnecting hetergeneous equipment. The result of this situation is that the user has a difficult task in developing strategies for its environment in order to get unscathed through the product jungle of the market[6].

The research and standardization efforts have been materialized in the ISO-Open System Interconnection Reference Model.

The layered model has two main objectives:

- to provide a logical framework to bring order into a very complex domain,
- to separate functions characterizing a certain layer in order to provide independence between standards and corresponding products at different layers.

The reference character of the ISO-OSI model has and will have a dominant role in the future of standards and products in data communication since it imposes a rigorous discipline for the development of products and systems to achieve compatibility. Many organizations (CCITT, IEEE) and products suppliers (DIX etc.) have adopted the model and are referencing their systems and products to the model.

The paper outlines the experience and problems coming up from a pilot project in networking which has been sponsored by the German Ministry of Research and Technology. The scope of the project was the development of a heterogeneous network based on ISO-OSI reference model and the related standardization output.

First we outline the main characteristics of the hardware and software characteristics and the network embedment in the national and international public networks.

Chapter 3 focusses on some general conceptual problems of the ISo-OSI model encountered in the design of the network. Then we discuss the practical and conceptual problems in each layer and we describe the adcpted solutions.

Some main points of concern and general conclusions are summarized in the last chapter of this paper.

We assume that the reader of this paper is familiar with the concepts and the terminology used in the ISO/TC97/SC16 documents.

2. HMINET2 - a network based on standards

HMI is a nuclear research institute in West-Berlin. The requirements for networking and distributed processing have been identified at the beginning of 70's. The result was the development of a local area network (HMINET-1) which was based on a design closely influenced by the local environment at that time. The network was a result of a cooperation between HMI and SIEMENS AG. and was installed at different places in the world[9]. The experience gained in the operation of HMINET-1 has influenced the decision to start the design of a new network called HMINET-2. The main aspects which have influenced this decision are:

- New computer types in the HMINET-1 environment impose a large implementation effort.
- New operating-system versions require changes in the network software.
- Requirement for on-line communication with other similar institutions in Germany or elsewhere.
- The requirement of a global concept which covers network and real-time applications in order to minimize the implementation effort.

These considerations and the new impacts and know-how in network technology have determined the basic aims of the HMINET-2 design:

1) - the manufacturer independence by adopting accepted standards,
2) - design of an open-ended network architecture,
3) - high interconnectivity and flexibility by allowing computer to participate at different network technologies using the same standard application
4) - compatibility with the national public network to allow communication to the outside world.

The developments in the standardization organizations, the evolution of the ISO-OSI reference model and its implication in the data communication market, the CCITT recommendations and their impact on the development of European networks are some of the facts which have influenced the decision to develop a network based on standards.

The computer types in HMI and the corresponding operating systems are depicted in the following table:

Host type	No. of Hosts	O.S.	Supplier
S7880	1	BS3000 (IBM compat.)	SIEMENS
VAX	2	VMS	DEC
PDP11 40-70	25	RSX 11M	DEC
R-30	2	ORG	SIEMENS

Outside HMI, in the Berlin area and in other institutions of interest for HMI users, a large variety of computer types are directly connected to the German public network (DATEX-P). Some of them are: IBM, CD, UNIVAC, S7700 etc.

The high degree of heterogenity explains also why the design had to rely on a reference model (ISO/OSI) and the corresponding standards.

The network topology and its embedment in the national and international public networks is outlined in fig. 1.

The adopted communication architecture and the related standards are depicted in fig. 2.

3. Conceptual problems

There are a number of issues which are not clear in the ISO-OSI reference model specification[4] for a network designer.

Some of them are:

1. Layer independence.
The adopted layering technique is characterized by two major concepts:
-The layer service which is the set of capabilities offered at the boundary of a layer to a user in the next higher layer. Note that the service is an abstraction by which the capabilities offered by a layer (in using all lower layers) are specified and that the service definition is independent of any particular implementation.
-The protocol which defines the rules of interactions between entitities which are situated in the same layer but pertain to different systems.
It is obvious that by the definition of the service offered by a layer and the definition of the service offered by the lower layer the functionality of a layer is completely specified. Note that different protocols may carry out this functionality.
Although these architectural concepts aim to layer indepedence the services defined in the related standards for each layer do not provide completely this goal. This is mainly due to the fact that the services are defined as a three party communication. The three communicating entities are the two users of the service and the layer below as service provider.
The implication of this fact is that the specifications of the services provided by each layer define the capabilities offered by the layer and the behaviour of the two users of the service in the layer above.

A neutral service definition without the involvement of the behaviour of the entities in the layer above is probably the only way to achieve the aimed layer independence.

2. Multicast communication
The ISO-OSI model provides provisions for point-to-point communication only. A large class of applications requires multicast communication regimes (distributed databases, mailing and teleconferencing systems etc.). At the present time the user of the model has to solve the communication aspects for multicast applications outside the model.
Since one of the aims of the model is to relieve the users of the model of communication oriented aspects, for this class of applications the model failed its aim.

3. Layer entities
Another practical and architectural problem is the fact that in the OSI Reference Model the existence of entities in the next higher layer is assumed at connection set up time (e.g. Session Entities for the Transport Layer in the establishment phase). This assumption is not true for most implementations if the implementator cares for implementation effiency and so does not implement a multitude of dummy processes which have to wait to be activated. That means that before a CONNECT indication may occur the creation of an entity in the Session Layer has to be performed. It is not clear from the service specification which entity in which layer has to enter the termination phase if the entity cannot be created or when deadlock situations occur.

4. Dynamic change of quality of service
The present documents specify the negotiation of the service quality only at connection set up time. There are many cases where a dynamic change of the quality of service is required. In the existing documents a quality of service may be changed only by involving the termination of the connection and then by re-establishing a new connection with the new service quality. This schema is too rigid and too costly.
A practical problem in the network design is also the criteria choice on how different quality of services at different layers can be maped.

3.1 Layer 1 to 3

As already mentioned the X25 LAP B recommendation was adopted and provided by the host manufacturer for the first three layers.

The practice has shown that even if a standard is available the manufacturer are reluctant in providing it. The reluctance is motivated by the options available in a standard and also in the ambiguities contained in it. These ambiguities appear through the informal description technique of the standard. Although the informal description eases the readability of standard, a formal methodology accompaning the informal one will minimize false interpretations and implementation effort. Since the first three layers are provided by different manufacturers in the HMINET-2 a lot of effort was put in testing, certification and alleviation of incompatibilities of the products supplied by the manufacturers. This task was eased by the existence of the requirement that all X.25 products have to be fully compatible with the adopted version of the X.25 in the German public network (DATEX-P). We learned that a certification authority and appropriate testing mechanisms and procedures are vital in the development of the network.

The certification task has accompanied the whole project and even now for new communication links to hosts connected to other national public networks differences appear between national X25 implementations (e.g. facility field).

A major practical and architectural problem is the visibility of the X.25 services. The question is "where the upper layers access the X.25 layer 3 services, in host or in the front-end?" (fig. 3)

Usually between the host operating system and front-end a manufacturer specific protocol is implemented (fig.3a). Adopting the ISO-OSI model in the network design means that the upper layers have to use the services and the characteristics of the layers below. The second solution (fig3b) has the advantage that all layer 3 characteristics: flow control, error detection and recovery, addressing are available in host for the upper layers. Since the standards in transport layer are based on backpressure, error reporting etc. the second solution eases the implementation and design of the network.

Disadvantage of this solution is the fact that it is contradictory with the front-end concept of relieving the main frame from the communication aspects.

We choose the second solution since standard products in the upper layers were not available from the manufacturers at that time and have had to be designed and implemented in HMI (fig. 4).

3.2 Layer 4

The scope of the layer 4, also called transport layer is to ensure an end-to-end communication between processes situated in different hosts. The present available ISO DP 8073 identifies 5 classes of protocols and mainly mirrors the compromize between ISO and CCITT outputs.

If class 0 and 1 are supposed to support usual PTT applications (teletex etc.) class 2 to 4 are characterizing the user concerns of cost effectiveness and enlarged interconnectivitiy with networks based on a connectionless type of service. The main practical problems encountered in the network design are:

a) Choice of the class and options to be adopted. This decision is influenced by the environmental characteristics and the scope of the network. The multitude of choices and the fact that a manufacturer decision towards a certain class and set of options is inpredictable at the present time the transport layer design is a difficult task.

b) Cost effectiveness. If one of the scopes of the layer 4 is to be cost efficient then it has to provide additionally a service which will allow the User of the Transport Service to interrupt the Network Connection (for which he has to pay) without interrupting the life of the Transport Connection. That means that the Transport entities will exist even if the corresponding Network Connection is discarded. Such a situation may occur when an application transmits data from time to time and does not want to pay for maintaining the Network Connection for the time when no communication occurs.

c) Authorization. If the Transport Layer has an end-to-end significance it has to provide an authorisation mechanism for the access in the end system from remote. In the present specification no protection mechanisms (e.g. user identification, passwords etc.) are mentioned and that implies that resources may be used by everybody everywhere. An intended or unintended user misbehaviour may use all resources of the remote system. In the current specifications this misbehaviour cannot be detected[5].

Some of the above items are identified in the DP8073 but considered for further study. At least the accounting and TC user identification seems to be vital for each operational network. The decision to implement a transport layer which offers the functionality of class 1 protocol is motivated by the HMINET and BERNET environment and scope.

The time scale of the project development did not allow to wait for a standard of the transport layer. We have adopted the message link protocol (MLP) a German research environment standard which is equivalent with the ISO class 1.

The accounting problems introduced by multiplexing of transport connections over a X.25 network connection, and the fact that HMINET is a compus network (no transmission costs are charged for local communication) are some other arguments for choosing a protocol functionally equivalent with class 1.

Again the formal description of the protocol was an important aid towards compatible implementation in the different hosts[1].

The emergence of the LAN technology in data communication have influenced the decision to reconsider the implemented layer 4 protocol. Since the tendence is a decentralization of the network in closed LANs for specific applications and the HMINET-2 use as a back-bone network (fig. 1), connection and connectionless services are required at the transport layer boundary. The most suitable class in DP8073 specification is class 4.

The advantage of a rigorous layered architecture for the network implementation is obvious since the changes introduced do not influence the layers above and below.

3.3 Session layer

The scope of the session layer is to offer a synchronization mechanism for entities residing in the layers above.

The design of this layer in HMINET-2 relies on the requirements of the standard applications offered.

The main functionality is a checkpoint/restart mechanisms used for data transfer between peer application entities.

Depending on the reliability class required by the application the frequency of checkpoints is negotiated at the session establishment time.

The main difference between the ISO-OSI documents on session and our design and implementation consists in the perception of the session functionality. If the ISO/SC16 documents are specifying a session layer which offers only a mechanism for synchronization which is triggered by the processes in the layers above, the session layer in HMINET-2 provides the necessary mechanism for reliable communication and synchronization inside the session layer. By this means the applications processes are relieved from communication reliability concerns and synchronization problems.

The evident implication is that data is buffered in the session layer and that the checkpoints refer to session data units which size are session specific and negotiable at the session establishment time. The independence between the session data unit and the application data unit is from our experience an important aspect to achieve the layer independence. The session data unit acts like a container where the application data units are put into for transfer. An application data unit can be transferred using one or more session data units or a session data unit may contain more than one application data units.

The above mechanism has two other important side-aspects which are:

- it offers a flexible mean for resource administration in communication between different hosts. The buffer size for the session data units transfer are negotiable at the session establishment time and are dependent on the communication host types and their load.

- it offers in certain cases a performance improvement if by one session data unit more than one application data are transferred through the network (e.g. file transfer application).

To summarize the implemented mechanism: depending on the application type which initializes the session a certain session data unit size and the checkpoint frequency is proposed to the remote system (session entity).

Depending on the local resources and parameters the remote system accepts or proposes in return its choice. The initiator session entity may now decide if in this conditions the application requirements can be fulfilled or not. In the later case the session is discarded and the application process may decide to establish a new session with decreased quality of service or to try latter in the expectation that the resource set in the session layer will be able to satisfy its requirements.

3.4 Application and presentation layer

The facilities offered by the network can be classified in three categories:

1) standard network facilities conforming the ISO-OSI model (CBMS, virtual file),
2) facilities conforming other standards (terminal access CCITT X3, X28, X29),
3) user software package relying on layer 4 or 5.

We will consider only the first two categories since they are of general interest.

3.4.1 The Computer Based Message System DINAMIT

The DINAMIT system provides four main facilities for the network user:

- mail service, where letters can be sent to one, to a group or to all network users,
- an on line access to a library of documents and help files for the use of the network,
- a network status service where information of general interest about the hosts connected and network status at the service request time is available,
- network management capabilities for the whole network[3].

The system is a fully distributed application where its users may send or receive messages from each terminal connected to the network (i.e. locality independent).

Four types of processes are involved in the system (fig. 5):

- an user agent process on each host from which the DINAMIT system is accessable,
- a post-station process for user message switching. The number of post station processes and their assignment to a certain host is dependent on topological and efficiency criteria.
- a message base for the storage of the messages to be forwarded.
- an user record base for each user of the system, where information about messages sent to him is available (fig. 5).

A message to be sent is delivered by the UAP to the post-station process to which the UAP is connected. The post-station process will store the message in its message base and will inform the addressed user(s) record base(s) about the existence of a message for him in the PS message base. The user(s) for whom the message is destinated will be informed about the existence of a message as soon as he is accessing the DINAMIT system at any of the user agent processes.

The presentation layer functionality is implemented by adopting standard data formats between the communicating processes and by encoding/decoding the standard data representation into the local one.

Note that DINAMIT is a typical example of a distributed application in the ISO-OSI environment, where different distributed processes are involved.

Although the ISO-OSI model describes only a point-to-point type of communication between autonomous application processes of the same type, some comments about the feasibility of the model for applications which are functional distributed are probably interesting:

- there is a need of multicast and broadcast communication type to support such applications. This facility has to be supported by the session layer and below in order to relieve the applications and presentation layer from communication oriented concerns,
- establishing and discarding connections for the transfer of small amounts of data is a very costly and inefficient mechanism. A datagram or fast connect/ disconnect service visible in the upper layers will be usefull for a number of applications,
- the synchronization between concurrent accesses to ensure the consistency of distributed information is a service which is mandatory for a large number of functional distributed applications (mail systems, distributed databases etc.). Mechanisms like two-phase commit, time stamps based have to be offered by the session layer.

3.4.2 The virtual file system

The virtual file concept was introduced[10] in order to alleviate the incompatibilities of the different data management system types in networks with a high degree of heterogeneity or for the design of networks with a non-predictable population of hosts (open systems). The concept was adopted in the national and international standardization bodies (ISO, DIN etc.) and was implemented in HMINET and BERNET[8].

The main aim of this approach is to define a standard logical file structure in each host in the network and to provide the different systems with translation mechanisms between the new logical structure and the existing local structures. With this concept, equivalent with the definition of netwide data management system, the user who accesses data somewhere in a network has only one interface; the interface to the virtual file system. The virtual file can be described as a tree structure with n hierarchical levels. Each level i ($1 \le i \le n$) consists of a set of file access data units (FADUs) at level i-1 or below (fig. 6). A file access data unit is an accessable piece of information that has a semantic meaning.

Note that the depth of the tree is open ended and it is user application dependent.

It is obvious that the advantage of introducing an uniform structure is that we can introduce an uniform set of FADU access services and one protocol (i.e. the same services and protocol support file transfer as well as data units access within a virtual file). The depth of the virtual file is negotiable between the two application entities and uniform conventions on authorization, access control etc. are introduced in the network. The common set of services and the related protocol are defined in the nested phases (ISO terminology: regimes):

There are some differences between the implemented virtual file system in HMINET - BERNET environment and the ISO-VF system specification[11].

- the implemented file structure is a subset of the ISO one and consists in the restriction that the arc length between the FADUs is always 1. The depth is negotiable between the systems involved in an application connection.
- for efficiency reasons the implemented system provides the capability of accessing FADUs in different virtual files stored at a certain host within one application connection. The ISO specification provides one application connection per accessed file. The reasoning is that since multiplexing is provided by the transport layer (cost efficiency) then maintaining one application connection per vitual file will not influence the costs. But since the first two classes of the transport protocol are not multiplexing and since there is an inherent sequentiality within most programs accessing data in different files, we decided to provide the mechanism depicted in fig. 7b rather than the ISO one (fig. 7a):
- another difference between the two approaches is that the HMINET-BERNET implementation provides a distinct separa-

tion for recovery for data transfer failures (check-point/restart in the session layer) and the check point /restart mechanism in the application layer related to the accessed structure. In our approach the application entities are not concerned with recovery from failures in the data transfer; the failures being captured within the session layer.

The data types supported by the presentation layer as standard transfer syntax encompass: characters, integers, reals etc. The data type set is defined open-ended and more complex structures for new applications like: graphics, document transfer, remote job entry etc. are in development.

The formal specification of the virtual file system[2] has accompanied the implementation work and has provided the precise basis for the implementation phase in the different computer system types.

The implemented virtual file structure is flexible enough to accommodate the requirements of the traditional file transfer and remote data access (record access) systems and at the same time to map data structures used in applications like graphical systems (metafiles), document access systems etc.

New enhancements of the virtual file protocol for concurrency control have been specified and are in development. The enhanced protocol is based on a time stamp mechanism for a distributed database management system[7].

3.4.3 The terminal access system DIA (CCITT X3, X28, X29)

The decision to support in HMINET-2 the CCITT 3X recommendations was motivated by its national and international dissemination although these standards do not rely on the ISO-OSI model.

The 3X recommendations describe the protocol for start-stop terminals in a X25 network.

The specification was influenced by the initial thoughts that packet-switching networks will support only terminal-host communication and that the network nodes will offer PADs (packet assembly-disassembly) as a common communication carrier service. The initial PAD specification for DCE (data communication equipment) has precipitate the invasion of products like PAD terminal concentrators and implementation of PAD in hosts.

This was motivated by the costs for the PAD/terminal connections and the flexibility in using the same terminal in local mode or as a terminal for a remote host.

Another important aspect to be observed is the fact that the 3X recommendations mainly describe a protocol and that the service definition is poor if not inexistent. The result is that the host behaviour is not specified and is implementation dependent (e.g reset behaviour, echoing etc.).

The DIA system in HMI is offered on each host, in terminal concentrator and in the switching node (fig. 8).

4. Conclusions

There are some aspects for general interest we have learned in the project development:

A) The ISO-OSI model is an efficient tool for the development of the complex hardware and software of a network.

   Adopting the same ISO-OSI reference terminology and design concepts in a large team of network designers and implementators has minimized the understanding overhead.

B) A strict layering architecture in the network design and implementation is mandatory for future changes and integration of new standards and products.

   A network based on the standardization output minimizes in long terms the maintenance and integration work since it can be expected that more and more communication standards will be provided by the computer manufacturers as parts of their operating systems.

C) An active participation in the standardization work has shorted the information path standardization output - implementation.

D) The use of formal description techniques in the specification phase is mandatory in order to achieve compatible implementations by different teams on different machines.

E) The development of testing procedures and reference implementations as certification centers is a necessity for heterogeneous networks and has to be considered as part of the network design from the beginning.

Literature:

1 Bochmann G.v., "Formalized specification of the MLP"
Report Univ. of Montreal June 1979

2 Bochman G.v. et al., "Formalized specification and analysis of the Virtual File System"
HMI Report B367 Feb. 1982

3 Bauerfeld W., et al., "DINAMIT - an adaptable, distributed computer based message system"
to be published

4 ISO/TC97/SC16 Draft International Standard 7498 1982

5 Lenzini L., Popescu-Zeletin R., Vissers C.
"State of the art study on the standardization of level 4" Report for the Commission of European Communities"
Brussel 1981

6 Mier, Edwin E. "High level protocols and the OSI reference model" Data Communication 1982

7 Popescu-Zeletin R., Weber H. "The logical architecture for D-DBMS in the ISO-OSI framework"
Proc. GI Congress Berlin 1983 Springer Verlag

8 Popescu-Zeletin R., et al. "The virtual file specification - final draft - "HMI Report B333 1980

9 Popescu-Zeletin R., Baum D., Butscher B. " A local computer network in a research environment: The HMINET Proc. Computer networking symposium NBS 1979

10 Popescu-Zeletin R., Bauerfeld W. "A virtual file concept for heterogeneous computer networks" Proc. AICA congress BARI Italy 1979

11 ISO/TC97/SC16/WG 5 Working documents on file transfer access and management. N1190, N1222, N1223, N1224 revised 1983

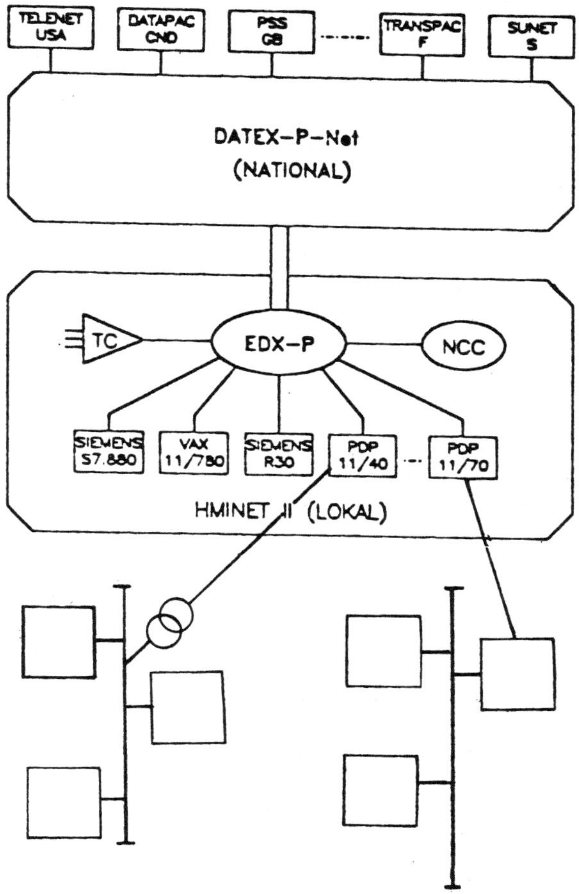

Fig.1

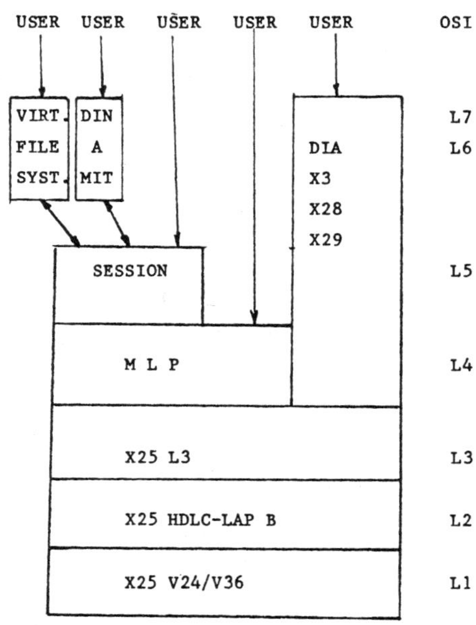

Fig.2

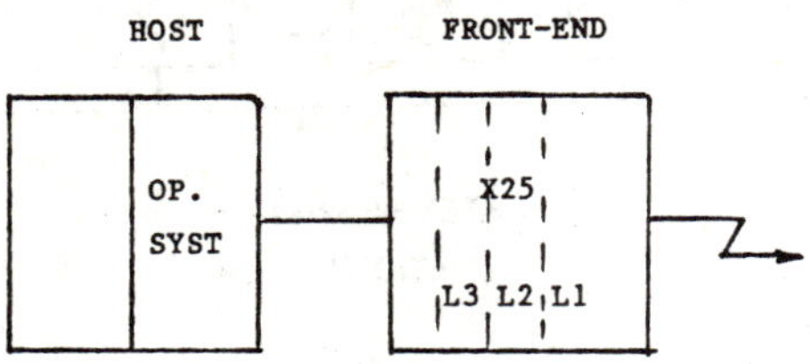

Fig.3a

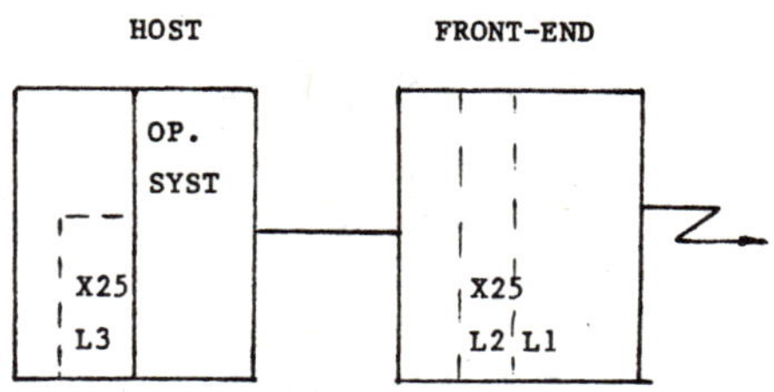

Fig.3b

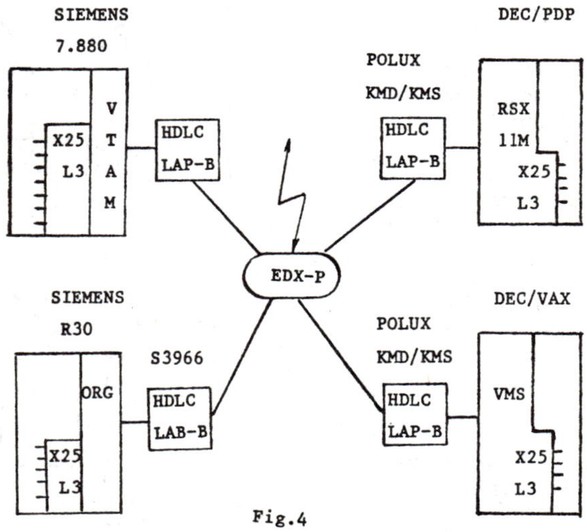

Fig.4

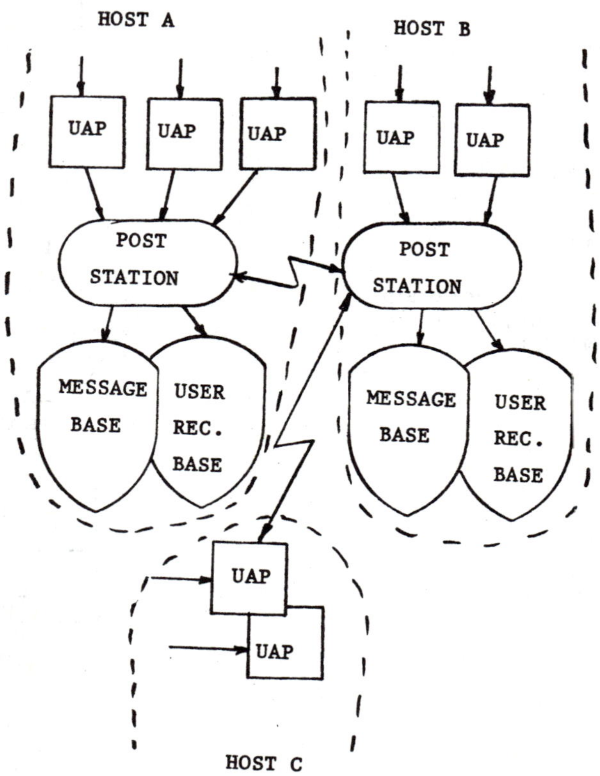

Fig.5

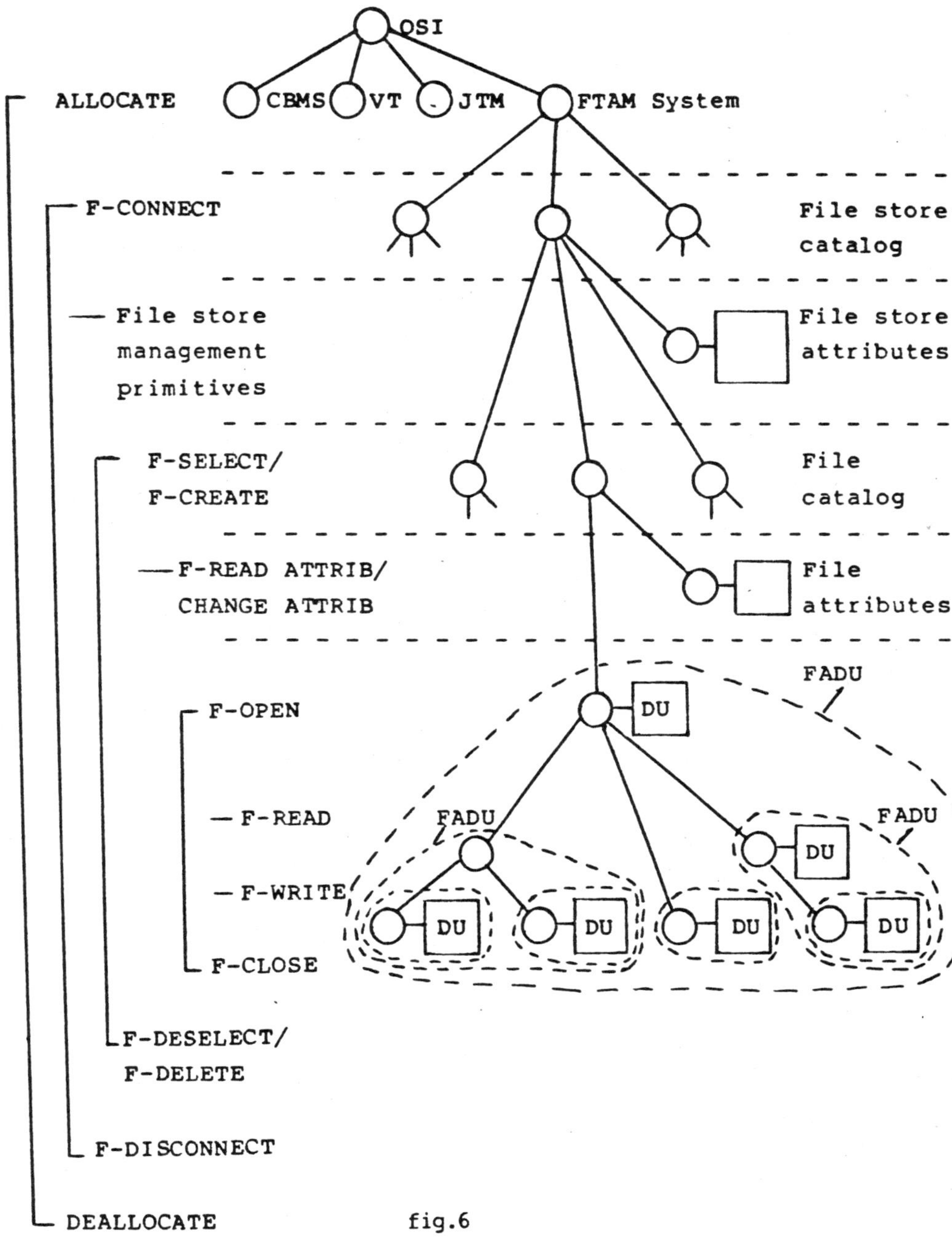
OSI
ALLOCATE
CBMS
VT
JTM
FTAM System
F-CONNECT
File store
catalog
File store
management
primitives
File store
attributes
F-SELECT/
F-CREATE
File
catalog
F-READ ATTRIB/
CHANGE ATTRIB
File
attributes
FADU
F-OPEN
DU
F-READ
FADU
FADU
F-WRITE
DU
DU
DU
DU
DU
F-CLOSE
F-DESELECT/
F-DELETE
F-DISCONNECT
DEALLOCATE

fig.6

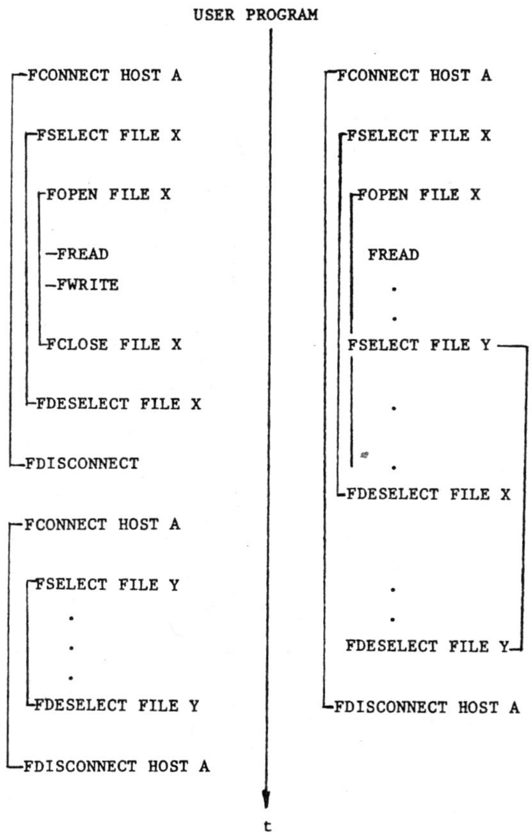

Fig.7a

Fig.7b

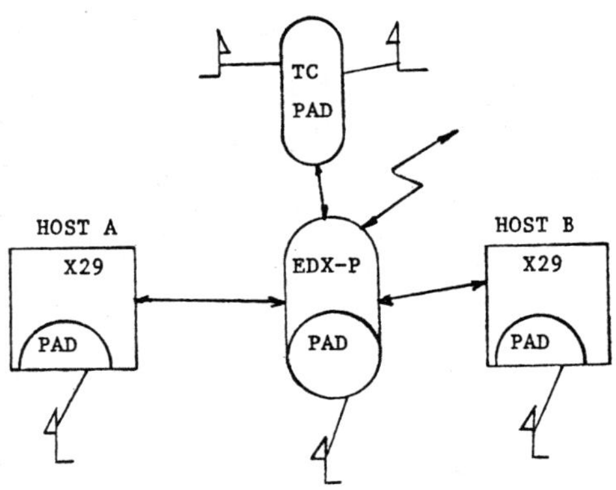

Fig.8

Exception Handling in Communication Protocols

M. Stella Atkins

Computer Science Department,
The University of British Columbia.

This paper describes structures used for exception handling in multi-process implementations of the X.25 and X.29 protocols. Each protocol layer is implemented as a collection of cooperating processes. These are structured in one of two alternative ways, reflecting differences in the type of exceptional situations that may occur.

Within each of the **lower** protocol layers, one process takes the form of a Finite State Machine. In these lower level protocols, where it is difficult to identify "normal" transitions, there are no special exception cases; we treat all transitions as being equally likely to occur.

For **higher** level protocols such as the X.29 protocol, exceptions occur less frequently. Here. transmitting and receiving are performed by two independent processes, and exception handling is performed by an auxiliary process which is invoked as needed. This multi-process structure matches the functionality of the protocol, and results in software which is easy to program and easy to understand.

1. Introduction

The CCITT Recommendation X.25 [2] defines a multi-layer protocol for interfacing computer equipment to a packet-switched network. Each X.25 protocol layer can be described as a Finite State Machine (FSM) making appropriate state transitions on receipt of packets or timeouts [1].

The CCITT's Virtual Terminal Protocol X.29 [6], here referred to as Datapac's Interactive Terminal Interface protocol (ITI), establishes a data structure that it views as representing the terminal. A remote terminal user may therefore interface with a host-side application program over the Datapac network via the host-side X.25 and ITI protocols. These protocols have been successfully implemented on a small timesharing system using a multi-process operating system called Verex, linking it to Canada's Datapac network.

The Verex operating system [8] is a descendent of Thoth[3], in which processes communicate via messages. The message-passing process model is a simple and unifying approach to synchronisation, data transfer, concurrency, and distribution of function across processors and memories.

Using multiple processes communicating via messages such as are found in the Thoth and Verex operating systems it is possible to model the action of the lower-level protocol finite state machines. When no special exception cases are identifiable, the process executing the Finite State Machine can then be conveniently implemented as a combination of a "server" process and a Finite State Machine. This process provides all the necessary synchronisation of transmitting and receiving, leading to efficient handling of all transitions. Deering has shown [7] in his X.25 implementation using Verex that such structuring is feasible. The resulting software is produced quickly and models closely the protocol descriptions contributing to its understandability and maintainability .

Scotton applied similar techniques [9] for his implementation of the ITI protocol in Verex, but recognized several disadvantages in using these techniques for the higher level protocols. We therefore propose a new structure for higher level protocols, where exceptional cases appear less frequently, and a "normal" case can be identified.

In this paper we first outline the process and message-passing environment supported by Verex. We then illustrate how this environment can be used to provide implementations of the X.25 protocol, and describe Deering's implementation. We discuss the exception handling mechanisms used in this implementation, where exceptions are treated as the rule, and the problems in extending this to an implementation of a higher-level protocol such as the ITI protocol.

We then describe the novel exception-handling mechanism employed in the ITI implementation. This structure employs separate independent processes for transmitting and receiving together with an auxiliary exception-handling process to coordinate transmitting and receiving when an exception occurs.

We show how this structure overcomes the problems of the server model, and conclude with a summary of the major aspects of the design.

2. Implementation Environment

This section is abstracted from [6], and is included for readers unfamiliar with the Thoth and Verex operating systems. Verex is structured as a kernel and a collection of processes [8]. The kernel provides process creation and destruction, interprocess message-passing and low-level device support. Processes provide the bulk of the operating system services, such as memory management, a file system, terminal support, interactive session management, and network access. Application programs execute as processes which obtain services by sending messages to system processes.

Central to the design of Verex is the use of multiple processes to support concurrent and asynchronous behaviour. To make multi-process structuring attractive, the implementation guarantees that processes are cheap to create and destroy, that process switching is efficient, and that message-passing is fast. Short, fixed-length messages are sent directly to processes - there are no connections and no ports. Each process has a unique, global identifier and a single FIFO queue for incoming messages.

The kernel provides the following message-passing primitives:

Send (**message, id**)

sends the specified message to the process identified by **id** and suspends the sending process until a reply is received. The contents of **message** are changed by the reply.

id = **Receive** (**message**)

retrieves the first message from the incoming message queue and returns in **id** the process identification of the sender. If the queue is empty, the receiver is suspended until a message arrives.

Reply (**message, id**)

returns a reply message to the process identified by **id.** This enables the sender to resume execution.

The **Send, Receive** and **Reply** message primitives, although not the only message primitives supported within Verex, form the basis for most of the interprocess communication.

The message-passing primitives described above support the **remote procedure call** style of interprocess communication. Sending a message and awaiting its reply is much like passing arguments to a procedure and receiving its results. However, processes that receive messages are more powerful than procedures: they can reply to the messages in any order, or even forward them to other processes for reply.

These message facilities are often used to establish a client/server relationship between processes, as described by Cheriton [5]. A **client** process requests some service by sending a message to a **server** process, and awaiting a reply. The request message contains all the necessary fields to specify the service required; the reply message contains the results of servicing the request. The client is given the simple procedure-like interface of **Send,** whereas the server can use the greater flexibility of a receiver to provide sophisticated scheduling and interleaving of services.

An example of a server-based facility is the Verex I/O system [4]. Processes obtain input and generate output by sending requests to file servers. A **file server** is any process which implements the Verex file access interface; it may provide disk storage, device access, or any other source/sink of data that can fit the model. All system servers, including file servers are structured so that they execute a repeated loop; first waiting to **Receive** any message, then processing it quickly so as not to block receipt of other messages.

3. Implementation of Finite State Machines

There are at least two alternative techniques for implementing a FSM using multiple processes - as a so-called **sequential automaton,** or as a Verex-like **server.** These are well known to compiler writers, and the implications of their use in implementing protocol FSM's are described briefly below.

3.1 Finite State Machine as a sequential automaton

In this method of implementing a FSM, a "normal" set of states and transitions is identified, such as states 1,2,3 and 4. The FSM is implemented by coding the transitions from one normal state to the next normal state as sequential statements. All other transitions and states are treated as exceptional, in the sense that they are non-normal. On encountering a message which would cause a non-normal transition, the FSM undergoes a transition to an exceptional state. In the implementation, control is diverted to the section of code handling this exception, and eventually control is returned to the appropriate place in the normal flow.

The advantages of this kind of implementation are the clear distinction between "normal" and "non-normal" transitions, and the readability of the control flow in the sequence of statements.

However, the technique has two major disadvantages. First, it involves the use of "exception trapping" mechanisms, including long jumps to transfer flow of control to other non-sequential states, with appropriate context-saving and restoring. Second, as Deering points out in [7],

"In implementations of a full duplex protocol for an error-prone circuit, it is difficult and perhaps meaningless to identify the "normal" flow of control - exceptions are the rule."

3.2 Finite State Machine as a server

An alternative to the above technique for implementing a FSM is to encode the current state explicitly in a global state vector instead of in the current position in a sequence of statements (the program counter). The control flow is implicit in the sequence of values taken on by the state variables. The

FSM may then be coded as a server executing a repeated loop consisting of a single **Receive** statement followed by a conditional branch depending on the message type and state in combination. This conditional branch may contain as many permutations of state and message type as required.

This FSM structure sacrifices some readability but avoids the use of exception-trapping mechanisms. It also avoids problems associated with identifying the "normal" flow of control - all states and messages are treated as equally likely.

Two major factors influenced our choice of this structure for our X.25 implementation. First, the usual form for servers is that all the messages are received at a single place, and that subsequent processing of the message is determined by a branch on the message type. We had a great deal of experience with such servers, which would be helpful in using this design for our X.25 implementation. Second, in the X.25 protocol, certain messages such as the "Clear" request, cause the protocol FSM to return to the same state, regardless of what state it was in before. The FSM modelled as a server with an initial branch on message type would reflect this situation cleanly and efficiently.

4. The X.25 implementation

The process structure of the Verex X.25 packet-level protocol implementation is shown below in Fig.1.

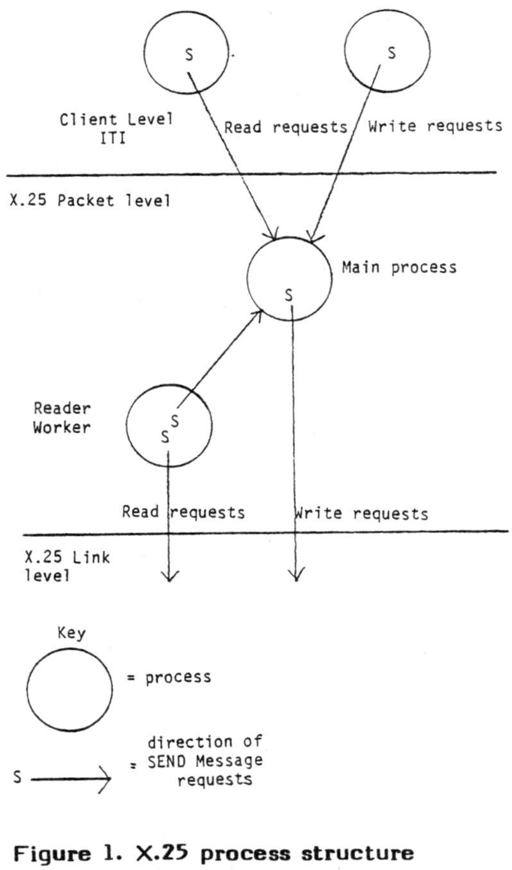

Figure 1. X.25 process structure

The Main process acts as a Verex server, accepting client requests for service and also accepting notifications from its reader worker when data is ready. The reader worker is used to await data from the protocol layer below; it prevents the Main process from being blocked on the data. The Main process also acts as the protocol FSM, changing state according to the data received from the reader worker. A writer worker process was not used in this implementation because the lower level protocol guaranteed to reply immediately to write requests, so the Main process would not block on a write for any length of time.

The Main X.25 process is structured as shown in Fig.2.

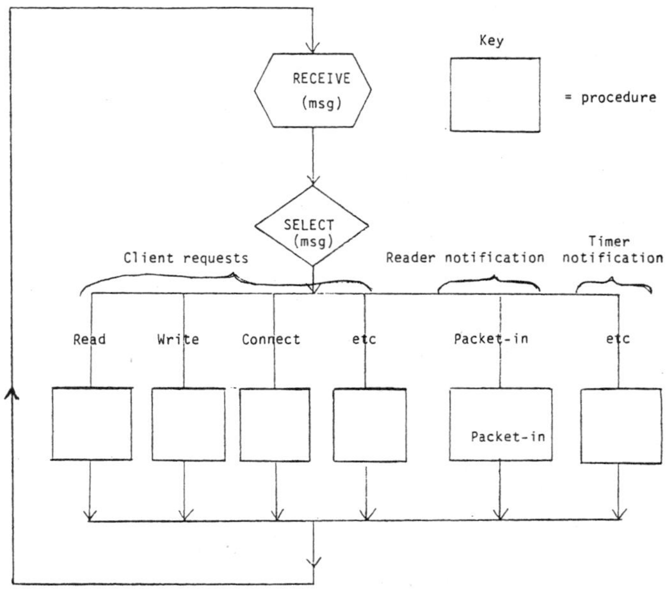

Figure 2. Structure of the X.25 server

Within the procedure **Packet_in,** the X.25 server is coded as a protocol FSM, branching on each combination of state and message type as shown below in Fig.3.

The exception situations are therefore treated as efficiently as the normal situations - no special context-saving and recovery is needed, nor are any longjumps performed.

5. The ITI implementation as a server

Having succesfully implemented the X.25 protocol as a FSM server, we tried to apply the same tecnnique to a higher-level protocol. The Datapac Interactive Terminal Interface (ITI) [DATA78] was initially implemented in this way by Scotton [SCOT81]. ITI acts mainly as an I/O filter, transmitting read/write requests from its client (called the application) through to X.25. In this implementation exceptions occur when the underlying network fails in some way, or when the remote user wishes to communicate a "break" signal. As with X.25, the ITI Main process executes a repeated loop with a single **Receive** statement. It maintains the

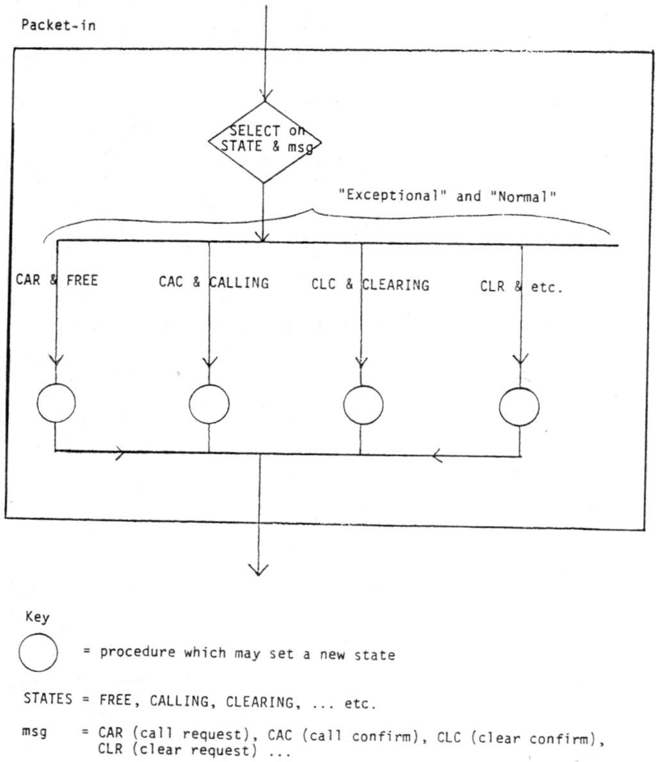

Figure 3. Structure of the X.25 FSM

state vector which is updated as events occur. Extra worker processes, a reader and a writer, are required to handle delays in reading and writing to X.25.

Although the network can fail at any time, it is not considered necessary for the ITI server to be informed of this event immeditely (i.e. asynchronously). Instead, the application is unaware of any disruption to the i/o service and executes normally until a read or write operation is requested. When this occurs, the ITI reader worker receives, synchronously, the exceptional information concerning the failure of the underlying network layer. The ITI server attempts to provide error recovery from this situation, by allowing the user to reconnect by logging in again. The application is blocked until either the transport connection is re-established, in which case the application continues normall , or until a timeout occurs, when an end-of-file condition is returned to the application.

This synchronous scheme cannot however be used to communicate a break signal from the remote user, as notification cannot wait until the user requests an i/o operation. For example, if a user initiates a long compilation, then notices an error and presses the break key, a response is required within a short finite period, say half a second.

5.1 Process destruction for asynchronous exceptions

There are several alternatives for handling this kind of exceptional, asynchronous event. The most obvious is for the X.25 server to send a message to the main ITI process. However, this kind of upward communication from server to client is not allowed in Verex, because of potential deadlock or abuse. The usual practise in Verex is to use process destruction. In this technique, the lower level process is given the process id of a "victim" to be destroyed when an exception occurs. The higher level process receives notification of this destruction through another process, an "undertaker", which is blocked explicitly awaitin the victim's death.

A variant of this scheme was used in Scotton's implementation of ITI but it was considered to be clumsy, involving two extra processes whose only function was to relay a message from the lower level to the ITI Main process (which is usually blocked awaiting any message). Also the overhead of process destruction and recreation was not insignificant.

5.2 Interrupt switch for asynchronous exceptions

A second solution for handling asynchronous exceptions, suggested by Cheriton, was devised where ITI put itself in the position of being always ready to receive a message from the lower level, regardless of whether or not the application had a read request outstanding. This was acheived by adding another state variable to both the ITI and X.25 servers. This acted as a switch to exert flow control on the movement of data from the lower level X.25 to the higher level ITI. When the switch was "ON", X.25 would return both data and interrupts; when "OFF", X.25 would return break signals only. Unfortunately, this scheme incurs the overhead of 4 extra process switches on each read request - 2 to set the switch on and off. This overhead can be reduced by setting a default for X.25 to set the switch "OFF" automatically after satisfying every read request. Then ITI's Main process controls the switch setting so that when there is an application level read request, it requests data from X.25 setting the switch "ON".

This solution has been successfully implemented; however, there are certain disadvantages with this scheme for asynchronous exception-handling. First, the solution is specific to the ITI-X.25 interface - it can't be generalised to solve other asynchronous communication problems. Second, we have two separate mechanisms for exception situations - those encountered synchronously and treated as first level branches by the FSM, and those encountered asynchronously. Third, there is an overhead of two extra process switches for each read request from ITI to X.25.

5.3 An exception-handler process for asynchronous exceptions

We therefore designed a new solution for handling exceptional asynchronous events encountered by ITI.

This solution requires an extra "exception handler" process EH, which registers its process id with the lower level process. Registration is similar to the notification of the victim's id in the initial scheme. EH then blocks awaiting an exceptional event to occur at the lower level by performing a **Send** request to the lower level process.

When an asynchronous exception occurs (such as an interrupt from the remote user), X.25 makes a

Reply to EH. EH then takes control as necessary, by initiating further read requests via the reader worker.

6. The ITI implementation as an I/O filter

Having designed an exception handling process to handle asynchronous exceptions encountered by ITI, we observed that the other type of exceptional event - that of failure of the underlying network - could also be efficiently handled using an exception handler process. Further, the same exception handler process could be used to handle both types of exception reported from the lower level.

We then found that the two major functions of ITI's Main process - that of coordinating action on receiving interrupts and that of reconnection - were taken over by the exception handler process.

We therefore decided to restructure the ITI processes as a reader worker, a writer worker, a timer and an exception handler process, as shown below in Fig. 4.

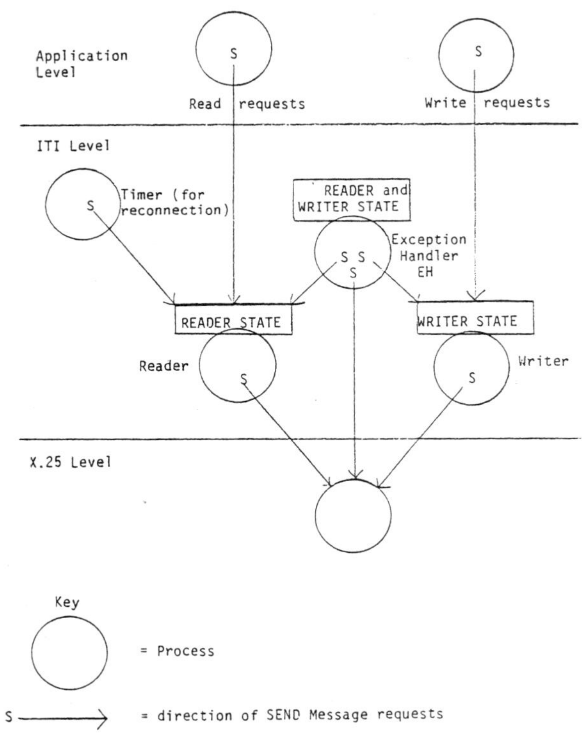

Figure 4. ITI as an I/O filter

This structure reflects the major functionality of ITI, that of an I/O filter, better than the server model. Furthermore, it is structured more efficiently for the normal case (no interrupts or network failures) by actually **reducing** the process switches from 5 to 3 on each read/write request.

Exception processing occurs as follows. When an exception occurs, EH takes control by receiving a **Reply** from X.25 which then "de-registers" EH. EH makes a copy of the relevent state information from the reader and writer workers, and then issues further read/write requests as appropriate, until the exceptional situation has been dealt with. EH then re-registers with X.25 and is ready to handle further exceptions. Exceptional events occurring across the X.25-ITI interface during this processing are queued up in X25 until there is a registered exception handler process ready to deal with them.

6.1 Recovery after network failure

There is one exception handler process, EH, for each X.25 virtual circuit. If a network failure on a virtual circuit is recorded, the EH associated with the failed virtual circuit is notified immediately. It tears down the virtual circuit and suspends itself by executing a **Send** request to the process which would be invoked to handle a reconnection. If a timeout occurs before the remote user has reconnected, the timer destroys the suspended session, causing the user to be logged out.

If the user attempts to reconnect via a new X.25 virtual circuit, another EH process is created for this circuit. The reconnection sequence involves a check of the remote user's status - if it is suspended, the old EH associated with the torn-down virtual circuit is unblocked with a **Reply.** The old EH resets its session to the new X.25 virtual circuit, and wakes up the reader and the writer, completing reconnection before destroying the new EH. The reader and writer then continue exactly as if the underlying network had not failed, replying with new data to the suspended application.

7. Conclusions

Two mechanisms for handling exceptions in multi-process protocol implementations have been described. The first mechanism reflects the use of combining the role of a server with a finite state machine. This structure is particularly efficient for the lower level protocols such as X.25, where it is difficult or impossible to define a normal flow of control.

For higher level protocols where exceptional situations occur less frequentl , it is more efficient to structure according to the normal flow of control. The server model is not so efficient in these situations - instead, the protocol is restructured as an i/o filter with a special exception handler process. This structure combines effects of both synchronous and asynchronous exceptions; it can be generalised as a tool for other asynchronous problems, and it does not add overhead to the normal case. In fact it actually **reduces** overhead in the normal case through avoiding unnecessary context saving of global state information, and reducing the number of process switches on each read/write request.

These mechanisms can be generalised to programs other then protocol implementations, and to systems other than Verex.

Acknowledgements

I am very grateful to David Cheriton for suggesting these studies of exception mechanisms, and for his continued interest and support of this work. I am also indebted to Steve Deering for the discussions that gave rise to many parts of this paper, and for his helpful comments throughout the production of this paper.

References

[1] Bochmann, G.V. **Finite state description of communication protocols** Computer Networks 2, 4/5 (October 1978), 361-372.

[2] CCITT Recommendation X.25 **Interface between DTE and DCE for terminals operating in the packet mode on public data networks** March 1976.

[3] Cheriton, D.R., Malcolm, M.A., Melen, L.S., and Sager, G.R. **Thoth, a portable real-timeoperating system** Communications of the ACM 22, 2 (February 1979), 105-115.

[4] Cheriton, D.R. **Distributed I/O using an object-based protocol** UBC Computer Science Technical Report 81-1, University of British Columbia, January 1981.

[5] Cheriton, D.R. **The Thoth System: Multi-Process structuring and Portability** Elsevier North-Holland, New York, 1982.

[6] The Computer Communications Group; TransCanada Telephone System. **Datapac Interactive Terminal Interface (ITI) Specification** Trans Canada Telephone System, Ottawa, Ontario, October 1978.

[7] Deering, S.E. **Multi-process structuring of X.25 software** UBC Computer Science Technical Report 82-11, University of British Columbia, October 1982.

[8] Lockhart, T.W. **The design of a verifiable operating system kernel** UBC Computer Science Technical Report 79-15, University of British Columbia, November 1979.

[9] Scotton, G.R. **An experiment in High level protocol design** University of British Columbia, Department of Computer Science, MSc. Thesis, December 1981.

Protocol Performance and Optimization

Chairman

J. Field

Controlling Window Protocols for Time-Constrained Communication in a Multiple Access Environment *

James F. Kurose** Mischa Schwartz*** Yechiam Yemini**

Columbia University
New York, New York 10027

Abstract

For many time-constrained communication applications, such as packetized voice, a critical performance measure is the percentage of messages which are transmitted within a given amount of time after their arrival at a sending station. We examine the use of a group random access protocol based on time windows for achieving time-constrained communication in a multiple access environment. First, we formulate a policy for controlling protocol operation in order to minimize the percentage of messages with waiting times greater than some given bound. A semi-Markov decision model is then developed for protocol operation and three of the four optimal control elements of this policy are then determined.

Although the semi-Markov decision model can also be used to obtain performance results, the procedure is too computationally expensive to be of practical use. Thus, an alternate performance model based on a centralized queueing system with impatient customers is developed. Protocol performance under the optimal elements of the control policy shows significant improvements over cases in which the protocol is not controlled in this manner. Simulation results are also presented to corroborate the analytic results.

1. Introduction

During the past ten years, numerous research efforts have been directed towards developing protocols for efficiently sharing a single multiple access communication channel among a community of distributed users; a survey of these efforts can be found in [16]. A primary performance objective of these protocols has been to minimize average message delay, i.e., the average time between a message's arrival at the sending station and its reception at the destination station.

Recently, there has been considerable interest in supporting *real-time* or *time-constrained* communication applications such as packetized voice [4] [7] and distributed sensor networks [5] in a multiple access environment. The communication requirements of time-constrained applications differ significantly from those of traditional multiple access communication in two respects. First, a certain amount of message loss is usually tolerable. Secondly, a message which is not successfully transmitted within a certain amount of time after its arrival at the sending station is considered lost, regardless of whether or not it is eventually received at the destination station. One consequence of these differences is that the primary performance objective is no longer to minimize average message delay but rather to maximize the percentage of messages successfully transmitted within the time constraint. These fundamentally different communication characteristics and performance objectives suggest that previously developed multiple access protocols may not be well suited for time-constrained applications.

In earlier work [11] it was noted that in addition to its traditional role as an arbiter of channel sharing, a multiple access protocol also serves as a *distributed scheduling mechanism* by (implicitly or explicitly) imposing a global transmission order on all messages distributed among the stations in the network. This scheduling function was shown to critically affect the distribution of message delays and thus the time-constrained performance of the protocol as well. A random access protocol, based on a generalization of time window protocols [6] [17] was proposed which provided a family of scheduling disciplines based on message arrival times. The performance of this protocol, which required that *all* messages be sent, was examined for the cases in which messages in the network were sent on a global FCFS, LCFS and RANDOM basis.

In this paper, we relax the constraint that all messages be transmitted, and examine one policy for controlling protocol operation in order to maximize the percentage of messages with delays below a given time constraint. In the following section we review the basic operation of the

* This work partially supported by the Defense Research Projects Agency Project N00039-82-C-0247, NSF grant ECS-81-08776 and ONR grant N00014-82-K-0508

** Department of Computer Science

*** Department of Electrical Engineering and Department of Computer Science

time window protocol and define the different elements which comprise a protocol control policy. In section 3 a semi-Markov decision model of protocol operation is developed and three of the four optimal elements of the control, policy are then determined. A heuristic is presented for the final policy element. Although the semi-Markov decision model can also be used to obtain performance results, the procedure is too computationally expensive to be of practical use. Thus, an alternate performance model based on a centralized queueing system with impatient customers is developed in section 4 and protocol performance is examined.

2. Group Polling and the Time-Window Protocol

Many of the protocols which have been proposed for sharing a multiple access channel belong to the class of group polling [8] or tree protocols [15]. Their operation is based on the principle of granting transmission rights to a group of stations (the *enabled* stations) in the hope that only a single station in the group is *ready*, i.e., has a message to send. Depending on the manner in which the enabled group is determined, group polling can often allocate the channel more efficiently than standard hub polling [14]. Group polling protocols operate by selecting some criterion, e.g., a range of station addresses [8] [2] or an interval of time [6] [17], such that all stations satisfying the given criteria (e.g., having an address or a message arrival within specified range) are in the enabled group. The manner in which this criteria is determined and possibly modified in order to isolate a single ready station in the enabled group will be discussed shortly. For time-constrained communication, since the distribution of message delay is of primary importance, it is natural to base protocol operation on group polling techniques that grant transmission rights based on message arrival times. Let us now briefly review the operation of such a protocol.

The protocol operates in a synchronous fashion. All stations continuously monitor the channel and begin by selecting some interval or *window* of time in the past according to some policy. In the following sections, a policy for selecting this initial window will be formulated, but for now let us simply assume that some policy exists, that all stations follow this policy, and thus all stations select the same window. Once a window has been selected, one of three possibilities can then occur. One possibility is that no stations have a message arrival in the selected initial time window. This situation is shown in figure 1a, in which message arrival times at stations throughout the network are shown below the time axis. In this case, no stations are enabled, no messages are transmitted and the channel remains silent. Once the channel remains silent for an amount of time equal to the end-to-end propagation delay of the channel, t_0, all stations know that no other stations have arrivals in this time interval. The stations can then determine a new initial time window and repeat the channel access procedure.

The second possibility is that exactly one station has a message arrival in the initial window. In this case, this station begins transmitting its message without interference. The above process is then repeated upon termination of the message transmission. Finally, if more than one station has an arrival in the initial window, then two or more stations transmit messages (figure 1b) and a collision occurs. If there is a collision, then it is detected by all stations within t_0 time units. Stations then continue to monitor the channel and attempt to resolve this collision by splitting the initial window in half and selecting one of the two halves (figure 1c). Since all stations follow the same policy, they select the same half of the split window to be the new time window and the group polling procedure is then repeated. If no station has an arrival in the selected half of a split window, then the channel remains idle and all stations then select the other half of the split window, immediately split this window (since it is known to contain two or more message arrivals), choose one of the halves of the newly split window and repeat the above procedure using this half of the window. This splitting process continues until a single message is finally transmitted.

Thus, the result of each windowing process, i.e., the selection of an initial window and its subsequent splitting (if any), always eventually results in either the start of a single message transmission or, if the initial window contains no message arrivals, the start of a new windowing process. Note that each step (choosing or splitting a window and transmitting any arrivals in the window) in the process takes t_0 units of time, the time required for all stations to determine whether a single message transmission, no transmission or a message collision has occurred.

All stations perform this windowing process and thus all stations know the width and starting time of every interval of time in the past which is known to contain either no message arrivals or arrivals that have aready been successfully transmitted. Since these intervals are known to contain no untransmitted message arrivals, the stations can remove these intervals of time from further consideration. Thus, the stations might view the time axis as shown below in figure 2. The shaded regions in figure 2 indicate those intervals of time which are known to contain no arrivals of untransmitted messages.

Note that the opportunity for controlling protocol operation arises only at those times when an initial window must be selected. Assuming the protocol maintains some state information (such as a record of its past history as in the time axis in figure 2), then a selection of

- the position of the initial window

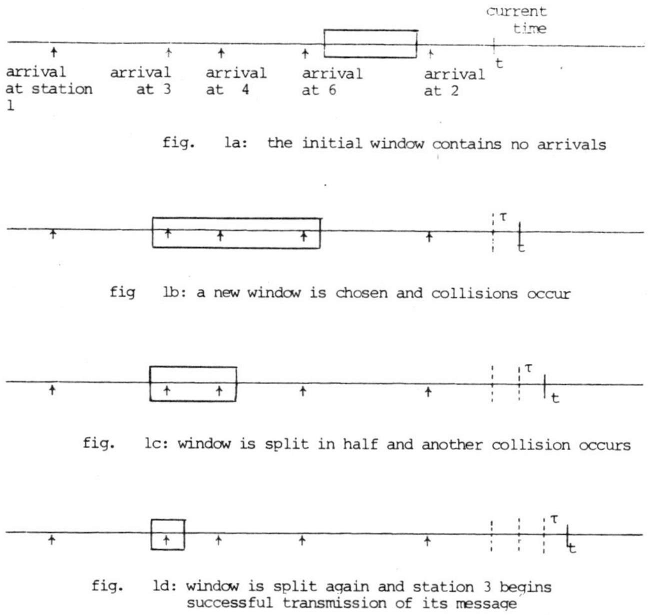

Figure 1: Operation of the time window protocol

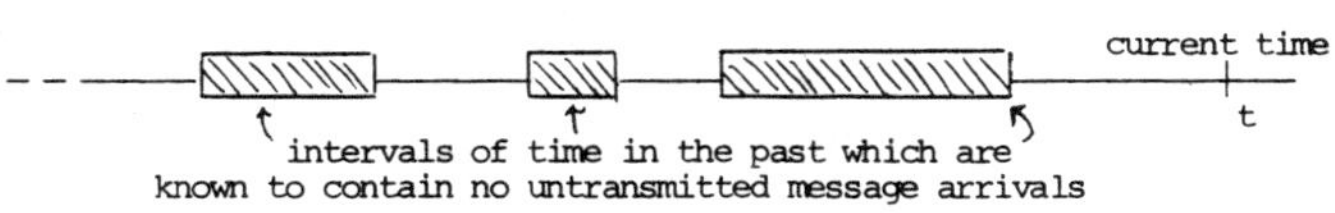

Figure 2: A station's view of the time axis

- the length of the initial window

- a procedure for splitting the window should collisions occur

must be made, based on the current state, from some set of alternatives. Once an alternative for operation has been selected, the probabilistic evolution of the protocol is determined until the next time an initial window must be chosen. The selection of an alternative for action (i.e., specifying (1) through (3) above) given the current state is known as a *decision* and the set of all decisions is known as a *policy*.

The problem we now want to address is how to select those alternatives for operation that will maximize the percentage of messages with delays below the given time constraint. A message's delay (or waiting time) will be defined as the amount of time between its arrival at the sending station and the beginning of the windowing process immediately preceding and resulting in, its own successful transmission. Thus, a message's delay does not (by definition) include the time required for the single windowing process resulting in its transmission. However, the delay *does* include the windowing time for the other message transmissions since its arrival; this point will be further discussed in section 4.

3. Controlling the Time Window Protocol

In this section we address the problem of selecting policy elements (1) - (3) in order to maximize the percentage of messages with a delay below a given bound. First, we develop a state space representation suitable to encode the necessary past history of the protocol. This state space description is then used as a basis for a semi-Markov decision model [9] of protocol operation. The usual approach for finding the optimal policy is to choose some initial policy and then to iteratively obtain better and better policies. Unfortunately this iterative process can be computationally quite expensive and moreover may provide little insight into the operation of the protocol itself. Our approach here will be to use our understanding of the protocol to infer elements (1) and (3) of the optimal policy and then to prove that no policy iteration would yield a better policy. A simple closed form characterization of (2) does not appear possible; this problem will be further discussed in section 4.

3.1 A State Space Description and Pseudo Time

Let us assume that time is discrete in units of Δ (where Δ can be arbitrarily small but finite) and is small enough so that the probability of more than one message arrival (anywhere in the network) can be assumed to be zero. One straightforward state space approach is simply to encode for each Δ unit of time in the past, whether or not it may still contain an untransmitted message arrival. However, this approach leads to a complicated state space which also grows exponentially in size with each Δ.

An alternative approach is to introduce the notion of *pseudo time*, determine the optimal policy elements (1) and (3) within a state space based on pseudo time and then to relate these results back to actual time. The relationship between actual time and pseudo time is shown below in figure 3. Pseudo time is defined such that each unit of pseudo time in the past is associated with a unit of actual time in the past which may still contain an untransmitted message arrival. With no loss of generality, we can require that if t_1 precedes t_2 in actual time then the pseudo time associated with t_1 precedes the pseudo time associated with t_2. In this case, the introduction of pseudo time essentially compresses the actual time axis by removing those intervals of time known to contain no untransmitted message arrivals.

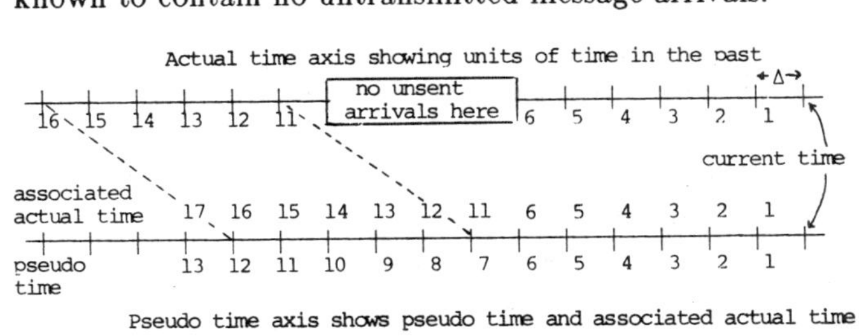

Figure 3: Actual time and pseudo time

Each state in pseudo time thus simply corresponds to the total amount of time which may still contain message arrivals. One possible pseudo time state space description is thus:

$$\mathbf{S} = \{ 0, 1, 2, 3 \ldots \} \quad (3.1)$$

where a particular state, i, indicates that i units of time may still contain untransmitted message arrivals.

This state space description can be further refined as follows. Let K (in units of Δ) represent the imposed time constraint. Clearly, transmitting a message with a delay greater than K (in actual time) is useless work since the message will be lost at the receiver with probability 1. Thus the protocol should never send a message with a delay greater than K. When an initial window is chosen, all messages with a delay greater than K can therefore be discarded *by the sending station*. Thus, in addition to policy elements (1), (2) and (3) of section 2, the optimal policy will also:

4. discard any messages with a delay greater than K. These messages can be effectively discarded by marking the actual time intervals containing possible arrivals which would have a delay greater than K as if the intervals were known to contain no untransmitted arrivals.

As a result of policy element (4), there are never more than K units of actual time (and hence pseudo time) possibly containing untransmitted message arrivals. Thus the pseudo time state space can be further refined to:

$$\mathbf{S} = \{ 0, 1, 2, \ldots K\text{-}1, K\} \quad (3.2)$$

3.2 Optimal Elements of the Window Control Policy

In this section we establish the following theorem which states that the window control policy elements (1) and (3) which maximize the percentage of messages with delays less than K, result in successfully transmitted messages being sent on a global (network-wide) FCFS basis:

Theorem 1: In the case that all message lengths are identically distributed and given policy element (4), the optimal selection of policy elements (1) and (3) is independent of policy element (2) and can be characterized as follows:

1. The beginning of an initial window should be placed at the point in time closest to, but not exceeding, K units of time in the past (where K is the imposed time constraint) which may contain untransmitted messages.

3. the older half of a split window is always selected first.

Note that a message is lost unless the windowing process which results in its successful transmission begins within K units of time after its arrival. Intuitively, since all the message lengths are identically distributed, it would seem reasonable to transmit that message with a delay closest to, but not exceeding, the time bound; this is exactly what (1) and (3) above specify. A similar scheduling policy, minimum slack time scheduling [3], can be easily proven optimal in the deterministic case that all arrival times are known in advance. The present case is somewhat more complicated since only probabilistic information concerning arrival times is known and since any decision influences the future evolution of the system.

In establishing Theorem 1, the following definitions will be useful:

- actual delay of a message. The amount of time between the current time and the arrival time of the message.

- pseudo delay of a message. The amount of time between the current time and the pseudo time associated with the actual arrival time of a message. Note that while a message's actual delay always increases with time, the pseudo delay may both increase and decrease in time, depending on the behavior of the window mechanism.

- actual loss: fraction of messages not successfully transmitted with an actual delay less than K. Since the loss will be a function of the policy, we will write actual loss(P) to indicate the actual loss under policy P.

- pseudo loss: fraction of messages not successfully transmitted with a *pseudo delay* less than K. Pseudo loss(P) indicates the pseudo loss under policy P.

- one-step pseudo loss: the expected number of messages which have a pseudo delay less than K when a decision is made, but have a pseudo delay greater than K (and hence be lost under policy element 4) when the next decision is made.

In order to establish Theorem 1, we will first establish the following lemmas, which will require the following assumption:

Assumption 1 : The distribution of arrival times measured in actual time and in pseudo time is the same, i.e., the removal of intervals of time and the concommitant shifting of actual arrival times (to get the pseudo arrival times) preserves the distribution of interarrival times. For the case of Poisson arrivals, the removal of an initial window containing 0 or 1 message arrivals preserves this property exactly. In general, however, if one half of a split window is removed, then the interarrival time distribution may not be exactly preserved.

Lemma 1 : For any policy P: actual loss(P) $\geq$ pseudo loss(P)

Proof: By the definition of pseudo time, the pseudo delay of a message is always less than or equal to the actual delay of a message. Thus if a message's pseudo delay exceeds K, then its actual delay also exceeds K.

Lemma 2 : Given policy element (4), any policy with policy elements (1) and (3) as in Theorem 1 preserves the following property of all messages which are not lost:

pseudo delay of a message = actual delay of a message

Proof: Lemma 2 can be inductively established. Suppose the above property holds when a decision is made. If this property does not hold when the next decision is made, then the selection of the first window must have been such that there was a message which arrived between K units of time in the past and the start of the first initial window. However, by hypothesis, the policy contains elements (1) and (3) as in Theorem 1 and thus no such message can exist. Thus the above property is preserved by each decision.

Lemma 3 : Let $\{P^w\}$ be the set of all policies which choose the same *size* window when in the same state (i.e., the set of all policies with the same second element). Let $P^w_{ms} \in \{P^w\}$ be the single policy with elements (1) and (3) as in Theorem 1. Then P^w_{ms} minimizes the one-step pseudo loss over all policies in $\{P^w\}$.

Proof: Let us define the *critical messages* associated with a decision as follows. When a decision is made at time t' in state i, a probabilistic amount of time, σ, is required for the windowing process and message transmission (if any). The critical messages associated with the decision made at t' are those messages with a pseudo arrival time after t'-i but before $t'+\sigma$-K. That is, a critical message is one with a pseudo delay less than i at t' which would have a pseudo delay greater than K at $t'+\sigma$ (when the next decision is made) if it is not transmitted. The one-step pseudo loss can thus be expressed by the following expected value:

one-step pseudo loss =
E [number of critical messages - prob. that a critical message is transmitted] (3.3)

By assumption 1, all units of pseudo time are statistically identical with respect to message arrival times. Thus, for a given window size, the time between two consecutive decisions is independent of both the *position* of the first initial window and the procedure for choosing halves of a split window. Thus, for a given window size, the number of critical messages associated with a decision is independent of policy elements (1) and (3). Now, since P^w_{ms} always selects the message with a pseudo delay closest to, but not exceeding K (i.e., the message that will be critical if *any* messages are critical), P^w_{ms} maximizes the second term in equation 3.3. Thus P^w_{ms} minimizes the one-step pseudo loss.

Lemma 4 : Given policy element 4 in section 3.1, a policy which minimizes the one-step pseudo loss also minimizes the pseudo loss.

Lemma 4 relates the short term pseudo loss to the long term average pseudo loss and relies on results from decision theory. The proof of lemma 4 can be found in appendix A. Given lemmas 1 through 4 we can now establish theorem 1:

Proof of Theorem 1: Let $\{P^w\}$ be the set of all policies which have the same second policy element and let $P^w_{ms} \in \{P^w\}$ be the policy with elements (1) and (3) as in theorem 1. We want to show that no policy in $\{P^w\}$ has an actual loss less than P^w_{ms}. Suppose there exists some policy, P^w_α which has an actual loss less than that of policy P^w_{ms} :

$$\text{actual loss}(P^w_\alpha) < \text{actual loss}(P^w_{ms})$$

By lemma 2, we then have

$$\text{actual loss}(P^w_\alpha) < \text{actual loss}(P^w_{ms}) = \text{pseudo loss}(P^w_{ms})$$

and then by lemmas 3 and 4: actual loss(P^w_α) < pseudo loss(P^w_{ms}) = $\min_{P' \in \{P^w\}}$ pseudo loss(P') and thus specifically since $P^w_\alpha \in \{P^w\}$:

$$\text{actual loss}(P^w_\alpha) < \text{pseudo loss}(P^w_\alpha)$$

which contradicts lemma 1. Thus P^w_α cannot exist and thus P^w_{ms} is the optimal policy.

An important consequence of theorem 1 (stated in lemma 2) is that there is no difference between pseudo time and actual time. Thus, there are no "gaps" in time (the shaded regions in figure 2) between those intervals of actual time still possibly containing untransmitted messages. Thus the state space need not be a large and complicated encoding of all the intervals of time known to contain no untransmitted message arrivals. Rather, only a single piece of information need be maintained by the protocol - that point in time closest to, but not exceeding K units of time in the past which may contain untransmitted messages. This value will be known as *t_past*. Under the optimal protocol, it is further known that *all* time between t_past and the current time may contain message arrivals. Figure 4 provides an example of the operation of the optimal protocol and the manner in which t_past is maintained.

4. A Queueing Model of Protocol Performance

The analysis developed in this section is based on viewing the messages distributed among the stations throughout the network as customers in a *distributed* queue. If we view channel activity as a function of time, the window protocol results in alternate use of the

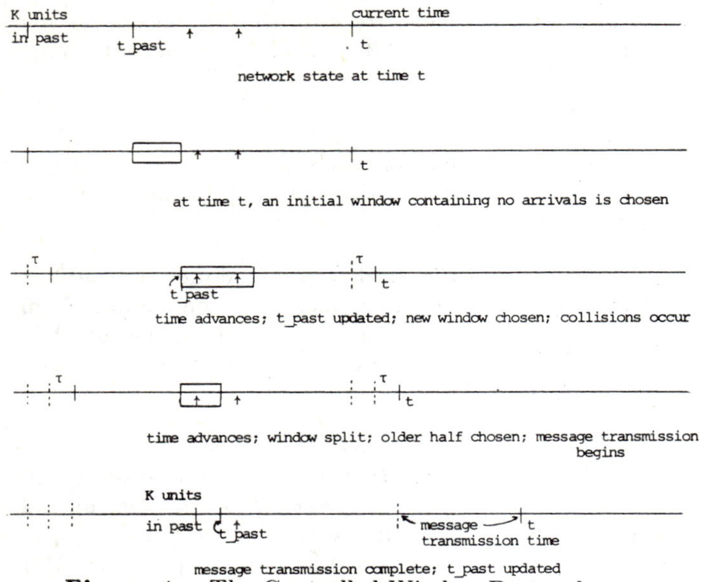

Figure 4: The Controlled Window Protocol

channel for the windowing process (to determine the message to be transmitted) and for the successful transmission of that message. Suppose we consider the time required by the windowing processes immediately preceding, and resulting in, a message's transmission (i.e., its scheduling time) to be part of its *service* time. The scheduling time component of a message's service time is thus the time between either the end of the most recent message transmission or its own arrival time (whichever is more recent) and the start of its own successful transmission. In this case the distributed queue is equivalent to a centralized queue in which a message's service time consists of two components: the scheduling time component and the actual transmission time component.

4.1 An M/G/1 Queue With Customer Loss

A consequence of policy elements (1), (3) and (4) is that all successfully transmitted messages are sent on a FCFS basis. Furthermore, as a result of policy element (4), messages are lost at the sender (i.e., never sent) only when their waiting time (as defined in section 2) exceeds the given time constraint. Thus, the operation of the optimal policy can be modeled as a FCFS queue in which messages at the front of the queue are lost (denied service) if their waiting time in the queue has exceeded the time constraint; this model is shown below in figure 5a

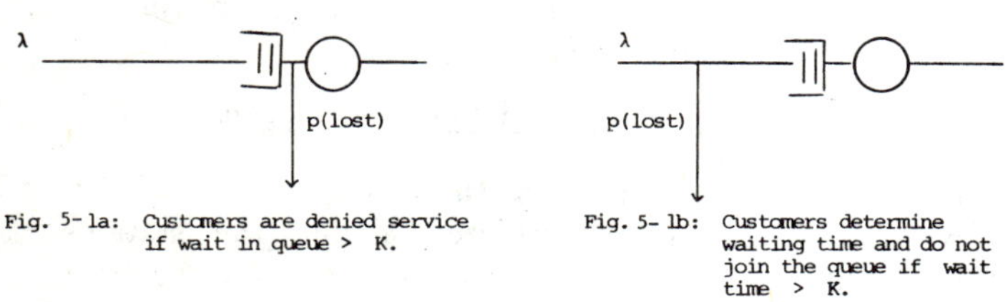

Figure 5: Two Models of a Queue With Customer Loss

In terms of server utilization, it makes no difference whether customers are lost upon arrival at the front of the queue or whether they somehow determine their waiting time and join the queue if and only if their waiting time is less than the specified time constraint. Thus, the probability that the server is busy is the same in the model in figure 5a as in the model in figure 5b. We will model the distributed queue using the M/G/1 queueing system shown in figure 5b. It should be noted that this model is only approximate since the "service" times are not truly independent. This second queueing model was recently studied in [1] for the M/G/1 case for the waiting time distribution of customers entering service. If we are only interested in the probability of message loss, an alternative approach can considerably simplify the analysis for the M/G/1 case.

Let us define F(w,t) as the PDF of the unfinished work in the queue at time t:

$$F(w,t) \triangleq P(\text{ unfinished work} < w)$$

Note that the unfinished work in the queue corresponds to the waiting time an arriving customer would experience under FCFS scheduling. By elementary continuity arguments, the PDF of the unfinished work at time t+Δt can be characterized in terms of its value at time t as follows:

$$F(w,t+\Delta t) = (1-\lambda\Delta t)F(w+\Delta t,t) +$$

$$\lambda\Delta t(1-\mu_1(w-K))\int_0^w B(w-x)\frac{\partial F(x,t)}{\partial x}dx + \tag{4.1}$$

$$\lambda\Delta t(\mu_1(w-K))\{\ c_1\int_0^w B(w-x)\frac{\partial F(x,t)}{\partial x}dx + (1-c_1)F(w+\Delta t,t)\ \}$$

where K is the time constraint, B(x) is the service time PDF of a customer, μ_1(w-K) is the unit step function at K and c_1 = F(K,t).

The first term on the right hand side of equation 4.1 relates the value of F(w,t+Δt) to the value of the PDF at time t in the case of no message arrivals in Δt. The second term is for the case of one message arrival and unfinished work at time t+Δt less than or equal to K. The final term is for the case of one message arrival and unfinished work at time t+Δt greater than K; the values of c_1 and 1-c_1 represent, respectively, the probability that an arriving customer found its waiting time to be less than or greater than K. Rearranging the terms in equation 4.1, taking the limit as Δt approaches 0 and then (assuming equilibrium exists) taking the limit as t approaches infinity, results in the following pair of integro-differential equations for the distribution of unfinished work in the queue:

$$0 = \frac{dF(w)}{dw} - \lambda F(w) + \lambda\int_0^w B(w-x)d_xF(x) \quad (0<w\leq K) \tag{4.2a}$$

$$0 = \frac{dF(w)}{dw} - \lambda c_1 F(w) + \lambda c_1\int_0^w B(w-x)d_xF(x) \quad (K < w) \tag{4.2b}$$

Let $f_{w<K}(w)$ be the derivative of the solution to equation 4.2 (i.e., the waiting time density (pdf))in the region $0<w\leq K$ and let $f_{K<w}(w)$ be the waiting time density function in the region $K<w$. Then by conservation of probability, we have:

$$\int_0^K f_{w<K}(w)dw \ + \ \int_K^\infty f_{K<w}(w)dw \ = \ 1 \qquad (4.3)$$

At this point, we could solve (4.2) for $f_{w<K}(w)$ and $f_{K<w}(w)$ using equation 4.3 to determine the unknown constants. The solution to equation 4.2a can be shown [10] to be:

$$f_{w<K}(w) \ = \ P(0) \sum_{i=0}^{\infty} \rho^i \beta^i(w) \qquad (4.4)$$

where:
- P(0) is the probability that the server is idle

- $\rho = \lambda \bar{x}$, where λ and $\bar{x}$ are, respectively, the arrival rate and average service times of customers.

- $\beta(w)$ has the form of the residual service time distribution of an M/G/1 queue with no loss, i.e., the distribution of the remaining work that an arriving customer would find for a customer in service.

- $\beta^i(w)$ is the i-fold convolution of $\beta(w)$.

The solution of equation 4.2b is considerably more complex; fortunately, it need not be solved. Note that the second term on the left of equation 4.3 is simply the probability that an arriving customer finds a waiting time greater than K and thus does not join the queue and is lost:

$$\int_K^\infty f_{K<w}(w)dw \ = \ p(loss) \ = \ 1 - p(accepted) \qquad (4.5)$$

The loss probability can be related to P(0), the probability that the server is idle, using the simple conservation of flow argument shown in figure 6. The average rate of customers joining the queue is given by λp(accept) and the average rate of customers leaving the queue after service is given by the probability that the server is busy times the rate at which the server services these customers. By conservation of flow, the average arrival rate and departure rate must be the same and thus:

$$p(accept)\rho \ = \ 1 - P(0) \qquad (4.6)$$

Using equations 4.3 - 4.6 we can now determine the probability of message loss:

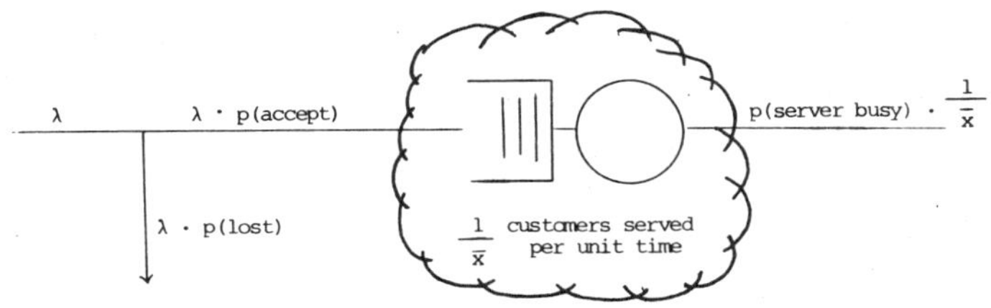

Figure 6: Flow Conservation

$$p(loss) \ = \ 1 - \rho^{-1} + \frac{1}{\rho + \rho^2 z(K,\rho)} \qquad (4.7)$$

$$\text{where} \ \ z(K,\rho) \ = \ \sum_{i=0}^{\infty} \rho^i \int_0^K \beta^i(w)dw$$

As a check of equation 4.7, note that in the limit that K approaches infinity, p(loss) approaches 0. As K approaches 0, p(loss) approaches 1-P(0). That is, the probability that a customer is lost approaches the probability that the server is busy, as would be expected since as K approaches 0, a customer would only enter service if the queue was empty.

Equation 4.7 thus gives the probability of message loss under optimal policy elements (1), (3) and (4). Note that we have not yet specified policy element (2) which determines the initial window length. The values chosen for (2) will affect both $\bar{x}$ (and thus ρ) and $\beta(w)$ in equation 4.7. Unfortunately, computing the optimal value of policy element (2) would require solving the set of equation (A1) in the appendix and thus is computationally too expensive to be of practical use; similar problems have been encountered in other protocol models based on semi-Markov decision analysis [12]. Thus, rather than compute the optimal values for (2), let us examine the performance of the protocol using a heuristic rule for (2).

Specifically, let us assume that (2) is chosen to minimize the *average* amount of time required by the windowing process to schedule a message. Even if the window sizes are selected in this manner, determining the first moment and distribution of the message scheduling time is not an easy task. In [11] these values were approximated by exactly determining the average scheduling time for two arrival rates and fitting a function to these endpoints to approximate the average scheduling time for intermediate arrival rates. This average scheduling time was then used as the mean of a geometrically distributed service time. The performance results obtained using these analytic approximations were shown to coincide closely with simulation results.

A final complication in evaluating equation 4.7 is that the average scheduling time (and thus message service time) depends on the fraction of messages actually entering the queue and eventually receiving service, i.e., the scheduling time components of $\bar{x}$ and $\beta(w)$ are dependent on p(loss). However, since the scheduling delay

Figure 7: Performance Results

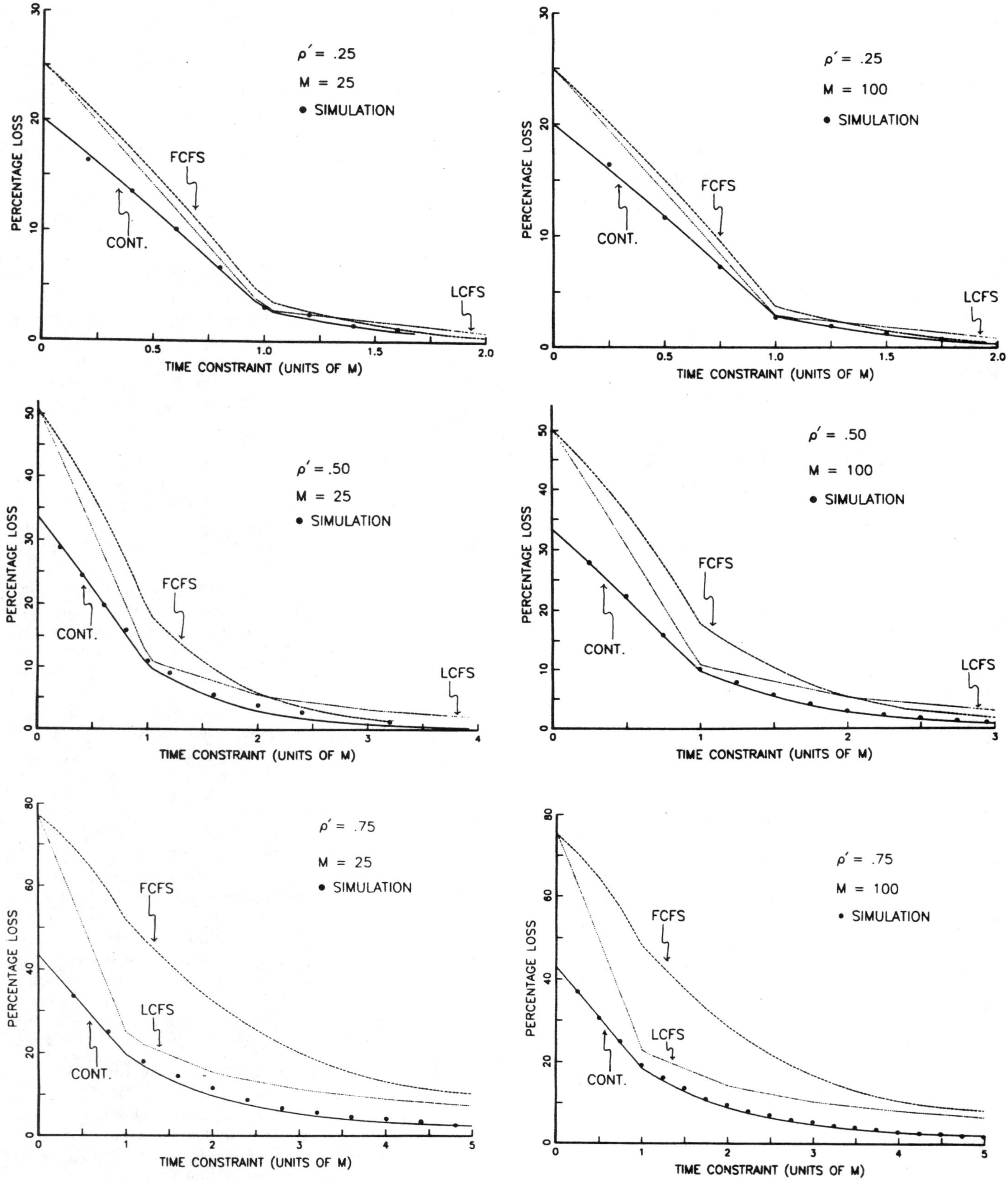

is known to be exactly 0 for the case that K=0, $\bar{x}$, β(w) and p(loss) can be computed exactly at K=0. The values of $\bar{x}$ and β(w) at K=ϵ (ϵ close to 0) can then be closely approximated using the exact fraction of messages entering service for K=0; these values can then be used to compute the loss at K=ϵ. In this fashion the loss at the nth value of K can be iteratively computed using the loss at the (n-1)st value of K to compute $\bar{x}$ and β(w).

4.2 Some Numerical Results

In figures 7 we present some numerical results for the performance of the controlled protocol and compare these results with those from [11] in which the protocol provided FCFS and LCFS service and messages were lost only at the receiving stations. Performance results are given for various values of M and ρ', where M is the fixed message length in units of the end-to-end propagation delay of the channel, t_0, and ρ' is the arrival rate of all messages (lost and transmitted) times

As expected, these results show significant performance improvements over the FCFS and LCFS results. Two factors contribute to this increase in performance. First, the optimal policy elements (1) and (3) have been used; the critical role of these two policy elements was demonstrated in [11]. However, the increase in performance probably primarily results from the inclusion of policy element (4). Note that as a result of this policy element, the channel is used only for "useful" work. That is, if the protocol sends a message then, due to element (4) and our definition of waiting time, that message will be accepted at the receiving station with probability 1. Thus, unlike the protocols in [11], the channel is *never* used for the transmission of messages which are lost at the receiving station.

Recall that our definition of waiting time in section 2 does not include a message's *own* scheduling time as part of its waiting time. This definition only approximates the truer (and more traditional) definition of waiting time: the time between a message's arrival at a sending station and the start of its successful transmission. The waiting time approximation was introduced to avoid considerable complication to the analyses of sections 3 and 4. In the simulation results shown in figure 7, messages were considered lost when their *true* waiting time exceeded the time constraint. (Note that in this case it is possible for messages to be lost at both the sending and receiving stations.) The close agreement between the analytic results and the simulation results indicate that the waiting time approximation as well as the other approximations and assumptions underlying the analysis are indeed reasonable.

5. Conclusion

In this paper we have examined the problem of controlling a group random access protocol based on message arrival times in order to maximize the percentage of messages with delays below a given bound. First, we identified four policy elements which comprised a policy for controlling protocol operation. A semi-Markov decision model was then developed and three of the four optimal policy elements were determined within this model; these elements were found to be both intuitive and simple. A simple closed form characterization of the final optimal policy element was not found.

Although the decision model was shown to be sufficient to provide performance results, it was found to be too computationally expensive to be of practical use. Thus an alternative performance model, based on a queueing system with impatient customers, was developed. A heuristic was then adopted for the final policy element. Protocol performance was then examined and found to be superior to cases in which it was not controlled using optimal policy elements (1), (2) and (4).

Finally, several extensions of this work seem promising to pursue. First, note that our *definition* of a policy (i.e., elements (1) through (4)) is only one policy by which the protocol can be controlled. Introducing additional policy elements (e.g., not necessarily splitting a window in half), may result in further performance improvements. Secondly, the protocol discussed in this paper operates in a synchronous manner. Since the synchronization of distributed stations is often a difficult task, it would be desirable for the protocol to operate in an asynchronous manner. It would be interesting to explore different approaches for achieving this asynchronous operation and the effect of these approaches on the time-constrained performance of the protocol. Molle [13] has recently investigated several aspects of this problem. Finally, the present protocol requires that all stations select initial windows of the same size. This may not be possible in practice and in some cases may not even be desirable! For example, if different stations have different priorities, then one form of priority be can achieved by permitting stations to choose different initial window sizes. Determining a policy for choosing these window sizes based on station priority and analyzing the performance of such a policy is an interesting, but potentially difficult, problem for future work.

1. Francois Baccelli and Gerard Hebuterne. On Queues With Impatient Customers. Performance '81, 1981, pp. 159-179.

2. J. I. Capetanakis. "Generalized TDMA: The Multi-Accessing Tree Protocol." *IEEE Transactions on Communications COM-27* (Oct. 1979), 1476-1484.

3. E.G. Coffman. *Computer and Job Shop Scheduling.* J. Wiley and Sons, N.Y. N.Y., 1976.

4. D. Cohen. Issues in Transnet Packetized Voice Communication. Conference Report, Proceedings of the

Fifth Data Communications Symposium, Snowbird, Utah, 1977.

5. , MIT Lincoln Laboratories. *Workshop on Distributed Sensor Networks*, Lexington, Mass., 1982.

6. R. G. Gallager. Conflict Resolution in Random Access Broadcast Networks. Proc. of the AFOSR Workshop in Communication Theory and Applications, AFOSR, 1978.

7. I. Gitman. "Analysis and Design of Hybrid Switching Networks." *IEEE Transactions on Communications COM-29*, 9 (September 1981), 1290-1300.

8. J. F. Hayes. "An Adaptive Technique for Local Distribution." *IEEE Transactions on Communications COM-26* (Aug. 1978), 1178-1186.

9. Ronald A. Howard. *Dynamic Probabilistic Systems, Volume 2: Semi-Markov and Decision Processes.* J. Wiley and Sons, N.Y. N.Y., 1971.

10. L. Kleinrock. *Queueing Systems Volume I: Theory.* J. Wiley and Sons, N.Y., N.Y., 1975.

11. J.F. Kurose and M. Schwartz. A Family of Window Protocols for Time-Constrained Applications in CSMA Networks. Proceedings, IEEE INFOCOMM '83, 1983, pp. 405-413.

12. S.S. Lam and L. Kleinrock. "Packet Switching in a Multiaccess Broadcast Channel: Dynamic Control Procedures." *IEEE Transactions on Communications COM-23* (Sept. 1975), 891-904.

13. M. Molle. Asynchronous Multiple Access Tree Algorithms. ACM SigComm 1983 Proceedings, ACM, March, 1983.

14. M. Schwartz. *Computer Communication Network Design and Analysis.* Prentice Hall, 1977.

15. A. S. Tanenbaum. *Computer Networks.* Prentice Hall, Englewood Cliffs, N.J., 1981.

16. F. Tobagi. "Multiaccess Protocols in Packet Communication Systems." *IEEE Transactions on Computers COM-28* (April 1980), 468-488.

17. D. Towsley and G. Venkatesh. "Window Random Access Protocols for Local Computer Networks." *IEEE Transactions on Computers COM-31*, 8 (Aug. 1982).

Appendix A: Proof of Lemma 4

Let $P' \epsilon \{P^w\}$ be a policy with a decision, k', which for some state $s_i \epsilon S$ does *not* minimize the one step pseudo loss. Also define:

- p_{ij}^k to be the probability that state s_j immediately succeeds state s_i given decision k is made upon entry to state s_i.
- τ_i^k to be the average time from when a decision is made upon entry to state s_i to the time when the next decision is made, given decision k is made upon entry to state s_i.
- r_i^k to be the one step pseudo loss in state s_i, given decision k is made upon entry to state s_i.

Recall that $\{P^w\}$ is a set of policies which choose the same action for policy element (2), i.e., choose the same size initial window when in the same state. Since any two equal length intervals of time are statistically identical, then if policies P and P' are in $\{P^w\}$, and choose actions k and k' respectively when in state s_i then

$$p_{ij}^k = p_{ij}^{k'} \text{ and } \tau_i^k = \tau_i^{k'}$$

We now want to determine if P' minimizes the average pseudo loss even though it does not (by hypothesis) minimize the one step pseudo loss for state s_i. If P' does not minimize the average pseudo loss then there must exist a policy iteration [Howard 71] starting from P' which yields a policy with a smaller pseudo loss. To determine if such a policy iteration exists, we would normally have to solve the set of simultaneous equations:

$$v_n + g\tau_n^{k'} = -r_n^{k'} + \sum_{j=1}^{K} p_{nj}^{k'} v_j \qquad n=1,2 \ldots K \qquad \text{(A1)}$$

where $v_K=0$ and $\tau_n^{k'}$, $r_n^{k'}$ and $P_{ni}^{k'}$ are computed using the decisions of policy P' to determine the values of g and $\{v_j\}$. g is known as the *gain* under policy P' and can be related to the average pseudo loss; $\{v_j\}$ is known as the set of relative values. To determine if a policy iteration exists, we must examine the value of γ_i^k, defined below, for all possible decisions, k, in state s_i:

$$\gamma_i^k = -(r_i^k/\tau_i^k) + (1/\tau_i^k) \sum_{j=1}^{K} p_{ij}^k v_j \qquad \text{(A2)}$$

Fortunately, for the purposes of proving that P' does not minimize the average pseudo loss, we need not actually solve A1 (note, however, that a numerical value for the loss can be obtained from solving A1). Now, if we can show that there is some alternate decision, *k*, such that

$$\gamma_i^{k'} < \gamma_i^k$$

then P' does not maximize the gain and hence does not minimize the average pseudo loss [Howard 71]. By our above arguments, p_{ij}^k, and τ_i^k are independent of k for all $P \epsilon \{P^w\}$. Thus, A2 can be expressed:

$$\gamma_i^k = -c_1 r_i^k + c_2$$

where c_1 and c_2 are constant with respect to k and c_1 is positive. Since $r_i^k \geq 0$, the maximum value of γ_i^k occurs when r_i^k is minimized. By hypothesis, P' chooses k' such that r_i^k is *not* minimized and thus there exists some *k* such that r_i^k is less than $r_i^{k'}$. Thus there exists a policy iteration on P' and hence P' does not minimize the average pseudo loss. Thus, any policy which does not minimize the one step pseudo loss in every state does not minimize the average pseudo loss.

Incorporation of Multiaccess Links Into a Routing Protocol

Radia Perlman

Digital Equipment Corp. [TW/C11]
1925 Andover Street, Tewksbury, MA 01876

Abstract

Conventional routing protocols and algorithms work most efficiently on sparsely connected networks. Network topologies today include multiaccess links which include hundreds of nodes, all of which are capable of direct communication with each other. Some of these multiaccess links have broadcasting ability. This paper presents protocols and algorithms for efficiently dealing with the characteristics of various types of multiaccess links, when they are included as links in a general topology net.

Introduction

In this paper, the effect of various kinds of multiaccess links on routing protocols and algorithms are explored. The routing algorithms discussed are distributed routing algorithms, and an assumed goal is that the network be self-configuring. Properties such as broadcast capabilities and reliable broadcast capabilities will affect the requirements placed on the protocols and the performance of the algorithms.

The approach discussed in the paper uses the Routing Protocol alone to yield a self-configuring network. An alternative approach is for the Routing Protocol merely to route towards the proper multiaccess link, and assume that higher layers keep track of where nodes currently reside in the network.

First the paper will present the Routing Protocol approach, and then it will contrast it with the higher-layer approach.

Types of Multiaccess Links

Simple multiaccess link -- All nodes attached to this kind of multiaccess link are capable of direct communication with each other, but only in pairs -- each packet transmitted can be received by at most one node. An example of this kind of link is a Public Packet Switching Net.

Broadcasting multiaccess link -- All nodes attached to this kind of multiaccess link are capable of direct communication with each other. In addition, a single packet can be directed to and received by all or some particular subset of attached nodes. An example of this kind of link is a token bus.

Contention broadcasting link -- This type of link has the capabilities of a broadcasting link, but the link works best when protocols do not cause many nodes to simultaneously attempt to transmit. An example of this kind of link is a CSMA/CD link such as the Ethernet.

Reliable broadcasting link -- This type of link has the capabilities of a broadcasting link, with the additional ability to have all addressees piggyback an acknowledgment to a packet, directly on the transmitted packet. Theoretically this can be done with a token ring.

Responsibilities of the Routing Protocol

In ISO terminology, the routing protocols and algorithms lie within the scope of the Network Layer. The routing protocol has the following responsibilities:

1. It must discover and handshake with neighbors. This piece of the Routing Protocol will be referred to as the Link Dependent Sublayer, since its protocols and algorithms differ according to the type of link to which the node is attached.

2. It must distribute enough information around the net to allow routes to be computed. This piece of the Routing Protocol will be referred to as the Update Process.

3. It must compute routes based on the information made available through the Update Process. This piece of the Routing Protocol will be referred to as the Decision Process.

All three of these components of the Routing Protocol have in the past been designed for sparsely connected networks. In this paper we explore methods of optimizing these components of the Network Layer for various types of multiaccess links.

Computation of Routes

There are two basic distributed routing algorithms in wide use in current networks. One, referred to as the "Routing Vector Scheme", involves having each node A transmit to its neighbors a vector consisting of A's distances to each destination in the network. Node A computes its vector using the vectors received from its neighbors. This scheme was the original ARPANET routing algorithm [4][6].

The other, referred to as the "Link State Routing Scheme", involves having each node A construct a Link State Packet, consisting of the state of A's links to its neighbors. This packet is broadcast throughout the entire network, and stored by all nodes. Each node has a database of the latest Link State Packet from every node in the network. This gives enough information to compute paths in the network. This scheme is currently used in the ARPANET [4][5][6][7].

Endnodes and Routers

A major topological implication of the introduction of multiaccess links is that many nodes will be connected to the network only via the multiaccess link. In other words, a typical network will consist of several large multiaccess links, with a few paths connecting the links.

Nodes connected to the network via only one link are referred to as endnodes. An endnode that is connected to the network via a point-to-point link obviously will not need to forward packets on behalf of other nodes.

An endnode S that is connected to the network via one of the multiaccess links will also not need to forward packets for other nodes, since the set of neighbors S can reach is included in the set of neighbors N can reach, if N is a neighbor of S.

For many applications, such as when many nodes are low-cost personal computers, it is desirable that the majority of the nodes on the multiaccess links be kept as simple as possible, and thus desirable to free them from as much responsibility for participation in routing protocols and overhead as possible.

The following sections describe ways for the Network Layer to account for endnodes.

Endnode Routing Messages

For most applications, it is not necessary for endnodes to transmit routing messages.

In the Link State Scheme (described above in the section "Computation of Routes"), a link between A and B is actually reported twice, once in A's Link State Packet, and once in B's Link State Packet. There are two reasons why this duplication might be useful:

1. It can be used as a sanity check--if A reports a link to B, but B does not report a link to A, then the network can ignore the link, as potentially being fallaciously reported by a malfunctioning node.

2. It gives the network the flexibility of having the cost of a link be different in each of the two directions.

The first reason is less applicable in the case of an endnode than in the case of a router. If router R fallaciously claims a link to endnode A, and A does not exist at all in the network, the only harm is that router databases in the network will be cluttered with useless information. It will not cause incorrect routes. If R fallaciously claims a link to endnode A, and A does exist elsewhere in the network, as a neighbor to router Q, the routers will detect that something is wrong when two different routers claim attachment to an endnode.

The second reason is not applicable in the case of an endnode at all. Since endnode E is attached to the network via only one link, by definition, the cost of the link is irrelevant--any path with endpoint E must include that link. Changing the cost of that link will not affect the path.

Note that if an application is not concerned with either of the two reasons above, the routing protocol could halve the database requirements by having each link reported only once, even between routers. This is not done in current networks because the database room to be saved has not been worth the added complexity. However, in the case of endnodes, there is an inherent asymmetry that makes the decision as to which neighbor should report a link a simple decision. The endnode does not report the link.

In the Routing Vector Scheme, there are similar arguments against the necessity for generation of routing messages by endnodes. The only destination for which endnode E can be on the path is E itself, by arguments above. Thus neighbors of E will never use E for a path. If E reported a routing vector consisting of 0 distance to itself, and infinite distance to every other destination in the network, its router neighbors would calculate the same routes as if E reported its true distances to all destinations.

As a matter of fact, there is an advantage in the Routing Vector Scheme of endnodes not participating in routing calculation. Consider the following case:

```
A------B------C
```

When the link between B and C is up, C reports itself as 0 from itself. B reports itself as 1 from C. A reports itself as 2 from C. When the link between B and C breaks, B will now use its next closest neighbor, A, as its path to C, and report that it is now 3 from C. A will change its distance to C to be 4. This continues until A and B count so high that they realize C is actually unreachable. If endnode A instead reported itself as infinitely far from all destinations except itself (or if B assumed that, given that B knew A was an endnode), then B would know C was unreachable as soon as its link to C broke. This counting up behavior is a major disadvantage of this routing algorithm. Preventing endnodes from participating in the routing computation does not solve the problem, but it does alleviate it, especially in a network with a high percentage of endnodes.

Endnode E can either send out a routing vector consisting of 0 for itself and infinity for all other destinations, or E's router neighbors can act as though they had received such a message from E. Either scheme has the advantage that it is simple for E, and lowers routing overhead for the rest of the net.

Thus in either routing algorithm, generation of routing traffic by endnodes is unnecessary.

Endnode Simplicity

Endnodes on point-to-point links do not need to make routing decisions. Packets for all destinations just get passed over their single attachment to the network. Thus there is no reason for them to receive routing messages, to keep routing tables, or to do any routing computation.

Endnodes on multiaccess links can make routing decisions. Although all messages get transmitted on the same link, the endnode has a choice of specification of the neighbor to receive the message. For example:

```
                R1          R2-----D2
                 |           |
-------+--------+------+-----+-----
       |               |
       A               D1
```

If endnode A has a packet for D1, A is best off sending the packet directly to D1. If A's packet is for D2, A must forward it through a router. Router R2 is a better choice than R1.

Note that if A wants to be as simple as possible, it can always send a packet to any router, and that router can forward the packet to the destination, or to the real "best" router. Thus a very simple algorithm for A, that of sending the packet to any router on the multiaccess link, will result in correct, but possibly 1 hop suboptimal, routes. Thus one can trade off endnode simplicity for route optimality to determine the best strategy for a particular application.

Without complicating A very much, a simple caching scheme can be used, in which A notes from which neighbor a packet is received, and caches that information as the best next hop for a given destination. (Note that this is similar to the "backward learning" algorithm, which is based on the priciple that usually the best way for source S to reach destination D is by the same path from which D reaches S [8].)

In the example above, if A receives a packet directly from D1, A will put D1 as the best next hop for D1 in its cache. If A receives a packet from D2 through R2, A will put R2 as the best next hop for D2 in its cache.

There is one necessary addition to the caching scheme to prevent two endnode neighbors on a multiaccess link from forever sending traffic to each other through a router. The addition is that a router R should flag a packet when R is forwarding the packet between two endnodes on the same multiaccess link. If the source of the packet, A, and the destination, B, are both endnodes on a multiaccess link, R should flag packets it is forwarding between A and B. When B receives a packet with source A that is thus flagged by a router, B should put A as the best next hop to A in its cache, and send future packets for A directly to A.

There is an additional desirable addition to this scheme. For some applications, the entire network might consist solely of a single multiaccess link. In this case the Network Layer might be considered superfluous, unless one wants to provide for generalizing the topology in the future without completely redoing the network design. While the network consists solely of a multiaccess link, the Network Layer should provide for the capability of endnode communication without the necessity for a router. Also, even in a general topology net, all routers on a multiaccess link might fail, and it is desirable that endnodes on that multiaccess link still be able to communicate with other endnodes on that multiaccess link, even if they cannot reach nodes off that link.

This can be accomplished with a simple extension of the endnode caching scheme whereby the endnode, given no entry in the cache, and given no knowledge of any attached routers, attempts to reach the destination on the multiaccess link. So the rules for choosing a next hop, when A wishes to send a packet to destination B are:

1. If B is in A's cache, with next hop X, A should transmit the packet to X.
2. Else, if there is a router on the link, A should transmit the packet to that router for forwarding.
3. Else, transmit the packet to B.

Note that we have not specified how A knows that there is a router on the link. That is covered below, in the section "Link Dependent Sublayer".

Endnode Outages

When an endnode fails, routes in the network do not change. The endnode will become unreachable, but it is not essential to inform the rest of the net of that event. Nodes that wish to communicate with the endnode will discover its unreachability at the time of the attempted communication. The amount of traffic caused by nodes attempting to reach destination endnodes that are currently down will be far less than the amount of traffic necessary to keep the entire network informed at all times of the reachability of all endnodes. This is especially true if many of the endnodes are personal computers, with people often cycling the machines to change disks, etc.

Thus router neighbors of endnodes should not inform the rest of the network of link failure to an endnode.

However, sometimes an endnode will move to a different location in the network, in which case routes will be affected and the rest of the network must be informed.

The amount of time necessary to unplug an endnode from one link and move to another location ("MOVE-TIME") is likely to be on the order of minutes. Thus router neighbors of endnodes should remember the previous reachability of endnode neighbors for MOVE-TIME. Endnode outages shorter than MOVE-TIME will not result in any routing overhead.

MOVE-TIME might be so short, in some applications, that a large proportion of endnode outages will be longer than MOVE-TIME, and very little traffic overhead will be saved by the above scheme. An alternative is for router neighbor R1 to remember for a much longer time the previous reachability of an endnode neighbor E. If E moves to another location, its new router neighbors will inform the rest of the network of the new location of E. At that point R1, noting that some other router is claiming attachment to E, and noting that R1's link to E has been down, can inform the rest of the net that E is no longer attached to R1. However, this approach only works with the Link State Routing Scheme.

This approach does not work with the Routing Vector routing algorithm since that algorithm does not give sufficient information. Consider the following example:

```
              R1------R2------R3
              |
   ---------+-----+-------
            |
            E
```

In the Routing Vector Scheme, R1 will report a distance to E of 1, R2 will report a distance to E of 2, and R3 will report a distance to E of 3.

Suppose E goes down. By our rules for endnode outages, R1 will not change its report to R2. Thus R2 and R3 will not detect that any change has occurred.

Now suppose E moves to R3. R3 will now report that it is 1 from E. R2 will report that it is 2 from E, but that is the same value it had. Thus R1 does not detect any change based upon the information it hears from R2. Thus there is not enough information for R1 to discover that E has moved.

This is not a problem in the Link State Scheme. Under that scheme R3 would explicitly include E in its Link State Packet, and R1 would know that E was now a neighbor of R3.

Link Dependent Sublayer

In a conventional network, each node S periodically sends a status message to each of its neighbors N, so that N will know that S continues to be a neighbor, and that S is up.

The list of neighbors can be known beforehand, for instance by a manually entered table, or node S can inform its neighbors of S's identity by S sending explicit messages over each of its interfaces, identifying itself.

As networks grow in size it becomes increasingly inconvenient to expect network topology to exist in manually entered tables. It is desirable to add a new node to a network without reconfiguring the software in existing nodes.

On a conventional point-to-point link it is not necessary to know the neighboring node's address or identity in order to communicate. Thus in a net with only point-to-point links it is easy to have a self configuring net. As each node comes up, it handshakes with its neighbors to determine their identity.

On multiaccess links, a packet must be addressed, so that it can be determined which node (or nodes) is supposed to receive the packet. Thus conventional methods for having a self-configuring net do not work on multiaccess links. However, multiaccess links make very large networks economically viable, making self-configurability very important.

Public Packet Switching Net

In a PPSN, there is no low-level mechanism for discovering the address of other attached DTEs. Thus when one uses a PPSN as a multiaccess link in a private network, where the nodes in the private net are DTEs on the PPSN, there must be a table in each DTE, or some high-level directory service that will maintain the list of attached nodes, since it is not possible to communicate with another DTE without knowing the other DTE's address on the PPSN.

A separate packet must be sent to each addressee. Thus the mechanisms to be discussed below of maintaining reachability information on broadcast forms of multiaccess links are inapplicable on a PPSN.

Broadcast Links

On a broadcast link there is the capability of sending a packet to a logical address meaning it should be read by some subset of the nodes on the network. This gives nodes on the link the capability of finding each other with no foreknowledge of their neighbors' addresses. All that is needed is knowledge of the single well-known logical address "all nodes".

To make oneself known, one periodically broadcasts a hello message, to the logical address "all nodes". On point-to-point links, it is not necessary to send periodic hellos if there is traffic flowing on that point-to-point link. However, on a multiaccess link, traffic sent to addresses other than "all nodes" may not be received by all the nodes, so the periodic hello is necessary.

To discover the membership of a multiaccess link, one listens to all the hello messages broadcast to "all nodes".

Multicast links such as busses can degrade in ways in which connectivity is not two-way, or not transitive. For instance, if A's transmitter is weak, and B's receiver is weak, A might be heard by all nodes except B, and B might be able to hear all nodes except A. Thus for routers on the link, it is important not only for R1 to hear a hello from R2, but to know that R2 has heard hellos from R1.

Thus a hello message from R1 should include the list of nodes from which R2 has heard hellos.

As discussed in the section "Endnode Simplicity", endnodes do not need to know the complete membership of the link. Thus the hello messages should really be broadcast to "all routers", and not "all nodes". This will unburden the endnodes from receiving and processing all the hello messages.

Endnodes do need to know the address of one of the routers on the link, however, if one exists. The method of informing the endnodes of the existence of at least one router is that the routers should have a very simple algorithm (for instance, highest address), for choosing which of them should be the "designated router". The designated router should periodically issue its hello message to the logical address "all endnodes".

This, and the simple algorithm presented in "Endnode Simplicity", enables endnodes to communicate without keeping a large database of current nodes on the link, and without keeping separate timers for each of the neighbors in order to time them out for nonreceipt of hello messages.

This algorithm allows a network to be self-configuring.

Contention Broadcasting Link

The algorithm presented above, for determining the link membership in a self-configuring manner, does not cause many nodes to simultaneously seek to acquire the channel. Each node on the network asynchronously sends periodic hello messages.

An algorithm that required all nodes on the link to acknowledge upon receipt of a packet would synchronize traffic, and lower the usable bandwidth of a contention broadcasting link.

Because the algorithm presented in the previous section does not synchronize traffic, it is also applicable to contention broadcasting links.

Reliable Broadcasting Link

A reliable broadcasting link has all the capabilities of a broadcasting link, so the algorithm presented for broadcasting links is certainly applicable.

However, the reliable broadcasting ability of this type of link can be used to refine the algorithm and cut down on routing overhead.

On this type of link, nodes can be sorted according to some simple scheme, such as numerical address. The node with the highest address can be designated as the "designated node". It is the responsibility of the designated node to issue a hello message, listing all known nodes on the link, and having a trailer of bits for acknowledgments, one for each node on the link. Other nodes on the link are responsible for flipping their bits, acknowledging their presence.

If a new node comes up, it issues a hello message to the logical address "all nodes". The designated node can then include the new node in the hello message list. If, however, the new node should be the designated node, then the old designated node will rebroadcast the old hello message, and the new node can take over the responsibility of being designated node, given a membership list by the old designated node.

Nodes that do not acknowledge as the hello message goes by are dropped from the membership list. If the designated node fails to send a hello message within an agreed-upon time, then the next highest node takes over designated node responsibility.

By utilizing the properties of this kind of link, traffic overhead from hello messages is dramatically reduced, because only one node needs to periodically send hello messages.

Update Process

Public Packet Switching Net

In a Public Packet Switching net, it might be expensive to maintain virtual circuits between every pair of nodes for the purpose of exchanging routing messages, especially on links that are not currently being used for traffic.

One method of alleviating this situation is not exchanging information to and from endnodes. Many private networks that utilize PPSNs use the link solely as a final hop in the network, not as a general link for forwarding traffic. In those networks, there is no need for exchanging routing information over the PPSN, since the nodes on the PPSN are endnodes.

Another method of alleviating this situation is by hierarchical routing [6].

In hierarchical routing, a network is divided into subnetworks known as "areas". Level 1 routing maintains routes within an area. Level 2 routing maintains routes to areas.

Some private networks use a PPSN to connect dispersed pieces of their network. The only route from one subnetwork to another is through the PPSN. With this topology, each subnetwork can be declared an "area". Level 1 routing messages would not cross the PPSN link, because that link is not included in any area. With this topology, level 2 routing messages are unnecessary as well, since the level 2 routing can be static. As stated in the section "Link Dependent Sublayer", manually entered tables are necessary in order to find neighbors on a PPSN. Thus the identity of and location of each of the "areas" might as well be manually entered and maintained as well.

Since the only path between areas is through the PPSN, there is no need to keep current knowledge of which areas are reachable. When there is traffic for an area, it will be discovered if the area is indeed unreachable.

Broadcast Link

The capabilities of a broadcast link are very valuable for the update process, since a routing message must be sent to all of one's neighbors, in either the routing vector or the link state routing schemes. Routing messages, instead of being sent individually to each neighbor, can be broadcast to the logical address "all routers".

The latest routing message from each node must be reliably received, however. This is not a problem, of course, in the case of a reliable broadcasting link, since the nodes can acknowledge a routing message without overhead.

One method on links which do not have reliable broadcast is to require acknowledgments from all nodes. This means that each transmission of routing information requires at least n messages, with n being the number of routers on the broadcast link. One message is required for a node to transmit its routing message. The other n-1 messages are acknowledgments of the message from the other nodes on the link. This method has the disadvantage on a contention link of causing n-1 nodes to simultaneously attempt to transmit.

Another method is to frequently retransmit routing messages, at intervals of RETRANSMIT-TIME, so that a node that missed a message would receive the retransmission, and not require acknowledgments. This method requires less traffic than the explicit acknowledgment scheme if n*(RETRANSMIT-TIME) is more than the average time between routing messages. However, depending on timer settings, this method might be less responsive in the event of lost messages.

A third method is a compromise between the two approaches above, and involves having a node acknowledge all Routing Messages received on the link at once, in one big packet.

Routing messages from each node must be numbered with sequence numbers, or timestamped. In the Link State Scheme, each node in the network must receive the latest Link State Packet from all nodes in the network. In the Routing Vector Scheme, each node needs to have received the latest Routing Vector from all its neighbors.

In the Routing Vector Scheme, this approach works as follows. The designated router D (see section on Link Dependent Sublayer) periodically broadcasts, to the logical address "all routers", a packet (known as a "Sequence Numbers Packet") listing all nodes on the multiaccess link, together with the sequence number of the latest routing message received from each of those nodes. If node B has issued a later routing message than the one listed in D's packet, B must reissue its latest routing message. If node A has not received B's latest routing message, as evidenced by the fact that D's Sequence Numbers Packet lists a larger sequence number for B than the one stored in A's database, then A issues a Sequence Numbers Packet, which will cause B to send its latest routing message in response.

The Link State Scheme is similar. In this scheme D's Sequence Numbers Packet must list all nodes in the network. Suppose one entry is node S, with sequence number n. If node A has a larger sequence number on its stored Link State Packet from S, A should respond by transmitting its Link State Packet from S. If node A has a smaller sequence number on its stored Link State Packet from S, A should respond by transmitting a Sequence Numbers Packet, as a request for more recent information. Note that if designated router D missed the latest link state packet from node S, all routers on the link will respond by retrasmitting S's Link State Packet. This can be a problem on a contention link, but the scheme can be refined by adding random delays.

On a multiaccess link a node can go down and come back up again without the outage being detected by the other nodes on the link. The sequence numbers packet scheme has the advantage of enabling a new node to request complete information upon restart.

Decision Process

Routing Vector Scheme

The routing vector scheme has the problem of being slow to terminate when paths get worse, as discussed in the section "Endnode Routing Messages". In the example:

```
A------B------C
```

A and B count up, one hop at a time, until they realize that C is unreachable.

This looping behavior is much worse with higher connectivity. Consider the case:

```
----+---+---+---+---+---+---+----
    |   |   |   |   |   |   |
    A   B   C   D   E   F   G------H
```

When the link between G and H is up, G reports its distance to H as 1, and nodes A through F on the multiaccess link report their distances to H as 2. When the link between G and H breaks, G changes its distance to H to be 3. Then one by one the other nodes on the link change their distances to H to be 3. Only when all of them have reported their new distance of 3, and all of them have received reports from all the other nodes, can they start, one by one, updating their distances to H to be 4. With n nodes on the link, it takes at least n messages (more if messages get dropped) to increase the distance by 1.

This disadvantage of the Routing Vector Scheme argues that the Link State Scheme is a preferable routing scheme in the presence of multiaccess links, unless the vast majority of nodes on the multiaccess links are endnodes that do not participate in routing calculation.

Link State Scheme

In the Link State Routing Scheme, each node has a complete database of Link State Packets, listing all links in the network. From this database, various algorithms, such as Dijkstra's algorithm (used in the current ARPANET), can be used to compute paths in the network [1][4].

In general, (and in particular in the case of the Dijkstra algorithm used in the ARPANET), the computational complexity of route calculation in the network increases with the number of links in the network.

A multiaccess link with n nodes can be considered topologically as n nodes, each with links to the other n-1 nodes, yielding n*(n-1)/2 links.

Another way of looking at this topology is by viewing the multiaccess link itself as a pseudonode, with links to each of the n nodes. This yields a star topology of n+1 nodes and n links.

To accomplish having the multiaccess link appear as a pseudonode to the routing algorithm, the designated router must give the link a unique ID. This can be accomplished by having part of the ID be the ID of the designated router, and the rest of the ID being a number assigned by the designated router. In its hello messages on the link, the designated router informs the other attached routers of the ID of the link, say L.

Each router R on L (including the designated router) reports a single link in its link state packet, being a link to "node" L. Then the designated router issues an additional Link State Packet, on behalf of "node" L, claiming links to each of the nodes on the link.

Assuming r routers and e endnodes on a multiaccess link, this saves database room proportional to e+(r-1) in each of the r link state packets from the r attached routers, since each of them only reports a single link, to "node" L, instead of reporting their e+(r-1) links to all the nodes on the multiaccess link. Only the Link State Packet from "node L" contains a list of the e+r links of nodes attached to the multiaccess link.

It also saves traffic overhead since the size of the Link State Packets is dramatically reduced. And it also saves CPU, since routing algorithms to compute paths tend to be proportional to the number of links in the net.

Summary of Approach

Multiaccess links dramatically change the types of topologies in networks. In traditional networks, each node had a very small number of neighbors. With multiaccess links, each node might have hundreds of neighbors.

Typical topologies will consist of several multiaccess links, each with hundreds of nodes. A few point-to-point links will merge all of the multiaccess links into one huge network.

Many recommendations were made in the paper for modifications to be made to traditional routing algorithms and protocols for this new environment. Recommendations were:

1. Distinguish between routers and endnodes.

2. Do not have endnodes generate routing messages.

3. Do not have endnodes receive routing messages.

4. Do not have endnodes participate in routing calculation.

5. Optionally have endnodes implement a simple caching scheme to eliminate one-hop suboptimal routing.

6. Routers should not inform the network of endnode outages, except if the outage is long-lasting, or if the router can detect the endnode has moved elsewhere in the network.

7. Have nodes on multiaccess links handshake with neighbor routers via broadcasted hello messages to the group "all routers".

8. Have routers broadcast routing messages to the group "all routers", instead of sending a copy to each neighbor. On channels that do not have reliable broadcast, use Sequence Numbers Packets for a periodic summary of acknowledgments.

9. Use the Link State Routing Scheme preferentially over the Routing Vector Routing Scheme because of the latter's looping problems, which are exacerbated by high connectivity such as on multiaccess links.

10. Consider a multiaccess link with n nodes as logically being n+1 nodes and n links instead of n nodes with n*(n-1)/2 links.

Higher-Layer Approach

The approach taken by Xerox is to assign each link in the network (point-to-point as well as multiaccess) a "network number". Their Routing Protocol routes towards links, and assumes that higher layers will know at which link a node resides [3].

When a node comes up, it registers at a "clearinghouse", so that other nodes will be able to know where it resides. If there are multiple clearinghouses (so that a single clearinghouse will not be a single point for network failure), the clearinghouses must have a protocol to ensure that their databases remain consistent.

This approach yields a simpler and more efficient Routing Protocol, since it is not necessary to discover or maintain the membership of the multiaccess links. However, it has the following disadvantages:

1. It is less self-configuring, since a "network number", unique to the network, must be assigned to a link before adding it to a network. The philosophy behind 48 bit IDs is that each node in the world has a unique 48 bit ID that it can use no matter in which network it is attached [3]. Thus with 48 bit IDs and the approach taken in the rest of the paper, a node can be attached anywhere in a network without administrative assignment of any numbers.

2. Nodes that are connected to the network via multiple links will have multiple addresses, one for each link. This has multiple consequences. First, the link by which the node is addressed affects the route to the node. Choosing the wrong link can result in a highly nonoptimal route. Second, if a link fails, a node might be reachable, but only if the correct link is addressed. Third, a node has to be consistent about which address it puts into the source field for itself, since the destination node's higher layers might have trouble matching packets to an ongoing conversation if the source field changes.

3. Endnodes have the additional burden of finding, registering with, and querying the clearinghouses. The endnode-clearinghouse protocols for accomplishing this must be considered in measuring the complexity of the architecture.

4. Clearinghouses must exist for the network to operate. This adds to the cost of a network.

5. A clearinghouse-clearinghouse protocol must exist for ensuring consistent databases.

On the other hand, it can be argued that

higher layers do not wish to find nodes, but wish to find objects, that can move from node to node. Thus a clearinghouse is necessary in order to locate objects. If that is true, then the last three items above are needed anyway.

If the network consists almost entirely of multiaccess links, and if a clearinghouse capability is in place for location of objects, the higher-level approach is simpler and more efficient. However, if the clearinghouse capability is not in place, or if the network contains large numbers of point-to-point links, the approach given in the rest of the paper is simpler and more efficient, especially for endnodes.

References

[1] A.V. Aho, J. E. Hopcroft, and J. D. Ullman [1974]. "The Design and Analysis of Computer Algorithms", Addison-Wesley, pp 208, 220.

[2] V. Ahuja, "Routing and Flow Control in Systems Network Architecture," IBM Systems Journal, Volume 18, Number 2, 1979.

[3] Yogen Dalal and Robert Printis, "48-bit Absolute Internet and Ethernet Host Numbers", Seventh Data Communications Symposium, 1981.

[4] J. McQuillan, et.al., "The New Routing Algorithm for the ARPANET", IEEE Transactions on Communications, May 1980.

[5] Radia Perlman, "Fault-Tolerant Broadcast of Routing Information", IEEE INFOCOM 83, April 1983. Also to be published in "Computer Networks".

[6] Radia Perlman, "Hierarchical Routing and the Subnetwork Partition Problem", Fifteenth Hawaiian International Conference on System Sciences, January 1982.

[7] Eric Rosen, "The Updating Protocol of ARPANET's New Routing Algorithm,", Computer Networks, February 1980.

[8] Andrew Tanenbaum, [1981]. "Computer Networks", Prentice-Hall Inc., p. 203.

[9] H. Zimmerman, "OSI Reference Model - The ISO Model of Architecture for Open Systems Interconnection", IEEE Trans. on Comm., April 1980.

Theoretical Performance Analysis of Sliding Window Link Level Flow Control for a Local Area Network

E.Arthurs
G.L.Chesson
B.W.Stuck

Bell Laboratories
Murray Hill, New Jersey 07974

ABSTRACT

A transmitter sends packets over a local area network to a receiver. The receiver has a finite amount of storage capacity for buffering messages. A *sliding window protocol* is employed to insure all packets are delivered without error in order of arrival. Mean throughput rate and packet delay statistics are studied as a function of model parameters. Simulation data are presented.

1. Introduction

At the present time there is great interest in communication over logical abstractions of physical circuits (so called *virtual* circuits) within local area networks. *Protocols* control the transfer of data from transmitters to receivers over the virtual circuit to insure no loss of data, and take appropriate actions in event of a wide variety of failures. References on this subject are found elsewhere (e.g., Tanenbaum, 1981, pp.187-196).

Examples of such mechanisms are stop-start protocols where the transmitter stops until the receiver acknowledges receipt of the message (e.g., Binary Synchronous Communications (IBM)), Digital Equipment's product line for Digital Network Architecture (Wecker,1980; Tanenbaum, 1981, pp.172-174), IBM's product line for Systems Network Architecture framework(Green, 1979; Atkins, 1980), the Defense Advance Research Project Agency Transport Control Protocol (Tanenbaum, 1981, pp.373-377) or CCITT's X.25 (Tanenbaum, 1981, pp.167-172).

In our opinion, at the present time there is a great deal of guidance required to engineer such systems to achieve predictable traffic handling characteristics (cf the current literature: Bux, Kuemmerle, Truong, 1980; Easton, 1980; Fayolle, Gelenbe, Pujolle, 1978; Kleinrock, 1978A, 1978B; Reiser, 1979; Sunshine, 1976, 1977; Traynham, Steen, 1977; Yu, Majithia, 1979; Luderer, Che, Marshall, 1982; Luderer, Che, Haggerty, Kirslis, Marshall, 1981).

Here we report on a novel technique for upper and lower bounding mean throughput rate based only on zero contention mean packet processing and transmission times. Furthermore, the bounds obtained are the *best* possible bounds, i.e., they are *achievable* given only mean times for packet handling under no load. The control of the flow of data for the protocol adopted here is found in the open literature (Knuth, 1981; Tanenbaum, 1981, pp.148-164) and is called a *sliding window link level flow control protocol.* It is representative of a great many protocols currently in use, each of which differs in detail in terms of error handling, but not in terms of pacing the flow of data between the transmitter and receiver (cf Schwartz, 1982, for an analysis of a protocol with the same control of flow of data but a different acknowledgement strategy). Most importantly, the analysis is *tractable,* i.e., it can be checked quickly in actual field operations.

We test the sensitivity of our *assumptions* as well as numerical *parameters* by comparing mean value analysis results against results based on a Jackson network analysis and on simulation results. In all cases, the results suggest that buffering *two* packets at the receiver buys virtually all the benefit of buffering more than two packets, and is superior to buffering only *one* packet at the receiver. This is well known to many digital systems engineers: the contribution here is rigorous analysis to substantitate this folk lore.

2. Model Description

The system that motivated this work is described elsewhere (Fraser, 1979; Chesson, 1979, 1980; Luderer, Che, Haggerty, Kirslis, Marshall, 1981; Luderer, Che, Marshall, 1982). An illustrative hardware block diagram is shown in Figure 1. A number of devices are interconnected via *Data Terminal Equipment (DTE)* to a *local area network* switching system. The devices communicate with one another in three phases: first, a full duplex virtual circuit is set up between two devices, second, communication exchange takes place, and third, the full duplex virtual circuit is taken down. Communication takes place as follows:

[1] One device, called the transmitter, takes a variable length message, decomposes it into a series of fixed length packets, appends a variety of control bits to each packet, and transmits it over the network. The transmitter holds each packet in local storage until an acknowledgement is received that the packet was correctly received.

[2] The receiver processes each packet, removes control bits, and groups packets into messages, plus sends an acknowledgement of proper receipt back to the transmitter.

In a local area network, the fraction of packets that are lost or garbled by the network is typically quite small; the impact on traffic handling characteristics of lost packets is ignored from this point on.

In a well engineered local area network, the packet delay due to the network is typically quite small compared to the packet handling at the sender and receiver; from this point the local area network delay for each packet is assumed to be an additive constant delay. There are a variety of other phenomena, such as hardware and software failures, higher level protocols, and so forth that are ignored from this point on in the interest of brevity.

2.1 Flow Control Policy

Initially, the transmitter starts a packet sequence counter, denoted C, at zero. Messages are transmitted in order of arrival; packets within

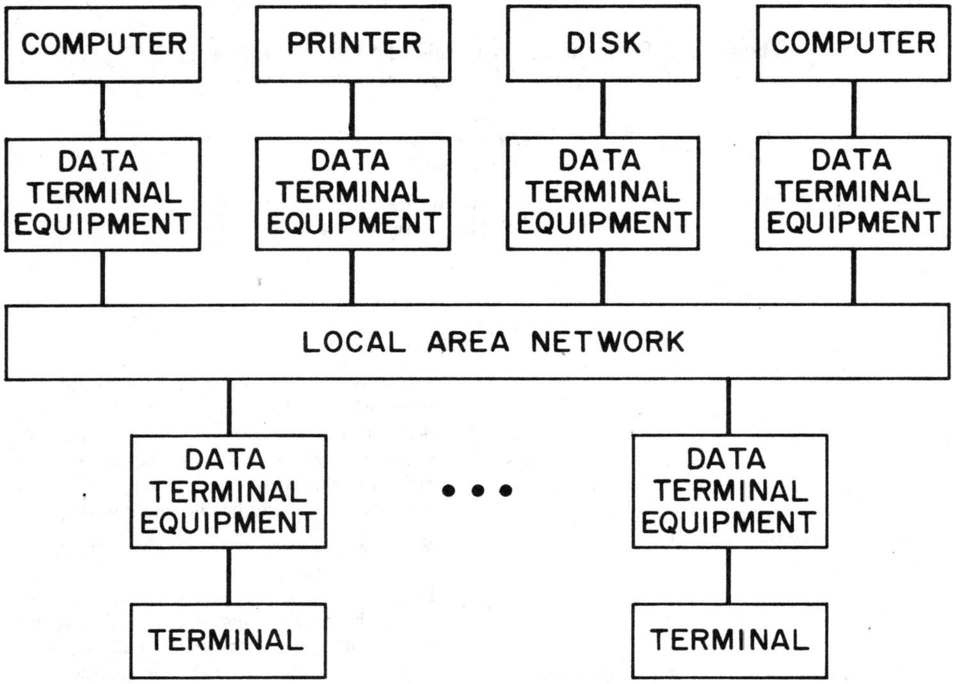

Figure 1.Hardware Block Diagram

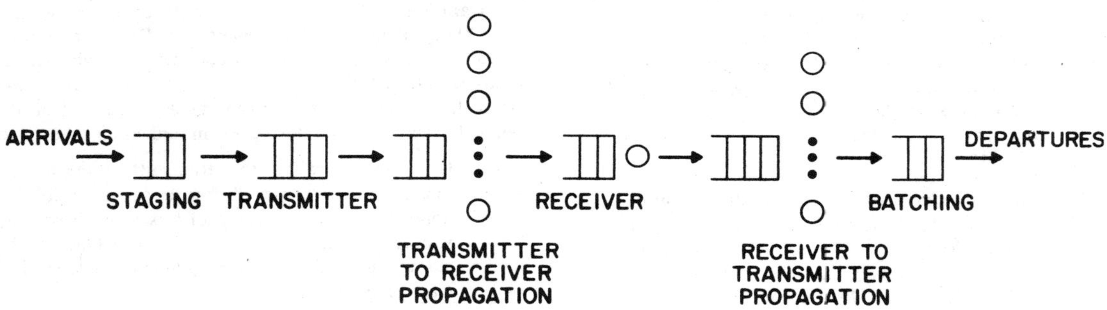

Figure 2.Queueing Network Block Diagram

messages are transmitted in order over the virtual circuit. Each packet has a sequence number that is used to pace the flow of data from the source to the sink. Each time the transmitter sends a packet, C is incremented by one; each time the transmitter receives an acknowledgement, C is decremented by one and flushes this packet from its transmitter buffer. The maximum number of packets that can be buffered by the receiver is called the *window* denoted W. The largest the transmitter packet sequence counter can be is W: the transmitter knows the receiver can buffer at most this many packets. Each packet holds one receiver buffer; when the packet sequence counter strikes W the transmitter ceases to send messages, until a minimum number of acknowledgements are received. A start/stop protocol would have a window of size one (W=1): the transmitter would send the first packet of a message and wait for a positive acknowledgement before sending the next packet, and so forth. A double buffering protocol would have a window size of two (W=2).

How frequently should the receiver acknowledge packets? Ideally it should be done after each packet; however, if this requires an unacceptable amount of processor time at the transmitter or at the receiver or both, then acknowledgements could be batched. The normal operating regime is where control packets are much less frequent than data packets; here we focus on the data packet processing time alone.

2.2 Queueing Network Model

The queueing model of this system (Figure 2) follows the above description quite closely.

2.2.1 Queues and Servers The system consists of a staging queue (with no server), a transmitter queue (with one server), a transmitter to receiver queue (with W servers), a receiver queue (with one server), and a receiver to transmitter queue (with W servers)

2.2.2 Packet Flow Through Queueing Network A packet migrates from one queue to another: packets arrive at an external queue where they are staged, before migrating to the transmitter queue, then through the transmitter to receiver queue, then to the receiver queue, then finally to the receiver to transmitter queue, before leaving the system; a packet is in the system if it is in the transmitter or receiver queue (waiting or in execution), or in the propagation queue from the transmitter to the receiver and vice versa.

2.2.3 Service Required for Each Step of Packet Communications Each packet requires some processing time by the transmitter, denoted T_{trans}, including both packet processing time and transmission time. Each packet propagates from the transmitter to receiver, in a mean time denoted $T_{trans-rec}$. Each packet requires receiver processing time, denoted T_{rec}. Each receiver acknowledgement packet propagates from the receiver to the transmitter in a time interval denoted $T_{rec-trans}$. The receiver and transmitter processing times are assumed to include the time to handle acknowledgement processing.

2.2.4 Flow Control Policy Arriving packets are stored in the staging queue. If there are less than W packets in the system, the packet immediately enters the transmitter queue; otherwise, the packet waits in the staging queue.

3. Mean Throughput Rate Bounds (cf Reiser, 1979; Fayolle et al, 1978)

The first step in the analysis is to construct a state space for this system, denoted by Ω. If we imagine observing* the system in operation at a given instant of time, say t, we would note at most four kinds of activities in process, one for each of the steps. Let the four tuple $\underline{J}=(J_{trans}, J_{trans-rec}, J_{rec}, J_{rec-trans})$ denote the state of the system, whose components are nonnegative integers, with each component denoting the number of packets either queued or in execution at that instant. The statement that the system is in state $\underline{J}$ at time t then means that at the time of observation, there were *concurrently* in progress J_{trans} packets at the transmitter (both queued and in processing), and so forth. Not all values for $\underline{J}$ are possible. Since we wish to determine the behavior of the system under load, we will assume we have an external staging queue to the system that contains $J_{staging}$ packets, while there can be at most W packets in the system:

$$J_{trans} = \min[J_{staging}, W - J_{trans-rec} - J_{rec} - J_{rec-trans}] \qquad (1)$$

Our goal is to determine the maximum mean throughput rate of packet transmission through this model. We assume that there are always sufficiently many packets waiting in the staging queue such that $J_{staging} \geq W$, i.e., there are W packets circulating in the system:

$$W = J_{trans} + J_{trans-rec} + J_{rec} + J_{rec-trans} \qquad (2)$$

If this maximum mean throughput rate is unacceptably low, then operating at a lower mean throughput rate (in order to achieve acceptable packet delay) will also be unacceptable.

* As an aside, it is interesting to note that the system state is intrinsically *distributed* in the transmitter, the receiver, and the channel; due to the finite propagation time of signals between the transmitter and the receiver, it is *impossible* for *either* to observe the total system state at a given instant of time, say t

3.1 Analysis

The mean throughput rate is denoted by λ. The mean number of packets in execution in the transmitter and in the receiver equals the mean throughput rate multiplied by the total mean execution time (Little, 1961; Conway, Maxwell, Miller, 1967, pp.18-19). We denote by $E(.)$ the time average of the argument, and write:

$$\lambda T_{trans} = E[1 - \delta_{0,J_{trans}}] \leq 1 \qquad (3a)$$

$$\lambda T_{rec} = E[1 - \delta_{0,J_{rec}}] \leq 1 \qquad (3b)$$

$$\delta_{ij} = \begin{cases} 1 & i = j \\ 0 & i \neq j \end{cases} \qquad (3c)$$

Since only one packet is in execution at the transmitter or the receiver at any one time, the above inequalities immediately give us

$$\lambda \leq \min\left[\frac{1}{T_{trans}}, \frac{1}{T_{rec}}\right] \qquad (4)$$

The mean number of packets in propagation from the transmitter to receiver is

$$\lambda T_{trans-rec} = E[J_{trans-rec}] \qquad (5a)$$

while the mean number of packets in propagation from the receiver to transmitter is

$$\lambda T_{rec-trans} = E[J_{rec-trans}] \qquad (5b)$$

Our goal is to find upper and lower bounds on mean throughput rate, subject to meeting state space constraints.

If we add equations (3a), (3b), (5a), and (5b), we see

$$E[1 - \delta_{0,J_{trans}} + J_{trans-rec} + 1 - \delta_{0,J_{rec}} + J_{rec-trans}] \qquad (6)$$
$$= \lambda[T_{trans} + T_{trans-rec} + T_{rec} + T_{rec-trans}]$$

However, since

$$1 - \delta_{0,J_{trans}} \leq J_{trans} \qquad 1 - \delta_{0,J_{rec}} \leq J_{rec} \qquad (7)$$

we find that

$$\lambda[T_{trans} + T_{trans-rec} + T_{rec} + T_{rec-trans}] \qquad (8)$$
$$\leq E[J_{trans} + J_{trans-rec} + J_{rec} + J_{rec-trans}] = W$$

Combining (4) and (8), we find

$$\lambda \leq \min\left[\frac{1}{T_{trans}}, \frac{1}{T_{rec}}, \frac{W}{T_{trans} + T_{trans-rec} + T_{rec} + T_{rec-trans}}\right] \qquad (9)$$

To get a lower bound on the mean throughput rate, we realize that

$$\lambda[T_{trans} + \frac{T_{trans-rec}}{W} + T_{rec} + \frac{T_{rec-trans}}{W}] \qquad (10)$$
$$= E[1 - \delta_{0,J_{trans}} + \frac{J_{trans-rec}}{W} + 1 - \delta_{0,J_{rec}} + \frac{J_{rec-trans}}{W}] \geq 1$$

The lower bound on the right hand side arises from realizing that if $J_{trans}=J_{rec}=0$ then the right hand side is one, while if either J_{trans} or J_{rec} is greater than zero then the right hand side is lower bounded by one. This allows us to show

$$\lambda \geq \frac{W}{W[T_{trans} + T_{rec}] + T_{trans-rec} + T_{rec-trans}} \qquad (11)$$

3.1.1 Interpretation of Upper Bound on Mean Throughput Rate The physical interpretation of the upper bound on mean throughput rate is as follows

- If the transmitter is the bottleneck, then

$$\lambda_{upper} = \frac{1}{T_{trans}} \qquad (12a)$$

- If the receiver is the bottleneck, then

$$\lambda_{upper} = \frac{1}{T_{rec}} \qquad (12b)$$

- If the number of buffers is the bottleneck, then

$$\lambda_{upper} = \frac{W}{T_{trans} + T_{trans-rec} + T_{rec} + T_{rec-trans}} \qquad (12c)$$

3.1.2 Interpretation of Lower Bound on Mean Throughput Rate The physical interpretation of the lower bound is that at most one packet at a time is being handled by the system.

3.2 Negligible Local Area Network Delay

As an example, let us assume that $W=1$ and $T_{trans-rec}=T_{rec-trans}=0$, i.e., the local area network delay is negligible compared to the mean time required at the transmitter and receiver to handle a packet, which is typical in *local area networks* (cf Luderer et al, 1981, 1982). If we do so, we see

$$\frac{1}{T_{trans}+T_{rec}} \leqslant \lambda_{\max} \leqslant \frac{1}{T_{trans}+T_{rec}} \quad W=1 \tag{13}$$

In words, the maximum rate of transmitting packets is the reciprocal of the sum of the mean time spent by the transmitter plus the mean time spent by the receiver.

Increasing the number of buffers from one to two, $W=1$ to $W=2$ always increases the maximum mean throughput rate, and now we see

$$\frac{1}{T_{trans}+T_{rec}} \leqslant \lambda_{\max} \leqslant \min\left[\frac{1}{T_{trans}},\frac{1}{T_{rec}}\right] \quad W>1 \tag{14}$$

Furthermore, this increase is maximized for $T_{trans}=T_{rec}$, and then the upper bound *doubles* in going from one buffer to more than one buffer. Why is this so? By having more than one buffer, both the transmitter and receiver can simultaneously be filling and emptying a buffer, allowing greater concurrency or parallelism compared with the single buffer case. We also note that allowing more than two buffers, e.g., *infinite* buffers, will not increase the upper bound on the maximum mean throughput rate any further; intuitively, we only have two serially reusable resources, the transmitter and receiver, and double buffering keeps them both busy simultaneously.

The lower bound on mean throughput rate, is identical to the upper bound for $W=1$. Why is this so? There may be significant fluctuation about the mean values shown above, and in the limit of one big swing about the mean value all of the messages will pile up at one stage in the network and nothing will be transmitted until buffers become available.

3.3 Nonnegligible Local Area Network Delay

If the local area network delay is not negligible compared to the packet processing at the transmitter and receiver, the upper bound on mean throughput rate will increase as a linear function of the amount of buffering available at the receiver, until either the transmitter or the receiver becomes a limiting bottleneck. Figures 3A, 3B, and 3C plot these upper and lower bounds, as well as the results of an Jackson queueing network analysis (e.g., Kelly, 1976, 1979), for the special case where

$$T_{trans} = T_{rec} \quad T_{trans-rec} = T_{rec-trans} \tag{16}$$

for three different cases, where the propagation delay is much smaller, equal, and much larger than the mean processing time at either the transmitter or receiver.

Introducing a Jackson network model requires additional information about the *fluctuations* about the mean packet service times at each step. This allows us to study the sensitivity of our findings to our *assumptions* as well as to the actual numerical values of model parameters.

The fraction of time the queueing network model predicts the system to be in state $\underline{J}$ is denoted by $\pi(\underline{J})$ where

$$\pi(\underline{J}) = \frac{1}{G} T_{trans}^{J_{trans}} \frac{T_{trans-rec}^{J_{trans-rec}}}{J_{trans-rec}!} T_{rec}^{J_{rec}} \frac{T_{rec-trans}^{J_{rec-trans}}}{J_{rec-trans}!} \tag{17}$$

The system partition function denoted G is chosen to normalize the probability distribution:

$$\sum_{\underline{J}} \pi(\underline{J}) = 1 \tag{18}$$

where the summation is carried out over all feasible system states.

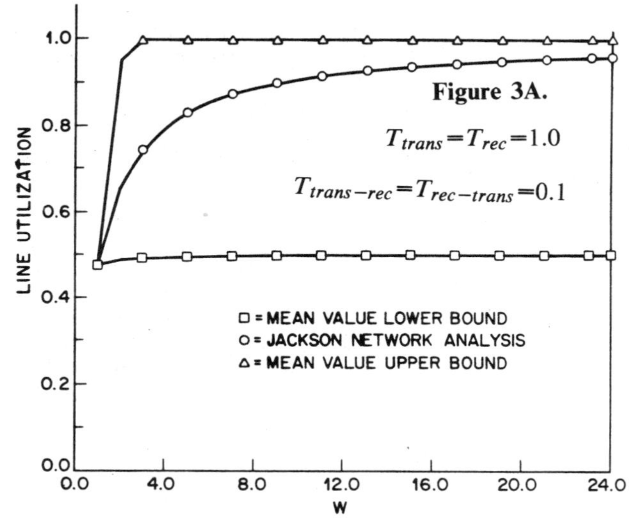

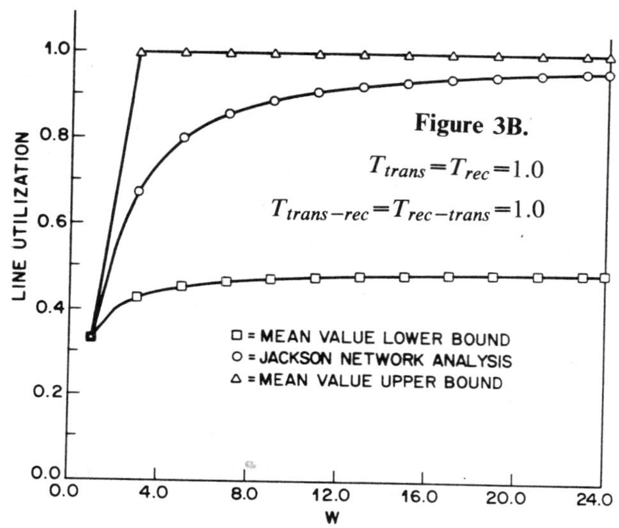

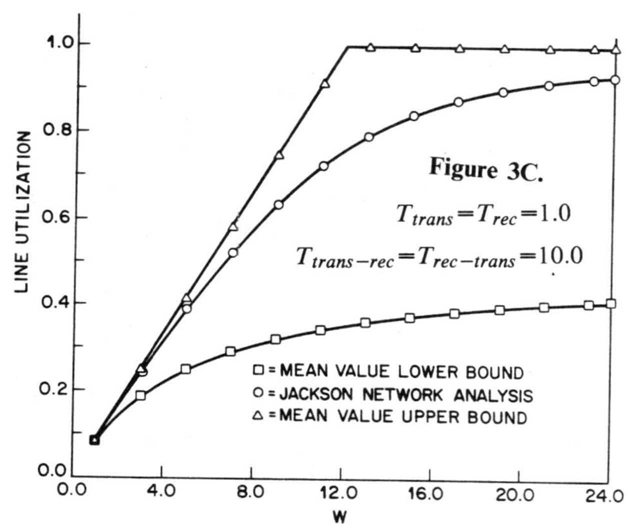

Two regimes are evident, one where the buffers are the bottleneck and the mean throughput rate grows linearly in the number of buffers, and one where the receiver is the bottleneck and the mean throughput rate is independent of the number of buffers; we saw exactly these same regimes in bounding mean throughput rate. As is evident from the figures, the Jackson network analysis tracks quite closely the mean value upper bound on throughput rate.. Since the Jackson network analysis assumes the packet processing times are *exponentially* distributed, i.e., with significantly greater fluctuation in processing times than might occur in practice, and since the agreement (at this level of analysis) between the mean value upper bound and the Jackson network is quite close, this suggests using the mean value upper bound as a guide to setting flow control parameters, because it is quite straightforward to analyze.

4. Simulation Results

We complement the above theoretical analysis with simulation results for packet delay. Eleven thousand packets were generated and sent through a GPSS simulation (IBM, 1971; Schriber, 1974; Appendix). The first one thousand were used as a warmup, and data was examined to insure that stationarity had set in before starting to gather and record data that is presented below. The statistics gathered for the next ten thousand packets were segmented into ten groups of one thousand each; the observed variability was felt to be within statistical fluctuations, and the uniformity of the statistics across the ten samples suggested that long term time averaged statistics were in fact meaningful. The packet interarrival times were exponential random variables; the transmitter, receiver, and channel propagation times were constant. The results below are a sample of some of the data gathered. We assume the channel propagation delay is zero here, and the transmitter and receiver require one time unit each per packet.

Table 1--First Two Moments of Packet Delay Statistics

Mean Interarrival Time	*Mean Arrival Rate*	*W=1,B=1* *Mean Delay*	*W=1,B=1* *Standard Deviation*	*W=2,B=1* *Mean Delay*	*W=2,B=1* *Standard Deviation*
6.67	0.15	3.366	4.085	2.088	0.257
4.00	0.25	3.378	3.453	2.169	0.375
2.80	0.36	4.248	3.194	2.292	0.546
2.20	0.45	4.983	3.316	2.442	0.741
1.70	0.59	--	--	2.745	1.080
1.30	0.77	--	--	3.748	2.052
1.10	0.91	--	--	7.141	4.562

Table 2--Percentiles of Packet Delay Statistics

Mean Interarrival Time	*Mean Arrival Rate*	*W=1,B=1* *90th Percentile*	*W=1,B=1* *95th Percentile*	*W=2,B=1* *90th Percentile*	*W=2,B=1* *95th Percentile*
6.67	0.15	6.395	10.610	2.393	2.722
4.00	0.25	8.145	10.635	2.710	2.930
2.80	0.36	8.670	10.675	2.915	3.400
2.20	0.45	9.615	11.295	3.365	3.955
1.70	0.59	--	--	4.025	4.820
1.30	0.77	--	--	6.585	7.965
1.10	0.91	--	--	11.300	13.557

As is clear from the above tables, to within statistical fluctuations the delay characteristics for $W=2,B=1$ and $W=1,B=1$ appear to differ greatly. Furthermore, the delay statistics for $W=2,B=1$ and $W=7,B=1$ (which are not presented here in the interest of brevity) appear to be virtually identical, to within fluctuations. The main difference in the delay characteristics for the double buffering and infinite buffering case was the startup transient in each: as congestion rises, both systems will always be started up, and the impact of this transient is apparently negligible for the numbers investigated above.

5. Summary

Granted the modeling assumptions described earlier for a single virtual circuit connecting one device to another over a local area network, it appears that double buffering (W=2) window flow control offers performance superior to single buffering (W=1) and performance comparable to larger (W>2) buffer sizes. This was suggested from mean value bounds on mean throughput rate, and substantiated from a Jackson network analysis and a simulation analysis.

Appendix--GPSS Simulation

We have been asked to include a more detailed description of the simulation referred to in the body of the text. Figure A is a source code listing of the GPSS simulation program. The transmitter and receiver each require a mean amount of processing per packet. The sequence of transmitter and receiver packet processing times are constant. The channel propagation time has a given mean value; the sequence of channel propagation times are constant. The packet interarrival times are independent exponentially distributed random variables with a given mean interarrival time The remaining parameters are the window size and the batch size.

The table below summarizes the parameters, the source code statement that defines each parameter, and the value of each parameter in Figure A.

GPSS Simulation Parameter Summary

Parameter	*Statement*	*Value*
$E(T_{trans})$=E(TRANS)	10	100
$E(T_{rec})$=E(REC)	20	100
$E(T_{trans-rec})=E(T_{rec-trans})$= E(TRANS-REC)=E(REC-TRANS)	16	0
W=WINDOW	3	7
B=ACKNOWLEDGEMENT BATCH SIZE	5	1
MEAN INTERARRIVAL TIME	1	280

References

[1] J.Atkins, *Path Control: The Transport Network of SNA,* IEEE Transactions on Communications, **28** (4) 527-538 (1980).

[2] W.Bux, K.Kuemmerle, H.Linh Truong, *Balanced HDLC Procedures: A Performance Analysis,* IEEE Trans. Communications, **28** (11), 1889-1898 (1980).

[3] G.L.Chesson, *DATAKIT Software Architecture,* 20.2.1-20.2.5, Proceedings International Communications Conference, Boston, Massachusetts, 1979.

[4] G.L.Chesson, A.G.Fraser, *DATAKIT Network Architecture,* COMPCON'80, 25-28 February 1980, San Francisco, California, IEEE Catalog Number 1491-0/80, pp.59-61

[5] R.W.Conway, W.L.Maxwell, L.W.Miller, **Theory of Scheduling,** Addison-Wesley, Reading, Massachusetts, 1967; Little's formula, pp.18-19.

[6] M.C.Easton, *Batch Throughput Efficiency of ADCCP/HDLC/SDLC Selective Reject Protocols,* IEEE Trans.Communications, **28** (2), 187-195 (1980).

[7] G.Fayolle, E.Gelenbe, G.Pujolle, *An Analytic Evaluation of the Performance of the "Send and Wait" Protocol,* IEEE Trans.Communications, **26** (3), 313-319(1978).

[8] A.G.Fraser, *DATAKIT--A Modular Network for Synchronous and Asynchronous Traffic,* 20.1.1-20.1.3, Proceedings International Communications Conference, Boston, Mass., 1979.

[9] P.E.Green, *An Introduction to Network Architecture,* IBM Systems Journal, **18** (2), 202-222 (1979).

[10] IBM, *General Information--Binary Synchronous Communications,* **IBM Systems Reference Library,** GA27-3004-2.

[11] IBM, *MSP/7 Binary Synchronous Communications: Program Logic Manual,* GY34-0012-1.

[12] IBM, *IBM General Purpose Simulation System Users Manual,* **IBM Systems Reference Library,** White Plains, NY, 1971, GH20-0326-04.

[13] F.P.Kelly, *Networks of Queues,* Advances in Applied Probability, **8,** 416-432 (1976).

[14] F.P.Kelly, **Reversibility and Stochastic Networks,** Wiley, Chichester, 1979.

[15] L.Kleinrock, *Principles and Lessons in Packet Communications,* Proceedings IEEE, **66** (11), 1320-1329(1978;A).

[16] L.Kleinrock, *On Flow Control,* Proc.Int.Conf.Communications, Toronto, Canada, 27.2-1--27.2-5, June 1978;B.

[17] D.E.Knuth, *Verification of Link-Level Protocols,* BIT, **21,** 31-36 (1981).

[18] J.D.C.Little, *Proof of the Queueing Formula* $L=\lambda W$, Operations Research, **9** (3), 383-386(1961).

[19] G.W.R.Luderer, H.Che, W.T.Marshall, *A Virtual Circuit Switch as the Basis for Distributed Systems,* Journal of Telecommunication Networks, **1,** 147-160 (1982).

[20] G.W.R.Luderer H.Che, J.P.Haggerty, P.A.Kirslis, W.T.Marshall, *A Distributed UNIX System Based on a Virtual Circuit Switch,* ACM Operating Systems Review, **15** (5), 160-168 (8th Symposium on Operating Systems Principles, Asilomar, 14-16 December 1981), ACM 534810.

[21] M.Reiser, *A Queueing Network Analysis of Computer Networks with Window Flow Control,* IEEE Trans.Communications, **27** (8), 1199-1209(1979).

[22] T.J.Schriber, **Simulation Using GPSS,** Wiley, NY, 1974.

[23] M.Schwartz, *Performance Analysis of the SNA Virtual Route Pacing Control,* IEEE Transactions on Communications, **30** (1), 172-184 (1982)

[24] C.A.Sunshine, *Factors in Interprocess Communication Protocol Efficiency for Computer Networks,* AFIP NCC, pp.571-576(1976).

[25] C.A.Sunshine, *Efficiency of Interprocess Communication Protocols for Computer Networks,* IEEE Transactions on Communications, **25,** 287-293(1977).

[26] A.S.Tanenbaum, **Computer Networks,** especially Section 4.2, pp.148-164, Prentice-Hall, Englewood Cliffs, NJ, 1981.

[27] K.C.Traynham, R.F.Steen, *SDLC and BSC on Satellite Links: A Performance Comparison,* Computer Communication Review, 1977

[28] S.Wecker, *DNA: The Digital Network Architecture,* IEEE Transactions on Communications, **28** (4), 510-525 (1980).

[29] L.W.Yu, J.C.Majithia, *An Analysis of One Direction of Window Mechanism,* IEEE Trans.Communications, **27** (5), 778-788(1979).

```
*LCC    OPERATION  A,B,C,D,E,F,G
*
*  FULL DUPLEX LINK LEVEL HIGH/LOW FLOW CONTROL
*  WITH CHANNEL PROPAGATION DELAYS
*
        SIMULATE
 1      FUNCTION    RN3,C24
0          0           .1           .104         .2          .222
.3         .355        .4           .509         .5          .69
.6         .915        .7           1.2          .75         1.38
.8         1.6         .84          1.83         .88         2.12
.9         2.3         .92          2.52         .94         2.81
.95        2.99        .96          3.2          .97         3.5
.98        3.9         .99          4.6          .995        5.3
.998       6.2         .999         7            .9997       8
*
* INTERARRIVAL TIMES IID EXPONENTIAL ARRIVALS
*
 1      GENERATE    280,FN1
*
* QUEUE 1--TRANSMITTER QUEUE
*
 2      QUEUE       1
 3      TEST E      Q3,K7,5
 4      LOGICS      1
 5      TEST E      Q3,K6,7
 6      LOGICR      1
 7      GATE LR     1
 8      SEIZE       1
 9      DEPART      1
 10     ADVANCE     100
 11     RELEASE     1
 12     TABULATE    4
*
* QUEUE 2--FORWARD AND REVERSE CHANNEL
*
 13     QUEUE       2
 14     SEIZE       2
 15     DEPART      2
 16     ADVANCE     0
 17     RELEASE     2
 18     TABULATE    5
*
* QUEUE 3--RECEIVER
*
 19     QUEUE       3
 20     ADVANCE     100
 21     SEIZE       3
 22     DEPART      3
 23     RELEASE     3
 24     TABULATE    6
 4      TABLE       M1,100,10,40
 5      TABLE       M1,100,10,10
 6      TABLE       M1,200,50,40
 25     TERMINATE   1
*
*  GENERATE 10000 EVENTS
*
        START       1000
```

Figure A.GPSS Simulation Source Code

Data Network Application I

Chairman

F. Ferrante

A MESSAGE HANDLING SYSTEM FOR PUBLIC NETWORKS

Toshihiko Nakayama, Yoshihiro Shimazu and Katsuhiko Haruta

Musashino Electrical Communication Laboratory, NTT
3-9-11, Midoricho, Musashino-shi, Tokyo 180, JAPAN

ABSTRACT

As a message handling system installed in the public communication networks, SSC (Store and Processing Service Control Facility) provides convenient communication processing services using storage and conversion technologies. The SSC conversion facilities, including media conversion from teletex codes to facsimile image, increase the communicable terminal range. Mailbox services, using four different kinds of personal Message Boxes in the SSC, bring about much benefit to personal communications. The SSC service requesting procedures facilitate multi-address delivery, timed delivery and automatic conversions. The SSC is a prototype which realizes the Message Handling Systems being studied in CCITT. The system is under developmental research in the NTT Laboratory.

This paper describes the basic SSC development concept, the relationship to the CCITT standard, the SSC service outline and the field trial system configuration.

1. INTRODUCTION

Nippon Telegraph & Telephone Public Corporation (NTT) is promoting construction of the Information Network System (INS), in which telecommunications and computers are integrated[1]. The INS will make cheaper, more convenient and diversified telecommunications services available to customers. In the INS, any given terminal equipment will be able to communicate information freely with different categories of terminals through selecting communication processing functions incorporated into the network.

Domestic public communication networks in Japan are now provided by telephone, telex, facsimile and the DDX (Digital Data Exchange) networks in NTT. Each network is available for such sole use communication as telephone and facsimile.

As the first stage to achieve the INS, the DDX is to be expanded throughout the country to cope with potential demands for non-telephone services. Circuit switched service started in December 1979, and is scheduled for all major cities in Japan by the end of 1987. Packet switched service started in July 1980, and will be extended to cover all municipalities by the end of fiscal 1987.

However, many facsimile terminals are connected to telephone network. Low speed data terminals, which have low communication traffic, may also be accommodated in the telephone network due to cost effectiveness considerations. Therefore, the communication processing center will bring about greater user benefit to integrate services all over the different networks, providing such communication processing services as temporary information storage, transmission speed conversion, recording document size conversion, media conversion, etc.

As one of the communication processing centers, the SSC (Store and Processing Service Control Facility) has been developmentally researched in the NTT Laboratory. By storage and conversion technologies, the SSC provides many convenient telecommunication services, including communications between the different categories of terminals and mailbox services.

This paper describes the basic SSC development concept, the relationship to the CCITT standard, the SSC service outline, and the field trial system configuration in the INS Model System.

2. APPROACHES TO NETWORK SERVICE ENHANCEMENT

The SSC is a center for service facilities enhancement in public networks and is designed to offer a variety of message communications services to data terminals and facsimile terminals accommodated in the DDX, telephone and telex networks[2,3] (Fig.1). The main SSC service features are communication range increase and facilitating personal communications by storage and conversion technologies. Since these communication processing facilities are used commonly by indefinite terminals, services will be provided at sufficiently low cost.

2.1 Communication Range Increase

In the existing communication networks, only communication between the same kind of terminals in the same network is usually possible. Therefore, customers are requiring communications between different category terminals. SSC makes this possible by storage and conversion techniques. That is, the messages are once received by the SSC according to originating terminal attribute and are then delivered in accordance with destination

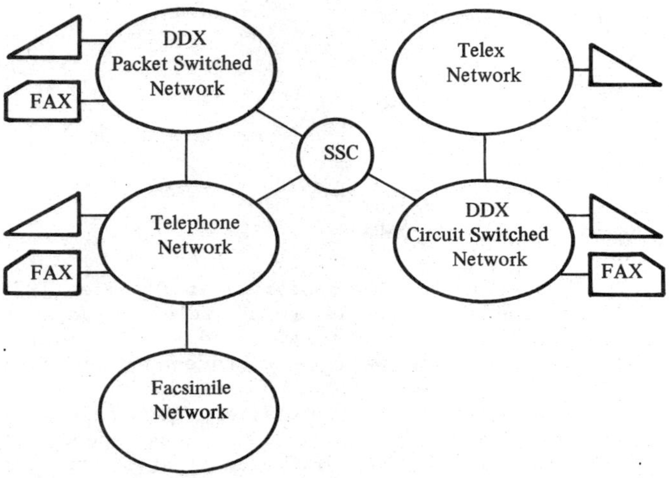

Fig. 1 Inter-Network Communication via SSC

terminal attribute. Provided that the several networks have the same service center in common, inter-networking services between the networks can be made possible.

(1) Network Interface and Subscriber Data Arrangement

Automatic conversion by using the subscriber attribute information registered in the networks, without demanding detailed instructions from a user, is preferable. To fulfill these conditions, common signaling data links, through which the SSC retrieves the subscriber data, including the terminal attribute data registered in each network, are necessary between the SSC and each network.

Each network will have Gateway Switches, with which the communication processing nodes are connected. The communication processing nodes include the voice storage centers[4] and the facsimile storage centers[5] besides the SSCs. The Gateway Switches will have the following commonly used functions for the communication processing nodes;

- Call distribution to various communication processing nodes.
- Subscriber data base management and interconnection compatibility check referring to the data base.
- Communication processing charge accounting and recording.

(2) Media Conversion

The media conversion functions for the SSC are significant from the following two viewpoints.

- Increase in communicable terminal categories.
- Communication cost reduction by making transmission and storage information amount as small as possible.

Table 1 Communication Media Comparison

Content Category	Typical Volume Unit	Information Amount for a Unit (bytes)	Typical Transmission Speed (bits/sec)
Simple message	line	50	300 or less
Document, like teletex	page (CCITT A4)	3,000	2,400
Facsimile image	page (CCITT A4)	35,000	48,000
Voice (carried as data)	minute	240,000	32,000

The communication media are classified into data, image and voice, as shown in Table 1. Among them, the character to text conversion is one of the most effective media conversion functions. While facsimile terminals are widely used in Japan, the Kanji (Chinese ideograph) character terminals or communicating Japanese word processors are expected to become widespread. Since the facsimile text information amount is much larger than the character text information amount, the document edited by the word processor should be transmitted in the character code form, rather than by facsimile image form after printing out. Therefore, when a Kanji character terminal has to send documents to a facsimile terminal, the communication cost can be reduced by character to facsimile media conversion at the nearest point to facsimile terminal after transmitting the character text over a long distance.

More widespread and more economical interconnection among terminals of different categories will be possible by the advancement of other recognition and conversion technologies. Therefore, the SSC has open ended architecture, which enables introducing the modularized conversion element according to the conversion technology advancement.

(3) Method Dealing with Diversified Terminals

Terminal Class

Terminals are classified according to their protocols (Fig.2). Layered and modularized protocol handling structure is necessary to economically support diversified terminal protocols and easily enable to add new terminal classes. In this structure, each terminal attribute is defined as a set of protocol elements collected from each protocol layer one by one. According to this definition, the SSC can communicate with a certain terminal choosing a necessary protocol element for each protocol layer.

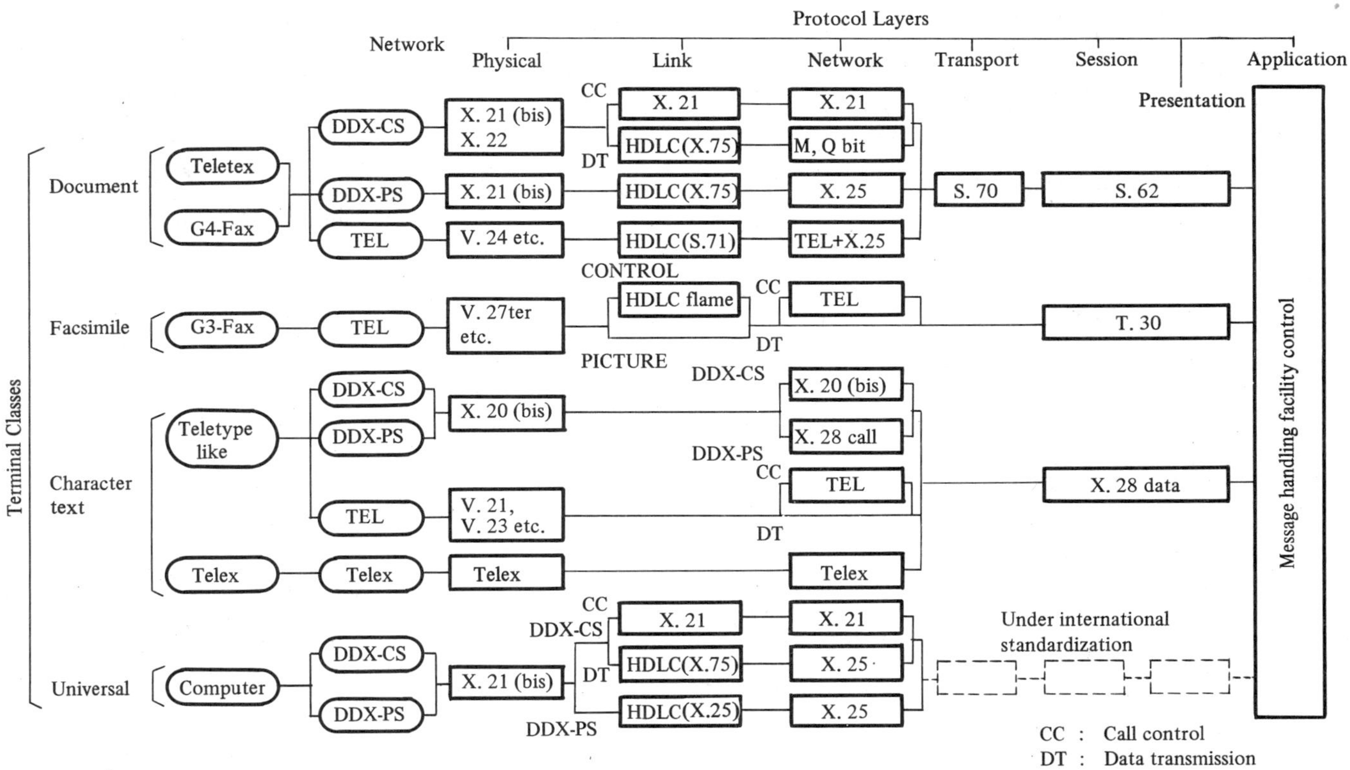

Fig. 2 Terminal Classes and Protocol Structure for SSC

However, since some existing terminals do not completely fit the layered protocol model, their terminal classes should be specially defined according to their protocol similarity in the layered model. In the early development stage, the supported terminals will be restricted to those with standard protocol and message communication oriented characteristics, such as teletex terminals.

Service Control Procedure

For message handling services, it is required to specify the protocols concerning such service control procedures as multi-address, mailbox, media conversion and delivery time, which are not specified between the terminals. These have to be specified as the application level protocols in order to minimize the functional modification to existing terminals and switching systems in the networks. By the application level protocol, the service control information is transmitted together with user messages collectively. Though some operators for data terminals may want to send a service request to the SSC using conversational procedure, the SSC adopted a collective input for control information, considering that a facsimile terminal without a keyboard printer cannot control conversational procedures.

It is difficult to unify the service control procedure among the existing terminals, since the input/output functions concerning man-machine interface differ among those terminals. Therefore, it is effective to compensate man-machine interfaces by the SSC in order to improve the service control procedures corresponding to the terminal characteristics. In fact, the procedures were improved by means of such additional functions as collective address in multi-address designation, on-line service parameter registration like the CCITT X.28 protocol.

In the case of an intelligent terminal, it is effective to edit the service control information on the terminal site by the aid of the terminal local processing functions.

2.2 Mail Box Services Facilitating Personal Communication

Throughout the extended communication range, mailbox services using storage techniques facilitate personal communications.

(1) Highly Reliable Communications

Instead of terminal storage, a user can use highly reliable storage supervised by the network, without the necessity to attach/detach his own storage in such form as flexible magnetic disks to/from the terminal. Even when a terminal is not operative, for such local terminal reasons as being in trouble, power off, storage detached and operator absent, communications using the network storage are possible.

It is dangerous for a user to leave the terminal when his own storage memory is left in it, since the storage can be easily extracted from the terminal and it can be copied without permission. On the contrary, the information stored in the network facilities has higher security.

Another reliable support for personal communications is notification of request handling states or of the results, using network facilities. A user need not positively collect this information by only terminal to terminal communications.

(2) Convenient Personal Communication

Since no proxy will be allowed for confidential personal communications, a person himself must send and receive messages, even though he is untrained in using the terminal. It is necessary, therefore, that terminal operation for the communication be as simple, brief and infrequent as possible. For example, whenever a person wants to send a message to plural people and to send it at a designated time, he has only to operate the terminal once to activate the SSC. On the contrary, in case of message receiving, since receiving time is unknown, it is preferable that the message can remain in the network storage until the designated person operates the terminal to retrieve the message from the network storage, for himself.

In mailbox services, personal storage is independent from a terminal. Even when a user is away from his own terminal, for instance on a business trip, he can read out messages received in his personal storage and he can transfer them to some other terminals, through an appropriate terminal near by.

Mailbox services are also convenient, even when the messages are to be read by indefinite people. In this case, the SSC saves a user from such laborious work as accepting requests and sending required messages through his terminal. That is, a user only has to register the messages to his personal storage, so that the SSC can automatically send them according to the requests.

3 RELATIONSHIP TO CCITT'S MHS STANDARDIZATION

The standards of computer based store and forward message services in association with public data networks are being studied in CCITT SG VII as Message Handling Systems (MHS). Standard recommendations concerning the basic part of MHS services and relevant protocols will be produced in 1984. The SSC will be a prototype for the MHS realization.

3.1 MHS model

The MHS model is composed of Users, User Agents (UAs) and Message Transfer Agents (MTAs), as shown in Fig.3. A User is either a person or a computer application process, and it sends a message or receives one. The UA is the functional component of the MHS model that interacts directly with a user and represents him to other Message Handling Service users. The UA is a set of computer processes that interacts with the Message Transfer System (MTS) on behalf of the user by means of messages. The MTS comprises a number of MTAs. Operating together, the MTAs relay messages and deliver them to the intended recipient UAs. The collective assembly of UAs and MTAs is called the MHS.

3.2 Physical mapping

The SSC has UA functions and MTA functions, as shown in Fig.4. The UA part of the SSC provides the following functions.

- Communication with user terminal via switching networks, and sending/receiving messages together with service control information between user and its personal storage, called Message Boxes (described in 4.1).
- Management of the user's message boxes, which are allocated to each user. Each user may have several message boxes.

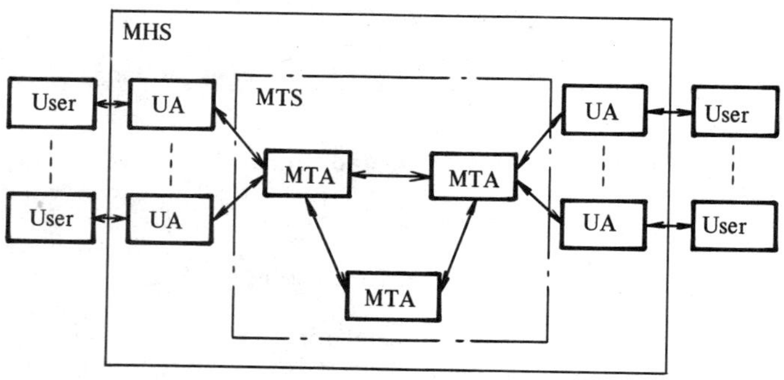

Fig. 3 MHS Model Functional View

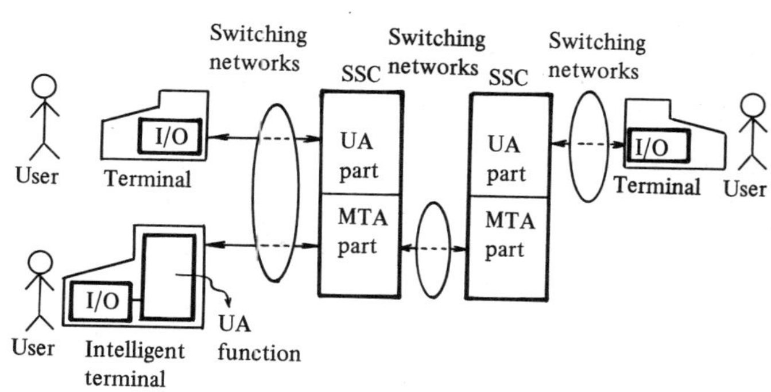

Fig. 4 Physical Mapping

In case the user terminal is an intelligent terminal, UA functions, such as message storage management, may be attached in the user terminal. Such terminal may communicate directly with the MTA part of the SSC. It can also communicate to the SSC UA part, independent from the terminal UA part. The MTA part of the SSC provides the following functions.

- Communication with other SSCs or MHSs MTA part via switched networks and relaying messages on a store and forward basis.
- Message transfer between message boxes which may exist in either the same SSC or different SSCs.
- Media conversion, which is performed under message transfer between message boxes if necessary.

3.3 Necessary protocols

Except application layer protocols, necessary protocols are specified with networks and terminals. As application layer protocols, the following CCITT's MHS protocols are applicable to the SSC, as shown in Fig.5.

P1 protocol : between the MTA parts of the SSCs
P2 protocol : between the UA parts of the SSCs or of terminals
P3 protocol : between the MTA part of the SSC and the user terminal with UA functions
P4 protocol : between the UA part of the SSC and the user terminal without UA functions

4. SSC SERVICES

4.1 Service Scheme

The SSC services are summarized as mailbox based services, as illustrated in Fig.6, in order to produce the above mentioned features. The storage in the SSC is partitioned into Message Boxes (MBs) for each user. Using these message boxes, the SSC communication service outline is shown in Fig.7. In order that a user can use his MBs as his agent, his MBs should be independent from any terminal in the public networks. However in the SSC, each MB is logically connected to a designated terminal, called a home terminal (HT), for the following reasons.

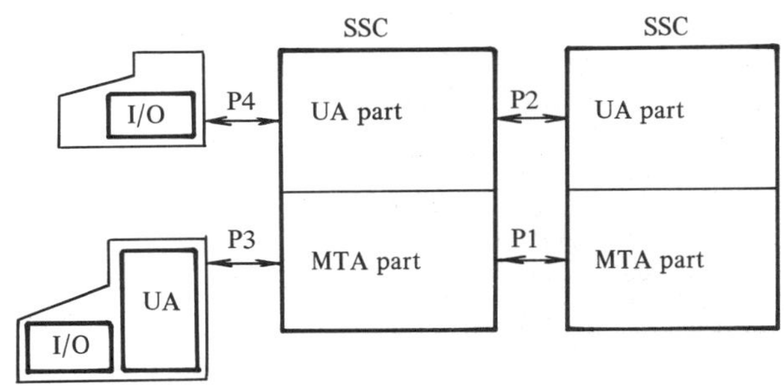

Fig. 5 Application Layer Protocols for SSC

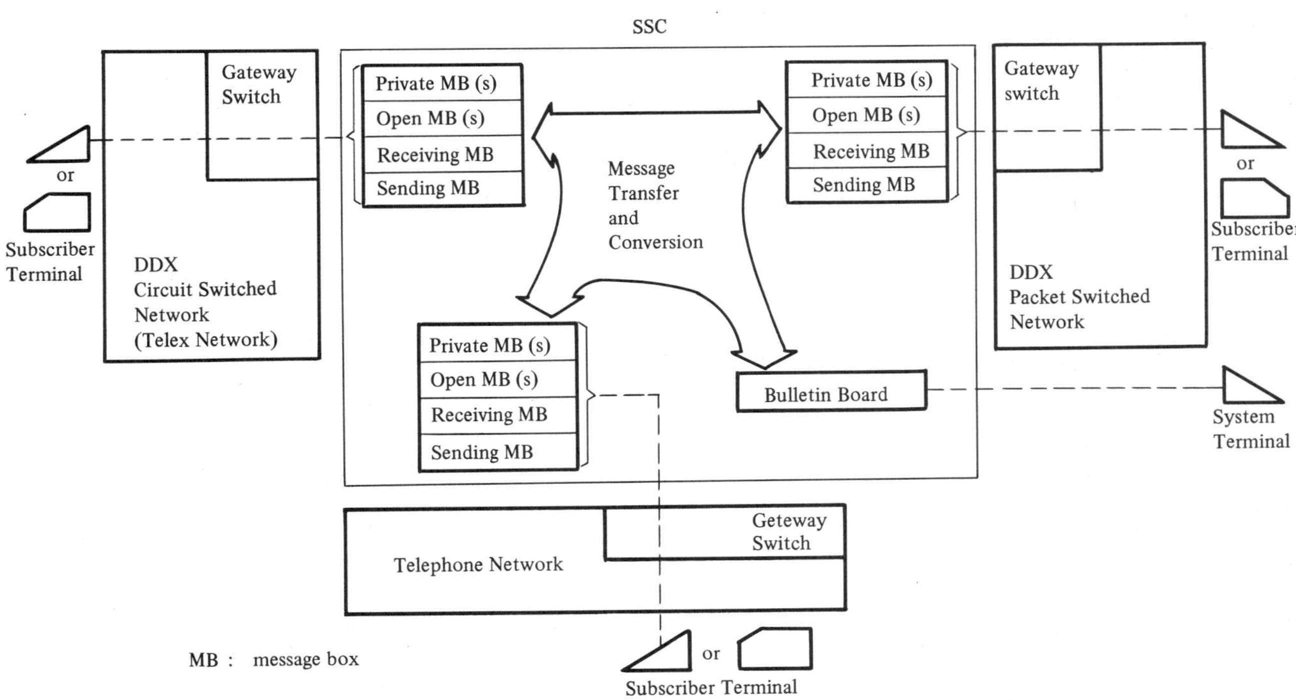

Fig. 6 Message Box Arrangement Concept

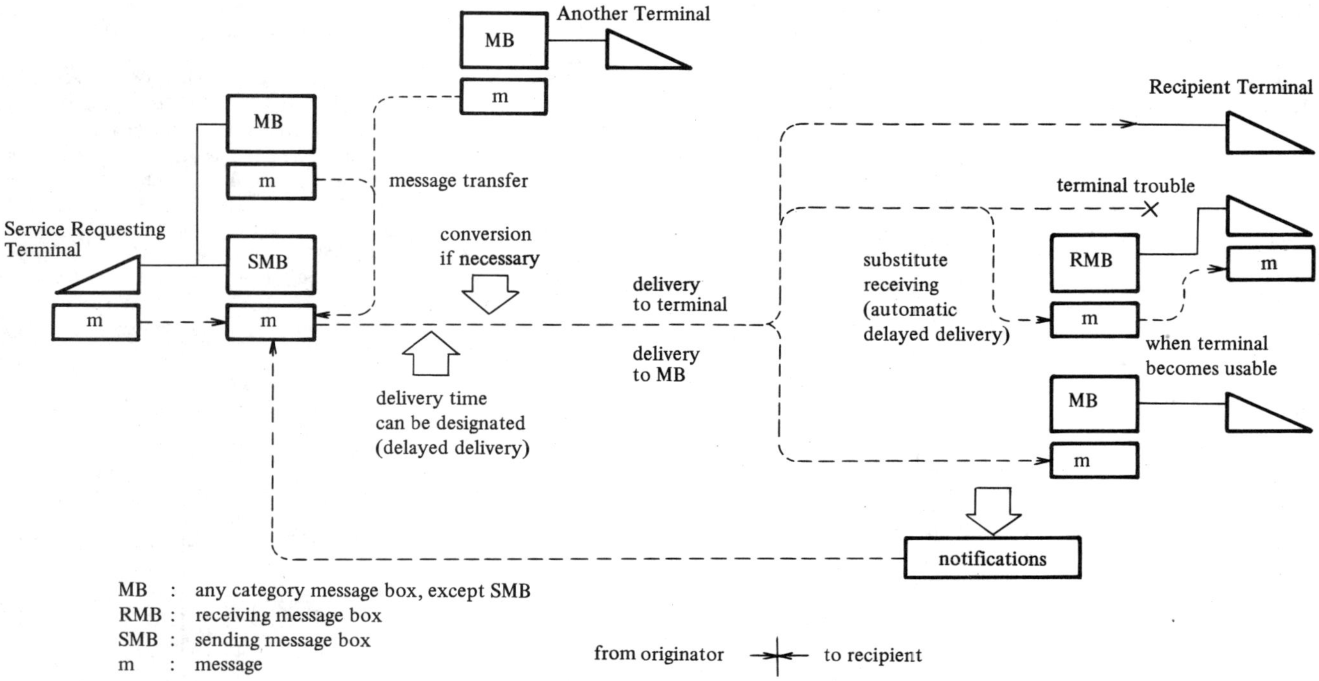

Fig. 7 SSC Service Outline

Table 2 Message Box Characteristics

Message Box Category	Purpose	Supervision by Home Terminal*				
		Create/ Cancel	Name	Accessible Terminal Restriction	Writing Lock by Password	Reading Lock by Password
Private MB	privately communicating	◎	free	◎	◎	◎
Open MB	openly reporting	◎	free	○	◎	○
Bulletin Board	advertisement to large number of people	×	fixed by SSC	×	×	×
Receiving MB	automatic message receiving substituting home terminal	×	fixed at '1'	○	×	○
Sending MB	inquiry for sending request handling status or results	×	fixed at '0'	◎	×	○

* Supervision needs supervising key password for each MB
◎ Possible
○ Possible, but not recommended
× Impossible

There will be some confusion, if individual MB administration, including creation, cancelling and change, is allowed by all terminals. Each MB can be freely named by its owner. Since a network routes a call by a destination address indicated by a subscriber line number or a terminal number, a destination address for a message should include a subscriber line number as well as an MB name.

Message boxes are segregated into the following four categories in accordance with their purposes (Table 2).

Private Message Box (PMB)

A user can store, receive or send private messages, including confidential messages, into or from his PMB(s). In order to protect each PMB from access from indiscriminate people, it can be locked by passwords. The passwords should be managed by the user for himself.

Open Message Box (OMB)

An OMB accommodates information required to be positively read out by others. When open messages are required to be sent, a message requiring person can derive information from the OMB instead of the information owner. The OMB owners should propagate their OMB's names beforehand, since the accessible people are restricted to the range of people who know his terminal number and the OMB name. A more positive report, or advertisement to a wide range of people, can be stored in the common OMB provided by the SSC's virtual terminal. This kind of OMB is called Bulletin Board.

Receiving Message Box (RMB)

An RMB cannot be locked by a password, when information is written in it, since it is open to receive information. The receiver can transfer the received messages in the RMB to his PMB, if necessary.

Another RMB feature is automatic delayed delivery. If the destination terminal is busy or in trouble, messages arriving at it are once received by the RMB on behalf of the terminal. When the terminal becomes usable, the SSC delivers the stored messages to the terminal.

Sending Message Box (SMB)

An SMB is somewhat different from above mentioned message boxes. It is virtually provided to a user, so that a user can handle some auxiliary functions helping communications with the same procedures as those for other message box communications.

For the period after a user sends a request to the SSC, until the SSC starts to deliver the message, the message is effectively stored in the sending terminal SMB. When the delivery is completed, the SSC writes the notifications based on the communication results in the SMB, after erasing the original message. If the user wants to cancel the requirement before its delivery, especially when the delivery time was designated, he has only to erase the message in the SMB according to the ordinary message erasing procedure.

4.2 Service Request Procedure

As mentioned above, the SSC service control information is transmitted in the application protocol level as a service access command. These commands are composed of four different function parts, as follows.

[Function Indicator] / [Destination Address Group] / [Message Address Group] / [Parameter Group] +

Function Indicator

A function Indicator has three functional variations. One is a message box communication request, such as message delivery, message retrieval and delivery status inquiry. Second is a maintenance request, such as message box creation, cancel and profile change. Third is a utility request, such as abbreviated address registration. In the following, an access command for a message box communication request is discussed.

Destination Address Group

The basic form of a destination address is as follows.

[Home Terminal Number] . [Message Box Name] . [Key Password for Writing]

For multi-address delivery, all addresses are connected by the delimiter ",". If a message is wanted to be directly delivered to a terminal, message box name and password are omitted. A key password is needed if the message box writing is locked by a password.

Message Address Group

A message address group is needed when transferring or reading messages in message boxes, instead of inputting them from the terminal. A message address group is generally composed of four parts, as follows.

[Home Terminal Number] . [Message Box Name] . [Key Password for Reading] . [Message Number]

For plural message addresses, message addresses are connected, but separated by ",". A key password is needed if the message box reading is locked by a password. Each message number was assigned by the SSC when the message was stored in the message box. The user is able to know the message number by reading the message box directory.

Parameter Group

Other additional service conditions, such as delivery time, are designated as parameters.

4.3 Service Control Sequence and Delivery Notification

Service control sequence is composed of three phases illustrated in Fig.8. In phase one, when the SSC received an access command, the SSC checks

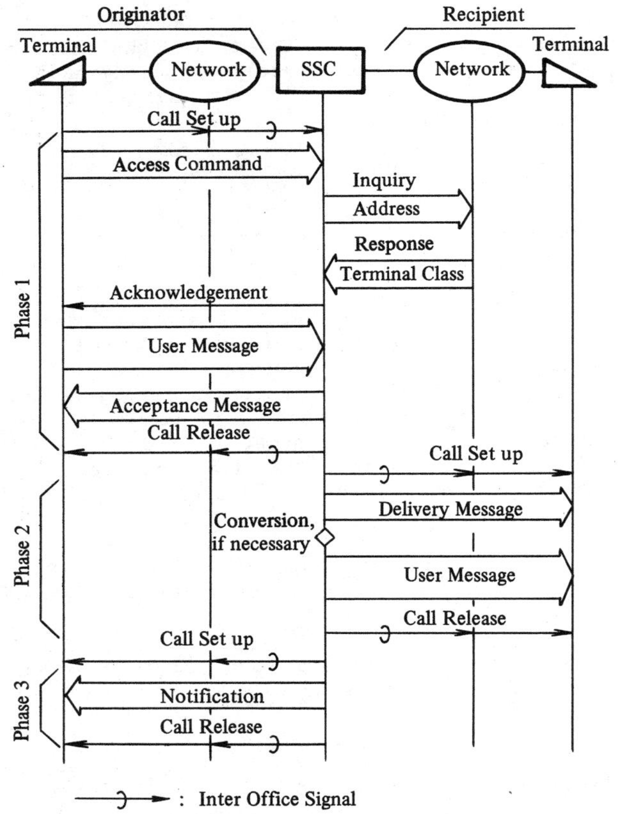

Fig. 8 Service Control Sequence Example

syntax for the access command formula, terminal class identity, message box name existence, password coincidence and necessity for media conversion, etc. If any check is no good, the SSC prompts the requesting person to retry by indicating error occurrence. If all checks are good, the SSC replies with an acceptance message, including an acceptance number. After the message delivery completion in phase two, the delivery notification is reported. Normally, in the SSC, notifications are written in the SMB and remain in it so that the requesting person can read them at a convenient time. However, non-delivery notifications are forced to deliver to the terminal in phase three, as well as being stored in the SMB directory, in order to help the user's quick response.

Notifications are classified as follows.

- Receipt Notification(RN) : This shows the message has been delivered to the destination terminal.
- Delivery Notification (DN) : This shows the message has been delivered to the message box.
- Non-Delivery Notification (NN) : This shows that the delivery attempt has resulted in failure.

4.4 Security Consideration

In order to use a message box as a user agent, the user wants to read and write his message box via any terminals, though he does not want it to be read by any other person except him. To answer these inconsistent requirements, the SSC proposes the following scheme.

Accessible Terminal Restriction

The SSC makes it possible for each message box to restrict accessible terminals, readable and writable, respectively.

Password Application

The SSC provides the following three password categories.

- Writing Password : When a user desires that no message should be stored in his message box by any other person, he can lock it by a writing password.
- Reading Password : The lock by this password is used to prevent any unidentified person from reading messages in the message box.
- Supervision Password : The supervision password is validated when a user changes the message box profile including password registration and change. Furthermore, the message box profile change is restricted to the HT.

Quick Response to Message Stolen

The maintenance of such passwords is put in the user's hand. If the message is stolen because the key password had leaked for some unexpected reason, it is necessary that the user immediately change passwords. For this purpose, the SSC records the information for each message stored in a message box concerning what terminal read the message last. A user can determine this information in the directory for each message box.

5. FIELD TRIAL IN THE INS MODEL SYSTEM

After confirming the fundamental technologies in the laboratory experimental system[3], the SSC field trial system, illustrated in Fig.9, is going to be implemented. As the first development stage, this system is connected to the DDX circuit switched network. It provides message handling services to the data terminals, including teletex terminals and digital facsimile terminals accommodated in the DDX network. Considering cost effectiveness, the SSC facilities are controlled by the central processor in the switching system, where the SSC service control programs, such as message box services, are added.

Interface control equipment interfaces various networks and communicates to various terminals supporting each terminal protocol. Therefore, this equipment is modularized according to the handling protocol. The equipment extracts the object messages from received information and sends them to the magnetic disk storage.

If necessary, conversion facilities are used. One of the most effective conversion facilities in the field trial system is media conversion from teletex codes to facsimile image. Conversion

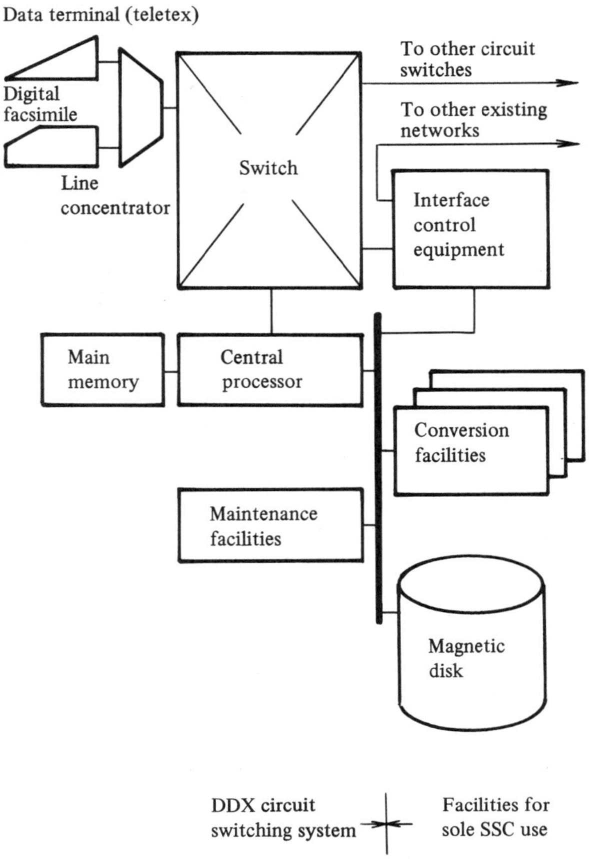

Fig. 9 SSC Field Trial System Configuration

facilities are also modularized according to the conversion categories, such as code conversion and media conversion. When new technologies will make new conversion category economically possible, they will be added as conversion modules.

This field trial system will be shown to the people as one of the new telecommunications service facilities in the INS Model System, which is going to be constructed in the Musashino and Mitaka area in Tokyo. The SSC will start experimental operation in the middle of 1984. Then, the communicable terminal range will be gradually expanded, connecting to the DDX packet switched network, telephone network and telex network, and expanding convertible terminal attributes.

6. CONCLUSION

This paper describes a message handling system SSC, which is installed in the public networks. The SSC provides profitable communication processing services using store and convenient technologies. The prime objectives of the communication processing services include communicable terminal range increase and offering convenient mailbox services, such as multi-address delivery and delayed delivery. These purposes were accomplished in the SSC.

Over all SSC services are summarized in the mailbox services, introducing the Message Boxes as personal storage. In the service requesting procedures, necessary conversions are automatically executed. The owner's supervision for each message box, such as creating it, erasing it and locking it by passwords, will also facilitate personal communications. The SSC matches the Message Handling Systems being studied in CCITT.

In the field trial scheduled in 1984, the SSC will start to provide these services to the teletex terminals and digital facsimile terminals in the DDX circuit switched network. Then, the communicable terminal range will be gradually expanded, connecting to the DDX packet switched network, telephone network and telex network, and expanding convertible terminal attributes.

ACKNOWLEDGEMENT

The authors wish to express their gratitude for guidance and encouragement received from Dr. M.Kato, Dr. K.Tsukada, Mr. M.Itoh and Mr. R.Mohri. They also wish to express their thanks to the SSC experiment group members.

REFERENCES

(1) Y.Kitahara: Information Network System----Infrastructure for an Advanced Information Society------, Japan Telecommunications Review, April 1982, pp96-103

(2) K.Tsukada, Y.Yoshida, K.Yukimatsu and H.Ohnishi: Integrated Services Data Switching Network, Proc. of 6th DCS, pp159-165, 1979

(3) S.Matsushita, K.Haruta, T.Kambayashi and T.Okada: Message Handling Facilities for Public Use in DDX, Proc. of 5th ICCC, pp127-132, 1980

(4) T.Morisawa, H.Miyabe and M.Ohyama: Voice Storage Communication Facility for the Information Network System, GLOBECOM'82, C3.2, 1982

(5) T.Kamae: Development of a Public Facsimile Communication System Using Storage and Conversion Techniques, NTC'80, 19.4, 1980

NOVANET
COMMUNICATIONS NETWORK FOR A CONTROL SYSTEM*

by J. R. Hill, J. R. Severyn and P. J. VanArsdall

Lawrence Livermore National Laboratory
University of California
P. O. Box 5508, L-492
Livermore, California 94550

ABSTRACT

Novanet is a control system oriented fiber optic local area network that was designed to meet the unique and often conflicting requirements of the Nova laser control system which will begin operation in 1984. The computers and data acquisition devices that form the distributed control system for a large laser fusion research facility need reliable, high speed communications. Both control/status messages and experimental data must be handled. A subset of NOVANET is currently operating on the two beam Novette laser system.

INTRODUCTION

This paper first looks briefly at the laser and its control system in order to see how this generates the design constraints for the network. Next, we present a system overview of NOVANET, followed by detailed descriptions of the hardware and software. The experience gained from operating NOVANET on the Novette laser system and some performance data concludes our discussion.

Nova Laser System

For the past several years, scientists at Lawrence Livermore National Laboratory have built and operated a series of neodimium-glass laser systems that are used to study Inertial Confinement Fusion (ICF). The largest of these, the Nova laser system, is scheduled to begin operation in 1984 (Figure 1). Nova's ten 74 centimeter diameter beams will concentrate 100-150 terawatts for 100 picoseconds - 3 nanoseconds on to a target and the resulting fusion reaction will be studied. The fundamental 1.06 micron light from the lasers will be doubled and tripled by inserting potassium dihydrogen phospate (KDP) crystals between the final laser amplifiers and the target. Each arm of Nova consists of an optical path of approximately 250 meters containing amplifiers, rotators, and spatial filters. This path is aligned by 1000 stepper motors which move mirrors and other beam line components. The laser amplifiers are driven by 4000 flashlamps which are fired by a total of 9 megaamps at 25 kilovolts.

Figure 1. Nova Laser Fusion Experimental Facility

Nova Control System

Operation of the Nova laser is made possible by a distributed control system. It consists of three Digital Equipment Corporation (DEC) VAX-11/780 control computers, fifty DEC LSI-11 microcomputers, and various data collection instruments including solid state Charge Coupled Device (CCD) cameras and transient digitizers (Figure 2). Operators communicate with the control system through consoles which contain three color graphic video monitors; the center monitor is overlaid with a transparent touch sensitive panel. Buttons are drawn on the color monitor, and the operator touches the area over

---

* Work performed under the auspices of the U.S. Department of Energy by the Lawrence Livermore National Laboratory under Contract No. W-7405-eng-48.

the button to effect the operations. The two side monitors are used to display status information (Figure 3). The control system also collects and stores for later analysis the 5 megabytes of laser and target performance data that is generated by an experiment.

A high speed array-processor is attached to one of the VAX computers to speed up image processing for alignment. An interactive system such as this needs an operator response time of less that one second and the distributed architecture allows us to meet this goal.

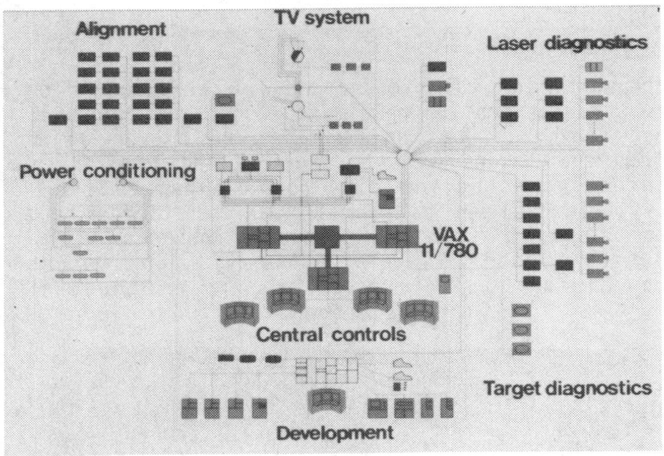

Figure 2. Nova Distributed Control System

Figure 3. Nova Control Console

In addition to the three control VAX computers, there is a separate VAX for development and testing.

NOVANET

Novanet Requirements

The design of NOVANET is closely intertwined with the design of the Nova control system, but in general, the control system architecture specifies the design requirements for the network. NOVANET must handle a wide variety of message types: Control messages (100 bytes) and data messages (100K bytes) can be sent at arbitrary times. The control messages often occur as a result of operator interaction, so they require rapid response.

In contrast, the much larger data messages can tolerate somewhat longer transmission delays. A further difference here is that control and status messages usually involve processor-to-processor communications (typically VAX to LSI-11) while data transfers often occur directly from the data acquisition device. To effect this, the protocol must be suitable for connecting processors and instruments directly to the network.

The pulse power system that energizes the laser flash lamps generates large amounts of Electro Magnetic Interference (EMI), and the control room must be isolated from the 25 kilovolt pulses present in the laser bay for safety.

System reliability must be very high since laser operation is expensive and with 200 nodes separated by as much as 1 kilometer, network diagnostics and repairs could consume a large part of the time allocated to operating the laser.

Novanet Overview

NOVANET is the local area network that we designed to solve the unique data communications problems associated with the control system described above (Figure 4).

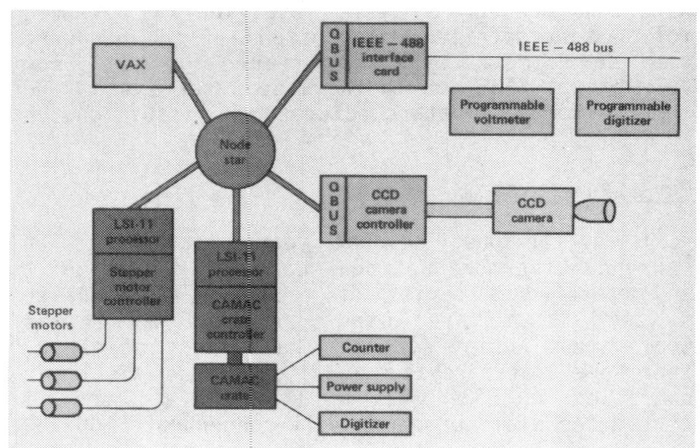

Figure 4. NOVANET Network Schematic

We now present an overview of the NOVANET network, followed by more detailed hardware and software descriptions. NOVANET utilizes the simple addressing structure of a bus topology. However, limitations on the number of optical taps on a fiber bus before the power reduction inhibits reliable communications forces the physical topology to be a star. Each node is connected point to point with the central "node star" which simply retransmits each message to all nodes. Thus NOVANET's topology is logically a bus, but physically a star. Having been forced into the star topology, we made use of it in several ways. The central node star allows us to split the network in multiple independent subnetworks which improves performance. In addition, the node star provides a central summary of network operations.

NOVANET nodes exist in three flavors: the Master Slave Controller (MSC) is the network interface for processors (VAX and LSI-11), the Q-Bus Device Interface (QBDI), and the Multiple Device Interface (MDI) are used to connect instruments directly to NOVANET. Each of these will be described in detail later. The NOVANET hardware transfers data using Direct Memory Access (DMA) techniques to minimize processor loading and maximize data transfer rates. The DMA transfer facilitates down-line loading of programs to the remote LSI-11s.

The NOVANET protocol was chosen to support both instrument and processor nodes. The link level protocol is 10 megabits per second asynchronous 50 bit packets with the hardware supplying handshaking and error detection (Figure 5).

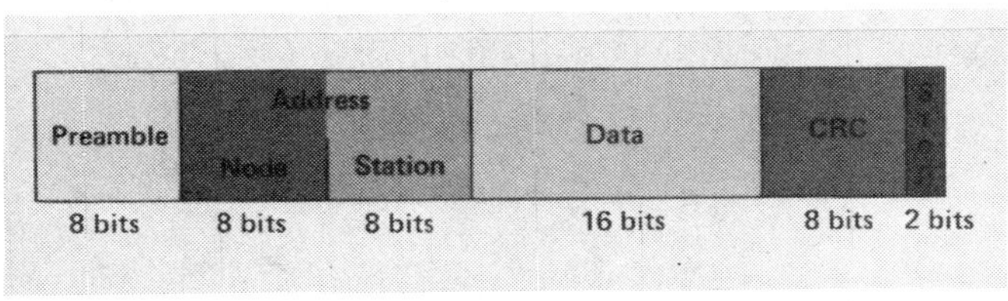

Figure 5. NOVANET Link-Level Protocol Packet

The network level utilizes rotating mastership for collision avoidance and two communications modes (active and passive).

For the active mode, the hardware requests network mastership and initiates the data transfer immediately after becoming master. The passive mode arms the hardware but does not initiate the transfer. In NOVANET, we use the active mode for writes and the passive mode for reads. When the network is idle, the current network master is continually polling to see whether some other node wishes to become network master. This is equivalent to a token passing scheme for collision avoidance. In the event of multiple masters on a segment, we use a backoff and wait for a random amount of time to regenerate a single master (token). This multiple master problem is not as rare as one might expect; it happens whenever subnetworks are recombined into a single network.

Novanet Hardware

NOVANET hardware is built around the Hewlett Packard fiber optic transmitters and receivers which are run at a line speed of 10 megabits per second. The hardware operates in half duplex mode which allows a single forty bit serializer/deserializer to format the packets for transmission and to decode them during reception. An eight bit Cyclic Redundancy Check (CRC) is included as part of each packet; CRC generation and checking is performed by the hardware. In order to operate instruments that are connected directly to the network, the hardware provides a handshake for each fifty bit packet. The polling and the rotation of mastership is also managed by the hardware, making this transparent to the network users. Polling is restarted immediately after the completion of a data transfer by the current master. The logic for these functions and for the Direct Memory Access (DMA) data transfers is performed by three state machines. A protocol state machine that is built from 2910 bit slice electronics with micro code in bipolar fusible link Read Only Memory (ROM) controls the other two. The basic clock frequency for the 2910 is 5 megahertz. The second state machine is built from a counter and more ROM. This one controls the serializer/deserializer that assembles the fifty bit packets. A third state machines manages the Q-Bus interface, generates interrupts, and detects and returns status through the device registers. The ROMs also contain micro-diagnostics for maintainability. It is possible for multiple masters to exist on a network as mentioned above. The hardware can detect this condition since the message collisions cause CRC errors in almost every packet. When this happens, all masters stop transmitting and begin listening. Each node that is capable of becoming a network master will wait a random time before listening for a poll. If there is no activity on the network, the node will begin polling. This scheme ensures that a single network master will be regenerated whenever multiple masters appear or if the current master should disappear.

We shall now describe the three flavors of network interface hardware. First let us consider the Master Slave Controller (MSC).

This is used to connect processors such as VAXs and LSI-11s to NOVANET. It is the only type of card that can become a network master and thus initiate an active transfer. The NOVANET interface can listen to the network, receive a message and continue polling even when its host processor is halted, since the lower levels of protocol are all implemented in the network hardware whose operation is largely independent of its host. The MSC is built on two quad-sized DEC Q-Bus boards and has eight control and status registers. All Q-Bus DMA and interrupt control logic is resident on the MSC. The master slave controller is compatable with the eighteen bit extended addressing mode, and the multi-level interrupt structure of the LSI-11/23. It may be connected to the VAX Unibus by using a commercial Unibus to Q-Bus converter.

The Multiple Device Interface (MDI) is used primarily to connect Charge Coupled Device (CCD) cameras directly to NOVANET. It consists of three cards that fit into an Augat card cage together with the CCD camera's memory and controller. The MDI electrically regenerates a Q-Bus and acts as the Q-Bus master. It allows a processor node (usually a VAX) to directly access the control and status registers of a remote CCD camera via NOVANET.

The MDI cannot become a network master; hence, a camera cannot initiate a data or control transfer. It also includes a sixteen bit parallel data port that is functionally equivalent to a DEC DRV-11 interface.

The Q-Bus Device Interface (QBDI) is electrically identical to the MDI, but it is built on one quad-size DEC Q-Bus board. Thus, the QBDI acts as a bus master in the quad-wide backplane where it regenerates the Q-Bus signals from NOVANET commands. If a Q-Bus device is plugged into the backplane, remote processors have access to it, almost as if it were in their address space. This versatility allows many standard Q-Bus devices to be connected directly to NOVANET for use by a remote processor. A very useful function of the QBDI is to use commercially available Q-Bus interface boards as gateways to other networks. We have been very successful in using a Tektronix IEEE-488 Q-Bus interface card to connect Tektronix 7912AD transient digitizers to NOVANET. This allows the digitizers to be located near the experiment while the operator can control them and display images on the consoles.

The node star is the central point of the NOVANET network (Figure 4). It is not a network node; it is simply a repeater that broadcasts each message to all nodes on the network. All nodes are physically connected point-to-point to the node star by the fiber optics. Since the node star is central to the network, it provides NOVANET with some additional capabilities.

The most important of these is the ability to split NOVANET into multiple independent subnetworks. This allows the control and status messages to maintain their short response times while the large volume data transfers that monopolize the network for several seconds take place. Furthermore, distinct subsystems can have separate subnetworks which improves performance and enhances minimal subsystem interdependancies. The node star is constructed of 4 x 16 crossbar switches which facilitate this segmentation into subnets.

The point-to-point connections to the node star make it easy to monitor network activity and optical power for each node and thus facilitate the location of faulty nodes. In addition, the node star has the ability to electrically isolate a malfunctioning node to permit operation of the remainder of the network. These node star control and status functions are available both on a front panel for manual operation and as registers in the address space of a dedicated micro-computer for computer control. In any star network, the central node is a location for single point failure, but our node star is designed to be as simple as possible for high reliability. In addition, it is constructed of many identical printed circuit boards for board replacement maintainance.

The final component of NOVANET is a network analyzer. Some type of device that can monitor network traffic at the bit level is very valuable during the hardware debugging, verification, and initial installation phases of operation. Since we are not using an industry standard protocol, we built our own link analyzer for NOVANET. It consists of a custom designed network interface, coupled with a commercially available Biomation data analyzer and a Tektronix display monitor. This approach is more cost effective and faster than designing and building the entire instrument ourselves. We found the NOVANET analyzer most useful during the initial stages of network installation.

Novanet Software

NOVANET software consists of device drivers and auxiliary control routines and programs (Figure 6). As is the case with most network

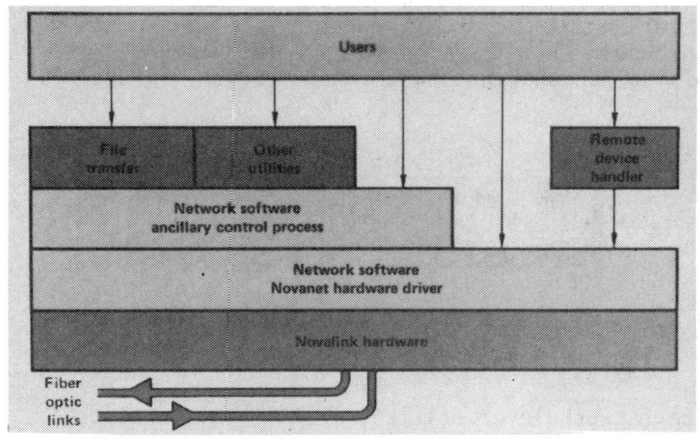

Figure 6. NOVANET Layered Software

software, NOVANET software protects the users and the hardware from each other. It synchronizes user requests with the operating system and with the network interface and programs the hardware for the DMA transfers. Diagnostics and the gathering of operational statistics are further software tasks. Software also allows the users to communicate with the network at a sufficiently high level that the irrelevant details of network operation are not troublesome. In the case of NOVANET, the network hardware is half duplex, but network software allows the user to view it as being full duplex. This is implemented in the drivers by using separate queues for active and passive functions and giving the active queue higher priority. An active transfer request will displace a passive transfer request that is pending, replacing it when the active transfer is completed. The software is designed and implemented in a variety of languages, but it is all modular by functionality for maintainability. It also allows users access to different levels of the network software. NOVANET hardware provides error detection with CRCs and timeouts; the software uses these hardware features to provide error correction by retransmission.

There are device drivers for the VAX-11/780 running VMS and for LSI-11/23 running in stand-alone mode. There is also an LSI-11 driver that runs under RSX, but it is not used now and so will not be discussed. Above the drivers, there are high level language interface routines, a variety of specialized interface modules, and a gateway handler to the IEEE-488 bus.

The VAX/VMS driver is written according to the template for device drivers included in the VMS documentation. It interfaces with the users through the VMS SYS$QIO system service which provides parameter checking, a status return mechanism, and other input/output (I/O) functions that are common to all device drivers. The VMS driver contains software hooks to allow it to operate with an optional Ancillary Control Process (ACP) that provides additional network functionality.

The LSI-11 stand-alone driver is functionally equivalent to the VAX/VMS driver and is structurally similar to it for maintainability. It makes use of the extended eighteen bit address space and the multilevel interrupt structure in the LSI-11/23.

In both the VAX/VMS and the LSI-11 there are software modules that sit above the device drivers and provide additional features and utilities for users. In the LSI-11, these are primarily interfaces to Fortran, Praxis (a Pascal/Ada like language developed at LLNL), and LSI-11 Macro. The VAX/VMS high level software consists of the language interfaces as in LSI-11 version, some driver arbitration software, a gateway handler to the IEEE-488 bus and a utility to down-line load programs into an LSI-11. The driver arbitration software uses semaphores to allow several processes to time share a network node while guaranteeing exclusive access when necessary. The IEEE-488 gateway handler controls a Tektronix IEEE-488 Q-Bus interface board to allow a user program to access IEEE-488 instruments from the VAX. The handler performs the raising and lowering of the IEEE-488 control lines and, in general, implements the lower levels of IEEE-488 protocol. The handler allows the user to send ASCII string messages to specific devices without regard to the details of the IEEE-488 protocol. The LSI-11 downline loader program allows LSI-11 programs to be developed on the VAX and the executable image can then be loaded into LSI-11 for operation. If an LSI-11 crashes during an experiment, it can be rebooted from an operator console.

Novanet Experience on the Novette Laser System

Although the Nova laser is scheduled to begin operation in 1984, the Novette laser facility consisting of two Nova beams has been operating since June of 1982. The Novette control system is a subset of the Nova control system and consists of one VAX-11/780, twenty LSI-11/23s, four transient digitizers, five CCD streak cameras and two consoles.

The NOVANET that links Novette together mirrors this configuration and consists of four VAX-11/780 nodes, twenty LSI-11/23 nodes, five MDI nodes for the CCD cameras, and two QBDI nodes for the transient digitizers. A two board node star completes the network hardware. The maximum length of optical fibers in Novette is 100 meters.

We have experienced a few NOVANET problems while operating Novette. The most serious of these is diagnosing network faults. The network users are interested only in a success/failure status for network transactions; hence, they discard the rest of the information that is returned. This makes the diagnostic task much more difficult and almost always requires a team effort to locate even the simplest of errors. Many times, the solution is as simple as applying power to a machine that has been unplugged. We have had a few node interfaces fail, but once the defective node is located, repairing it (off-line) is facilitated by the micro-diagnostics included in it. Another, more subtle problem is that of network performance. When used properly, the network performs very well. However, a user can easily write programs that slow network transfers to the point of unacceptability. Placing each subsystem on its own independent subnet helps locate the culprits and allows the rest of the network to maintain high performance. More instruction to the network users will help to eliminate this problem.

Novanet Performance

NOVANET performance is sufficient for the Nova and Novette control systems as viewed from the operator consoles. While this type of measurement is always the bottom line in any type of system performance, a more detailed study of the interaction of various parts of the system is in order. The line speed of NOVANET is ten megabits per second. The overhead of the fifty bit packets, the handshake for each packet, and the line turn around time yields a data rate of 640 kilobits per second. We measured the VAX/VMS overhead for a transfer and found it to be about 0.5 milliseconds and the time for a one word DMA transfer to be 1.2 milliseconds. We also measured the end-to-end transfer rate for a 64 kilobyte transfer from a CCD camera to a VAX and found it to be about 1.0 seconds and from a CCD camera to an LSI-11 about 0.7 seconds. These figures are consistent with the 640 kilobits per second data rate stated above. The difference between the VAX and LSI-11 is that the VAX's Unibus is being shared with a lot of devices such as disks, other network cards, and terminals which slow down the DMA transfers. In monitoring control system performance on Novette, we find that the network transfer time is a small part of the total control system time. Typical control and status messages are 100 bytes long and thus their end-to-end time is under ten milliseconds. The QBDI network interfaces contain error counters that may be read by a processor node. For a network of ten nodes, the measured error rate is approximately 10^{-2}

errors per second. Combining this with our transfer rate, we see an error rate of $2.5 \times 10^{-9} - 10^{-8}$ errors per bit. This is somewhat misleading, however, as our traffic tends to be bursty and much of the time the network is polling where errors are much less problematic than those that occur during a data transfer.

Our Novette experience has led us to consider some minor changes in NOVANET for the Nova control system. We will write a more complete network diagnostics package. Error reporting will be incorporated into the network software instead of leaving this to the users since our experience indicates that they will not report sufficient information for easy diagnosis and correction. This becomes more important for the larger Nova system (approximately 200 nodes compared to Novette's 31). Network status displays will be integrated with the diagnostics package and will provide on line performance and error statistics as well as the current network configuration. The Nova control system has three VAX-11/780 computers which allows us to split the Unibus load into three parts. This increase in Unibus bandwidth and processor power will improve NOVANET's performance which in turn will enhance the perfomance of the entire control system. There is also the possibility of reconfiguring the node star from the VAXs to allow dynamic segmentation of the network. We are currently reevaluating the need for a network Ancillary Control Process (ACP) to provide multiplexing, blocking and more services to the users. Multiplexing on Novette is accomplished by multiple network nodes, but the larger Nova control system makes this solution less desirable.

SUMMARY

In summary, the NOVANET fiber optic local area network was designed to meet the diverse need of the control system for the Nova laser fusion experiment. Our experience on the smaller Novette laser system indicates that NOVANET will meet the communications requirements for Nova.

GLOSSARY

Bus	A network topology in which all nodes share a common data pathway.
CRC	Cyclic Redundancy Check. A method for detecting communications errors that is performed by the NOVANET hardware.
Device	An instrument or memory which has no local intelligence (no processor) which can be controlled by a processor via NOVANET.
LSI-11	A micro computer manufactured by Digital Equipment Corporation used to control stepper motors in the Nova laser system.
Node	An addressable location on NOVANET through which an instrument or a computer may communicate with others.
Nodestar	The central hub for the NOVANET network.
Segment/ Subnetwork	The Nodestar can be split NOVANET into multiple independent subnetworks. These subnetworks are called segments.
Shot time	The time when the laser is fired and the Inertial Confinement Fusion experiment takes place.
Star	A network topology in which all nodes are connected to a central hub.
VAX-11/780	A minicomputer manufactured by Digital Equipment Corporation used as the main control computers for the Nova laser system.

BIBLIOGRAPHY

J. R. Severyn, P. J. VanArsdall, G. J. Suski, "NOVANET - Multiple Computer/Multiple Device Fiber Optic Communication System", CLEO/ICF Conference 1980.

J. R. Hill, J. R. Severyn, P. J. VanArsdall, "Fiber Optics Links Control System for the Nova Laser", UCRL-87751, for Photonics Spectra, June 18, 1982.

Laser Program Annual Report - 1979, UCRL-50021-79, Lawrence Livermore National Laboratory, Livermore, California.

Laser Program Annual Report - 1980, UCRL-50021-80, Lawrence Livermore National Laboratory, Livermore, California.

"Introduction to Local Area Networks," Digital Equipment Corporation, 1982.

Electronics Engineering Department Quarterly Report No. 2 - 1980, UCRL-50025-80-2, pgs. 9-16, Lawrence Livermore National Laboratory, Livermore, California.

ACCESS AND COMMUNICATION CONTROLS
IN AN ACCOUNTING INFORMATION SYSTEM

by Avi Rushinek and Sara F. Rushinek

University of Miami,
Coral Gables, Florida

Abstract

This paper involves the exploration of two very important security controls in a computerized accounting information system: (1) access controls, and (2) communication controls. The various specific access and communication controls are examined, analyzing their roles in an accounting information system's computer network.

The growing use of computers in the accounting information systems of the business environment, along with the presence of growing computer fraud, necessitate managements to implement stricter access and communication controls.

Introduction

Used in the broadest sense, "controls" are methods and/or procedures used by and within an organization to safeguard its assets. The importance of controls in an Accounting Information System (AIS) or the Electronic Data Processing (EDP) System is both prudent and understandable when one considers the following factors: First, an automated AIS is likely to process more data than the manual one -- increasing the number of both potential errors and potential problems. Computerized AISs also gather, process, and store data in non-readable (by the human eye) forms, thus eliminating the possibility of observation to check for data accuracy and integrity. The audit trail has also been blurred in the use of AISs due to its nature of taking one system entry and sending it simultaneously to several different places in the entire system, according to Moscove and Simkin (1981). Other control considerations, or the need for them would be: (1) Management has come to rely increasingly on computer generated reports, and many major financial decisions are made on the basis of these reports. (2) Tremendous amounts (if not all) of a company's resources are controlled by AISs and/or EDP systems.

Analysis, Synthesis and Discussion

Some of the primary objectives of controls are: (a) to insure that transactions are processed in accordance with management's authorization; (b) to insure that transactions are processed and recorded properly; (c) to insure that transactions which are not processed or recorded correctly, or transactions which are not processed in accordance with management's authorization are detected; and (d) improper transactions that are detected are corrected to the extent possible, as stated by Harrison (1981).

Exposures are risks or threats that an organization is subjected to. Controls should seek to prevent, eliminate, and/or minimize costs and problems associated with exposures. Any action leading to an exposure is known as a cause of the exposure. A good control system will reduce, minimize, or preclude some of the more typical exposures such as: (1) destruction or loss of assets; (2) interruption of business; (3) bad management decisions; (4) unreliable record keeping; (5) unreliable data; and (6) possible competitive disadvantage. There are three categories of exposure reduction/control. The first category is that of Preventative - which (hopefully) keeps the cause or causes of exposure from occurring. The second set of controls falls under the heading of Detective Controls. Once a cause of exposure has taken place, this type of control has then to detect it. Thirdly, Corrective Controls present and provide information needed to determine the causes of exposures and the corrections of them, as discussed by Harrison (1981).

Summary, Conclusions and Implications

This paper reports on two important areas of control concerning computer usage in an accounting information system: (1) access controls, and (2) communication controls. Both sets of controls encompass a vast array of subset controls, each equally as vital as the next.

Access and communication controls are designed to: (1) insure that transactions are processed in accordance with management's authorization; (2) insure that transactions are processed and recorded properly; (3) insure that transactions which are not processed or recorded correctly, or transactions which are not processed in accordance with management's authorization are detected; and (4) insure that improper transactions that are detected are corrected to the extent possible. The various access and communications controls were examined, and each of their advantages and disadvantages were analyzed.

The implications of this research is fairly clear. With the growing use of computers in the accounting information systems of the business world, coupled with the corresponding growth of computer crimes being prepetuated not only by "outsiders", but also by intelligent (though misguided perhpas) employees; management must give strict attention to the necessary and applicable access and communication controls available for implementation in their computerized accounting information system. Adherence to this advice can save millions of dollars of a company's most important or valuable resources, which in turn, can be invested toward the advancement of a company's computer technology.

References

Available upon request.

Workshop
Commercial Network Security—Does Anyone Care?

Chairman

E. Burke

Panelists

B. Schanning
D. Tocher
G. Hopkins
M. Muntner
J. Yao

COMMERCIAL NETWORK SECURITY -- DOES ANYONE CARE?

Edmund L. Burke

Data General Corporation
Research Triangle Park, North Carolina

Since World War II, the US government has had a comprehensive way to deal with communication security. Under pressure from commercial interests, the government moved in the 70's to make some communication security technology available in the form of the Data Encryption Standard.

DES has been available for some time, yet there is little interest in the marketplace. The lack of interest could stem from unawareness or unconcern with security or from the feeling that data security is not the weak point in the system.

This session will investigate the techniques and vulnerabilities of commercial network security. Panel members will present their experiences with developmental and product activities aimed at providing security in a business environment. The panel will try to stimulate discussion on why there has been no market and what technical characteristics that market should have.

Network Security Considerations in BLN

J. Yao

Bell Laboratories
Naperville, Illinois 60566

ABSTRACT

In a heterogeneous computer network, resources on each node are protected by the local security mechanism. Network services allow local resources to be accessed remotely from other nodes. Without appropriate network security measures, each node is vulnerable to attack from the network. This paper analyzes the heterogeneous Bell Labs Network (BLN) environment and lists the potential network security risks. By assessing the risks, counter-measures are proposed for minimizing potential exposure. These counter-measures are part of a global network security mechanism being implemented for BLN.

1. INTRODUCTION

In a heterogeneous network, each node is protected by its own security mechanism that is administered locally. Hence, some nodes are more secure than others. Without networking, only the local users are affected when the local security is breached. However, when these systems are interconnected via a network, other nodes can be exposed to attack from a less secure node. This paper describes the Bell Labs Network (BLN) [1] environment and lists the potential network security risks. By assessing the risks, counter-measures are being implemented to minimize potential exposure.

BLN interconnects heterogeneous computing systems throughout the various Bell Laboratories locations. The systems that are interconnected include IBM MVS (TSO, JES2, and JES3), IBM TSS and UNIX™ on DEC PDP 11/70, VAX 11/780 and Western Electric 3B20S. These systems are geographically distributed in Illinois, Ohio, Pennsylvania and New Jersey. BLN is a packet-switched network that supports various physical transport mechanisms including the Network Systems Corporation HYPERchannel™, dial-up links and dedicated links.

The goal of BLN is to allow users easy access to all geographically separated computing resources.

The host-to-host networking services provided include file transfer, magnetic tape reel-to-reel transfer, remote job submittal, and distribution of various types of output [2]. Central to these networking services is the ability to move information from one system to another. In BLN this service is provided by the File Transfer System [3].

2. NETWORK ENVIRONMENT

Before listing the potential security threats, it is necessary to understand the network environment provided by BLN. This section describes the network services provided to the users, how the file transfer system supports these services, and the different local security mechanisms on each node.

2.1 Network Services

BLN facilitates the sharing of resources among users on different nodes. The batch network services include:

- File Transfer – Transfer a file with options to create, replace, or append to the target file. A request for a file transfer from any source node to any destination node can be initiated at any node on the network.
- Transient Output Routing – Redirect transient output files to a remote site. After the transient file is transferred to the destination node, it is outputted (e.g. printed, plotted, punched, etc.).
- Remote Job Submission – Submit a system job to a remote execution system. After the job is transferred to the destination node, it is submitted to run on the destination system.
- Service Request Notification – Notify one or more users (via mail) of the network service completion status. If the service did not complete successfully, an explanation is given.

BLN also supports interactive network management and job inquiry commands used to monitor and control the network [4]. With these network services, resources on a node are now accessible via the network. These resources include CPU cycles, storage devices (e.g. memory, disk) and other I/O devices (e.g. tape drives, phototypesetter), etc. In particular, requests can come in from a remote node to read or write files, access other devices, and/or execute a job or command.

2.2 File Transfer System

The batch network services provided in BLN are built on top of a File Transfer System (FTS). A file transfer involves four or more nodes:

- initiator – the node on which the file transfer request is made,
- source – the node on which the source file resides,
- destination – the node on which the destination file resides, and
- notification – one or more nodes on which a user is notified of the service completion status. These nodes are specified with the transfer request, and need not be the same as the initiator, source or destination nodes.

However, since notification only involves sending network generated mail to a user about the completion status of file transfers, the following discussion will only concentrate on the first three nodes, i.e. initiator, source and destination. In most cases, the initiator is the same as the source or destination. However, this restriction is not imposed by the FTS. In addition, to support other networking services and to make the FTS more flexible, the FTS allows a request to also specify:

- a pre-transfer program to be executed at the source before the file transfer, e.g. a pre-transfer program may be used to perform code conversion for the source file, and
- a post-transfer program executed at the destination after the file transfer, e.g. a post-transfer program may submit the file just received to run on the local system.

Therefore, a file transfer request in the FTS can be generalized to involve the following network resources:

1. At the initiator:
   - request to use resources on the source and destination nodes
2. At the source:
   - run the pre-transfer program
   - read from the source file and transfer it to the destination file
3. At the destination:
   - write to the destination file with the source file data received
   - run the post-transfer program

2.3 Local Security

Security for most computing systems used within Bell Labs is controlled by login ID. Before a user can use a system's resources, he/she must have a valid login ID on the system. Furthermore, to gain access to the system, a user must login and provide the proper password and be authenticated by the system. Once logged on, the user can run programs and commands, and access files on the system. The computer time used will be charged to this user's account. Files created by a user are then owned by the user.

To facilitate the sharing of files by users belonging to the same group, the group ID is also used to control file access. A user can belong to several groups, although only one group ID can be active at a time.

Access to files is controlled by login ID and group ID. For each file, the owner can specify the read, write and execute permissions for self, group members, and other local users (on the same system). In accessing a file, if the login ID matches that of the owner, the read, write and execute permissions for the owner will be used. Otherwise, if the user's group ID matches that of the group, the group permissions will be used. If neither the login ID nor the group ID matches, the file will be accessed with the permissions for other local users.

3. SECURITY RISKS

After analyzing the BLN network environment it is possible to identify potential security risks. This is accomplished by first understanding the security clearance process for a file transfer request.

3.1 Request Clearance

Since a file transfer request involves resources on the initiator, source and destination nodes, and access to resources on each node is controlled by the local security mechanism, the security clearance for a file transfer should be distributed in the three nodes. In particular, the following questions should be asked:

1. At the initiator:
   - Is the initiating user permitted to make such a network request?
2. At the source:
   - Is the initiating user permitted to run the pre-transfer program on this node?
   - Is the initiating user permitted to read the source file?
3. At the destination:
   - Is the initiating user permitted to write to the destination file?
   - Is the initiating user permitted to run the post-transfer program on this node?

What should be the criteria for answering these questions? Without networking, the local security mechanism uses login IDs to control resource accesses by local users. With networking, network users should also be given controlled access to these resources. These network users are logged in on remote nodes, with remote login IDs. How does the local security mechanism control accesses by these network users?

3.2 Potential Risks

If no network security checks are performed, and a node always answers "yes" to the clearance questions listed in the previous section, this node may be subject to attack from other nodes on the network. Potential risks are listed as follows:

- Data Exposure – Unauthorized copying of files and browsing of public files.
- Data Damage – Unauthorized over-writing or deletion of files.
- Execution Cycle Stealing – Running a remotely submitted job without a valid login ID, password and account number.
- Communication Wire-tapping – Exposure of data on physical links and in intermediate switching nodes.
- Malicious Host – Security on an insecure host may be compromised, making it possible for it to masquerade as another host. Or a node may become insane, flooding the network with extraneous traffic.
- Misuse of Network Management Services (NMS) – To preserve the integrity of the network configuration, the execution of NMS commands must be controlled, and in some cases (e.g. route change) limited to authorized network operators only.

4. COUNTER-MEASURES

In this section, we will assess the threats to assets and describe counter-measures adopted by BLN to minimize potential exposure.

4.1 Data Exposure

Since login ids are controlled by the local system administrator, data public to local users are not always public to all network users. It is necessary for each system to control network users who are allowed to browse at local data. For a file transfer request, an initiating user requests to read a file at the source node, and to transfer it to the destination node. The network software has to determine if the initiating user is permitted to access the source file.

If the initiating user has a login id on the source node, the network software will allow the user to read the source file using the permissions for this local login. Without a local login, read access by a network user must be restricted. By default, no read access is permitted. The system administrator can give users from other nodes the capability to read certain public files. All read access attempt violations will be logged in a security log for auditing by a security officer.

4.2 Data Damage

Since login ids are controlled by the local system administrator, files that are writable by local users need not be writable by all network users. Receiving junk files in public directories is an annoyance, and can tie up storage resources if not promptly removed. Worse yet, public files can be accidentally or maliciously overwritten by other network users. It is therefore, necessary to control where data received from network users can be written.

For a file transfer, an initiating user is requesting to write data from the source node to a file in the destination node. The network software has to determine if the initiating user is permitted to write to the destination file. Since local security mechanisms protect resources via login ids, if the initiating user has a login id on the destination node, the network software will allow the user to access the destination file using the permissions for this local login. Without a local login, write access by a network user must be restricted. By default, no write access is permitted. The system administrator can give users from another node the capability to write into certain public directories. All write access attempt violations will be logged in the security log for auditing by a security officer.

4.3 Execution Cycle Stealing

Assets on a system include CPU cycles and various storage and output devices. Access to these resources is controlled by the login process. For a remote execution request, an initiating user is requesting to execute a program on a remote node. The network software has to determine if the initiating user is permitted to execute on the remote node.

Since access to a system is controlled by the login process, if the initiating user has a login id on the remote system, he/she should be able to execute on the remote system as if logged on. Without a local login, execution by a network user must be severely restricted. By default, no execution is permitted. The system administrator can control the list of system-certified programs that can be executed by users from trusted nodes. All execution attempt violations will be logged in the security log for auditing by a security officer.

4.4 Communication Wire-Tapping

There is a potential threat that data, when transmitted in clear-text, may be exposed on the links, and in intermediate nodes in a packet-switched network. When data for node or user authentication is exposed, it can compromise the security of that node. Therefore, authentication data, like passwords or secret keys should never be transmitted in the clear by the network software. Indeed, digital signatures [5] can be used for node and user authentication.

To prevent exposure of data on the communication links, it is possible to install hardware encryption boxes on both ends of a link. In a packet-switched network, where data may be exposed on an untrusted intermediate node, it may be necessary to have end-to-end encryption of data. The file transfer system should allow the user to specify encryption pre-processing and decryption post-processing.

4.5 Malicious Host

On each node, the system administrator can give certain trusted nodes more capabilities than others, e.g. permission to read all public files. Therefore, it is necessary for each node to authenticate request messages from other nodes. Message authentication can be achieved via digital signatures. Each node has a secret key which it uses to sign its request messages. At the destination, the message is authenticated by decryption using the originator's public key. The originator must be trusted to safeguard its secret key, so other nodes cannot masquerade as the originator. Request messages from untrusted nodes will be rejected. The system administrator determines the trustworthiness of a node by examining its local security mechanism and system administration practices. For example, a trusted node must authenticate its users, protect its secret key, protect its file system, etc.

4.6 Misuse of Network Management Services

Commands for monitoring and controlling the network can affect network functionality and user jobs. Some examples are: the change route, disable link, and delete job commands. To preserve the integrity of the network configuration, the execution of these commands must be controlled, and in some cases (e.g. route change) limited to authorized network operators only. It is necessary for the system administrator to control the network users who can execute each command.

5. CONCLUSION

The BLN network security and protection problem is defined in this paper. Within BLN, resources on each node are protected by the local security mechanism. Network services allow local resources to be accessed remotely from other nodes. Without appropriate network security measures, each node is subject to attack from other nodes. Therefore, it is necessary to extend the local security mechanism on each host, to provide for global network security. This is accomplished by assessing the security risks and adopting appropriate counter-measures, to minimize potential exposure.

The key feature of the Bell Labs Network Security is decentralized control - each system can determine its own security needs and control network access accordingly. The existing local security mechanisms of a system are maintained, and the network will interface to this local security mechanism to prevent compromising local security. The local System Administrator controls the sharing of system resources by users from other systems. In particular, the System Administrator can specify what data can be read, written, and what programs can be executed by network users. Local users can specify a list of network users who can access resources under their login ids. For data privacy, users can also request end-to-end encryption for their file transfers. Digital signature is used to authenticate messages from another node. This prevents one node from masquerading as another. Finally, all network security violations are logged for auditing.

REFERENCES

[1] K. E. Coates, D. L. Dvorak, and R. M. Watts, "An Overview of BLN: A Bell Laboratories Computing Network," Proceedings of the Seventh Data Communications Symposium, Mexico City, Mexico, October 1981, pages 224-229.

[2] K. E. Coates and K. E. Mackey, "Architecture for User and Network Management Services in a Heterogeneous Computer Network," Proceedings of the Fifteenth Hawaii International Conference on System Sciences, Honolulu, Hawaii, January 1982, pages 636-645.

[3] B. Gopinath, K. Sabnani, A. Y. Teng, and J. Yao, "A File Transfer System for Scheduling File Transfers in the Bell Labs Network," Proceedings of IEEE INFOCOM 83, San Diego, California, April 1983, pages 279-287.

[4] K. E. Coates and K. E. Mackey, "The Evolution of Network Management Services in the Bell Labs Network: Throes and Aftermath," Proceedings of COMPCON '82, Washington, D. C., September 1982.

[5] R. L. Rivest, A. Shamir, and L. Adleman, "A Method for Obtaining Digital Signatures and Public Key Cryptosystems," Communications of the ACM, February 1978, pages 120-126.

Reliable Data Networks

Chairman

B. Stuck

A METHODOLOGY FOR THE DESIGN OF RELIABLE COMMUNICATION NETWORKS IN DISTRIBUTED PROCESSING SYSTEMS

Hossein Besharatian

M/A COM RESEARCH CENTER
1350 Piccard Dr , Rockville. Maryland. 20850

ABSTRACT

The combined problem of the communication network design and resource allocation is studied for Disributed Data Processing (DDP) networks. The reliability measure for a distributed data processing system is used in order to enhance network reliability.

A model is proposed to determine an optimal DDP network and to allocate resources that maximize the reliability measure of the network. The model takes into consideration network topology, resource avaliability and channel capacity. It is shown that the model may be represented by a linear programming model.

1 INTRODUCTION

A geographically distributed organization often has a need for a unified information system that enhances proper and efficient management of its resources. This usually needs a set of geographically distributed computer systems that interact through a communication network [1.2.3.4]. In such a case the following questions usually arise:

1) How should the resources be allocated across the computer sites?

2) How should the communication network be designed?

3) What should be the size of a computer system that will be installed at each organizational site?

In this paper we attempt to answer these questions. A framework for an evaluation tool is introduced that [4.5.6]:

1) Can be used to compare alternative distributed data processing systems with respect to reliability problems;

2) Provide a means to use optimization methods in an iterative design improvement process; and

3) Provide a tool to use sensitivity analysis to determine the effect of changes in system parameters.

The formulation of the reliability measure for a distributed data processing system is the main focus of this paper [7.8.9]. A reliability index is defined for a potential path between any pair of nodes in the system. The expected reliability index is defined for every individual pair of nodes and will be formulated to represent the reliability measure of the system. Finally, a set of properties will be presented to justify the use of this factor as a measure of reliability. The reliability measure completely provides the salient information about the network [10,11]. Hence, for the first time it is computationally feasible to study the effects of demand (load), links reliability, degradation of capacity, and other factors upon the ability of network system to provide the desired level of performance.

To define the reliability problem, it is necessary to develop expressions for the reliability measures, link communications capacity, site capacity, and request volume [12,13], The reliability measure is an objective function, while the remaining three constitute constraints. A reliability measure can be generated by taking the expectation of a reliability index. defined for each pair of nodes which depends on the number of messages issued from source to destination sites, and the weighted reliability factor between those sites. This measure provides a quantitative approach to measuring the reliability of a distributed data processing system that depends on the network architecture, data requirements, and processing distribution. The quantitative network evaluation permits a comparison of the performance of different network architectures with respect to the reliability measure. An example of a distributed data processing network is shown in Figure 1.

The problem of the distribution of the resources (question 1) and the size of computer system at each site (question 3) is known as the resource allocation. The communication network design problem(question 2) can, therefore, be broken down into two subproblems. The first problem is to determine which sites to interconnect (we will address this problem in our design of the network topology [14]). The second subproblem is to determine the capacity of each communication channel. This will be referred to as the channel capacity allocation problem.

The objectives of this work then are as follows:

1) To find a solution to the communication network design.

2) To find a solution to the resource allocation at each site.

3) To find a solution to the channel capacity allocation.

4) To investigate the effect of the resource and channel capacities on the overall design.

2. THE MODEL

The problem formulation and the derivation of expressions for the problem model are discussed briefly below.

2 1) PROBLEM FORMULATION

The problem addressed is formulated as follows:

GIVEN:

- A set of n geographically distributed computer sites ($N_1, N_2, N_3, .., N_n$)
- A set of service requests ($R_1, R_2, R_3, ..., R_n$)
- A set of available computer

system capacities $(S_1, S_2, S_3, \ldots S_n)$.

- The set of available channel capacities $(\lambda_1, \lambda_2, \ldots, \lambda_k)$.

- Site and channel failure probabilities (h). The parameter h is noted as the reliability index.

FIND:

- The allocation of the communication channel capacities. The set of channel apacity allocation variables is :

$$f = \{f_k, \; k = 1, 2, \ldots, k\}$$

where f_k is:

$$f_k = \sum_{i=1}^{n} \sum_{j=1}^{n} \sum^{p \in P_{ij}} f_m (R_i \, m^p_{ij}) \qquad (1)$$

Number m^p_{ij} is the portion of traffic (or number of messages) issued at the ith site, passed throughout the path p and processed at the jth site. Number f_k $(R_i \cdot m^p_{ij})$ is the portion of m^p_{ij} which is passed throughout the kth channel. The ratio of f_k/λ_k gives the utilization of channel kth.

- The allocation of computer system capacities. The set of resource capacity allocation variables is :

$$C_s = \{C_j, \; j = 1, 2, \ldots, n\},$$

where

$$C_j = \sum_{i=1}^{n} \sum^{p \in P_{ij}} R_i \circ m^P_{ij} \qquad (2)$$

Integer C_j is the traffic (or number of messages) issued at the ith site and processed at the jth site.

The objective is to maximize the reliability measure which is the sum of the following :

$$z = \max \left\{ \frac{1}{n} \sum_{j=1}^{n} \sum_{i=1}^{n} d_{ij} \right\} \qquad (3)$$

Where d_{ij} is called the weighted reliability index between the ith and jth sites. The value of d_{ij} is given by:

$$d_{ij} = \sum^{p \in P_{ij}} m^p_{ij} \circ h^p_{ij} \qquad (4)$$

Where m^p_{ij} is the portion of the traffic (or number of messages) issued at the ith site, passed throughout the pth path and processed at jth site. h^p_{ij} is the reliability index between the ith site and the jth site when path p is considered. P_{ij} is the set of possible paths between the ith and jth sites.

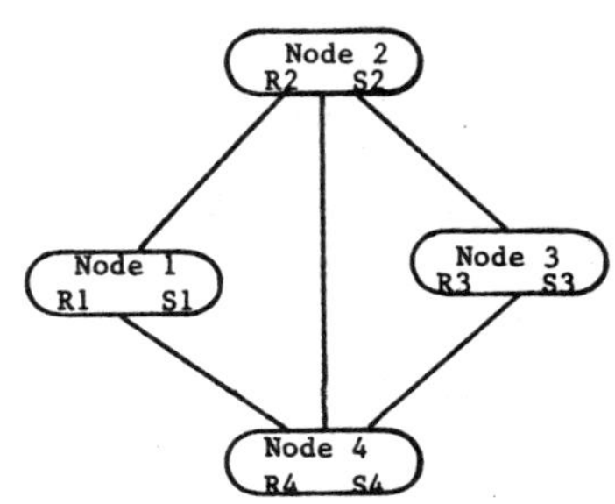

Fig. 1 FOUR NODES DISTRIBUTION DATA PROCESSING NETWORK

2.2. DERIVATION OF EXPRESSIONS FOR THE PROBLEM MODEL

Expressions for the problem model (Equation 1 to 4) are now derived in terms of the reliability index, and sets of C_s, λ, R, and f.

2.2.1. ISSUED REQUEST CONSTRAINTS

The number of messages issued per unit of time at site i will be distributed into the processing centers located at different sites to be processed. This distribution will be represented by:

$$\sum_{j=1}^{n} m_{ij} = \sum_{j=1}^{n}\sum^{p} m^{p}_{ij} = 1 \qquad (5)$$

for PEP_{ij}

Where m_{ij} is the portion of traffic (or number of messages) issued per unit of time at site i and processed at site j (Fig. 2.a).

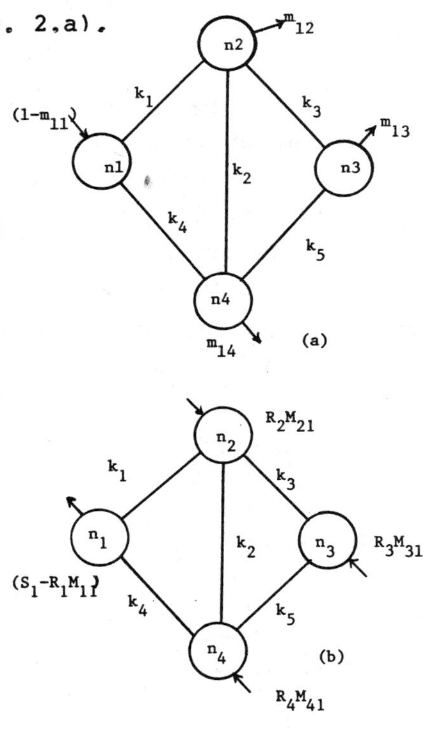

Fig. 2 TRAFFIC FLOW

2.2.2. PROCESSING CENTER CAPACITY CONSTRAINTS

The capacity of a processing center is defined as the maximum number of messages that will be processed per unit of time at the processing center (Fig. 2.b). The capacity constraint is given by:

$$C_j = \sum_{i=1}^{n} \sum^{p \epsilon P_{ij}} (R_i m^{p}_{ij}) \le s_j \qquad (6)$$

where s_j is the maximum number of messages processed by processing center at site j per unit of time. R_i is the total number of messages issued per unit of time at site i.

2.2.3 CHANNEL CAPACITY CONSTRAINTS

Since each channel in the communication network is considered to be a separate server, the notation λ_k is adapted as the maximum number of messages per unit of time that travel over the kth channel or line. We should recognize the fact that the routing procedure operating upon the message traffic will determine the relation between the set $\{\lambda_k\}$ and the set $\{m^{p}_{ij}\}$ in any real network. These two quantities are related by:

$$f_k = \sum_{\substack{i=1 \\ (i \neq j)}}^{n} \sum_{j=1}^{n} f_k (R_i m^{p}_{ij}) \le \lambda_k \qquad (7)$$

for PEP_{ij}

Where f_k $(R_i m_{ij})$ indicates the portion of the number of messages which travel over the kth channel, issued at site i and processed at site j. The routing procedure will indicate function f_k.

2.2.4. OBJECTIVE FUNCTIONS

Using the notation of the preceeding discussion, the total weighted differences given by Z (Eq. 3), is defined as the objective function:

$$Z = \max \left[1/n \sum_{i=1}^{n} \sum_{j=1}^{n} d_{ij} \right]_{\text{for all } m_{ij}} = \max \left[1/n \sum_{i=1}^{n} \sum_{j=1}^{n} \sum^{p} (h^{p}_{ij} \circ m^{p}_{ij}) \right]_{\text{for all } m_{ij} \text{ and } PEP_{ij}} \quad (8)$$

In trying to maximize the total weighted differences (Z), the designer should give the highest flow assignment to the channel with the highest reliability index.

Furthermore, let B_{st} denote the event that the path p exists between site s and site t. The following definition is given by Barllow[12.13].

$$P[B^{p}_{st} = 1] = h^{p}_{st} = E[B^{p}_{st}] \quad (9)$$

where B^{p}_{st} is defined as:

$$B^{p}_{st} = \begin{cases} 1 & \text{if path p between site s and site t is operational} \\ 0 & \text{if path p between site s and site t is not operational} \end{cases}$$

$E(B^{p}_{st})$ denotes the expected value of the B^{p}_{st}, and h^{p}_{st} denotes the reliability function of path p in the network for the source s and destination t.

Reliability index is therefore, expressed in terms of the site and channel failure probability [9,11,15].

3. THE DESIGN PROCESS

A design process to solve the problem formulated in the previous section is now presented. The main part of the optimization problem consists of an iteration process on the network data flow m^{p}_{ij}.

The design process consists of an optimum algorithm whose input/output description is shown in figure 3. The output of OPTIMUM is as follows:

- The optimal value for reliability measure Z.

- The optimal resource allocation:

  $C_{sopt} = \{C_{jopt}, j = 1, 2, \ldots, n\}$

  where C_{jopt} is the value of required resource capacity at site j found in the optimal solution,

- The optimal channel capacity allocation:

  $F_{kopt} = \{f_k, k = 1, 2, \ldots, K\}$

  where f_{kopt} is the value of required channel capacity on channel k found in the optimal solution.

The Algorithm OPTIMUM is now described. It consists of algorithms LOC-RA, DECOMP, INIT-M and ITER-M. Figure 4 shows the processing escription of the OPTIMUM algorithm.

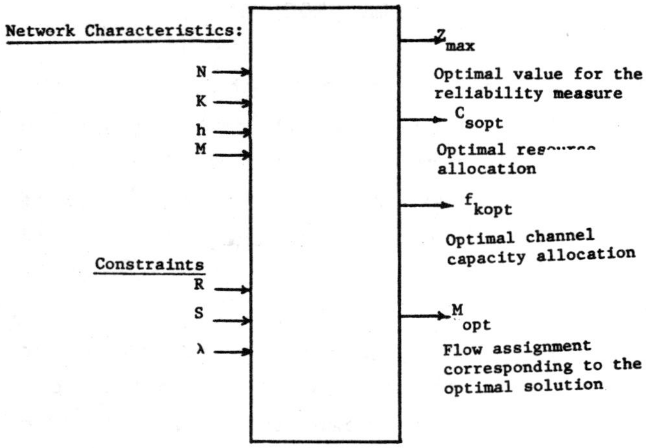

OPTIMUM ALGORITHM: INPUT/OUTPUT DESCRIPTION

Fig. 3

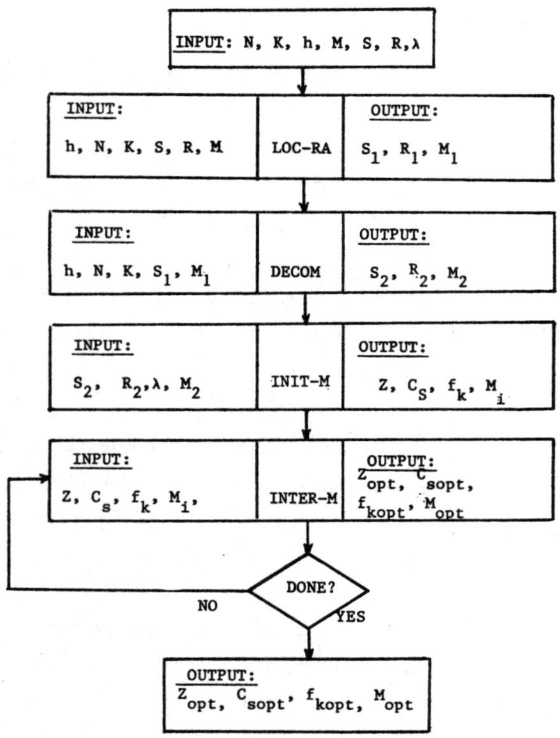

OPTIMUM ALGORITHM: PROCESSING DESCRIPTION

Fig. 4

3.1. ALGORITHM LOC-RA

By exploiting the properties of the linear programming and the result of property 1 (see Appendix A), an initial local resource allocation is obtained. The condition (10) is required for initial local resource allocation,

$$\Big[1/R_i \underset{p\epsilon P_{ij}}{} (H^p_{ij}) + 1/R_g \min_{p\epsilon P_{gi}} (h^p_{gj})$$

$$1/R_i \max_{p\epsilon P_{ij}} (h^p_{ij}) + 1/R_g \max_{p\epsilon P_{gj}} (h^p_{gj})\Big] \geq o \tag{10}$$

for all j, g, = 1, 2, - - - n, j ≠ i, g ≠ i

and

$$h_{ii} \geq \max_{p\epsilon P_{ij}} (h^p_{ij})$$

for all j = 1, - - - n, j ≠ 1

Where min (h^p_{ij}) means the smallest h^p_{ij} in the set of $p\epsilon P_{ij}$ and max (h^p_{ij}) means the largest h^p_{ij} in the set of $p\epsilon P_{ij}$.

When the reliability index at site i satisfies the condition of (10), then we will conclude that the processing center at site i gives the first priority to those messages which are issued at site i. This result is shown by:

$$M^*_{ii} = \min [1 \text{ or } S_i/R_i]$$

Algorithm LOC-RA will check condition (10) for each site, and will find the local resource allocation in case of satisfying condition (10).

3.2 ALGORITHM DECOMP

In the same way as we did for algorithm LOC-RA by using the properties of Linear Programming and the result of property 2 (see Appendix A), we may conclude that under condition (11) a new initial resource allocation is obtained. Therefore, the processing center located at sub-network N1 must provide the maximum service to the messages that are issued in the sub-network N1; and the same conclusion is true about sub-network N2. The results can be presented in the following form:

$$\begin{bmatrix}\text{The smallest}\\ \text{element of}\\ [1/R_1][H_{11}]\end{bmatrix} \circ \begin{bmatrix}\text{The smallest}\\ \text{element of}\\ [1/R_2][H_{22}]\end{bmatrix} \geq$$

$$\begin{bmatrix}\text{The largest}\\ \text{element of}\\ [1/R_1][H_{12}]\end{bmatrix} \circ \begin{bmatrix}\text{The largest}\\ \text{element of}\\ [1/R_2][H_{21}]\end{bmatrix} \qquad (11)$$

where $[1/R_i]$ is a diagonal matrix, the invers value of each element of which gives the number of requests issued at a node.

$$M_{t_{11}} = \min\left[1 \text{ or } S_{t_1}/R_{t_1}\right]$$

$$M_{t_{22}} = \min\left[1 \text{ or } S_{t_2}/R_{t_2}\right]$$

Algorithm DECOMP will check condition (11) for any sub-network which satisfies the requirements for property 2, and will find the initial resource allocation for that sub-network.

3.3 ALGORITHM INIT-M

This algorithm finds initial value of M_i (the initial feasible solution for linear programming). The output from algorithm INIT-M is the first solution which satisfies all onstraints. We may apply the phase-I of the simplex algorithm for INIT-M.

3.4. ALGORITHM ITER-M

The phase-II of the simplex method can be used here. This algorithm maintains the value of reliability measure corresponding to the optimal solution found so far. It decides that the iteration process has ended wherever the optimality conditions are satisfied.

4. SENSITIVITY ANALYSIS

The discussion in previous sections has emphasized on the evaluation and resource allocation of certain network topologies. after the values of h_{ij}, R_i and S_j were obtained for each network system. The R_i and S_j values are the responsibility of the user and can be indicated by the customer as to how these values may be specified. To date, however, the selection of the h_{ij} values has not been addressed. How does the designer produce an optimal or at least a good allocation of available resources, subject to the constraints of the specification and system architecture?

The objective as discussed in previous sections is, therefore, to maximize the reliability measure of the distribution data processing network which is subject to the data flow and system specification. When studying a system using a linear programming model technique. the sensitivity analysis can be used to acquire additional processing centers; and to determine which resourcs to acquire at what capacity. The linear programming model not only determines an optimum solution to implement, but becomes a tool for optimal planning and design.

By applying the sensitivity analysis, we want to know how far the input parameter values (i.e., R_i, S_j, or h_{ij}) can vary without causing violent changes in a compound optimal solution or the composition of a basic set.

5. SIMILAR PROBLEMS

The other network design problems can be posed as linear programs similar to problem model(Eq. 8). These are problems in which data between every pair of nodes in the network have to be transmitted to minimize average weighted delay. Applications are also found in network cost problems. Which deal with the problems of determining the minimum cost of data transmission within the data communication networks.

Flow assignment and optimum routing problems are also similar problems that can be posed as linear programs similar to the problem model, which deal with the problem of determining the minimum data flow to provide an optimum set of routes for the data transmission within the DDP system.

6. CONCLUSION

The problem of the combined communication network design and resource allocation for distributed data processing system was addressed. The reliability modeling tool which is presented in this paper, allows network designers to evaluate various network configurations during the design phase. In this model we choose data flow as a weighting factor to objective function because it relates our model directly to the first goal in network data communication which is data transmission.

A model was described which provided a framework and mathematical model for the computation of the reliability measure. This reliability measure was presented as a function of data flow (m). reliability index (h). channel capacity (λ). and information processing center capacities (R, S). This mathematical model dealt with identifying the best data flow assignment whose objective was maximizing the reliability measure.

A design methodology to solve the model was then presented. A Linear Programming (LP) model for the problem was presented. Several general algorithms were introduced to decrease the size of the problem model. In a real network, the cost of transmission and the delay time will be increased by increasing the distance between sites. Consequently, the first priority of processing should be given to the local requests. Therefore. in a real case. each network should have a more reliable processing capability for local requests versus non-local requests. That is to say. in a real case, the decompositon algorithm and other relevant methods will be very helpful in reducing the size of the problem model.

In linear programming problem requires the examination of all minimal paths in the graph between every pair of nodes. The solution of the problem model just mentioned is not computationally feasible for large networks. In a related study, two procedures for reducing the number of variables in linear programming was suggested based on the fact that the few minimal paths between any pair of nodes with the largest reliability index will exist in the optimal solution [7].

7. APPENDIX A

Here in this appendix we summarized some properties of function Z.

Property 1) Processing center at node i gives the first priority to those messages which are issued at node i.

Property 2) Processing centers in a subnetwork of a distributed data processing network must provide the maximum service to the requests that are issued in the same subnetwork.

Property 3) The value of the reliability measure for function Z is between Ø and 1.

Property 4) Increasing the channel capacity or service capacity will not decrease the reliability measure Z, i.e.,

$Z_{max}^* > Z_{max}$

where Z* is the new value of Z.

Property 5) Increasing the reliability index of network's component will not decrease the reliability measure of the DDP network ($Z_{max}^* \geq Z_{max}$).

Property 6) Adding a new channel to network will not decrease the reliability measure of the DDP network ($Z^*_{max} \geq Z_{max}$).

REFERENCES

[1] P.H. Enslow. Jr.. "What is a distributed data processing system?". Computer. January 1978.

[2] Donaldson. Hamish. "Designing a distributed processing system". Halsted Press Book, New York, 1979.

[3] Kahn, R.W. "Resource sharing computer communications networks", Proc. of IEEE-, PP. 1379-14Ø7, November 1972.

[4] Frank H. "computer networks" Networks. Vol. 5. PP. 69-73. 1975

[5] Chu, W.W. "Optimal file allocation in a muticomputer information system." IEEE Trans. of Computers, Vol. C-18, PP. 885-889, 1979.

[6] Barber D.L.A. and Davies. D.W. "Computer networks and protocols". Wiley; PP. 417-456, 1979.

[7] Besharatian H.. "Optimization of a reliability measure for distributed network systems" ,Ph.D. dissertation. George Washington University. Washington D.C.; 1983.

[8] Friedman, Arthur D. & Brewer, Melwin A. "Diagnosis & reliable Desgin ofDigital System " Computer Science. Inc., PP. 284-291, 1976.

[9] Hanseler, G.K., McAuliffe. G.K. and Wikou, R.S. "Exact Calculation of computer network reliability." Networks, Vol., 4,pp. 95-112. 1974,

[1Ø] Jordan, B. and Gonzalez, M.J. "A framework for the quantitative evaluation of distributed computer system." IEEE Trans. on Computers. Vol. c-29. No. 12. December 198Ø.

[11] Rai, S. and Aggraval, K.K. "An effective method for reliability evaluation of general network." IEEE Trans. Reliability, Vol. 27, PP. 2Ø6-211, August 1978.

[12] Barlow, R.E. and Proschan, F. "Statistical theory of reliability and life testing : Probability models." Holt-Rinehart and Winson, New York, 1975,

[13] Barlow, R.E. and Proschan, F. "Availability theory of multi-component systems." Academic Press., New York. 1969

[14] Frank. H. and Chou W. "Topological optimization of computer networks." Proceedings of IEEE. Vol., 60. PP. 1385-1397, November 1972,

[15] Wing. O. and Demetriou. P "Analysis of probailistic networks." IEEE communications Tech., Vol. 12, PP. 38-40, September 1964.

VERIFICATION OF A METHODOLOGY FOR DESIGNING RELIABLE COMMUNICATION PROTOCOLS*

Huai-An Lin** and Ming T. Liu

Department of Computer
and Information Science
The Ohio State University
Columbus, Ohio 43210

Charles J. Graff

U.S. Army Communications-Electronics Command

Ft. Monmouth, NJ 07703

Abstract

In this paper we present a new methodology for designing reliable communication protocols. This methodology enhances communicating processes with a synchronization mechanism so that they can detect and resolve the errors caused by collisions automatically. The major advantages of this new methodology include: (1) the "state explosion" problem involved in protocol validation is alleviated; and (2) the burden of handling errors due to collisions is removed from the protocol designer. There is a need to verify that this methodology is applicable to arbitrary protocols. In this paper we also discuss the application of a program verification technique to this methodology.

1. Introduction

A communication protocol is a set of rules governing the interaction among physically separated processes (to be called communicating processes in the following discussion) [14]. Reliability is a matter of serious concern in the design of communication protocols because they form the basis upon which a distributed system is built. By reliability we mean that protocols should possess certain "general properties" which include, as listed by Sunshine [17], freedom from deadlock, completeness to handle all the conditions that may arise, proper termination, etc. Ambiguities inherent in informal techniques used to design protocols are well known today. Consequently, formal techniques [3, 5, 17] have been employed to provide precise definitions of protocols and to provide systematic ways of examining errors that may occur during protocol execution.

As observed by Hailpern and Owicki [7], errors may occur during protocol execution because of (1) failures in communicating processes and in communication media; and (2) asynchronous operations of communicating processes, resulting in collisions.

Many researchers have devoted their efforts to handling errors of the first cause. However, very few people have investigated, to the best of our knowledge, the way of handling errors of the second cause (i.e., collisions).

In [11, 12] we have proposed a new methodology for designing reliable communication protocols, called Priority Driven Communication Protocol Design (PDCPD). This methodology aims to handle errors due to collisions. In this paper we will briefly review PDCPD. The methodology of PDCPD consists of two components:

1. An algorithm that exploits the coupling relationship [2] among communicating processes to produce a system state diagram. This diagram records, from the protocol designer's point of view, the "desirable" interactions of the communicating processes.

2. A synchronization mechanism which enables the communicating processes to detect and resolve collisions due to not conforming to the system state diagram.

In this paper we will only discuss the synchronization mechanism; the reader is referred to [12, 13] for the details of the aforementioned algorithm.

* Research reported herein was supported by U. S. Army CECOM, Ft. Monmouth, NJ, under Contract Nos. DAAK-80-81-K-0104 and DAAB07-83-K-K542. The views, opinions and/or findings contained in this paper are those of the authors and should not be construed as an official Department of the Army position, policy or decision.

** Author's current affiliation is Gould Inc., Gould Research Center, 40 Gould Center, Rolling Meadows, IL 60008.

We are also interested in the applicability of PDCPD. Even though we have tested PDCPD on several real protocols, including CCITT's X.21 Recommendation [4], to demonstrate its usefulness, we are still intrigued by the question of whether PDCPD is applicable to arbitrary protocols. To satisfy our curiosity, we have applied a Floyd/Hoare style of program verification technique [6, 8] to PDCPD and have proved that our methodology is useful for designing any protocol that operates in a certain environment [13]. Another purpose of this paper is, therefore, to present some highlight of our proof.

This paper is organized as follows: Section 2 presents the underlying principle of PDCPD. Section 3 defines the model used in PDCPD for protocol specification. This section also defines the environment in which PDCPD operates and gives a precise definition of collisions. The synchronization mechanism used by PDCPD to detect and resolve collisions is discussed in Section 4. Section 5 gives a brief description of the verification technique used to prove the applicability of PDCPD and the highlights of our proof. Finally, a summary is given in Section 6.

2. Motivation of PDCPD

As mentioned in Section 1, there are two sources of protocol execution errors: (1) failures in communicating processes and in communication media; and (2) asynchronous operations of communicating processes, resulting in collisions.

Many techniques have been developed during the last decade to handle the errors of the first cause. There are mechanisms, such as PAR (positive acknowledgement and retransmission), sequence numbering and connection management scheme (e.g., three way handshaking), which enable communicating processes to detect and recover from such errors.

A collision occurs when communicating processes initiate activities without proper coordination. (A formal definition of collision will be given in Section 3.) The traditional approach to detecting possible collisions involves exhaustively generating the reachable global states. (Each global state is composed of the states of communicating processes and the states of channels that transport messages between processes.) Once a collision is detected, the traditional approach requires the protocol designer to introduce extra states and transitions into the protocol state diagram in order to resolve this collision. However, the power of such an approach is severely limited due to the problem of "state explosion". Another difficulty of such an approach is that the protocol designer has to worry about all possible collisions, thereby increasing the complexity of his task and the possibility of introducing design errors.

PDCPD has been developed based on the belief that the protocol designer should not be burdened by the work of detecting and resolving collisions during the design phase. Instead, PDCPD should enhance the communicating processes with a synchronization mechanism so that they can detect and resolve collisions dynamically during the execution of the protocol. The details of this approach are described in the following sections.

3. Model, Environment and Collision

In this section we will define the model that PDCPD uses to specify protocols and the environment in which PDCPD operates. We will also give a formal definition of collisions and investigate their effect on communication.

Most formal techniques model a protocol as a set of finite state automata (FSA), with each FSA describing an involved process. Each FSA can be represented by a state diagram whose nodes represent process states and whose arcs represent transitions between states.

However, we have found another way to model protocols. Using the coupling relationship [2] among communicating processes, we presented in [12, 13] an algorithm that transforms the individual FSA into a single system state diagram. Although this algorithm has many similarities to a typical protocol validation technique, the problem of state explosion in our algorithm is largely alleviated because the states of channels are excluded from our representation of global states. Due to limits of space, we will not present the algorithm in this paper; the details can be found in [12, 13]. The system state diagram model, however, is defined below because PDCPD is developed based upon such a model.

We define a **protocol** @ as a state diagram with two or more states and satisfying the following five properties:

1. The states in @ have distinct labels

2. Each transition in @ is labelled with an event, which specifies the type of the transition and the name of the process that may **initiate** this transition. Output transitions of the same state have distinct labels (i.e., @ is deterministic).

3. There are an initial state and at least one final state. The initial state is not a final state.

4. Each state in @ has at least one output transition unless it is a final state. A final state has no output transition.

5. Each state in @ is reachable from the initial state by a directed path.

Informally, a transition in protocol @ represents an action to be taken by the communicating processes involved in @. We assume that when a process initiates a transition, it will transmits a

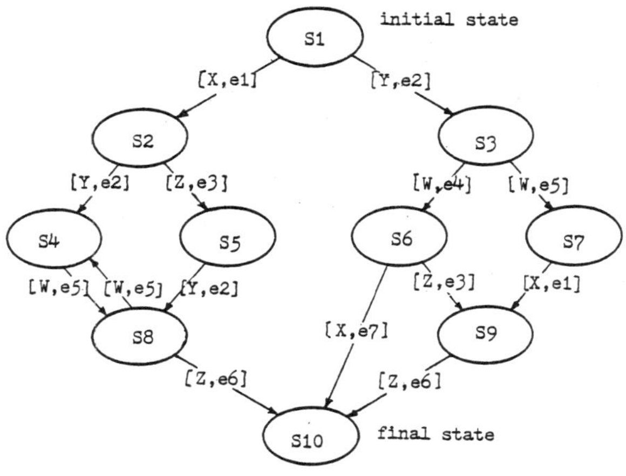

Figure 1: An example of protocol specification using system state diagram

signal (message) to the other processes to indicate the action it has taken. The scheme is described as follows. Suppose in @, X is a process, e is an event, and [X,e] is an output transition of state s. Then process X, having reached state s, <u>can</u> (actively) initiate transition [X,e]. Upon initiating [X,e], X also transmits a signal to the other processes to indicate this initiation. On the other hand, another process Y, having reached state s, <u>must</u> (passively) **follow** transition [X,e] if Y receives the aforementioned signal and has neither initiated nor followed any other output tranition of state s. A process is said to **take** a transition if it actively initiates or passively follows this transition. If [X,e] is a transition from state s to state s′, then a process will jump from s to s′upon taking [X,e] at s.

To illustrate the above model, Figure 1 depicts a simple, but unrealistic protocol which satisfies the above five properties. Four communicating processes X, Y, Z and W are involved in this protocol. Output transition labeled [X,el] of state sl indicates that process X may initiate event el at state sl, etc.

We assume that the environment in which PDCPD operates satisfies the following assumptions: (1) each pair of communicating processes is connected by a channel that is full-duplex, FIFO and free from failures; and (2) communicating processes are failure-free; i.e., they will never break down nor malfunction. These assumptions may sound too ideal to be possible. However, from the discussion in Section 2, we know that they can be achieved by the use of mechanisms such as PAR, sequence numberering, three way handshaking, etc.

Many types of errors can be caused by asynchrionious operations of communcating processes. Even as simple a protocol as that illustrated in Figure 1 may be subjected to errors of incompleteness, deadlock, ambiguity, etc. Due to the limit of space, we only describe one example in the following paragraph. (The reader is referred to [11] for more examples and other types of errors.)

We will use the protocol in Figure 1 as an example again. Let both processes X and Y start from the initial state sl. Suppose X and Y simultaneously initiate transitions [X,el] and [Y,e2], respectively. According to the signal exchange scheme, each of these two processes transmits a signal to indicate the transition it initiates. Let the signals transmitted by X and Y be denoted S_x and S_y, respectively. Having initiated [Y,e2], process Y reaches state s3. Suppose now Y receives signal S_x at s3, then Y is confused because transition [X,el], which is indicated by S_x, is not specified as an output transition of s3. Such a condition is an error of **incompleteness**. On the other hand, when process X receives signal S_y after it has initiated [X,el] and reached state s2, X will take the output transition [Y,e2] of s2 by mistake because it will think that [Y,e2], which is indicated by S_y, has been initiated by Y at state s2. Notice that the above error may occur even if X and Y do not initiate transitions simultaneously. For example, X may first initiate [X,el] at sl. Then, because of signal propagation delay, Y may initiate [Y,e2] at sl before it receives S_x. In such a case, a collision still occurs even though X and Y do not initiate the aforementioned transitions at the same time.

We call the above phenonmenon a **collision.** However, we need a more precise definition of collisions, which is described as follows. Given a protocol @, we use an **execution tree** to record all the directed paths from the initial state in @. Each vertex in the execution tree corresponds to a state, and each directed edge in the tree corresponds to a transition. (The execution tree for the protocol in Figure 1 is partially shown in Figure 2.) For ease of explanation, we will use the term of transition (as well as initiation, following and taking) with the same meaning on execution trees as on protocols. With the use of execution trees, we define a collision as a condition in which two or more transitions are initiated by different processes at the same vertex. Notice that this definition does not necessarily imply that a collision occurs if more than one transition is initiated at the same state by different processes. The reason is that the same state may appear at more than one place on a path (e.g., there are loops in the protocol). If different processes initiate transitions at different vertices along a path, it does not represent a collision even though the vertices may represent the same protocol state.

Since the sequence of transitions taken by a process forms a directed path of the protocol, we call this sequence the **path** of the process. An interesting observation on collisions is that the paths of communicating processes diverge if they collide, and the vertex of divergence indicates how they collide. As shown in Figure 2, the paths of processes X and Y diverge at the root vertex because they collide at the very beginning.

It is important to realize that collisions may not always be a form of errors in some protocols. However, from our experience with protocol design,

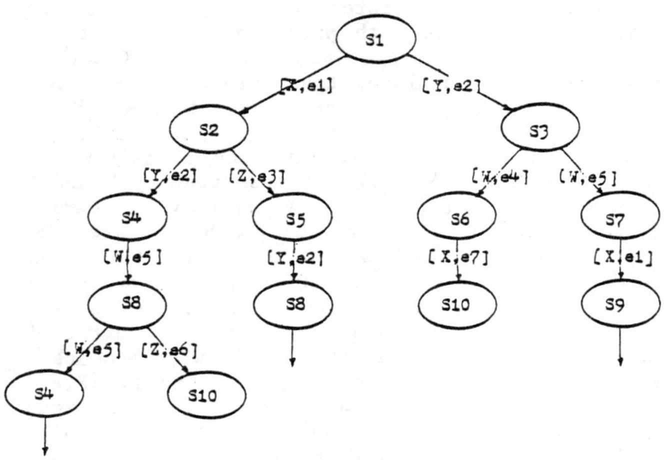

Figure 2: The execution tree for the protocol in Figure 1

almost every collision will result in an error of some type.

4. Synchronization Mechanism

We have mentioned that PDCPD tackles the problem of collisions by enhancing the communicating processes with a synchronization mechanism so that they can detect and resolve collsions automatically. The synchronization mechanism described in this section is developed based on the assumption that every collision is an error in protocol communication. The task of this synchronization mechanism consists of two parts: collision detection and collision resolution.

We have also observed that the paths of two communicating processes diverge if they collide. If each process can record its own path and the paths of the others, then the processes should be able to detect any occurred collision. Therefore, a necessary function of the synchronization mechanism is to help communicating processes record the paths of others. For this purpose, two items of information, **logical time** and **confirmation,** are necessary for a process to correctly record the paths of the other processes.

First, we define the logical time of a path to be the length of that path from the root, with each transition having one unit of length. The necessity of logical time can be seen from Figure 3. As illustrated in Figure 3(a), processes A and B collide at vertex N0 by initiating transitions [A,e1] and [B,e2], respectively. Let S_a and S_b denote the signals used by A and B to indicate the initiation of these two transitions, respectively. Assume that process A receives signal S_b at vertex N1. Because transition [B,e2], which is indicated by S_b, is also an output transition of N1, A will overlook the collision at N0. Similarly, assume that process B receives signal S_a at vertex N2. B will not detect the collision either because

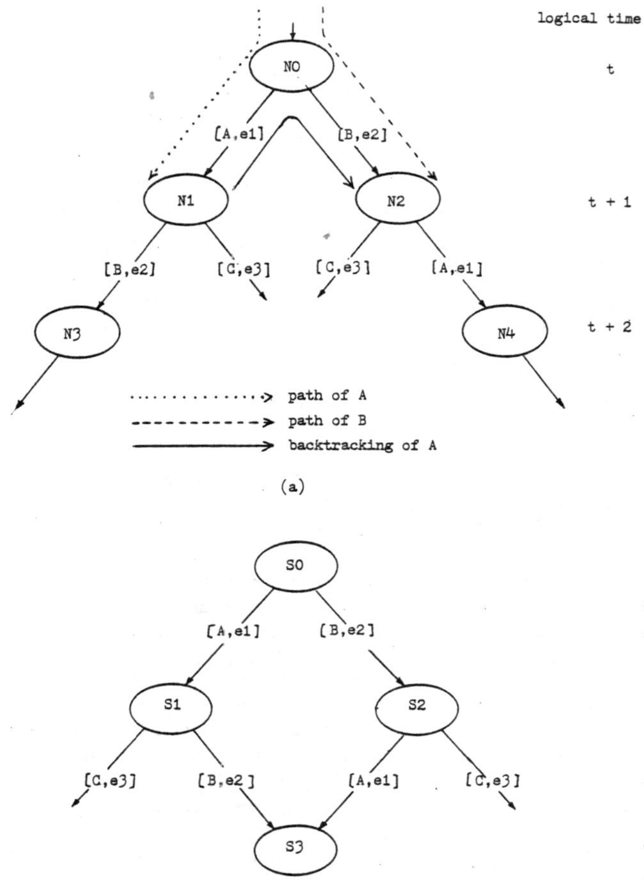

Figure 3: The use of synchronization mechanism

transition [A,e1], which is indicated by S_a, is also an output transition of N2. Notice that further transitions may not reveal the aforementioned collision. Figure 3(b) gives such a case. Suppose vertices N0, N1 and N2 in Figure 3(a) correspond to states s0, s1 and s2 in Figure 3(b), respectively. Then both vertices N3 and N4 in Figure 3(a) must correspond to the same state s3 in Figure 3(b) because both the output transitions [B,e2] of state s1 and [A,e1] of state s2 have the same destination state s4. In such a case, even though further transitions can continue, its meaning is in doubt, since the processes have failed to detect the aforementioned collision and collisions are regarded as erroneous in protocol execution. Such an oversight can be avoided, however, if the initiating process appends the logical time to each signal it transmits to tell the other processes "when" this transition is initiated.

The second item of information necessary for path recording is called confirmation. Confirmation is used by a process to report to the other processes the transition it takes at each state where there is more than one output transition. The necessity of confirmation can also be seen from Figure 3(a). Assume processes A and B have collided at vertex

N0, and [C,e3] is an output transition at both vertices N1 and N2, and process C does not report the transition it takes at N0 to process B. We also assume B has already detected the collision at N0. Then, when process B receives a signal indicating the initiation of transition [C,e3] with logical time t+1 at vertex N2, it represents two possibilities: (1) process C had taken transition [A,e1] at vertex N0 before it initiated transition [C,e3] at vertex N1; or (2) C had taken [B,e2] at N0 before it initiated [C,e3] at N2. However, this problem can be solved if process C transmits a special signal, which we call a confirmation signal, to indicate the transition it takes at vertex N0 to the other processes even though C inself does not initiate any transition. In general, we require a process to transmit a confirmation signal to the other processes to indicate the transition it follows at each vertex where there is more than one output transition.

From the above discussion, therefore, we can see that the combined use of the logical time and confirmation helps processes correctly record the paths of the others, thereby making collision detection possible.

To resolve a detected collisions, we use a **priority assignment** and a **backtracking scheme.**

Priority assignment is described as follows. For a given protocol @, we require the protocol designer to give a linear ordering among the output transitions of each state in @. If t is an output transition of state s, we use $Pty_@(s,t)$ to denote the priority level assigned to output transition t of state s. The priority level of each transition should be determined by its importance or urgency. Suppose [X,e1] and [Y,e2] are two distinct output transitions of state s in @. Then $Pty_@(s,[Y,e2])<Pty_@(s,[X,e1])$ indicates that handling [X,e1] is more important or more urgent than handling [Y,e2].

Having detected a collision, the processes use the priority assignment along with the backtracking scheme to resolve the collision as follows: Suppose the two transitions [A,e1] and [B,e2] have been initiated by processes A and B at the same vertex N, thereby resulting in a collision. Let the logical time of vertex N be t, and let N correspond to state s and $Pty_@(s,[A,e1])<Pty_@(s,[B,e2])$ (i.e., the priority of [A,e1] is lower than that of [B,e2] at state s). Then, when a process detects the aforementioned collision, it takes one of the following actions:

1. If this process has taken [A,e1], it backtracks to the vertex N where the collision occurs by discarding its path beyond N, and then follows [B,e2]. In order to let the other processes know its backtracking step, it also transmits a confirmation signal for [B,e2] with logical time t.

2. If this process has taken [B,e2], it does not need to backtrack because transition [B,e2] has precedence over transition [A,e1] at vertex N.

In the example of Figure 3, suppose that the priority of transition [B,e2] is higher than that of transition [A,e1] at vertex N0. Let S_a and S_b denote the signals transmitted by processes A and B when they collide at N0 by initiating [A,e1] and [B,e2], respectively. Then, when process A receives signal S_b at vertex N1, it detects the collision at N0. According to the collision resolution scheme it backtracks to N0, follows the transition [B,e2] at N0, and transmits a confirmation signal for [B,e2] with logical time t. On the other hand, when process B receives signal S_a at vertex N2, it also detects the collision at N0. However, it does not need to backtrack because [B,e2] has a higher priority than [A,e1] at N0.

In summary, the synchronization mechanism of PDCPD can help communicating processes detect and resolve collisions during protocol execution. Collisions can be detected by path recording. Two items of information, logical time and confirmation, are necessary for correct path recording. Once a collision is detected, a priority assignment and a backtracking scheme are used to resolve it.

PDCPD has been applied to several real protocols, including CCITT′s X.21 Recommendation [4], to demonstrate its usefulness and advantages. In the case of X.21, we have found that all the errors discovered in this protocol by various research groups are caused by collisions [15, 18, 19]. We have demonstrated that these errors can be easily resolved by the use of PDCPD. The details of this application are reported in [11, 12, 13].

5. Verification of PDCPD

In the previous section we have informally discussed the synchronization mechanism of PDCPD. We have used a simple example (illustrated in Figure 3) to demonstrate how communicating processes use the information of logical time and confirmation as well as the priority assignment and backtracking scheme to detect and resolve collisions. The reader may be suspicious, however, whether our methododlogy can be applied to more complex examples. One way to test the applicability of PDCPD is to apply it to real protocols, as we did to CCITT′s X.21 Recommendation. Nevertheless, the ultimate question is: Is PDCPD workable on arbitrary protocols? In this section we use a program verification technique to prove that PDCPD is applicable to designing any protocol which operates in the environment described in Section 3.

The reason for using program verification techniques stems from the observation that PDCPD is an algorithm, and that high-level programming languages provide a clear and concise means of describing algorithms. Furthermore, even though the current Floyd/Hoare style verification techniques are still clumsy to use, the process of verification provides a precise way to understand what an algorithm does. If the principles used in verification techniques are followed to develop algorithms, the well-structuredness of the algorithms can often be achieved.

The language we use for the specification of PDCPD is Hoare's <u>Communicating Sequential Processes</u> (CSP) [9]. CSP is a language for describing interprocess communication through the transmission and reception of signals (messages) instead of shared variables. This feature is suitable for the environment described in Section 3. Moreover, by using CSP's nondeterministic alternative commands, repetitive commands and I/O commands, we can specify the interactions among communicating processes in a concise and elegant way. Therefore, we adopt CSP as the language for specifying PDCPD. In order to model the asynchronous operations of communicating processes, however, we must eliminate the rendezvous assumption of CSP (i.e., a transmitting process is delayed until some process is ready to receive the signal) from our specification. The reader is refered to [9] for the details of CSP.

Figure 4 shows the specification of PDCPD written in CSP. We assume there are n processes $P_1, \ldots, P_n$ involved in a given protocol @. The entire system is specified as a concurrent program $[P_1 || \ldots || P_n]$. However, it is very difficult, if not impossible, to explain this specification without getting into a lengthy discussion. Due to the limit of space, we will omit this painstaking explanation, but the interested reader is referred to [13] for the detail of our specification. It is worth mentioning, however, that Figure 4 represents only one of many alternative ways for specifying PDCPD. We must say that our specification is concerned more with ease in verification than with efficency in execution.

Currently there are several verification systems for CSP [1, 10, 16], but all these systems are still quite difficult to use. Therefore, we have developed a verification system of our own, incorporating the advantages of the other systems. The interested reader is referred to [13] for the detail of our system. Here we only describe the basic scheme used by our system in proving concurrent programs.

Developing the proof of a concurrent program using our verfication system consists of two steps:

1. Developing proofs for each process. The proof of an individual process accounts for the process' effect on its local variables and the channels connected to it.

2. Combining the proofs of individual processes to derive the desired system properties.

The proof of an individual process basically follows the standard Floyd/Hoare techniques for proving sequential programs. To prove a sequential program S is like proving a theorem {P} S {Q} in a deductive system consisting of axioms and rules of inference that define the semantics of statements used in S. Informally, {P} S {Q} means that if assertion P is true before S is executed, then assertion Q is true when S terminates. In such a proof P is the assumption under which program S begins execution, and Q is the property that results from the execution of S, given P.

While combining individual proofs, our verification provides a means to identify the assumptions made by each process and has a rule of inference to examine whether all the assumptions support each other.

```
A Terminating Specification of PDCPD for a Given Protocol @:

            [P_1||...||P_n],

where P_1,...,P_n are n communicating processes involved in @.

Specification of an Individual Process P_i:

/ variable list:
    path_{i,i} :  the path of process P_i;
    path_{i,j} :  the path of process P_j recorded
                  by process P_i (i≠j);
    h-path     :  the path with the highest precedence among
                  path_{i,1},...,path_{i,n};
    ‖S‖        :  the cardinality of set S.

  abbreviation: Π_{i=1,...,n}S_i abbreviates S_1;...;S_n.

/ All the paths are empty before the program begins. /

path_{i,1},...,path_{i,n} :=Λ,...,Λ;

h-path :=Λ;

*[  / P_i receives a signal <[P,e],t> from P_j. /
  □_{P_j∈PROCESS_@ & P_j≠P_i}
    {path_{i,i}≠path_{i,j} ∨ ¬FINAL_@(State_@(path_{i,i}))} P_j?<[P,e],t> -->
      path_{i,j} := Path_{@,j}(path_{i,j},<[P,e],t>);
      [ h-path<_@path_{i,j} --> h-path:=path_{i,j} ]

    / P_i initiates event e at the end of path_{i,i}. /
  □_{e∈EVENT_@}{[P_i,e]∈OT_@(State_@(path_{i,i})) & h-path<_@path_{i,i}∘[P_i,e]} -->
      Π_{P_j∈PROCESS_@ & P_j≠P_i} P_j!<[P_i,e],|path_{i,i}|>;
      path_{i,i},h-path := path_{i,i}∘[P_i,e],path_{i,i}∘[P_i,e]

    / P_i "catches up" h-path by taking transition [P_k,e]
      which is on h-path. /
  □_{P_k∈PROCESS_@ & e∈EVENT_@}
    {path_{i,i}<h-path & [P_k,e]=Elem(h-path,|path_{i,i}|)
     & path_{i,i}∘[P_k,e]≮path_{i,k}} -->
    [ {‖OT_@(State_@(path_{i,i}))‖>1 ∨ FINAL_@(State_@(path_{i,i}∘[P_k,e]))} -->
        / P_i transmits a confirmation about transition [P_k,e]. /
        Π_{P_j∈PROCESS_@ & P_j≠P_i} P_j!<[P_k,e],|path_{i,i}|> ];
    path_{i,i} := path_{i,i}∘[P_k,e]

   / P_i backtracts to Common(h-path,path_{i,i})
     and transmits a confirmation about transition [P_k,e]. /
  □_{P_k∈PROCESS_@ & e∈EVENT_@}
   {path_{i,i}≮h-path & [P_k,e]=Elem(h-path,|Common(h-path,path_{i,i})|)
    & Common(h-path,path_{i,i})∘[P_k,e]≮path_{i,k}} -->
   Π_{P_j∈PROCESS_@ & P_j≠P_i} P_j!<[P_k,e],|Common(h-path,path_{i,i})|>;
   path_{i,i} := Common(h-path,path_{i,i})∘[P_k,e]
]
```

Figure 4: Specification of PDCPD

The unique characteristic of our verification system is the standardized use of assumptions constructed from history variables. Our verification system uses history variables that record the sequences of signals that are input and output of the communicating processes. Figure 5 depicts our scheme. Suppose P_i and P_j are two communicating processes. Then history variable $OUT_{i,j}$ denotes the sequence of output signals which process P_i has transmitted to process P_j while variable $IN_{j,i}$ denotes the sequence of input signals which P_j has actually received from P_i. Because communication channels are assumed to be FIFO and error-free, the existence of signal propagation delay implies that $IN_{j,i}$ must always be some initial subsequence of $OUT_{i,j}$. (Suppose A and B are two sequences and the length of A and B are denoted as |A| and |B|. Then we say A is an initial subsequence of B if |A|<=|B| and the two sequences have the same first |A| elements.) We have found that using this proof scheme helps reduce complexity in verifying many input/output-oriented concurrent programs.

The specification of PDCPD given in Figure 4 has been proved by our verification system. To present the proof of PDCPD, we must first define the following notation.

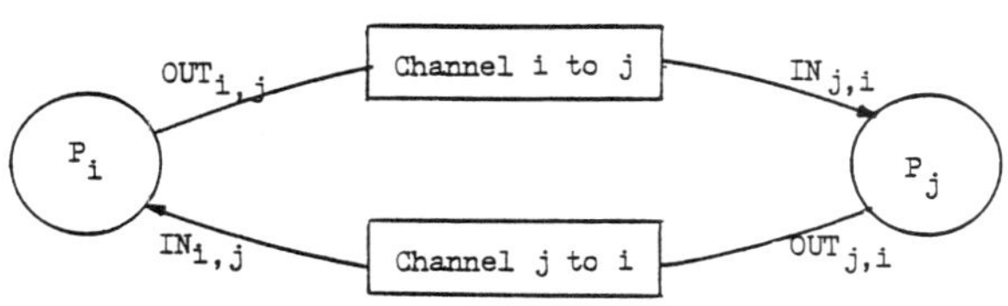

Figure 5: History variables

Given an arbitrary protocol @, let $STATE_@$, $EVENT_@$ and $PROCESS_@$ be the sets of states, events and processes in this protocol, respectively. We assume there are n communicating processes $P_1,\ldots,P_n$ involved in @; i.e., $PROCESS_@=\{P_1,\ldots,P_n\}$. We use $Tr_@$ to denote the transition function of @; i.e., $Tr_@$ maps $STATE_@ \times [PROCESS_@ \times EVENT_@]$ into $STATE_@$ such that if $[P_i,e_j]$ is a transition from s_1 to s_2, then $Tr_@(s_1,[P_i,e_j])=s_2$. We assume that $Tr_@(s_1,[P_i,e_j])$ is undefined if $[P_i,e_j]$ is not an output transition at state s1.

Let $FINAL_@$ be a boolean function over $STATE_@$ such that $FINAL_@(s)$=<u>true</u> if and only if s is a final state in @. We use $PATH_@$ to denote the set of paths from the initial state in @. We record a path of @ as a sequence of transitions. For example, [X,e1]∘[Z,e3]∘[Y,e2] (∘ denotes the concatenation operator) is a path of the protocol in Figure 1. If both P′ and P″ belong to $PATH_@$, then we say P′ is a **subpath** of P″ in @ if P′ is an initial subsequence of P″ and denote this condition by $P' \preccurlyeq P''$.

Let $State_@$ be a function mapping $PATH_@$ into $STATE_@$ such that if $P' \in PATH_@$, then $State_@(P')$ is the resulting state of P′. For example, we have $State_@([X,e1]\circ[Z,e3]\circ[Y,e2])=s8$ if @ is the protocol given in Figure 1. This function can be defined recursively as follows:

$$State_@(\Lambda) = s_0,$$

$$State_@(P' \circ [P_i,e_j]) = Tr_@(State_@(P'),[P_i,e_j]),$$

where Λ represents an empty path and s_0 is the initial state of @. Notice that $State_@(P')$ is defined if and only if $P' \in PATH_@$.

According to the synchronization mechanism described in Section 4, each process records the paths of the other processes in order to detect and resolve collisions. Restricted by our communication environment, a process can record the path of another process only from the signals received from the latter. We use $Path^*_{@,j}$ to denote a function such that if $IN_{i,j}$ is the sequence of signals which process P_i has received from process P_j, then in P_i the recorded path of P_j is the value of $Path^*_{@,j}(\Lambda,IN_{i,j})$.

The main body of the specification of an individual process in PDCPD (see Figure 4) is a big repetitive statement. Process P_i uses variable $path_{i,i}$ to record the path of itself, and uses variable $path_{i,j}$ to record the path of another process P_j. In the proofs of individual processes, we have proved that the following two assertions, among others, are loop-invariants (a loop-invariant is an assertion whose truth is preserved by each iteration of the repetitive statement) for process P_i:

$$\forall P_j \in PROCESS_@ \ \&\ P_j \neq P_i \cdot (path_{i,j}=Path^*_{@,j}(\Lambda,IN_{i,j})) \qquad \text{<L1>}$$

$$\forall P_j \in PROCESS_@ \ \&\ P_j \neq P_i \cdot (Path^*_{@,i}(\Lambda,OUT_{i,j}) \preccurlyeq path_{i,i}) \qquad \text{<L2>}$$

<L1> states that the recorded path of process P_j in process P_i is determined by the value of $Path^*_{@,j}(\Lambda,IN_{i,j})$, as already mentioned in this section. On the other hand, <L2> states that $Path^*_{@,i}(\Lambda,OUT_{i,j})$ is always a subpath of $path_{i,i}$. The proof of <L1> and <L2> is quite complicated and are omitted in this paper.

Having verified the above loop-invariants, we then combine the individual proofs to derive the desired system properites. We have proved that, when the concurrent program $[P_1||\ldots||P_n]$ terminates, the communicating processes satisfy the following two properties:

$$path_{1,1} = \ldots = path_{n,n} \qquad \text{<S1>}$$

$$\forall P_i \in PROCESS_@ \cdot (FINAL_@(State_@(path_{i,i}))) \qquad \text{<S2>}$$

<S1> states that, when the concurrent program terminates, the paths of the individual processes are all equivalent. According to our observation on collisions, this assertion is true only if all the collisions occurred during communication have been correctly detected and resolved. <S2> states that, when the program terminates, all processes reach a final state. The proof of these properties is given below.

According to the semantics of CSP, when the concurrent program $[P_1||....||P_n]$ terminates, all the guards of the guarded loop repetitive statement in process P_i must be false. Therefore, the proof of <S2> is obvious because predicate $\sim FINAL_@(State_@(path_{i,i}))$ is a part of a guard of the loop statement in P_i. Using the same principle, we also have

$$\forall P_j \in PROCESS_@ \;\&\; P_j \neq P_i \cdot (path_{i,j} = path_{i,i}) \qquad \text{<P1>}$$

We have proved that, when the aforementioned concurrent program terminates, all the transmitted signals must have been received (the proof of termination will not presented here). Therefore, when the program terminates, we have

$$\forall P_i \& P_j \in PROCESS_@ \; (IN_{i,j} = OUT_{j,i}) \qquad \text{<P2>}$$

Combine <P2> with <L1> and <L2>, we get

$$\begin{aligned} path_{i,j} &= Path^*_{@,j}(\Lambda, IN_{i,j}) && \text{(By <L1>)} \\ &= Path^*_{@,j}(\Lambda, OUT_{j,i}) && \text{(By <P2>)} \\ &\preccurlyeq path_{j,j} && \text{(By <L2>)} \end{aligned}$$

Then from <P1>, we get

$$path_{i,i} \preccurlyeq path_{j,j} \qquad \text{<P3>}$$

The above argument is also valid for process P_j; therefore,

$$path_{j,j} \preccurlyeq path_{i,i} \qquad \text{<P4>}$$

Then <S1> can be concluded from <P3> and <P4>.

Because the above proof does not use any property that is particular to the given protocol @, we have therefore proved that PDCPD is applicable to arbitrary protocols.

6. Summary

In this paper, we have presented a new methodology for designing reliable communication protocols, called Priority Driven Communication Protocol Design (PDCPD). We have discussed the synchronization mechanism which PDCPD uses to detect and resolve collisions. The synchronization mechanism utilizes two items of information, logical time and confirmation, to enable communicating processes to detect collisions. It uses a priority assignment as well as a backtracking scheme to help processes resolve collisions once they are detected. The advantages of using PDCPD for protocol design are that the design task can be simplified and that the validation complexity can be reduced.

We have also used Hoare's Communicating Sequential Processes (CSP) to specify PDCPD. This specification has been verified by a Floyd/Hoare style of program verification technique to prove that PDCPD is applicable to any protocol which operates in a certain environment. The verification has been divided into two stages. We first verify the individual processes, and the individual proofs are then combined to derive the desired system properties. Because the proof is independent of any particular property of the given protocol, we conclude that PDCPD is applicable to designing arbitrary protocols.

Bibliography

1 Apt, K.R., N. Francez and W.P. DeRoever "A Proof System for Communicating Sequential Processes", ACM Transactions on Programming Languages and Systems 2, 3, July 1980, 359-385.

2 Bochmann, G.V. "Finite State Description of Communication Protocols", Proceedings, Symposium on Computer Network Protocols, February 1978, F3.1-F3.11.

3 Bochmann, G.V. and C.A. Sunshine "Formal Methods in Communication Protocol Design", IEEE Transactions on Communications COM-28, 4, April 1980, 624-631.

4 "Recommendation X.21" (amended), CCITT, Document AP VI, No .55-E, Geneva, Switzerland, 1976.

5 Day, J.D. and C.A. Sunshine, editors "A Bibliography on the Formal Specification and Verification of Computer Networks Protocols", ACM SIGCOMM Computer Communication Review 9, 4, October 1979, 23-39.

6 Floyd, R.W. "Assigning Meanings to Programs", Proceedings, Symposia in Applied Mathematics XIX, American Mathematical Society, 1967, 19-32.

7 Hailpern, B. and S. Owicki "Verifying Protocols Using Temporal Logic", Proceedings, Trends and Applications: 1980 Computer Network Protocols, May 1980, 18-28.

8 Hoare, C.A.R. "An Axiomatic Basis for Computer Programming", Communications ACM 12, 5, May 1969, 576-580.

9 Hoare, C.A.R. "Communicating Sequential Processes", Communications ACM 21, 8, August 1978, 666-677.

10 Levin, G.M. "Proof Rules for Communicating Sequential Processes", PhD Thesis, Cornell University, Ithaca, N.Y., 1980.

11 Lin, H. and M.T. Liu "Priority Driven Communication Protocol Design", Proceedings, 3rd International Conference on Distributed Computing Systems, October 1982, 371-378.

12 Lin, H., M.T. Liu, and C.J. Graff "A Methodology for Reliable Communications Protocol Design", Proceedings, ICC83, Boston, Massachusetts, June 19-22, 1983, E5.2.1-E5.2.6.

13 Lin, H. "A Methodology for Designing Reliable Communication Protocols", PhD Thesis, The Ohio State University, Columbus, Ohio, September 1983.

14 Le Moli, G. "A Theory of Colloquies", Proceedings, First European Workshop on Computer Networks, 1973, 153-173.

15 Razouk, R. and G. Estrin "Modeling and Verification of Communication Protocols in SARA: The X.21 Interface", IEEE Transactions on Computers C-29, 12, December 1980, 1052-1083.

16 Soundararajan, N. and O-J. Dahl "Partial Correctness Semantics of Communicating Sequential Processes", Research Report No. 66, Institute of Informatics, University of Oslo, February 1982.

17 Sunshine, C. "Formal Techniques for Protocol Specification and Verification", Computer 12, 9, September 1979, 20-27.

18 Umbaugh, L.D. and M.T. Liu "A Comparison of Communications Protocol Validation Techniques", Proceedings, International Conference on Communications, ICC82, June 1982, 4C.4.1-4C.4.7.

19 West, C.H. and P. Zafiropulo "Automated Validation of a Communications Protocol: The CCITT X.21 Recommendation", IBM Journal of Research and Development 22, 1, January 1978, 60-71.

ANALYSIS OF RELIABLE MULTICAST ALGORITHMS FOR LOCAL NETWORKS[1]

by Paul V. Mockapetris

USC Information Sciences Institute

Marina del Rey, California

Abstract

Local networks offer unique opportunities for supporting multicast transmissions. This paper describes and analyzes several families of multicast algorithms for local networks. The algorithms examined provide reliable service by dealing with the effects of transmission errors.

Introduction

Local networks use transmission media that make all transmissions equally available to all network interfaces; point-to-point communication is simulated by having all network interfaces but the one at the desired destination discard the transmission. These systems have the potential capability of distributing a single transmission to many destinations at the same cost as a point-to-point transmission. This raw broadcast capability is used sparingly by existing networks because of the cost and difficulty of transforming the raw capability into services which are compatible with existing high level protocols and appropriate to processes' needs. This paper compares algorithms for implementing reliable broadcast transmissions (one to all) as well as reliable multicast transmissions (one to a selected subset of all) in the context of existing bus and ring local networks, and also discusses modifications to link level hardware which improve multicast performance.

[1]This research was supported by the Defense Advanced Research Projects Agency under contract no. MDA903-81-C-0355. Views and conclusions contained in this report are the author's and should not be interpreted as representing the official opinion or policy of DARPA, the U.S. government, or any person or agency connected with them.

Interprocess communication need not be restricted to a single destination; a source process often needs to distribute the same information to several destination processes. When the target processes are distributed among local network hosts, we would like to use the broadcast capability of the medium to improve performance. Two forms of this type of communication are broadcast, in which a given transmission goes to all destinations, and multicast, in which information is sent to a specified subset of all destinations.

Because high level protocols allow every process to act as one or more destinations, broadcast has few applications at the process level; essentially no information is relevant to all processes in a network. Applications which use broadcast algorithms, such as routing update systems[1], depend on addressing or some other mechanism to restrict the transmission. Thus broadcast services usually appear at a lower level of any system which supplies multicast services; should broadcast be needed at the higher level, it is treated as a special case of multicast. For example, network interfaces that recognize multicast addresses usually are based on a broadcast medium; interfaces that recognize a single broadcast address rely on host software to convert the broadcasts to multicast.

Whether implemented implicitly or explicitly, multicast transmissions are inherent in any application which includes a distributed database[2,3,4,5,6]. Multicast transmissions can search for an object among a set of server processes or inform all concerned processes of an event. Multicast queries enable multiple database servers to process queries in parallel. Multicast transmissions are useful in the update process; multicast allows for rapid update of redundant copies as well as rapid distribution of "ballots" in voting systems.

These goals imply the metrics which should be used to evaluate the effectiveness of any multicast system:

Speed

Multicast services should be able to provide significantly faster service than the equivalent set of one-to-one transmissions. There are two times of interest. The *distribution* time is the time it takes for all multicast set members to receive a particular distribution. This time is especially important if the purpose is to allow parallelism. The *completion* time is the time it takes for the sender to know that all destinations have reliably received the distribution. This time is of special interest in update operations, and is also important in queries or searches when failure is detected as an absence of responses to a query. Both times can be measured in the number of transmissions necessary to achieve the corresponding result.

Cost

Multicast operation have two types of cost: bandwidth on the medium and computation in the hosts. The bandwidth on the medium can be expressed as a transmission count. Host loading is measured in terms of the number of packet processing events (i.e. packet reception or transmission) that occur in the involved hosts. In a one-to-one transmission, the packet count is one, and the packet events are two, one for the sender and one for the receiver. With multicast, a given transmission will cost at least a transmission by the sender and receptions by every member in the multicast set.

Compatibility

Multicast transmissions should follow the form and usage of one-to-one transmissions where possible. At the process level, the main difficulty is in reporting the result of a transmission request; rather than a simple success or failure, a multicast transmission may encounter success with some members of the multicast set and failure with others. Parallel difficulties arise with protocol definitions and mechanisms for sequencing, flow control, connection management, etc.

Reliability

Some applications do not require absolute reliability. For example, a voting system may only need to generate a majority, and hence could use a slightly unreliable multicast facility. However, the majority of update and search applications are best served by reliable multicast. Even systems that have higher level error correction can benefit by avoiding the cost and delays associated with higher-level recovery mechanisms when databases are resynchronized.

Set definition

Existing mechanisms for defining the processes that belong in a particular multicast group are not very general. For example, the Ethernet[7] uses a special address for each multicast set; each host that contains processes in multicast sets must recognize the set address(es) as well as the unique interface address. The network interfaces designed for the DCS system[8] contained special hardware to allow wildcarding of selected components of a segmented address. In both cases, address slots in the interface represent a limited resource that must be managed. Both systems rely on well known multicast set addresses, and hence do not allow dynamic creation of new sets.

Several proposals have been made for improving this type of mechanism. Rowe[9], Pardo[10], and others have proposed more sophisticated address recognition schemes that would allow multicast addresses to contain the equivalent of a function. For example, a multicast address might contain a component similar to a conventional multicast address which identifies a set of eligible processes (e.g. all database servers for employee records), as well as an application-specific predicate component (e.g. which are inverted by age). Both components would have a standard format. The first component would be a well-known value; the second component would have a standard interpretation but process specific values. For example, in the database case mentioned above, there would be a bit in the second component corresponding to each type of inversion kept in the databases. Boolean functions[9,10] and regular expressions[11] have been proposed for the evaluation predicate.

Set definition mechanisms must often provide other parts of the multicast support with information regarding the multicast set's population. For example, systems which collect separate acknowledgment transmissions (ACKs) from each member of the multicast set must know how many members are currently in the set. If the predicate systems are used, sequence numbers must be updated in both members of the set that pass the predicate test as well as those that do not. Population information must track arrivals and departures from the multicast set. Ideally, we would like a scheme where the sender doesn't need this type of information unless required by the application (i.e. determining the number of processes that constitute a majority.)

Further work is needed in this area, and is beyond the scope of this paper.

Multicast implementations

Reliable multicast transmission can be decomposed into separate actions:

1. Assignment of a multicast set address.

2. A distribution transmission, and possibly retransmissions, that place the information to be multicast onto the medium.

3. Reception of the distribution transmission in the target hosts, followed by processing to discard duplicates and to route the information to target processes.

4. Generation and transmission of acknowledgments from receivers to the sending host.

5. Acknowledgment processing at the sending host.

This model illustrates the main performance issues in multicast.

The first of these is optimizing the performance of packet primitives in the network interface. Our goal is to optimize the multicast potential of the medium without incurring excessive cost in terms of processing events in the receivers of the distribution. This goal is achieved through measures to improve the probability that transmissions are successful and measures to rapidly discard irrelevant or duplicate transmissions. In this regard, multicast is more sensitive to the effects of errors than one-to-one transmission because although a failure may still double the cost, the cost of multicast increases with the size of the multicast set.

We also want to optimize the acknowledgment algorithm. In multicast, there is more distinct acknowledgment information than data to be acknowledged; hence special acknowledgment algorithms may be justified.

In the next two sections we examine these problems, and then compare the performance of several combinations of packet processing primitives and acknowledgment algorithms.

Packet primitives strategies and costs

Several techniques for improving interface performance are already in use in various systems. Interfaces should recognize multicast addresses instead of a single broadcast address; thus hosts that are not in the multicast set won't have to expend time to discard extraneous packets. Network interfaces can minimize packet loss through full duplex operation and by buffering strategies that allow reception of back-to-back packets from the medium. A fairly simple extension to this scheme would be to reserve a buffer for each multicast connection so that multicast distributions would never be discarded due to lack of resources.

In situations such as saturation, where the ACK reliability isn't a problem, but the distribution may still need retransmission, duplicate detection can be made automatic by using two multicast addresses and a variation on the alternating bit protocol[12]. In this scheme, called *parity*, the sender uses one address for the initial transmission *and all retransmissions* of a message, and then switches to the other address for the next message. The receivers change addresses whenever they successfully copy a new message. Receivers that miss a message stay with the old address and eventually receive a retransmission; receivers that copy a message are spared receiving any future retransmissions. The parity system requires restrictions on the packet lifetime and outstanding messages that are rarely a problem in a local network.

The ultimate in performance is achieved by a network interface that performs duplicate detection, ACK generation, and ACK reception without host intervention. These interfaces are referred to as *filter* interfaces in further discussion. The parity scheme is a primitive example of automatic duplicate detection; various interfaces, such as the Hyperchannel[13] and others[14] incorporate automatic ACK generation, though at a low level in the protocol hierarchy. A scheme for a high-level version is described by Mockapetris[11]. These acknowledgments are transmitted immediately following the distribution they acknowledge, and hence are called *prompt* ACKs.

Acknowledgment strategies and costs

The focus for acknowledgments is eliminating the cost of ACK transmissions, either by moving the cost into the network interface or by reducing the number of ACKs required. Four types of multicast algorithms are considered:

1. Simulation algorithms, which achieve the effect of multicast using separate one-to-one transmissions. These algorithms are primarily of interest as a baseline for comparison.

2. Multiple acknowledgment algorithms, which distribute the multicast text using some sort of one-to-many transmission, but collect ACKs via one-to-one transmissions. These algorithms are representative of today's systems.

3. Saturation algorithms, which rely on statistical arguments to avoid the need for acknowledgments.

4. Negative acknowledgment (NACK) algorithms, which require filtering and generate transmissions only when a transfer fails.

Simulation algorithms

The most straightforward way for a network which lacks any sort of one-to-many transmission capability to simulate multicast is for the sender to transmit separate messages to each destination and receive separate ACKs in return. Each destination requires two transmissions, so that a multicast set of N destinations requires 2N transmissions. Each transmission is created and received by a host, so a grand total of 4N packets are processed by all hosts. This method is usually the most expensive, but can be used with any medium or system of protocols. It requires all senders to maintain lists of multicast set members. Assuming that the receivers transmit ACKs as soon as they receive the distribution, approximately 2N-1 transmissions will take place before all receivers have the distribution. Lost packets, whether distributions or ACKs, will result in 2 additional transmissions and 4 packet events.

If all hosts have filter interfaces, prompt ACKs replace host-generated ACKs and save 50 percent of both metrics.

An alternate method is to use a software ring of destinations: the source transmits the message to the first destination, which forwards the message to the next destination, etc. The last destination returns the message or an ACK to the sender. If intermediate ACKs are not returned, a total of N+1 transmissions are required. The advantages of this scheme are the reduction in traffic, and that the sender needn't maintain a list of all destinations; each member need only remember the next member. Each member of the set can also add new members. The drawbacks of this scheme are its slowness, since all transmissions are made in series, and its unfavorable performance in the presense of transient errors or host failures. When a packet is lost, the entire cost is doubled. No performance advantage is gained by using filter interfaces in this scheme.

Separate acknowledgment algorithms

The archetypes of multicast algorithms for a local network rely on various types of one-to-many distribution followed by one-to-one ACKs. The message is distributed in one transmission; N ACKs are subsequently returned. The host event cost includes the distribution transmission and N receptions; acknowledgments generate 2N events unless filter

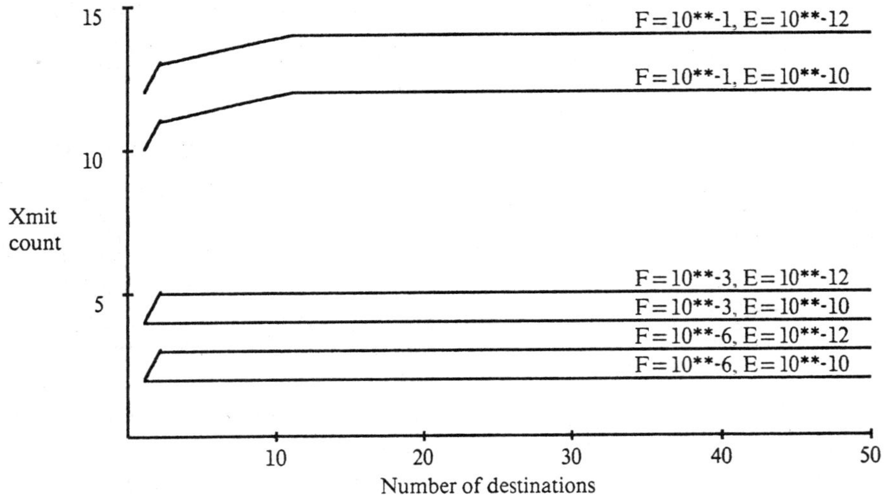

Figure 1 - Multicast saturation transmission counts

interfaces process the ACKs. In general, the cost of acknowledgments is greater than the cost of the message distribution.

The main variability in cost is due to the different number of hosts which may receive the one-to-many message. In a network with C hosts, a message addressed to the broadcast address is seen by all C hosts; if a multicast address is available, only the N destinations see the message.

These algorithms can be used with either a bus or a ring. However, the controlled access provided by a token system avoids the likely collisions between ACKs for a bus system. In systems where bus length reduces the effectiveness of carrier sense, some collisions are inevitable unless special pains are taken to spread out the ACKs; in the simplest CSMA system, these ACKs will often be precisely synchronized by the distribution transmission or other network traffic.

Saturation algorithms

Saturation algorithms do not use ACKs; instead they make a statistical argument about the probability of transmitting at least one copy of the message to every member of the multicast set. The basic principle is to transmit enough copies of the message to insure that at least one copy gets through to every destination.

If E is the probability that one or more destinations will not get the multicast (i.e. the desired overall error rate of multicast transmissions), and F is the the probability that a single network interface will fail to copy a multicast transmission (i.e. the link level error rate), then we wish to solve for M, the number of transmissions which are required to send to a set of N hosts with probability E of failure. The probability of success for each host is

$$1-F^M$$

hence for all N hosts

$$1-E = (1-F^M)^N$$

solving for M

$$M = \frac{\log(1-(1-E)^{1/N})}{\log(F)} \qquad (1)$$

Figure 1 graphs M rounded to the next higher integer for several combinations of E and F.

For N = 1, M is equal to log(F)/log(E), that is, the ratio of the exponents of the error rates. M grows very slowly as N increases. Intuitively, this is because each additional destination benefits from the transmissions required by the other destinations. Contemporary network designs typically strive for an error rate E of 10^{-10} to 10^{-12}, although few empirical measurements have been made. Hence choosing a value for E is not a problem. The problem is determining the correct value for F, the interface-to-interface probability of packet loss. F is affected by several factors:

1. Errors due to line noise, clock-recovery errors, transmitter-receiver errors, and other noise-related problems in the hardware.

2. Transmissions which are discarded due to half-duplex interfaces.

3. Transmissions which are discarded due to interfaces which have a "recovery" time following receipt of a message before another message can be received.

4. Transmissions which are discarded due to lack of buffer space in the interface or host.

The noise component is fairly well understood. Shoch[15] reports that measurements on the Ethernet showed that a poorly designed interface had an error rate of 10^{-3}, whereas a well-designed interface had an error rate of less than 10^{-6} The point-to-point communication links used in a ring do even better.

The remaining components are difficult to quantify because they are dependent on host and network load, and the retransmission policy followed by the sender. The preceding analysis depends on the fact that the transmissions are independent trials with a constant probability of success; even if this is a good assumption most of the time in real systems, it is almost impossible to know F exactly. Filter interfaces have a real advantage since they can eliminate these causes of packet loss. Conventional networks can still use saturation algorithms, but only at an artificially high value of F.

The packet events cost is very sensitive to the interface capabilities. A saturation algorithm used with a broadcast interface results in every host on the network having to process M packets; similarly a multicast address has every member of the multicast set processing M packets. In both cases, approximately M-1 of these packets are of no value and are discarded. A network of filtering interfaces is dramatically better because the duplicates are discarded by the interface.

These algorithms are also attractive in situations where the multicast set is large; in situations where collection of ACKs can be difficult; in situations where quick delivery is more important than host processing costs; and in situations where F is well known. Because this algorithm assumes that errors will occur, its behavior is the same whether or not errors occur.

Negative acknowledgment algorithms

The strength of the saturation algorithm is that it avoids the need for N ACKs; its primary weakness is its inability to deal with interfaces which are unable to receive due to buffering problems and other load-induced conditions which may persist for indeterminate time. The independent trials assumption at the heart of the theoretical model is very difficult to realize in practice.

This problem is avoided by negative acknowledgment (NACK) algorithms, which assume filter interfaces. Members of the multicast set which receive the message correctly don't transmit a prompt ACK; member of the multicast set which would like to be able to copy the message, but cannot, send a prompt NACK. The NACK demands a retransmission by the sender of the distribution message. Because NACK generation requires no resources, interfaces can always generate NACKs. Thus load-induced conditions are removed from estimates of F, and F is driven by the noise-related causes which presumably are random.

NACK algorithms relate to separate acknowledgment algorithms in that the termination conditions are equivalent under DeMorgan's law. A separate acknowledgment system terminates on the basis of a logical AND condition over the individual ACKs; the NACK algorithm relies on the logical NOR of NACK transmissions. The functional difference is that the NOR predicate can be deduced from any single destination which sends a NACK; the AND requires all results. In use this means that the NACK protocol doesn't need to know how many destinations are in the multicast set; this is somewhat of a disadvantage in that it cannot detect destination failures that lose state, such as a host crash and restart.

In a bus system, multiple destinations may wish to send a NACK, and these transmissions will collide. However, the presence or absence of a NACK is all the information which is required. Hence NACKs could use the same mechanism that is used to achieve collision consensus enforcement; the collision is equivalent to a NACK. In order to guarantee an acceptable level of reliability, the sender should retransmit until M transmissions have *not* resulted in NACKs (collisions); these extra transmissions are required for bit errors in the receivers which are not due to causes that the sender can detect.

In a ring network, the NACK system can be particularly reliable and effective. The sender transmits the distribution message followed by a "blank" message. If both return unchanged to the sender, then the multicast is complete. If any destination is unable to copy the distribution message, it overlays the blank message with a NACK. This scheme is superior to the *match/accept* bit scheme used in the RI[16] and LNI[8] in that it neither requires that the interfaces examine bits

Table 1 - Best case multicast algorithm comparison

Major algorithm	Option used	distribution time	completion time	packet events	per error events
Simulate	one by one	2N-1	2N	4N	4
	filter ACKs	2N-1	2N	N+1	1
	software ring	N	N+1	2(N+1)	2(N+1)
Separate ACKs	broadcast address	1	N+1	C+2N+1	C+2N+1
	multicast address	1	N+1	3N+1	3N+1
	filter ACKs	1	N+1	N+1	2
Saturate	broadcast address	1	M	M(C+1)	0
	multicast address	1	M	M(N+1)	0
	filter/parity	1	M	N+M	0
NACK	ring	1	1	N+1	N+1
	Ethernet	1	M	N+1	0

Legend:

N = number of destinations desired

C = number of hosts on network

M = result of saturation formula (1); assuming single message error rate of 10^{-3} and desired net error rate of 10^{-12}, M = 5

of media data before changing them nor is it sensitive to a small number of bit errors. Instead, the destinations simply emit a prompt NACK and its associated CRC.

The logical extension to this ring scheme is to encode whether the message is a multicast or not as a bit in the message; the interface hardware could invert the sense of prompt ACKs automatically.

Algorithm comparisons

Table 1 summarizes the algorithm comparisons. The distribution time, completion time, and packet events columns assume that no packets are lost. The "per error events" column is the maximum cost of recovering from loss of one packet.

Any system that uses a multicast distribution channel has equivalent best case distribution time. However, when errors occur, the distribution time is related to the completion time because some estimate of the completion time is presumably included in the retransmission interval. Hence if it is important to bound the distribution time even in the presence of errors, NACK and saturation algorithms offer the best performance.

In systems using existing technology, the two most practical choices are multicast with separate ACKs and saturation using parity. In terms of completion time, the saturation algorithm is equivalent in cost at N=4 and better for larger multicast sets; each additional member saves one message. In terms of packet events, saturation is equivalent at N=2 and grows better at a rate of 2N; if the cost of error correction is considered, saturation is always better for any multicast. Saturation also has the advantage that the sender need not keep track of the current membership in the multicast set; given M's insensitivity to N, the sender does not even have to track the size of the multicast set. The only disadvantage to saturation is the difficulty in including load-induced packet loss into the basic channel error rate. As VLSI network chips become available that include buffer management, this problem should become quite tractable.

The algorithm comparison also suggests some directions for future development. The filtering concept doesn't improve the completion time unless it includes an inversion of acknowledgment strategy from ACKs to NACKs. Given the surprising success of saturation, it might be more worthwhile to concentrate on strategies for priority buffering so that the saturation estimate of F is improved.

References

1. McQuillan, J.M., Richer, I., and Rosen, E.C., "The New Routing Algorithm for the ARPANET," IEEE Transactions on Communications, Vol. com-28, no. 5, May 1980.

2. Gifford, D.K., "Weighted Voting for Replicated Data," Proceedings Seventh Symposium on Operating Systems Principles, December 1979.

3. Gifford, D.K., "Violet, an Experimental Decentralized System," XEROX PARC Technical Report CSL-79-12, September 1979.

4. Rothnie, J.B., Goodman, N., and Bernstein, P.A., "The Redundant Update Methodology of SDD-1: A System for Distributed Databases (The Fully Redundant Case), report no. CCA-77-02, Computer Corporation of America, 1977.

5. Stonebreaker, M., "Concurrency Control and Consistency of Multiple Copies of Data in Distributed INGRESS," IEEE Transactions on Software Engineering, May 1979, pp. 188-194.

6. Thomas, R.H., "A Majority Consensus Approach to Concurrency Control for Multiple Copy Databases, ACM Transactions on Database Systems, June 1979, pp. 180-20.9

7. Xerox Corp., Intel Corp., and Digital Equipment Corp., "The Ethernet, A Local Area Network, Data Link Layer and Physical Layer Specifications," Version 1.0, September 1980

8. Mockapetris, P.V., Lyle, M.R., and Farber, D.J., "On the Design of Local Network Interfaces," IFIP Congress, August 1977, pp. 427-430.

9. Rowe, L.A., Birman, K.P., "Network Support for a Distributed Data Base System," Proceedings Fourth Berkeley Conference on Distributed Data Bases and Computer Networks, 1979.

10. Pardo, R., and Liu, M.T.,"Multidestination protocols for distributed systems," Proceedings of the Computer Networking Symposium, National Bureau of Standards, Gaithersburg, Maryland, 1979.

11. Mockapetris, .P, "Communication Environments for Local Networks," USC Informations Sciences Institute Research Report ISI/RR-82-103, December 1982

12. Bartlett, K.A., Scantlebury, R.A., and Wilkenson, P.T., "A Note on Reliable Full-Duplex Transmission over Half-Duplex Links," CACM, vol 12, no 5, May 1969.

13. Thornton, James E., "Overview of the HYPERchannel," Proceedings COMPCON, 1979.

14. Tokoro, M., and Tamaru, K., "Acknowledging ETHERNET," Proceedings COMPCON, Fall 1977.

15. Shoch, J.F., and Hupp, J.A., "Performance of an Ethernet Local Network: A Preliminary Report," Proceedings of the local area communication network symposium, May 1979, pp. 113-125.

16. Mockapetris, P. , D.J. Farber. "Experiences with The Distributed Computer System," Technical Report 116, Department of Information and Computer Science, University of California, Irvine.

ANALYSIS OF RELIABLE BROADCAST IN LOCAL-AREA NETWORKS *

J.W. Wong and G. Gopal

Department of Computer Science
University of Waterloo, Waterloo, Ontario
Canada N2L 3G1

Abstract

The performance characteristics of a reliable broadcast protocol in a local-area network environment are analyzed. This protocol involves a source broadcasting a message to all destinations and collecting replies from these destinations. Reliability is achieved by using Send-and-Wait protocols for transmitting broadcast and reply messages. A queueing model is developed and results on the throughput and delay of the broadcast operation are obtained by approximate analysis. Numerical results showing the effect of model parameters on throughput are provided.

1. Introduction

Many applications make use of broadcast and multicast messages, notably distributed databases and distributed processing systems. For performance reasons, it is important that broadcasting and multicasting can be efficiently provided by the communication network. These applications may also require that such an operation be reliable, i.e. when a message is broadcast from a site, all destination sites are certain to receive it. However, most work on performance analysis of reliable communication has been in the area of point-to-point protocols and not much has been done on broadcasts and multicasts.

The cost of providing a completely reliable broadcast in a network environment may be prohibitively expensive. There is therefore a need to provide a range of protocols with different levels of reliability and associated costs. Pardo has defined a number of protocols dealing with the ability to recover the system state after hardware failure, either in a communication link or at one of the sites [1]. Some protocols for broadcast over a satellite channel have been specified and analyzed [2,3] but the analysis of reliable broadcast on local-area networks has received little attention.

In many applications, a message is broadcast to cause some action to take place at the destinations, or to elicit a response. So, if we consider broadcasting from the application's point-of-view, it can be classified into the following four categories :

1. Message is broadcast to N destinations and no reply is expected :- This situation occurs when the source would like some action to be performed at all destinations, e.g. synchronization of clocks at all sites.
2. Message is broadcast to N destinations and the first reply is used :- When a user wishes to make use of some service which may be provided by several processes, the first process to respond is used.
3. Message is broadcast to N destinations and the first $n<N$ replies are used :- Distributed database systems which use Thomas' concurrency control algorithm for synchronization fall into this category [4].
4. Message is broadcast to N destinations and replies from all N destinations are collected and then processed :- This operation may be used by many concurrency control algorithms for distributed databases [4-10].

In this paper, we study the performance of the fourth category of broadcast in a local-area network. For this category, we consider the broadcasting of message and the collection of all replies as constituting an operation. From the application's point-of-view, it is of interest to study the throughput and delay characteristics of this operation.

Our analysis is based on a broadcast protocol which is designed to operate reliably in a failure-free local network environment. By failure-free, we mean no hardware/software failures. However, messages may be lost due to transmission error or buffer limitations. All essential functions such as error-recovery, sequencing and flow control are done end-to-end by the application process, e.g. at the application layer of the OSI reference model [11]. The lower protocol layers provide a service with minimum complexity; an unacknowledged datagram service is assumed. Furthermore, we only consider the information transfer phase of the broadcast operation. It is assumed that the connections (at the application layer) necessary for information transfer have already been established.

Our reliable broadcast protocol (with replies) is described in section 2. A queueing model of this protocol in a local-area network is developed in section 3. The throughput and delay of broadcast are analyzed in sections 4 and 5. Finally, sample results of this study are presented in section 6.

2. Broadcast Protocol

Consider the local-area network shown in Figure 1. It consists of a number of user machines connected to a transmission medium through network adapters. The transmission medium is a broadcast medium where a message transmitted by one adapter may be received by all other adapters. Typical network topologies where this broadcast mechanism is possible are ring and bus.

* This work was supported by the Natural Sciences and Engineering Research Council of Canada.

In each user machine, broadcast requests are generated by an application process. These broadcasts are processed one at a time. For each broadcast, a complete operation consists of first broadcasting a message to all destinations (application processes in other machines) and then collecting all the replies. To ensure reliable communication, Send-and-Wait protocols [12] are used to perform the broadcast, and collect the replies.

For the broadcast phase, the message is prepared by the source application process and and passed to the datagram server process for transfer to the adapter which then broadcasts it to all destinations. Some destinations may not receive the message successfully because of transmission error or buffer shortage. To recover from lost messages, an interval timer is set by the source at the time the message is passed to the datagram server. Meanwhile, a destination which receives the broadcast message successfully will process the message to formulate a reply. This reply will be returned to the source, constituting a positive acknowledgement. If the timer expires before all replies are received, a multicast message with address indicating those destinations which have not returned the replies is prepared and passed to the datagram server. The timer is again started and this operation is repeated until replies are received from all destinations. When all replies have been received, the next broadcast message is prepared for transmission. Each broadcast message has a one-bit sequence number for the receiver to ignore duplicate messages.

A similar Send-and-Wait protocol is used to collect each reply. In this case, the reply is point-to-point (i.e. from a destination to the source of the broadcast). Positive acknowledgement can be provided by the next broadcast message, or by a separate control message.

The timeout interval is an important parameter in the above protocol. If the timout interval is too long, network performance may suffer because retransmission of lost messages is delayed. If the timeout interval is too short, frequent retransmissions may occur resulting in queueing delay at the datagram server. Note that the datagram server is responsible for transferring messages to/from the network adapter only, and does not access the contents of the message.

3. Queueing Model

In this section, a queueing model is developed for the broadcast protocol and local-area network under consideration. For simplicity, we consider only the case of one source performing broadcast to N ($N > 1$) destinations and collecting replies from these destinations. The queueing model is depicted in Figure 2.

A broadcast message is first prepared by the source. The preparation time $\tilde{x}$ is assumed to be exponentially distributed with mean $\frac{1}{\nu_s}$. This message then visits the "network server" at the source. The service time at this server corresponds to the aggregate of (a) the time to transfer the broadcast message to the source adapter, (b) the transmission time on the medium, and (c) transfer time from a receiving adapter to its corresponding destination process. This service time is assumed to be exponentially distributed with mean $\frac{1}{\mu_s}$.

Note that a queue may be formed in front of the network server at the source. This may be due to retransmission at the expiration of timeout, or a new broadcast which has been prepared. At each destination, the loss probability of a broadcast message is assumed to be independent and identical, and is denoted by L_s. As mentioned previously, such loss is due to transmission error or buffer shortage. For those destinations where loss does not occur, the broadcast message is assumed to be received at the same time.

At each destination, if a broadcast message is received successfully and this message is not a duplicate of a previously received message, a reply message is generated (duplicate messages are assumed to require zero processing time). The time to formulate a reply is exponentially distributed with mean $\frac{1}{\alpha}$. The reply is returned to the source by way of the the destination adapter, the transmission medium, and the source adapter. Similarly, we assume that the preparation time of a reply message (denoted by $\tilde{y}$) is exponentially distributed with mean $\frac{1}{\nu_d}$ and the total service time at each "network server" from destination to source is exponentially distributed with mean $\frac{1}{\mu_d}$. Again, queues may be formed at these network servers because of retransmission of replies at expiration of timeout or availability of new replies. At the source, the loss probability of a reply is denoted by L_d. Successfully received replies are assumed to be acknowledged with zero delay. These replies will be collected at the source, and the time required is assumed to be negligible. When the replies from all N destinations have been collected, the preparation of a new broadcast will begin. Here we assume a non-empty broadcast queue waiting to be processed.

The timeout intervals at the source and destination are assumed to be constant and denoted by T_s and T_d respectively.

4. Analysis of Send-and-Wait Point-to-Point Protocol

Before analyzing the broadcast protocol, it is necessary to obtain results for the Send-and-Wait point-to-point protocol which is used to send back replies. This protocol has been studied by Fayolle et. al. [13]. However, their model treats all messages which are not acknowledged within the timeout interval as being lost. This is not suitable for the network environment that we are studying, since acknowledgements may be delayed due to the stochastic nature of network delays. Also, it is necessary to have a more detailed model for the network to reflect the congestion caused by small timeout intervals.

With probability $L_d^{m-1}(1-L_d)$, a reply message has to be transmitted m times before it reaches the source of the broadcast safely. Let ϕ_m be the delay experienced by a reply, given that it has to be transmitted m times before it reaches the source safely, and $\phi_m^*(\xi)$ be the Laplace transform of its probability density function (pdf). To get an expression for $\phi_m^*(\xi)$ we need to get the response time distribution at a destination network server. Let $\tilde{A}_d$ be the interarrival time at such a network server and $A_d^*(\xi)$ the Laplace transform of its pdf. We will approximate $\tilde{A}_d$ by $T_d+\tilde{y}$ (see Figure 3). $A_d^*(\xi)$ is then given by :

$$A_d^*(\xi) = \frac{\nu_d}{\xi+\nu_d} e^{-\xi T_d} \quad (1)$$

The network server is essentially a G/M/1 model [14]. For this model, we need to find σ_d such that

$$\sigma_d = A_d^*(\mu_d - \mu_d\sigma_d) \quad (2)$$

This can be easily calculated using fixed point iteration techniques. The response time at the network server is exponentially distributed [14] with mean $\frac{1}{\mu_d(1-\sigma_d)}$. Then

$$\phi_m^*(\xi) = \left(\frac{\nu_d}{\xi+\nu_d}\right)^m e^{-\xi(m-1)T_d} \frac{\mu_d(1-\sigma_d)}{\xi+\mu_d(1-\sigma_d)} \quad (3)$$

and the mean delay given m transmissions is :

$$E[\phi_m] = mE[\tilde{y}] + (m-1)T_d + \frac{1}{\mu_d(1-\sigma_d)} \quad (4)$$

Removing the condition on m, the Laplace transform of the pdf of delay experienced by a reply is

$$\phi^*(\xi) = \sum_{m=1}^{\infty} L_d^{m-1}(1-L_d)\left(\frac{\nu_d}{\xi+\nu_d}\right)^m e^{-\xi(m-1)T_d} \frac{\mu_d(1-\sigma_d)}{\xi+\mu_d(1-\sigma_d)} \quad (5)$$

and the mean delay is given by

$$E[\phi] = \frac{1}{\nu_d(1-L_d)} + \frac{L_d T_d}{(1-L_d)} + \frac{1}{\mu_d(1-\sigma_d)} \tag{6}$$

The throughput of the point-to-point Send-and-Wait protocol (denoted by θ) can be easily obtained from

$$\theta = \frac{1}{E[\phi]} \tag{7}$$

5. Analysis of Send-and-Wait Broadcast Protocol

We now proceed to analyze the performance of the broadcast operation. We will break up this operation into two phases, the first phase being the time it takes for the broadcast message to reach all destinations and the second phase the time after the completion of the first phase for all replies to get back to the source.

Similar to the case of the point-to-point protocol, the first phase is dependent on m, the number of transmissions required before all destinations receive the broadcast message successfully. Let $E[\tau_m(1)]$ be the mean time to complete phase 1 given m transmissions. The result for $E[\tau_m(1)]$ is analogous to Eq. (4) i.e.,

$$E[\tau_m(1)] = mE[\tilde{x}] + (m-1)T_s + \frac{1}{\mu_s(1-\sigma_s)} \tag{8}$$

where σ_s is the solution to $\sigma_s = A_s^*(\mu_s-\mu_s\sigma_s)$ with $A_s^*(\xi)$ being the Laplace transform of the pdf of interarrival time at the source network server. $A_s^*(\xi)$ is approximately given by

$$A_s^*(\xi) = \frac{\nu_s}{\xi+\nu_s} e^{-\xi T_s} \tag{9}$$

The second phase is complete when the last reply from the destinations is received by the source. We need to take the maximum of processing and reply delays over the N destination nodes, appropriately shifted according to the time at which each node receives the broadcast message. Since the loss probability L_s is typically small, the delay of phase 2 is heavily affected by the number of destinations which first receive the broadcast message successfully in the mth and in the $(m-1)^{st}$ transmissions. Let these numbers be k_1 and k_2 respectively. Also let $E[\tau_{m,k_1,k_2}(2)]$ be the mean delay of phase 2 given m, k_1 and k_2. $E[\tau_{m,k_1,k_2}(2)]$ can accurately be approximated by the mean of the maximum of processing and reply delays over the (k_1+k_2) destinations.

Let $G_1(y)$ and $G_2(y)$ be the cumulative distribution functions of the processing and reply delays for a destination which first receives the broadcast message in the mth and $(m-1)^{st}$ transmissions respectively.

$$E[\tau_{m,k_1,k_2}(2)] = \int_0^\infty \{1-G_1(y)^{k_1}G_2(y)^{k_2}\}\, dy \tag{10}$$

$G_1(y)$ can be obtained by inverting $G_1^*(\xi)$, the Laplace transform of the corresponding pdf. Since the processing delay at a destination is exponentially distributed with mean $\frac{1}{\alpha}$ and the Laplace transform of the reply delay pdf is given by $\phi^*(\xi)$ in Eq. (5), we have

$$G_1^*(\xi) = \phi^*(\xi)\frac{\alpha}{\xi+\alpha} \tag{11}$$

Inverting $G_1^*(\xi)$ exactly is tedious. Fortunately, we can take advantage of the fact that L_d is typically small to approximate $\phi^*(\xi)$. We thus have

$$G_1^*(\xi) = \tag{12}$$

$$\frac{\alpha}{\xi+\alpha}\,\frac{\nu_d}{\xi+\nu_d}\,\frac{\mu_d(1-\sigma_d)}{\xi+\mu_d(1-\sigma_d)}\left[(1-L_d) + L_d\frac{\nu_d}{\xi+\nu_d}e^{-\xi T_d}\right].$$

$G_1^*(\xi)$ can now be inverted easily to give $G_1(y)$.

To get $G_2(y)$, we note that destinations which first receive the broadcast message successfully in the $(m-1)^{st}$ transmission, start preparing the reply earlier by $T_s+\tilde{x}$ (see Figure 4). $G_2(y)$ can therefore be approximated by

$$G_2(y) = G_1\left(y + T_s + \frac{1}{\nu_s}\right) \tag{13}$$

Using Eq. (12) and (13) in (10), we can compute $E[\tau_{m,k_1,k_2}(2)]$.

Let τ be the total delay of the broadcast operation, i.e., the delay to broadcast the message and collect all N replies. Removing the condition on m, k_1 and k_2, we get,

$$E[\tau] = \sum_{m=1}^{\infty}\sum_{k_1=1}^{N}\sum_{k_2=0}^{N-k_1} Pr[m,k_1,k_2]\,\{E[\tau_m(1)] + E[\tau_{m,k_1,k_2}(2)]\} \tag{14}$$

where Pr [m, k_1, k_2] is the probability of m transmissions for all destinations to receive the broadcast successfully, and k_1 and k_2 destinations first receiving the broadcast successfully in the mth and $(m-1)^{st}$ transmission. Using straight forward probabilistic arguments, Pr [m, k_1, k_2] is given by

$$Pr[m,k_1,k_2] = \tag{15}$$

$$\begin{cases} (1-L_s)^N & m=1,k_1=N,k_2=0 \\ 0 & m=1,k_1<N \\ \binom{N}{k_1}(L_s(1-L_s))^{k_1}(1-L_s)^{N-k_1} & m=2,k_1\geq 1,k_2=N-k_1 \\ 0 & m=2,k_2\neq N-k_1 \\ \frac{N!}{k_1!k_2!(N-k_1-k_2)!}(L_s^{m-1}(1-L_s))^{k_1}(L_s^{m-2}(1-L_s))^{k_2}(1-L_s^{m-2})^{N-k_1-k_2} & m>2,1\leq k_1+k_2\leq N,k_1\geq 1 \end{cases}$$

Similar to Eq. (7), the throughput of the broadcast operation (denoted by γ) can be obtained from

$$\gamma = \frac{1}{E[\tau]} \tag{16}$$

This completes our analysis of the broadcast protocol.

6. Results and Discussions

Figure 5 shows throughput of the Send-and-Wait, point-to-point protocol as a function of the timeout interval for loss probabilities of .01, .04 and .08. It can be seen that the throughput drops drastically if the timeout interval is very small. This is due to the fact that the message is retransmitted frequently and this causes a queue to build up at the network server. For low loss probabilities, the throughput is not affected significantly by the length of the timeout interval as long as the interval is of sufficient length to prevent congestion in the network. For larger loss probabilities, the throughput declines as the length of the interval increases since retransmission of lost messages is delayed. It is possible to find an optimal timeout interval within this range.

Figures 6, 7, 8 and 9 are for the broadcast operation. In Figure 6, the source timeout interval is varied while keeping the destination interval fixed. Again, the curves are shown for three different loss probabilities. There are 5 destinations involved in the broadcast. The broadcast protocol exhibits the same throughput characteristics as the point-to-point protocol. Figure 7 shows throughput versus timeout for N=5 and N=10. The number of destinations does not affect the relationship between throughput and the length of the timeout interval. As expected, throughput is smaller for N=10, and decreases quite quickly as we increase the number of destinations (Figure 8).

Figure 9 seems to indicate that the loss probability does not affect the throughput very much. Note, however, that this is for a given set of parameter values and the relationship may vary for other values.

Some simulation results have been shown to assess the accuracy of the approximate analysis. These results indicate that the approximate analysis is very accurate, the worst error for the examples considered being less than 1%.

References

[1] Pardo, R.; "Interprocess Communication And Synchronization For Distributed Systems", Ph.D. Thesis, Ohio State University, 1979.

[2] Calo, S.B., and Easton, M.C.; "A Broadcast Protocol For File Transfers To Multiple Sites", IEEE Transactions on Communications, Vol. COM-29, No. 11, November 1981.

[3] Gopal, I. S., and Jaffe, J.;"Point-to-Multipoint Link Control Protocols for Satellites", IBM Research Report RC 9671, 1982.

[4] Thomas, R.H.; "A Majority Consensus Approach To Concurrency Control For Multiple Copy Databases", ACM Transactions On Database Systems, Vol. 4, No. 2, June 1979.

[5] Bernstein, P.A., Rothnie Jr., J.B., Goodman, N., and Papadimitriou, C.A.; "The Concurrency Control Mechanism Of SDD-1 : A System For Distributed Databases (The Fully Redundant Case) ", IEEE Transactions on Software Engineering, Vol. SE-4, No. 3, May 1978.

[6] Gray, J.; "Notes On Database Operating Systems", Operating Systems - An Advanced Course, Springer Verlag, 1978.

[7] Kaneko, A., Nishihara, Y., Tsuruoka, K., and Hattori, M.; "Logical Clock Synchronization Method For Duplicated Database Control", 1st International Conference On Distributed Computing Systems, Huntsville, Alabama, October 1979.

[8] Ellis, C.A.; "A Robust Algorithm For Updating Duplicate Databases", Proceedings of 2nd Berkeley Workshop on DDMCN, May 1977.

[9] Lin, W.K.; "Concurrency Control In A Multiple Copy Distributed Database System", Proceedings of 4th Berkeley Conference On DDMCN, August 1979.

[10] Badal, D.Z., and Popek, G.J.; "A Proposal For Distributed Concurrency Control For Partially Redundant Distributed Data Base Systems", Proceedings of 3rd Berkeley Workshop on DDMCN, August 1978.

[11] ISO/TC 97/SC 16 Open Systems Interconnection - Basic Reference Model, N537. Revised November 1980.

[12] Tanenbaum, A.; "Computer Networks", Prentice-Hall, Inc., 1981.

[13] Fayolle, G., Gelenbe, E., and Pujolle, G; "An Analytic Evaluation Of The Performance Of The Send And Wait Protocol", IEEE Transactions on Communications, Vol. COM-26, No. 3, March 1978.

[14] Kleinrock, L.; "Queueing Systems, Volume 1 : Theory", John Wiley and Sons, 1975.

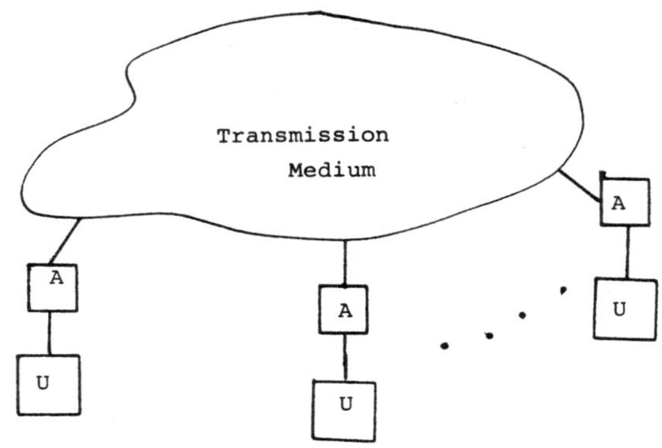

A Adapter
U User Machine

Fig. 1 Local area network

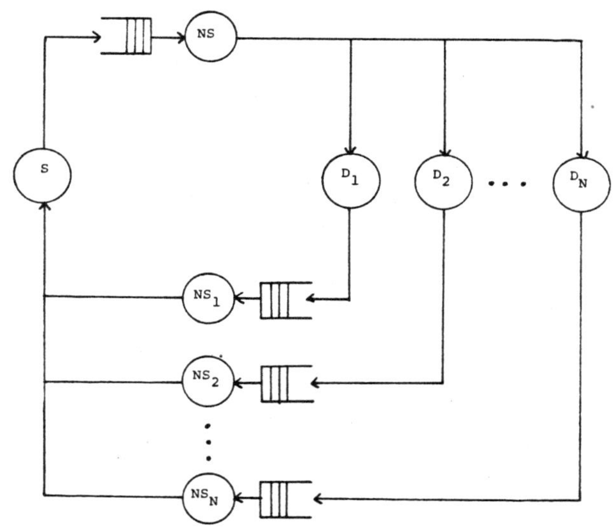

S Source
D Destination
NS Network Server

Fig. 2 Queueing model

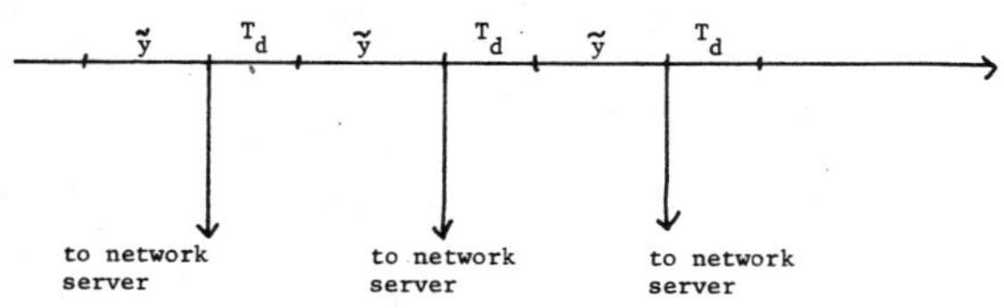

Fig. 3 Successive transmission times (point-to-point)

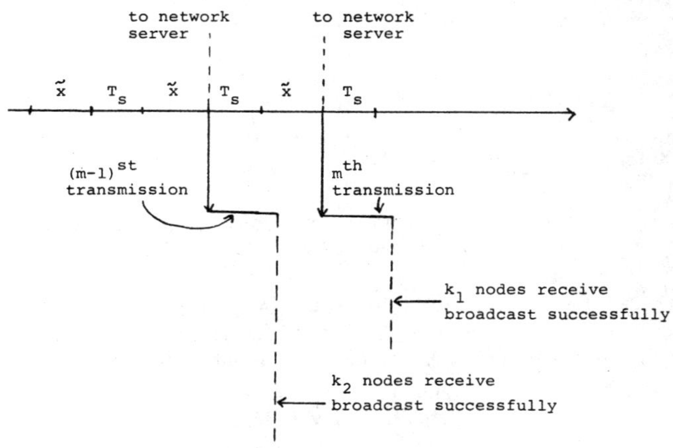

Fig. 4 Successive transmission times (broadcast)

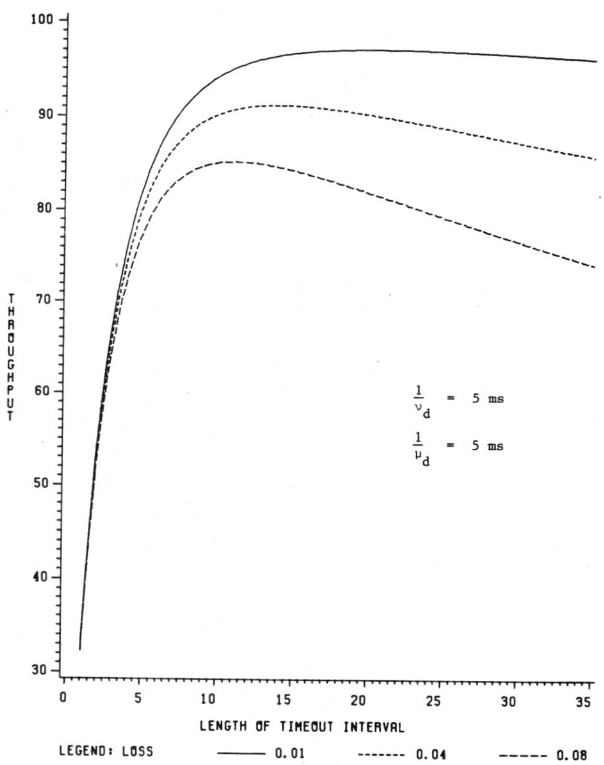

Fig. 5 Throughput vs. timeout (point-to-point)

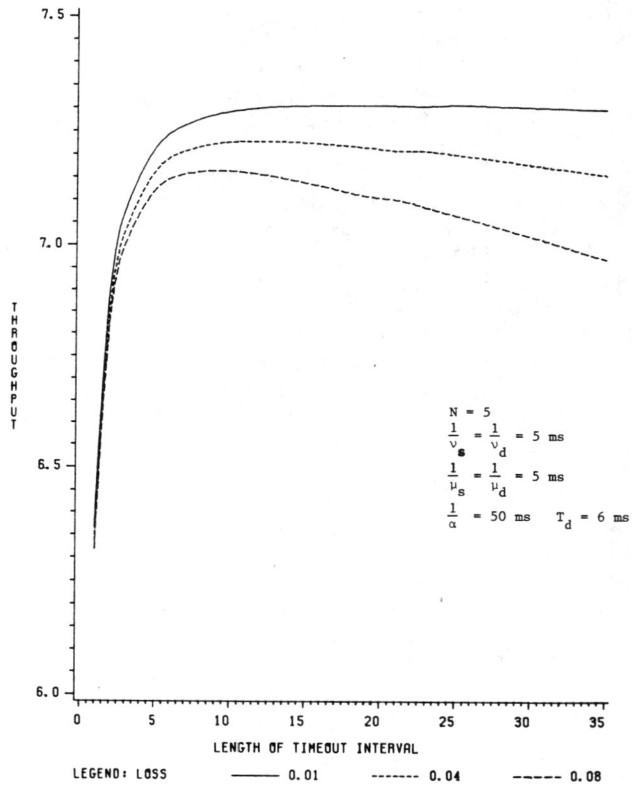

Fig. 6 Throughput vs. timeout (broadcast)

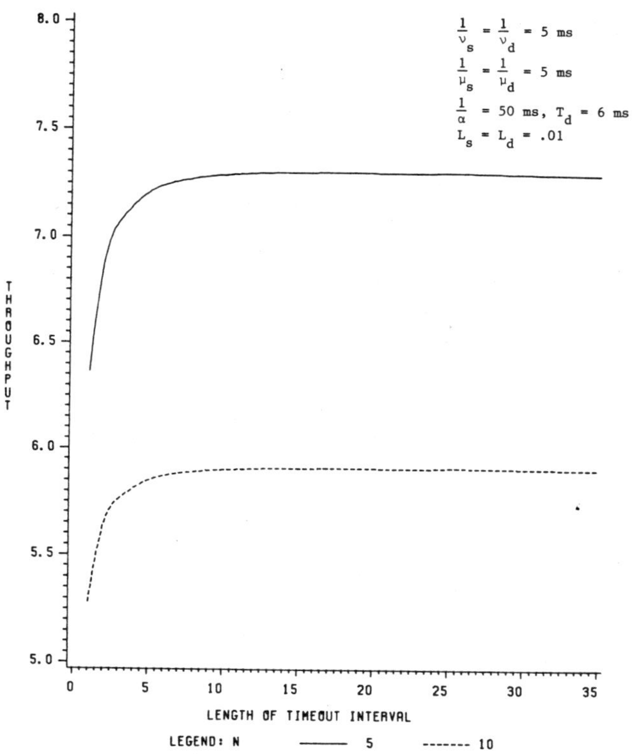

Fig. 7 Throughput vs. timeout (broadcast)

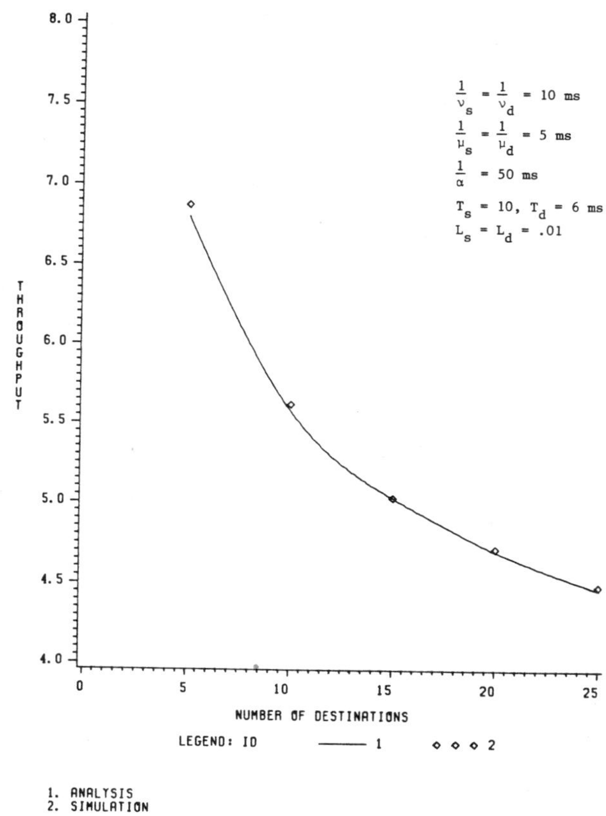

Fig. 8 Throughput vs. number of destinations

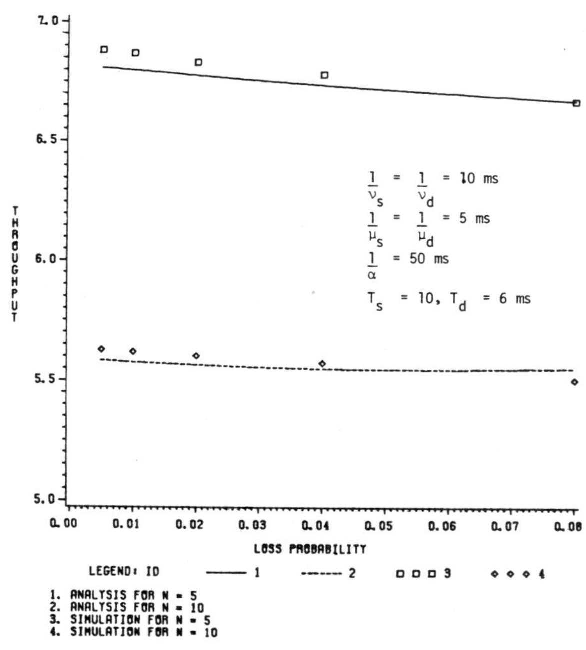

Fig. 9 Throughput vs. loss probability

Protocol Design and Analysis

Chairman

D. Oran

A DECOMPOSITION METHOD FOR THE ANALYSIS AND DESIGN OF FINITE STATE PROTOCOLS

Tat Y. Choi and Raymond E. Miller*

Georgia Institute of Technology
Atlanta, Georgia 30332

Abstract

Finite state automata have been applied with success to the modeling of Computer Network Protocols. The interaction of finite state machines can be very complex especially if the protocol involves a large number of states. To counteract the complexity of analysis and design, we propose an approach of decomposition. Through this approach, the protocol graph can be partitioned into subgraphs each having a unique entry node and zero or more exit nodes. The exit nodes of one subgraph can be connected only to the entry nodes of other subgraphs. From the standpoint of protocol analysis, the correctness of the entire protocol graph can be inferred from the correctness of individual protocol subgraphs. From the standpoint of protocol design, the individual protocol subgraphs can be designed to correspond to different phases of the protocol. If the individual protocol subgraphs are designed correctly and the connections between subgraphs conform to the structure discussed above, then we show that the entire protocol graph will operate correctly.

I. INTRODUCTION

The early eighties has seen the proliferation of different types of computer networks and their application in various areas. With this a variety of network architectures and protocols have arisen [1]. Whether the network under discussion be a local network offered by a computer manufacturer or a long haul network offered by a common carrier, the question confronting network architects remains the same: what principles can we draw on for the engineering of these systems? In this paper, we intend to address an important area of network architecture, that of protocol analysis and design. Despite the large number of networks in exis tence today and the experience gained from the implementation of these systems, the design and analysis of network protocols has remained ad hoc. Various efforts have been undertaken in the formal modeling of network protocols [2,3], yet these approaches have not solved the problem of complexity. Little has been done in the way of partitioning the analysis and design process, the use of canonical components for protocol design, or the establishment of practical theorems to aid in the analysis and design process [4,5]. To counteract the complexity of protocol analysis and design, we propose an approach of decomposition. Amongst the various ways of modeling protocols, we have chosen the finite state model for the following reasons. It is a simple, widely understood model, correctness conditions can be simply and completely stated, these conditions not only are decidable but usually have tractable algorithms for testing their validity, and it has been used with success in the modeling of many practical protocols. We realize that finite state models have their limitations, for example, a complete description of some protocols may require a large number of states. Yet, it is precisely the state explosion problem that we intend to solve in this paper, by showing that finite state protocols are conducive to structured techniques of analysis and design.

II. THE PROTOCOL MODEL

Protocols are modeled by processes exchanging messages through communication channels. In finite state protocols, the processes can be represented by finite state machines [6]. A commonly used model for finite state protocols is one based on the work of Zafiropulo, et. al. [7]. In this model, a finite state protocol is defined as follows:

<u>Defintion</u>: A <u>Finite State Protocol</u> FSP $= (S,M,\Sigma,O,\tau)$ consists of:

Permission to copy without fee all or part of this material is granted provided that the copies are not made or distributed for direct commercial advantage, the ACM copyright notice and the title of the publication and its date appear, and notice is given that copying is by permission of the Association for Computing Machinery. To copy otherwise, or to republish, requires a fee and/or specific permission.

*Work on this paper was supported in part by National Science Foundation Grant MCS-8103608.

i. $S = \{S_1, S_2\}$, two disjoint finite sets representing the states of processes P_1 and P_2 respectively.

ii. $M = \{M_{12}, M_{21}\}$, two finite sets, where M_{12} represents the messages that can be sent from process P_1 to process P_2 and M_{21} represents the messages that can be sent from process P_2 to process P_1.

iii. $\Sigma = \{\Sigma_1, \Sigma_2\}$, two finite sets of events on M of the following kind:

(1) for every message $x \in M_{ij}$, the sending of message x is denoted by $-x$. Every send event $-x$ is an element of Σ_i.

(2) for every message $x \in M_{ij}$, the receiving of message x is denoted by $+x$. Every receive event $+x$ is an element of Σ_j.

(3) a null or internal event is denoted by λ and λ is an element of Σ_i.

iv. $O = \{o_1, o_2\}$, where $o_1 \in S_1$ and $o_2 \in S_2$. o_1 and o_2 are the initial states for processes P_1 and P_2 respectively.

v. τ a transition function: $S_i \times \Sigma_i \rightarrow S_i$, i=1,2. The transition function for event $\sigma \in \Sigma_i$ at state s can be written as $\tau(s,\sigma)$. It represents the next state reached by a process after executing event σ at state s.

If $T' = \sigma_1, \sigma_2, \ldots, \sigma_n$ is a sequence of events, then let $T = \sigma T' = \sigma, \sigma_1, \sigma_2, \ldots, \sigma_n$.

<u>Definition:</u> An <u>extended transition function</u> $\tau(s,T)$ is defined for a state $s \in S_i$ and a sequence of events T by the following equation:

$$\tau(s,T) = \tau(\tau(s,\sigma),T')$$

<u>Definition:</u> A <u>Channel</u> C_{ij} is a FIFO queue connecting process i to process j. The contents of C_{ij} is labeled c_{ij}, it is a string of symbols from M_{ij} and represents the FIFO queue of messages being sent from process i to process j. Each entry in c_{ij} is an element of M_{ij}.

<u>Definition:</u> A <u>Global State</u> is a pair <S,C> where $S = (s_1, s_2)$ with $s_1 \in S_1$ and $s_2 \in S_2$ representing the current states of process P_1 and P_2 and $C = (c_{12}, c_{21})$ representing the current contents of channels C_{12} and C_{21}.

<u>Definition:</u> A <u>Stable State Pair</u> (s_p, s_q) is a pair derived from a global state <S,C> where $S = (s_p, s_q)$ and $C = (c_{12}, c_{21})$ with both c_{12} and c_{21} empty.

A binary relation $\vdash$ on global states is defined as follows:

<u>Definition:</u> A global state <S,C> $\vdash$ <S',C'> iff there exists i,j and c_{ij} satisfying one of the following execution rules:

i. $s_i' = \tau(s_i, -x)$ and $c_{ij}' = c_{ij} \cdot x$

ii. $s_j' = \tau(s_j, +x)$ and $c_{ij} = x \cdot c_{ij}'$

iii. $s_i' = \tau(s_i, \lambda)$ and $c_{ij}' = c_{ij}$

Except for the one execution rule applied, all other elements of <S',C'> are equal to the elements of <S,C>.

<u>Definition:</u> A global state <S,C> is said to be <u>reachable</u> from an initial state $\langle S_o, C_o \rangle$ iff $\langle S_o, C_o \rangle \vdash^* \langle S, C \rangle$ where $\langle S_o, C_o \rangle = \langle (o_1, o_2), (\Lambda, \Lambda) \rangle$† and $\vdash^*$ denotes the reflexive, transitive closure of $\vdash$.

<u>Definition:</u> A transition at state s for event σ is <u>specified</u> iff $\tau(s,\sigma)$ is defined.

<u>Definition:</u> A transition at state s for event is <u>executable</u> iff there exists a reachable global state $\langle (s_i, s_j), (c_{ij}, c_{ji}) \rangle$ with $s = s_i$ or $s = s_j$, and if σ is a receive transition $+x$, then for $s = s_i$, $c_{ij} = xY$ and for $s = s_j$, $c_{ji} = xZ$, with Y and Z being arbitrary.

<u>Definition:</u> A message x at state s is <u>live</u> iff there is a reachable global state <S,C> with $S = (s_i, s_j)$ and $s = s_i$ or $s = s_j$ and there exists an <S',C'> such that $\langle S,C \rangle \vdash^* \langle S',C' \rangle$ where $S' = (s_k, s_\ell)$ and if $s = s_i$, then $\tau(s_k, +x)$ is specified and executable and if $s = s_j$, then $\tau(s_\ell, +x)$ is specified and executable.

We now define the following four types of protocol errors.

i. <u>Unspecified Receptions:</u> A reception for message x at state s is unspecified iff it is not live.

ii. <u>Nonexecutable Interactions:</u> A transition $\tau(s,\sigma)$ at state s for event σ is nonexecutable iff it is specified and not executable.

iii. <u>State Deadlocks:</u> A state deadlock is a stable state pair $S = (s_i, s_j)$ such that there is no x for which $\tau(s_i, -x)$ or $\tau(s_j, -x)$ is specified and S is not a final system state.

iv. <u>State Ambiguities:</u> A state ambiguity is a pair of stable states $S = (s_p, s_q)$ and $S' = (s_p', s_q')$ such that either

1. $s_p = s_p'$ and $s_q \neq s_q'$ or

2. $s_p \neq s_p'$ and $s_q = s_q'$

A state ambiguity is a potential design error.

---

†Here we use Λ to represent the null string of symbols, which intuitively represents the empty queue.

Definition: A finite state protocol is said to be logically correct w.r.t. unspecified receptions, nonexecutable interactions and state deadlocks if and only if it is free from these errors.

Various techniques have been applied for the validation of finite state protocols [8,9]. The most common one being reachability analysis. Let the finite state machines for process P_1 and P_2 be represented by the finite state graphs g_1 and g_2 respectively. Then the protocol graph $PG(g_1,g_2)$ denotes the protocol between process P_1 and process P_2. The reachability tree RT (g_1,g_2) for the protocol graph $PG(g_1,g_2)$ can be constructed by successively generating reachable global states from the initial global state.

Definition: A finite state protocol is balanced if and only if the finite state graphs g_1 and g_2 representing process P_1 and P_2 respectively are isomorphic.

III. THE STRUCTURED PARTITION OF A PROTOCOL GRAPH

Let g be the finite state graph representing process P. For the purpose of protocol decomposition, we define a Structural Partition π of graph g into subgraphs as follows:

Definition: A partition $\pi = \{G_1,G_2,\dots,G_n\}$ of graph g into subgraphs is a Structured Partition if and only if it satisfies the following conditions:

i. each subgraph G_i contains a unique header node h and zero or more exit nodes e.

ii. any node v_i belonging to subgraph G_i can be connected to any other node belonging to the same subgraph.

iii. only the exit node e of a subgraph G_i can be connected to the nodes of other subgraphs and any such edge is connected to the header node h of other subgraphs G_j.

iv. a header node can also serve as an exit node e.

In the event that a node acts as both header and exit nodes, the same rules apply. The minimal subgraph is a single node, in which case the single node acts as both a header and exit node. The structured partition π of a graph g is not unique. The set of all structured partitions $SP = \{\pi_i\}$ of graph g forms a partially ordered set. The largest structured partition $\pi(I)$ of graph g is one that has a single block that includes the entire graph g. The smallest structured partition $\pi(0)$ of graph g is one in which there are as many blocks as there are nodes which means that every node v_i of graph g is a subgraph. From a smaller partition π of the graph g, we can construct a larger partition π' of graph g by forming the union of subgraphs of partition π such that the resulting subgraphs satisfy the structured requirements state above. The algorithm for constructing structured partitions can be found in [16].

In the following, we will refer to a graph g or subgraph G_i by its nodes $\{v_i\}$. By that we mean the graph or induced subgraph which includes all the nodes $\{v_i\}$.

Example 3.1

Consider the graph structure g for the call control phase of Recommendation X.21 as shown in Fig. 3.1 [10]. We have omitted state 13 since the final transition can occur as soon as state 12 (READY FOR DATA) is reached and is not considered to be part of the call establishment procedure. Recommendation X.21 provides many options which network implementors can choose from. We have chosen the option to include all the states thus omitting all bypassing links in the state diagram. In that case, the graph structure g = (1, 2, 3, 4, 5, 6A, 6B, 7/10, 8, 9, 10bis, 11, 12, 15). The smallest structured partition $\pi(0) = \{G_1, G_2, G_3, G_4, G_5, G_{6A}, G_{6B}, G_{7/10}, G_8, G_9, G_{10bis}, G_{11}, G_{12}, G_{15}\}$, where G_1 = (1), G_2 = (2), G_3 = (3), G_4 = (4), G_5 = (5), G_{6A} = (6A), G_{6B} = (6B), $G_{7/10}$ = (7/10), G_8 = (8), G_9 = (9), G_{10bis} = (10bis), G_{11} = (11), G_{12} = (12) and G_{15} = (15) are single node subgraphs. From the smallest structured partition $\pi(0)$, we can optionally construct a larger partition $\pi' = \{G_i'\}$ by forming subgraph $G_1' = G_1 \cup G_2 \cup G_8$ with the rest of the subgraphs remaining the same. Thus G_1' = (1,2,8), G_3' = (3), G_4' = (4), G_5' = (5), G_{6A}' = (6A), G_{6B}' = (6B), $G_{7/10}'$ = (7/10), G_9' = (9), G_{10bis}' = (10bis), G_{11}' = (11), G_{12}' = (12) and G_{15}' = (15). This partition will be needed in our later discussion.

IV. A STRUCTURE THEORY FOR FINITE STATE PROTOCOLS

Consider the protocol between two processes P_1 and P_2 connected by communication channels C_{12} and C_{21}. Let process P_1 be represented by the finite state graph g_1 which can be partitioned structurally into m subgraphs $\pi_1 = (G_1,\dots,G_m)$. Let process P_2 be represented by finite state graph g_2 which can be partitioned structurally into n subgraphs $\pi_2 = (G_1',\dots,G_n')$. Let subgraphs G_1 and G_1' be the initial subgraphs for g_1 and g_2 respectively, where they contain the initial node for each graph. Let G_i be the ith successor subgraph to G_1 in graph g_1 and G_i' be the ith successor subgraph to G_1' in graph g_2. We say that G_i' in g_2 is the corresponding subgraph to G_i in g_1. For balanced protocols, the corresponding subgraphs are quite obvious since graphs g_1 and g_2 are identical in structure. In other cases, we are referring to the pair of corresponding subgraphs that are reachable from the initial pair of subgraphs. Let $G_i \cup h$ denote the union of subgraph G_i with the header node h of its successor subgraph

G_j. Consider an arbitrary subgraph $G_i \cup h$ of $\mathcal{g}_1$, and its successor subgraph G_j. Its corresponding counterparts in $\mathcal{g}_2$ are subgraphs $G_i' \cup h'$ and G_j'. See Fig. 4.1. Between subgraphs $G_i \cup G_j$ and $G_i' \cup G_j'$, there are four regions of interaction. See Table 4.1. We can distinguish between two kinds of interactions.

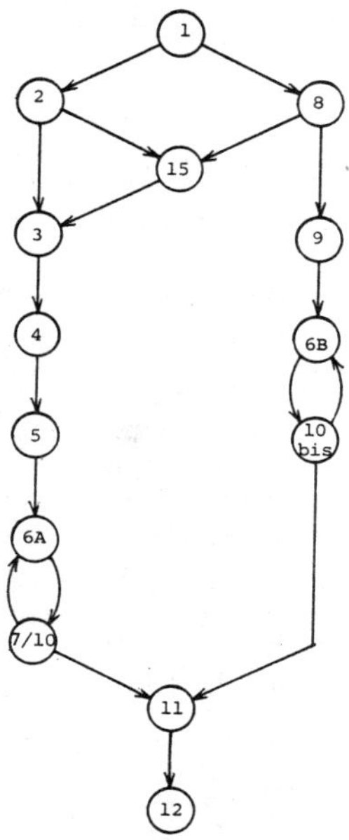

Fig. 3.1 The graph structure $\mathcal{g}$ for the call control phase of X.21 with state 13 omitted

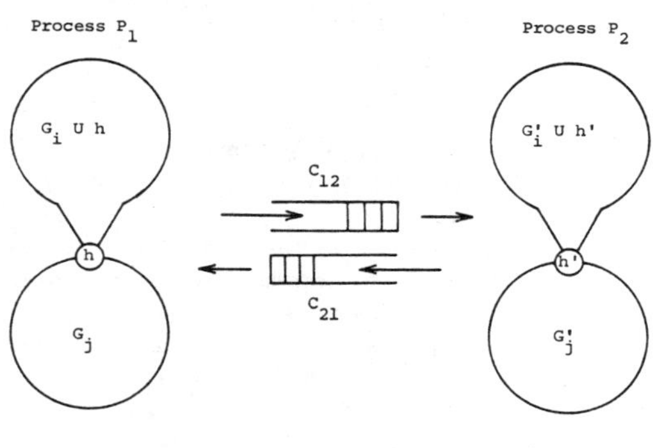

Fig. 4.1 The Protocol Subgraph $PG(G_i \cup G_j,\ G_i' \cup G_j')$

1. Expected Interactions

In both regions 1 and 2, while process P_1 is in subgraph $G_i \cup h$ or G_j, process P_2 is in its corresponding subgraph $G_i' \cup h'$ or G_j' respectively. When they exchange events in these subgraphs, we refer to them as the 'expected interactions' between subgraphs.

TABLE 4.1 Four Regions of Interaction

Regions of interaction	Process P_1	Process P_2
region 1	$G_i \cup h$	$G_i' \cup h'$
region 2	G_j	G_j'
region 3	$G_i \cup h$	G_j'
region 4	G_j	$G_i' \cup h'$

2. Cross Interactions

In regions 3 and 4, while process P_1 is in subgraph $G_i \cup h$ or G_j, process P_2 is in its corresponding successor or predecessor subgraph, namely, G_j' or $G_i' \cup h'$ respectively. This can happen as a result of one process racing ahead into its successor subgraph while the other process lags behind. By itself, this does not signify that a process in one subgraph will exchange events with another process in its predecessor or successor subgraph. However, if they do so, we refer to this as a 'cross interaction' between subgraphs.

In some instances, either process P_1 or P_2 can race ahead into successor subgraphs of G_j or G_j' while the other process lags behind in $G_i' \cup h'$ or $G_i \cup h$. In those cases, we can have 'cross interaction' between processes that are separated by more than one subgraph. Clearly, from the standpoint of a structured approach to protocol analysis and design, these are the interactions we want to avoid. In a well designed protocol, one would expect that whatever events are exchanged between subgraphs $G_i \cup h$ and $G_i' \cup h'$, they would be confined to those subgraphs, and once process P_1 or P_2 enters subgraph G_j or G_j', the other process will follow suit. In the following, we will state two different propositions under which 'cross interaction' is absent.

Proposition 4.1: If the set of events in protocol graph $PG(G_i \cup h,\ G_i' \cup h')$ is totally different from the set of events in $PG(G_j,\ G_j')$, then there can be no 'cross interaction' between the two subgraphs.

The reason for this is obvious. However, the above condition may not always be the case and we will have to rely upon the following proposition for no cross interaction.

Proposition 4.2: If the protocol given by the protocol graph $PG(G_i \cup h,\ G_i' \cup h')$ is correct, then all the messages sent by process P_1 in subgraph $G_i \cup h$ will be received by P_2 in subgraph $G_i' \cup h'$ and vice versa, i.e. there can be no cross interaction between the two subgraphs.

If there are no cross interactions between subgraphs, then the reachability tree of $PG(G_i \cup G_j, G_i' \cup G_j')$ is the union of the reachability tree of $PG(G_i \cup h, G_i' \cup h')$ and the reachability tree of $PG(G_j, G_j')$ over the global state $<(h,h'),(\Lambda,\Lambda)>$ plus a transition region. See Fig. 4.2. The transition region represents intermediate states where one process races ahead into subgraph G_j or G_j' while the other process lags behind in subgraph $G_i' \cup h'$ or $G_i \cup h$. It is generated as a result of connecting subgraph G_j to G_i and G_j' to G_i'. The correctness of the protocols given by $PG(G_i \cup h, G_i' \cup h')$ and $PG(G_j, G_j')$ guarantees the correctness of the transition region. This is because for any sequence of transitions through the transition region, there is an equivalent sequence through the union of the reachability tree of $PG(G_i \cup h, G_i' \cup h')$ and the reachability tree of $PG(G_j, G_j')$. By equivalent sequences, we mean the two sequences have the same set of events except the order in which they occur [11].

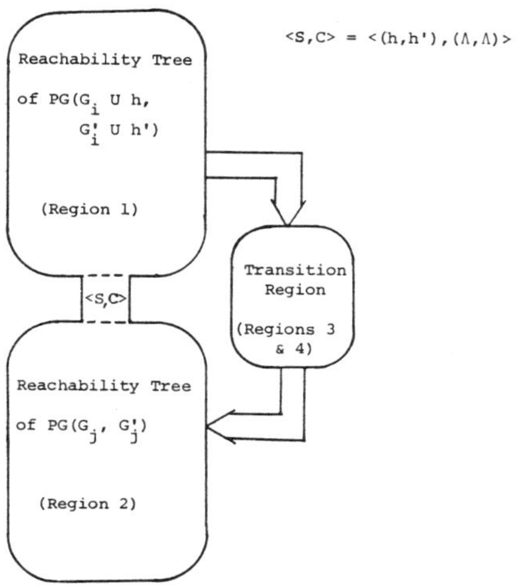

Fig. 4.2 Reachability Tree of $PG(G_i \cup G_j, G_i' \cup G_j')$

<u>Lemma 4.1</u>

The correctness of the protocols given by the protocol subgraphs $PG(G_i \cup h, G_i' \cup h')$ and $PG(G_j, G_j')$ implies the correctness of the protocol given by $PG(G_i \cup G_j, G_i' \cup G_j')$.

We now see that the converse is not necessarily true.

<u>Lemma 4.2</u>

The correctness of the protocol given by the protocol graph $PG(G_i \cup G_j, G_i' \cup G_j')$ does not imply the correctness of the protocols given by the protocol subgraphs $PG(G_i \cup h, G_i' \cup h')$ or $PG(G_j, G_j')$.

We will now generalize the situation to include multiple successor subgraphs to G_i and G_i'. Let $\{G_j^k\}$, $k = 1,\ldots,m$ be the set of successor subgraphs to G_i and $\{G_j'^{\ell}\}$, $\ell = 1,\ldots,n$ be the set of successor subgraphs to G_i'. Let $H_i = \{h_k\}$ be the set of header nodes of successor subgraphs $\{G_j^k\}$ and $H_i' = \{h_k'\}$ be the set of header nodes of successor subgraphs $\{G'^{\ell}_j\}$. We extend the term 'no cross interaction between subgraphs' to mean that process P_1 in subgraph $G_i \cup H_i$ should not exchange events with process P_2 in any subgraph $G_j'^{\ell}$. Similarly process P_2 in subgraph $G_i' \cup H_i'$ should not exchange events with process P_1 in any subgraph G_j^k. Let $PG(G_i \cup H_i, G_i' \cup H_i')$ be the protocol graph formed by the union of subgraph G_i and G_i' with the set of header nodes H_i and H_i'. See Fig. 4.3. For m successor subgraphs to G_i and n successor subgraphs to G_i', there are m x n combinations of header state pairs of the form (h_x,h_y'). Only a subset of these header state pairs are reachable. The existence of stable header state pairs of the form (h_x,h_y') in the reachability tree of $PG(G_i \cup H_i, G_i' \cup H_i')$ means that when process P_1 makes a transition into successor subgraph G_j^k, process P_2 can make a similar transition into subgraph $G_j'^{y}$.

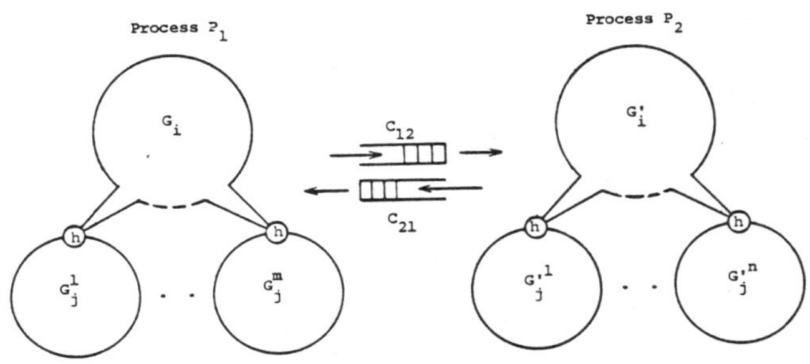

Fig. 4.3 The Protocol Subgraph $PG(G_i \cup G_j^1 \cup \ldots \cup G_j^m, G_i' \cup G_j'^1 \cup \ldots \cup G_j'^n)$

For multiple successor subgraphs the reachability tree of $PG(G_i \cup G_j^1 \cup \ldots \cup G_j^m, G_i' \cup G_j'^1 \cup \ldots \cup G_j'^n)$ is the union of the reachability tree of $PG(G_i \cup H_i, G_i' \cup H_i')$ with the reachability trees of protocol subgraphs of the form $PG(G_j^x, G_j'^y)$ where $(G_j^x, G_j'^y)$ is any pair of reachable successor subgraphs to $(G_i \cup H_i, G_i' \cup H_i')$, plus a set of transition regions, see Fig. 4.4.

<u>Lemma 4.3</u>

If the protocol given by the protocol graph $PG(G_i \cup H_i, G_i' \cup H_i')$ is correct and for every reachable stable header state pair (h_x,h_y') of $PG(G_i \cup H_i, G_i' \cup H_i')$, the protocol given by $PG(G_j^x, G_j'^y)$ is also correct, then the protocol given by $PG(G_i \cup G_j^1 \cup \ldots \cup G_j^m, G_i' \cup G_j'^1 \cup \ldots \cup G_j'^n)$ is correct.

Again, the converse is not necessarily true.

<u>Lemma 4.4</u>

The correctness of the protocol given by the protocol graph $PG(G_i \cup G_j^1 \cup \ldots \cup G_j^m, G_i' \cup G_j'^1 \cup \ldots \cup G_j'^n)$ does not imply the correctness of the protocol given by $PG(G_i \cup H_i, G_i' \cup H_i')$

or $PG(G_j^x, G_j'^y)$ where $(G_j^x, G_j'^y)$ is any pair of reachable successor subgraphs to $(G_i \cup H_i, G_i' \cup H_i')$.

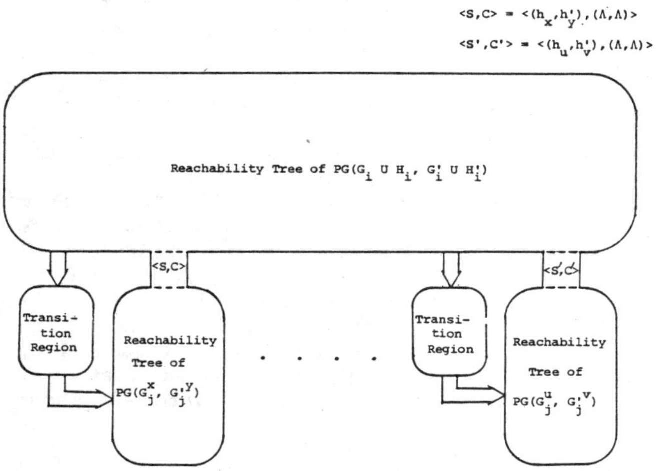

Fig. 4.4 The Reachability Tree of $PG(G_i \cup G_j^1 \cup .. \cup G_j^m, G_i' \cup G_j'^1 \cup .. \cup G_j'^n)$ where (h_x, h_y') and (h_u, h_v') are any reachable stable header state pairs of $PG(G_i \cup H_i, G_i' \cup H_i')$

Finally, we generalize the situation to include the entire protocol graph and arrive at the following theorems.

Theorem 4.1

Given a protocol graph $PG(\mathcal{G}_1, \mathcal{G}_2)$ where $\mathcal{G}_1$ representing process P_1 which can be partitioned into m subgraphs $\pi_1 = \{G_1, \ldots, G_m\}$ and $\mathcal{G}_2$ representing process P_2 which can be partitioned into n subgraphs $\pi_2 = \{G_1', \ldots, G_n'\}$, then the protocol given by the protocol graph $PG(G_1 \cup .. \cup G_m, G_1' \cup .. \cup G_n')$ is correct if

i. the initial protocol subgraph $PG(G_1 \cup H_1, G_1' \cup H_1')$ is correct, and

ii. if the protocol given by $PG(G_u \cup H_u, G_v' \cup H_v')$ is correct and (h_x, h_y') is a stable header state pair of $PG(G_u \cup H_u, G_v' \cup H_v')$, then the protocol given by $PG(G_x \cup H_x, G_y' \cup H_y')$ must also be correct where G_x is the successor subgraph of G_u with header h_x and G_y' is the successor subgraph of G_v' with header h_y'.

For balanced protocols, the processes P_1 and P_2 are represented by identical graph structures. In that case, there is a one-to-one correspondence between the subgraphs of process P_1 and the subgraphs of process P_2. If the protocols are well designed, the processes engaged in the protocol will not enter into different successor subgraphs. This means that for the protocol subgraph $PG(G_i \cup H_i, G_i' \cup H_i')$, the only stable header state pairs reachable will be of the form (h_x, h_x') where (h_x, h_x') are the header nodes of successor subgraphs to (G_i, G_i'). Under those circumstances, we have the following corollary to the theorem.

Corollary:

Given a protocol graph $PG(\mathcal{G}_1, \mathcal{G}_2)$ consisting of n subgraphs, if for each protocol subgraph $PG(G_i \cup H_i, G_i' \cup H_i')$, the only stable header state pairs reachable are of the form (h_x, h_x'), then the correctness of the protocols given by the individual subgraphs plus the header nodes of successor subgraph $PG(G_i \cup H_i, G_i' \cup H_i')$, $i = 1, \ldots, n$ implies the correctness of the entire protocol graph $PG(G_1 \cup .. \cup G_n, G_1' \cup .. \cup G_n')$.

The converse is not necessarily true.

Theorem 4.2

Given a protocol graph $PG(\mathcal{G}_1, \mathcal{G}_2)$ where $\mathcal{G}_1$ representing process P_1 which can be partitioned into m subgraphs $\pi_1 = \{G_1, \ldots, G_m\}$ and $\mathcal{G}_2$ representing process P_2 which can be partitioned into n subgraphs $\pi_2 = \{G_1', \ldots, G_n'\}$, the correctness of the protocol given by the entire protocol graph $PG(G_1 \cup \ldots \cup G_m, G_1' \cup \ldots \cup G_n')$ does not imply the correctness of the protocols given by the protocol subgraphs $PG(G_k \cup H_k, G_\ell' \cup H_\ell')$ where $(G_k \cup H_k, G_\ell' \cup G_\ell')$ is any pair of subgraphs reachable from the initial subgraphs $(G_1 \cup H_1, G_1' \cup H_1')$.

For balanced protocols, we have the following corollary to Theorem 4.2

Corollary:

Given a balanced protocol graph $PG(\mathcal{G}_1, \mathcal{G}_2)$ consisting of n subgraphs, the correctness of the protocol given by the entire protocol graph $PG(G_1 \cup \ldots \cup G_n, G_1' \cup \ldots \cup G_n')$ does not imply the correctness of the protocol given by the individual protocol subgraphs $PG(G_i \cup H_i, G_i' \cup H_i')$, $i = 1, \ldots, n$.

V. STRUCTURED PROTOCOL ANALYSIS AND DESIGN

Based on the theory discussed in section IV, we have developed a structured approach to protocol analysis and design. This approach provides a systematic method to the analysis and design of finite state protocols based on protocol subgraphs.

A. Structural Protocol Analysis

In the following, we restrict our analysis procedure to balanced protocols. This ensures that there is a one-to-one correspondence between the subgraphs of $\mathcal{G}_1$ and $\mathcal{G}_2$. We begin our analysis with the smallest structured partition $\pi(0)$ and whenever we detect the possibility for cross interaction between subgraphs, we form a larger partition until that cross interaction is eliminated. If the protocol graph is correct, then we arrive at a partition π in which all the protocol subgraphs are correct and there are no cross interactions between any two protocol subgraphs. This partition can be the largest structured partition $\pi(I)$ which means that we have to analyze the protocol graph as a whole.

Let $PG(g_1,g_2)$ be the balanced protocol graph to be analyzed, the structured analysis method for $PG(g_1,g_2)$ is given as follows:

Step 1: Let π_{curr} be the current structured partition of the protocol graph $PG(g_1,g_2)$ to be analyzed. Initialize π_{curr} to the smallest structured partition $\pi(0)$.

Step 2: For the protocol graph $PG(g_1,g_2)$ partitioned according to π_{curr}, construct the protocol tree $PT(T_1,T_2)$ by converting graphs g_1 and g_2 into trees T_1 and T_2 respectively using the following algorithms:

Algorithm 5.1

i. Let the initial subgraph G_1 of π_{curr} be represented by the root node of the tree T_1.

ii. Let the immediate successor subgraph G_i to G_1 in graph g_1 be represented by the immediate descendants to node G_1 in the tree T_1.

iii. For each successor subgraph G_i, let the immediate successor subgraph G_j to G_i in graph g_1 be represented by the immediate descendants to node G_i in the tree T_1.

iv. Repeat (iii) until every terminal node of the tree T_1 is either a duplicate node or a final node.

Using the same algorithm, we can construct tree T_2 for graph g_2. The protocol tree $PT(T_1,T_2)$ so constructed is equivalent to the protocol graph $PG(g_1,g_2)$.

Step 3 Starting with the root node G_1 and G_1' of the protocol tree $PT(T_1,T_2)$, construct the reachability tree for the protocol subgraph $PG(G_1 \cup H_1, G_1' \cup H_1')$. If the reachability tree $RT(G_1 \cup H, G_1' \cup H_1')$ contains protocol errors, then go to step 4, else go to step 5.

Step 4 For any protocol subgraph $PG(G_u \cup H_u, G_v' \cup H_v')$, if there are state deadlocks or unspecified receptions, then we have to distinguish between 'definite' protocol errors and 'potential' protocol errors. Let p be any node of subgraph G_u and q be any node of subgraph G_v'. Let h_x and h_y' be the header nodes of any immediate successor subgraphs G_i^x and $G_j'^y$ to G_u and G_v' respectively. Let X and Y denote any arbitrary sequences of messages. Table 5.1 makes the distinction between what are 'definite' protocol errors and what are 'potential' protocol errors. By potential errors, we mean those errors that may vanish as a result of forming larger partitions. This is because partition π_{CURR} is too fine and as a result we have cross interactions between subgraphs. By definite errors, we mean that they are errors not only for the protocol subgraph $PG(G_u \cup H_u, G_v' \cup H_v')$, but will also become errors for the entire protocol graph $PG(g_1,g_2)$ as well.

TABLE 5.1 Potential and Definite Protocol Errors

	Definite Protocol Error	Potential Protocol Error
State Deadlocks†	$<(p,q),(\Lambda,\Lambda)>$	$<(h_x,q),(\Lambda,\Lambda)>$
		$<(p,h_y'),(\Lambda,\Lambda)>$
Unspecified Receptions	$<(p,q),(X,Y)>$	$<(h_x,q),(X,Y)>$
	$<(p,q),(X,\Lambda)>$	$<(h_x,q),(\Lambda,Y)>$
	$<(p,q),(\Lambda,Y)>$	$<(p,h_y'),(X,Y)>$
	$<(h_x,q),(X,\Lambda)>$	$<(p,h_y'),(X,\Lambda)>$
	$<(p,h_y'),(\Lambda,Y)>$	$<(h_x,h_y'),(X,Y)>$
		$<(h_x,h_y'),(\Lambda,Y)>$
		$<(h_x,h_y'),(X,\Lambda)>$

† $<(h_x,h_y'),(\Lambda,\Lambda)>$ is regarded as a final global state of $PG(G_i \cup H_i, G_i \cup H_i)$.

If the state deadlocks and unspecified receptions in the reachability tree $RT(G_u \cup H_u, G_v' \cup H_v')$ are all definite protocol errors, then record these errors. Record the nonexecutable interactions and state ambiguities and go to Step 5. If the reachability tree $RT(G_u \cup H_u, G_v' \cup H_v')$ contains potential protocol errors, then construct a larger partition $\pi_{NEW} > \pi_{CURR}$ by forming the union of subgraphs G_u and G_v' with its successor subgraphs for which cross interaction is possible and in addition any other subgraph whose inclusion is required by the definition of a structured partition. Let π_{NEW} be π_{CURR} and go to Step 2.

Step 5 If the final global states for $PG(G_u \cup H_u, G_v' \cup H_v')$ are of the form $<(h_x,h_y'),(\Lambda,\Lambda)>$ where h_x and h_y' are the header nodes of successor subgraphs G_x and G_y' respectively, then the next set of protocol subgraphs we need to examine are of the form $PG(G_x \cup H_x, G_y' \cup H_y')$. For each protocol subgraph $PG(G_x \cup H_x, G_y' \cup H_y')$, construct the reachability tree $RT(G_x \cup H_x, G_y' \cup H_y')$. If it contains protocol errors, then go back to Step 4, else repeat Step 5 until all reachable pairs of subgraphs have been examined.

The structured technique described above simplifies the analysis process by looking only at subtrees $RT(G_u \cup H_u, G'_v \cup H'_v)$ of the entire reachability tree $RT(\mathcal{G}_1, \mathcal{G}_2)$ and omitting transition regions which for our purpose can be viewed as 'redundancies' in the reachability tree.

B. Structured Protocol Design

The theory discussed in section IV provides us with a definition for structured protocol design. By structured protocol design, we require the following:

i. the entire protocol graph $PG(\mathcal{G}_1, \mathcal{G}_2)$ is constructed from the union of protocol subgraphs $PG(G_i \cup H_i, G'_i \cup H'_i)$, $i = 1,\ldots,n$ with each protocol subgraph designed to correspond to some phase of the protocol.

ii. there are no cross interactions between protocol subgraphs.

iii. when one process makes a transition into one of its successor subgraphs, the other process will follow suit and make a similar transition into its corresponding subgraph.

The structured protocol design approach for $PG(\mathcal{G}_1, \mathcal{G}_2)$ is given as follows:

Step 1: Construct the initial protocol subgraph $PG(G_1 \cup H_1, G'_1 \cup H'_1)$ using, for example, the production rules of Zafiropulo [12]. Let subgraphs G_1 and G'_1 be the root nodes of trees T_1 and T_2 to be constructed.

Step 2: To determine which nodes in subgraphs $G_1 \cup H_1$ and $G'_1 \cup H'_1$ can act as header nodes $h_x \in H_1$ and $h'_x \in H'_1$ for successor subgraphs to G_1 and G'_1 respectively, use design rule 1.

Design Rule 1: Let p and p' be any node of subgraph $G_i \cup H_i$ and $G'_i \cup H'_i$ other than the header nodes h_i and h'_i. Let q and q' represent any nodes of subgraph $G_i \cup H_i$ and $G'_i \cup H'_i$ respectively including p and p'. If in the reachability tree of $PG(G_i \cup H_i, G'_i \cup H'_i)$, there exists a global state of the form $<(p,p'),(\Lambda,\Lambda)>$ without any accompanying global states of the form $<(p,q'),(X \text{ or } \Lambda, Y)>$ or $<(q,p'),(X, Y \text{ or } \Lambda)>$, then nodes p and p' can serve as header nodes h_x and h'_x for successor subgraphs G_x and G'_x respectively.

In order to avoid processes from entering into different successor subgraphs, use design rule 2.

Design Rule 2: Let (h_x, h'_x) be the header state pair for successor subgraphs to G_i and G'_i chosen using design rule 1. We disallow choosing any other stable state pairs of the form (h_x, h'_y) or (h_y, h'_x) as header state pairs for successor subgraphs to G_i and G'_i.

Step 3: For every header state pair (h_x, h'_x) chosen in step 2, construct the protocol subgraph $PG(G_u \cup H_u, G'_u \cup H'_u)$. Let the subgraphs G_u and G'_u be the immediate descendants to G_1 and G'_1 in trees T_1 and T_2 respectively.

Step 4: Using design rule 1 and 2, determine the new header state pairs (h_x, h'_x) for each protocol subgraph $PG(G_u \cup H_u, G'_u \cup H'_u)$ with $h_x \in H_u$ and $h'_x \in H'_u$.

Step 5: For each header state pair (h_x, h'_x), construct the protocol subgraph $PG(G_v \cup H_v, G'_v \cup H'_v)$. Let the subgraphs G_v and G'_v be the immediate descendants to G_u and G'_u in tree T_1 and T_2 respectively. If subgraph G_v and G'_v have appeared in trees T_1 and T_2 before, i.e. it is a duplicate node, then subgraph G_v and G'_v are terminal nodes of tree T_1 and T_2 respectively. If the protocol subgraph $PG(G_v \cup H_v, G'_v \cup H'_v)$ is a final subgraph, i.e. $H_v = H'_v = \phi$, then subgraph G_v and G'_v are terminal nodes of tree T_1 and T_2 also. Repeat steps 4 and 5 until every leaf of tree T_1 and T_2 is a terminal node.

Step 6: Finally, convert the protocol tree $PT(T_1, T_2)$ so constructed to the protocol graph $PG(\mathcal{G}_1, \mathcal{G}_2)$ by merging identical nodes in trees T_1 and T_2.

Using the structured design technique described above, we can construct complicated protocol graphs by connecting together relatively simple protocol subgraphs. This forms the basis for a building block approach to protocol design.

In the following, we will illustrate the above procedures with a practical example, We have chosen to use the call control phase of CCITT Recommendation X.21. Recommendation X.21 has been validated by different authors [13,14]. It is not our intention to revalidate this protocol but only to demonstrate how the structured approach would apply. We will not examine the issue of time limits and timeouts but only the logical correctness as given by the state diagram.

Example 5.1

The call control phase for circuit switched service is specified by the state diagram Fig. A-2 in Recommendation X.21 [10]. The state diagram can be translated into separate state transition graphs for the DTE and the DCE participating in the protocol. See Fig. 5.1. The four main interface circuits are T, C, R, I, [15]. s(t,c) and s(r,i) represent a send event by the DTE and DCE respectively, while r(r,i) and r(t,c) represent a receive event by the DTE and DCE respectively. Let g_1 and g_2 be the state transition graphs representing the DTE and DCE respectively. The PG(g_1,g_2) represents the protocol between the DTE and DCE. In this case, the two graphs g_1 and g_2 have an identical structure . The smallest structured partition of g is given by $\pi(0) = \{G_1, G_2, G_3, G_4, G_5, G_{6A}, G_{6B}, G_{7/10}, G_8, G_9, G_{10bis}, G_{11}, G_{12}, G_{15}\}$. See Example 3.1. From the protocol graph PG(g_1,g_2), we construct the protocol tree PT(T_1,T_2). Since both trees T_1 and T_2 have an identical structure, we will call it T. See Fig. 5.2.

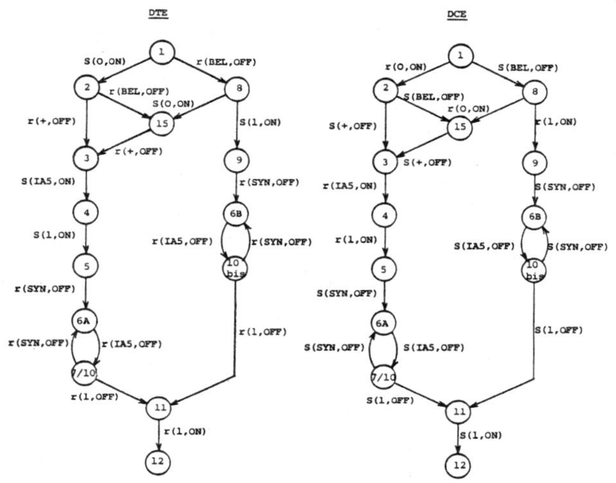

Fig. 5.1 The Protocol Graph PG(g_1,g_2) for the Call Control Phase of X.21

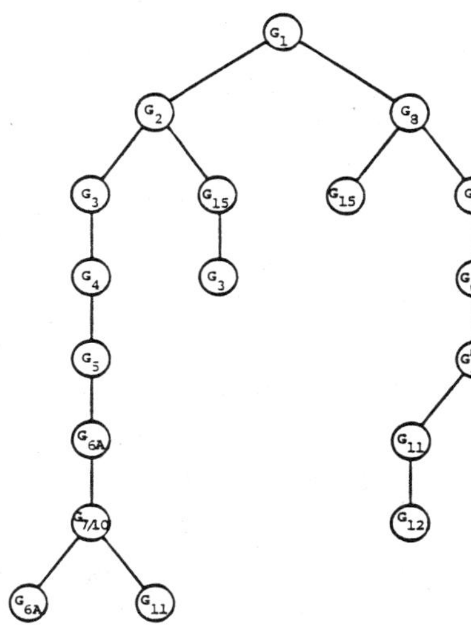

Fig. 5.2 The Tree T of Graph g

For structured protocol analysis, we will first examine the protocol subgraph PG($G_1 \cup H_1$, $G_1 \cup H_1$). See Fig. 5.3. Since the reachability tree of PG($G_1 \cup H$, $G_1 \cup H_1$) contains an unspecified reception of the form <(s_2,s_8), ([0,ON], [BEL,OFF])> which is a potential protocol error, we form a larger subgraph $G_1' = G_1 \cup G_2 \cup G_8$. The new partition so formed $\pi' = \{G_1', G_3', G_4', G_5', G_{6A}', G_{6B}', G_{7/10}', G_9', G_{10bis}', G_{11}', G_{12}', G_{15}'\}$ is given in Example 3.1. For the new partition π', we construct a new tree T' of g as shown in Fig. 5.4. The protocol tree PT(T_1',T_2') tells us that the protocol graph PG(g_1,g_2) is correct if the protocol subgraphs PG($G_i' \cup H_i'$, $G_i' \cup H_i'$), i = 1, 3, 4, 5, 6A, 6B, 7/10, 9, 10bis, 11, 12, 15 are correct. See Fig. 5.5. For the simple protocol subgraphs of Fig. 5.5, the validation can be done by sight.

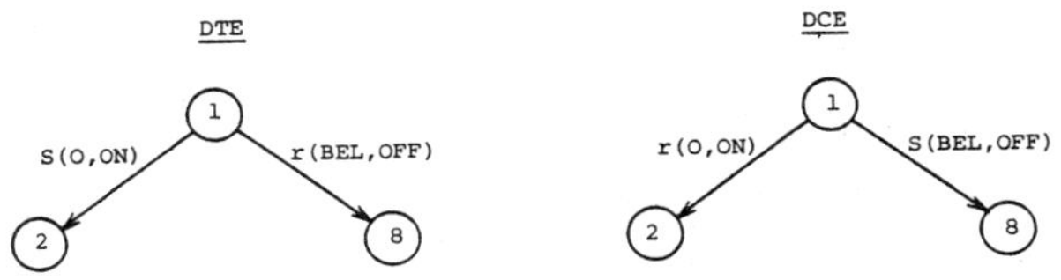

Fig. 5.3 The Protocol Subgraph PG($G_1 \cup H_1$, $G_1' \cup H_1'$)

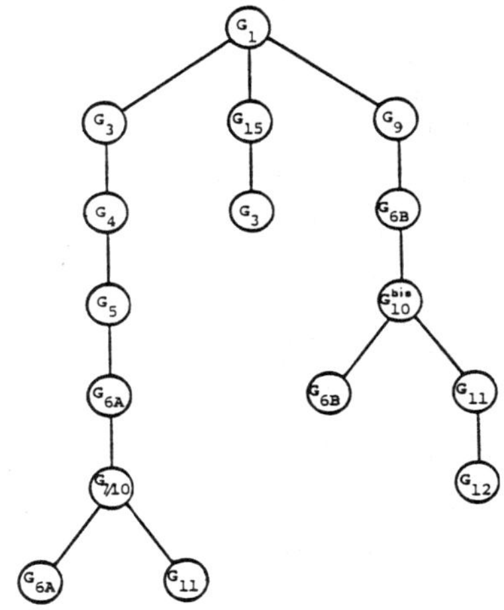

Fig. 5.4 The Tree T' of Graph g

For structured protocol design, we will first construct the protocol subgraph PG($G_1' \cup H_1'$, $G_1' \cup H_1'$) and let G_1' and G_1' be the root nodes of trees T_1' and T_2' to be constructed. Using rules 1 and 2 discussed above, we chose (s_3,s_3), (s_9,s_9), and (s_{15},s_{15}) to be the header state pairs of successor subgraphs to G_1'. Next we construct protocol subgraphs PG($G_3' \cup H_3'$, $G_3' \cup H_3'$) PG($G_9' \cup H_9'$, $G_9' \cup H_9'$), and PG($G_{15}' \cup H_{15}'$, $G_{15}' \cup H_{15}'$) and let subgraphs G_3', G_9', and G_{15}' be the immediate descendents to G_1' in trees T_1' and T_2'. Following the structured protocol design procedure described above, we build up trees T_1' and T_2'. The process terminates when we arrive at subgraphs G_{6A}' and G_{11}' which are duplicate nodes and subgraph G_{12}' which is a final node.

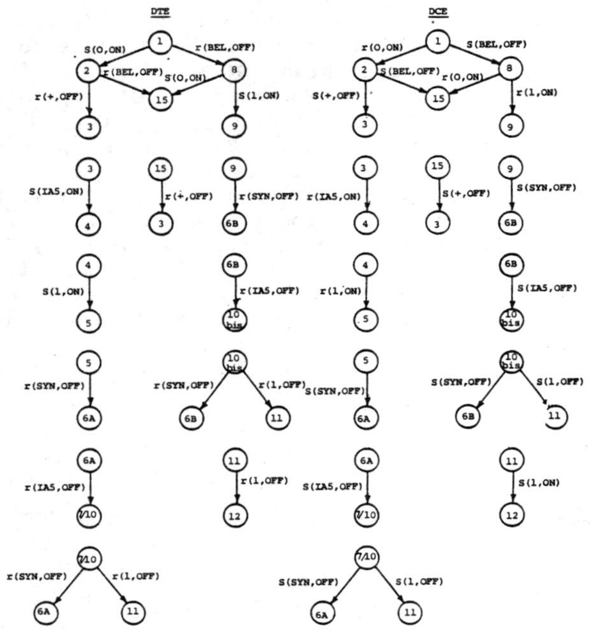

Fig. 5.5 The Protocol Subgraphs $PG(G_i' \cup H_i', G_i' \cup H_i')$

Finally, convert the protocol tree $PT(T_1^!, T_2^!)$ to the protocol graph $PG(g_1, g_2)$. The protocol so constructed is a structured protocol since it satisfies the three requirements stated above.

VI. CONCLUSIONS

In this paper, we introduced a 'Structured Partition' of a finite state graph into subgraphs and described the properties of such a partition. Based on the structured partition, we presented a structure theory for finite state protocols. We developed a structured approach to protocol analysis and design based on subgraphs. We applied the technique to the analysis of the call control phase of CCITT Recommendation X.21 and verified its correctness. We also found that the call control phase of Recommendation X.21 conforms with our requirements for structured protocol design.

The extension of the structure theory to protocols involving more than two processes can be done in a straightforward manner. In the limited space available, we have presented a summary of our work. A complete account is given in [16].

REFERENCES

[1] A. S. Tanenbaum, "Network Protocols," Computing Survey, Vol. 13, No. 4, Dec. 1981, pp. 453-489.

[2] C. A. Sunshine, "Formal Modeling of Communication Protocols," University of Southern California, ISI RR-81-89, March 5, 1981.

[3] National Bureau of Standards, "Formal Description Techniques for Network Protocols," Report No. ICST-HLNP-80-3, June 1980.

[4] T. F. Piatkowski, "An Engineering Discipline for Distributed Protocol Systems," Proc. INWG/NPL Workshop on Protocol Testing, Vol. 1, May 1981, pp. 177-215.

[5] H. Rudin and C. H. West, "Validation of Protocols using State Enumeration: A summary of some experience," Proc. INWG/NPL Workshop on Protocol Testing, Vol. 1, May 1981, pp. 371-375.

[6] G. V. Bochmann, "Finite State Description of Communication Protocols," Computer Networks, Vol. 2, Oct. 1978, pp. 361-372.

[7] D. Brand and P. Zafiropulo, "On Communicating Finite State Machines," IBM Research Report RZ 1053, Jan. 1981.

[8] C. H. West, "General Techniques for Communication Protocol Validation," IBM J. Res. Develop., Vol. 11, No. 4, July 1978, pp. 393-404.

[9] H. Rudin, et. al., "Automated Protocol Validation: One chain of development," Computer Networks, Vol. 2, No. 4/5, 1978, pp. 373-380.

[10] CCITT Recommendation X.21, Geneva, Switzerland, 1980.

[11] J. Rubin and C. H. West, "An Improved Protocol Validation Technique," Computer Networks, Vol. 6, 1982, pp. 65-73.

[12] P. Zafiropulo, et. al., "Towards Analyzing and Synthesizing Protocols," IEEE Trans. on Communications, Vol. COM-28, No. 4, April 1980, pp. 651-661.

[13] C. H. West and P. Zafiropulo, "Automated Validation of a Communications Protocol: the CCITT X.21 Recommendation," IBM J. Res. Develop., Vol. 22, No. 1, Jan. 1978, pp. 60-71.

[14] R. Razouk and G. Estrin, "Validation of the X.21 Interface Specification Using SARA," Proceedings of the NBS Trends and Applications Symposium, May 29, 1980.

[15] H. C. Folts, "Procedures for Circuit Switched Service in Synchronous Public Data Networks," IEEE Trans. on Communications, Vol. COM-28, No. 4, April 1980, pp. 489-496.

[16] T. Y. Choi, "A Structured Approach to the Analysis and Design of Finite State Protocols," Ph.D. Thesis, School of Electrical Engineering, Georgia Institute of Technology, 1983 (in preparation).

DYNAMIC SELECTION OF A PERFORMANCE-EFFECTIVE TRANSMISSION SEQUENCE FOR TOKEN-PASSING NETWORKS WITH MOBILE NODES

Yaron I. Gold and Shlomo Moran

University of Connecticut

Technion, Israel Institute of technology

ABSTRACT

We describe a distributed method for keeping down "token-passing" overhead in a mobile multi-access network, by performing local corrections in the token-passing sequence as they become necessary due to changes in node spatial configuration. These corrections involve only a subset of the nodes in the network, thus reducing the required computational effort. The method consists of three distributed protocols. The first is for detecting deterioration and identifying a subset of nodes that constitutes a "problem area", the second is to provide each node with the distances (propagation delays) to all other nodes, and the third is to use this topological information to construct a minimal spanning tree, from which a good "token passing" sequence can be derived. The second and third protocols may also have applications other than the one described here, such as position location, routing and broadcasting.

1. INTRODUCTION

Performance of distributed round-robin access-protocols with "tight" Round-Robin Token-Passing (e.g.: SOSAM [1,2]) depends on ΣR_o, the round-trip propagation delay between the nodes in the order of the round-robin sequence. An optimal sequence is one that minimizes ΣR_o. The corresponding optimal ΣR_o depends on node spatial configuration. It can be shown [3] that the optimal ΣR_o for a network with K nodes is bounded by $bK^{1/2}$, where b is a constant that depends on the distance between the two remotest nodes. As shown in [1,2], selecting an optimal sequence is equivalent to solving the "Travelling Salesman" problem which is NP hard. As long as the network consists of stationary nodes only (as in [1]), an optimal sequence can be computed once before network initialization, and used thereafter. (For a network with a large number of nodes a sub-optimal sequence can be determined using an approximation algorithm with linear time complexity [4]. With this algorithm ΣR_o will be bounded by twice the optimal ΣR_o). However, if the network contains mobile nodes (as in [2]) ΣR_o may deteriorate with time and may eventually exceed a critical value at which the access-protocol's decreasing performance advantage over topology-independent access-protocols no longer justifies its additional complexity. Recomputing the sequence "from scratch" at regular intervals may be prohibitively costly.

In this paper we present an efficient distributed method for preventing excessive deterioration of ΣR_o. The method is based on the assumptions that (1) ΣR_o deteriorates gradually, and that (2) the K nodes in the network are not always all involved in the configuration change that is responsible for the deterioration of ΣR_o. These assumptions allow the network to take advantage of the fact that prior to deterioration the sequence was close to optimal, and hence small local corrections, performed only when necessary, can restore

---

This research was supported in part by NSF grant ECS 8307186 and in part by United Technologies Corporation.

performance and never allow it to even get near the critical level.

According to our method nodes periodically probe the value of ΣR_o (using a method derived from the one used in [2] to update the scheduling function), and an alarm is generated when the value exceeds some threshold (say 3 times the upper bound on the optimal ΣR_o). The nodes then identify a "problem area" - a section of L ($L \leq K$) consecutive nodes in the sequence that are the main contributors to the deterioration, and apply a distributed algorithm to correct the order of these L nodes. These local corrections, with the number of participating nodes changing "by demand", involve much less computational effort than re-computing an optimal (or sub-optimal) sequence for all K nodes in the network. The idea is illustrated in Figure 1.

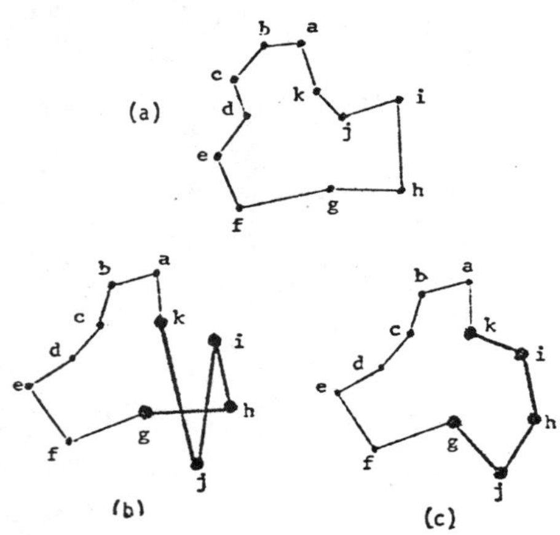

(a) "Token passing" sequence before deterioration.

(b) ΣR_o deteriorates due to configuration change. "Problem area" with L=5 is indicated in heavy lines.

(c) Sequence corrected in "problem area".

Figure 1 - Local Correction of Sequence

2. DETECTING DETERIORATION AND IDENTIFYING A "PROBLEM-AREA"

The following distributed protocol is executed by the nodes to obtain the necessary information about their relative spatial configuration. The protocol is similar (with only slight modification) to the one used by nodes to update the SOSAM scheduling function [2]. The two protocols are overlapping and hence the additional overhead is minimal. The protocol consists of a sequenced exchange of "trigger" messages. All "trigger" messages carry a code that distinguishes them from other types of messages, and also contain the source-index. The "trigger"s are broadcast by the nodes in two cycles. The first cycle is initiated by, say, node-1 which broadcasts the first "trigger", causing all nodes to suspend the regular access-protocol. Each node then broadcasts a "trigger" as soon as it receives that of the node immediately preceding it in the cyclic order. When the last node, which also precedes node-1 has broadcast and its "trigger" is received by node-1, a second cycle begins immediately. This cycle is almost identical to the first, except that each "trigger" contains an additional piece of information. This additional information, broadcast by each node-i, is the value of the propagation delay d(i,i+1), between node-i and the node immediately following it in the cyclic order (note: "+" and "-" in the context of node indices will always be modulo K). Node-i derives this information from the time that elapsed between the transmission of its own "trigger" and the reception of its immediate successor's "trigger": d(i,i+1) is equal to half that time (after deducting "trigger" duration and node response time). The last "trigger" in the second cycle also signals all nodes to resume their regular access-protocol. Each node has transmitted 2 "trigger" messages so that the total number of "trigger"s in the sequence is 2K.

At this point all nodes know the values of d(j,j+1) for all $1 \leq j \leq K$. A second distributed algorithm is now executed by the nodes to determine whether ΣR_o has deteriorated enough to generate an alarm, and in such a case - to identify the "problem area" that has to be corrected. This algorithm is outlined next:

Each node-i computes a set of values, R(i,j), which are the "path lengths" along the cyclic node sequence from each node-j to node-i:

$$R(i,j) = \sum_{m=j}^{i-1} d(m,m+1)$$

Each $R(i,j)$ is compared to a threshold value that is a function of the number of nodes, L, in the corresponding path: $L=i-(j-1)$. This threshold is predetermined by the designer and must be larger than twice the upper bound on the "shortest path" among the L nodes, which is proportional to $L^{1/2}$. Each node-i identifies the longest path for which $R(i,j)$ exceeds the corresponding threshold. This path will contain the "problem area". The nodes, each at its turn, broadcast messages indicating the identities of these paths, and the one with the smallest number, L, of participating nodes will be defined as the "problem area" and will be subject to correction. (Note: depending on network size and the number of nodes, it may be faster to have all nodes determine the "problem area" independently, using the same algorithm. This will eliminate the need to broadcast "partial results" by each node, with the price of redundant computation. Recall that all nodes share all the information needed to execute the algorithm).

3. SEQUENCE CORRECTION

In order to correct the sequence of L nodes, all $L^2/2$ pairwise inter-node propagation delays must be known. These values may be computed from the information obtained by the protocol in Section 2. As described in [2], each node-i computes a set of values, called D_o-values, from the time intervals measured between the "trigger" messages it receives. For each $j \neq i-1$ node-i determines $D_o(i,j)$ as the interval $[t_j, t_{i-1}]_i$ where t_j and t_{i-1} are the "trigger" messages originating at nodes j and i-1 respectively and being received by node-i in this order. (message durations are deductd). $D_o(i,i-1)$ is defined as 0 for all i. In addition to the D_o-values each node also knows the values $d(j,j+1)$ for all j (see Section 2). It can be shown that from these values each node-i can compute the "distances", $d(i,j)$, (in terms of propagation delay) from itself to every node-j:

for $j=i-1$:

$$d(i,i-1) = d(i-1,i) \quad \text{(broadcast by node i-1, see Section 2).}$$

and for $j \neq i-1$:

$$d(i,j) = \sum_{m=j}^{i-1} d(m,m+1) - D_o(i,j)$$
$$= R(i,j) - D_o(i,j)$$

The network now possesses the knowledge of all inter-node propagation delays. However, this knowledge is distributed among the nodes: each node knows the delays between itself and all other nodes. This information is enough for computing a sub-optimal sequence (which produces $\sum R_o$ that is at most twice as long as the optimal $\sum R_o$), as demonstrated by the distributed algorithm outlined below.

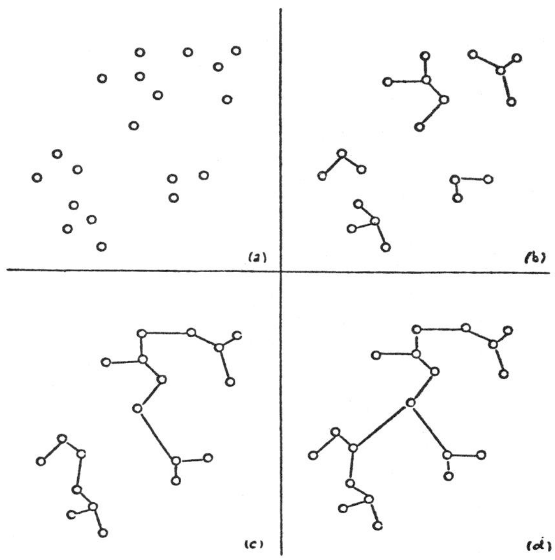

(a) Node configuration
(b) Connected components after 1st pass
(c) After 2nd pass
(d) complete minimal spanning tree after 3rd pass

Figure 2 - Construction of a minimal spanning tree.

First, a minimal spanning-tree over the L nodes in the "problem area" is constructed in the following distributed manner: each node first broadcasts the identity of its closest neighbour. All nodes use this information to construct adjacency lists, from which they learn about the connected components that were formed by the edges to the nearest neighbours. Each node then broadcasts the identity of its nearest neighbour in a <u>different</u> connected component, and the shortest edge between any two components is used to connect these components and is inserted in the adjacency lists. This process is repeated until all nodes are connected, as illustrated in Figure 2. It can be shown that the resulting graph is a minimal spanning-tree. The worst-case total number of messages required is $O(L \log_2 L)$. The sub-optimal sequence is then generated by traversing the minimal spanning tree using a Depth First Search algorithm (see [4]).

CONCLUSION

In this paper we described a distributed method for dynamically correcting the "token-passing" sequence in mobile networks that use a multi-access channel (e.g. - radio). The use of the protocols that constitute this method is not, however, limited to this particular application. For example, the protocol that provides all nodes with the distances (propagation delays) to all other nodes can be used for position location [5] or with distributed dynamic routing algorithms. The protocol for constructing a minimal spanning tree can be used for broadcasting.

REFERENCES

[1] Gold, Yaron I. and W.R Franta, "An efficient collision-free protocol for prioritized access-control of cable or radio channels", Computer Networks, Vol. 7, No. 2, April 1983, pp. 83-98.

[2] Gold, Yaron I., W.R. Franta and S.Moran, "A distributed channel-access protocol for fully-connected networks with mobile nodes", IEEE Trans. on Comp.Vol. C-32 No. 2, pp. 133-147, February 1983.

[3] Gold, Yaron I. and S. Moran, "A bound on the minimal token passing overhead in a radio network with an arbitrary node configuration", tech. report, Dept. of Computer Science, Technion, Israel Institute of Technology, 1982.

[4] Christofedes, N., "Worst-case analysis of a new heuristic for the travelling salesman problem", Manag. Sci. Res. Report 388, Carnegie-Mellon University, 1976.

[5] Yemini, Y., "Some theoretical aspects of position location problems," Proc. IEEE 20th Conf. Foundations Comput. Sci., 1979, pp. 1-8.

GRACEFUL PREEMPTION FOR MULTI-LINK LINK LAYER PROTOCOLS

M. Wm. Beckner
T. J. J. Starr

Bell Laboratories
Naperville, Illinois 60566

ABSTRACT

This paper discusses a powerful priority mechanism that can be used on a physical communication medium supporting multiple, independent, logical data links. This scheme allows a high priority message to immediately interrupt a lower priority message which is in the process of being transmitted, and yet will not require the re-transmission of the first part of the lower priority message; hence, the term *graceful* preemption. Graceful preemption may be extended to furnish multiple priority levels similar to existing processor interrupt structures which implement multiple levels. This protocol may serve a single processor which handles several different processes, or several independent stations that share a common bus. Hence, priority levels can be enforced without the need for a centralized bus "master" or "arbitrator" unit. As an example, the application of graceful preemption to the Integrated Services Digital Network (ISDN) link access procedure, LAPD, is discussed.

1. INTRODUCTION

Several processes requiring differing degrees of real-time performance can share a common communications link if a suitable priority structured protocol is used. This paper investigates the types of priority that may be employed. A link using **non-preemptive priority** will allow the current link-layer frame to complete and will then send the highest priority frame in the transmit queue. A link using **preemptive priority** will immediately abort the current frame when a higher priority frame enters the transmit queue; the aborted frame is repeated in full later. Preemptive priority provides the high priority frames rapid transmission at the cost of a greatly increased delay for low priority frames. This paper introduces the concept of **gracefully preemptive priority**. A link using this technique will immediately interrupt the current frame when a higher priority frame enters the transmit queue. When the higher priority frame completes, the interrupted frame resumes with no need for retransmission of its first part.

Graceful preemption is valuable when the rapid transmission of some frames must be ensured and yet it is desirable to minimize the delay for the lower priority frames. The only way for a non-preemptive link to ensure short delay for high priority frames is to severely restrict the maximum frame size (this may be inefficient) or to provide a high data rate (this may be expensive). While a preemptive link avoids these problems, it can greatly increase the delay of the lower priority frames. In effect, the capacity of a link may be reduced by using a preemptive priority because of the overhead imposed by retransmitting the preempted information. Thus, graceful preemption removes a constraint on frame size, allows the use of a lower speed link, and provides good delay performance for both low and high priority frames.

We have stated the desirable aspects of graceful preemption; the question remains as to how this concept is applied to existing link access procedures. Sections 2 and 3 of this paper show the details of implementing graceful preemption in an HDLC-based protocol. Section 4 presents the results of the simulated performance of the three types of priority mentioned above. Section 5 extends graceful preemption to the role of multiple access contention resolution.

This paper is an introduction to providing graceful preemption in existing HDLC-based link-layer protocols and does not address details such as how to handle all possible error conditions. Furthermore, the transmission of information with multiple priority levels is the main topic of this paper, and not the switching of this information.

2. GRACEFUL PREEMPTION

2.1 Origins

Graceful preemption is a direct result of our work with the Integrated Services Digital Network (ISDN) link access procedure, LAPD, used on the Digital Subscriber Line (DSL) D-channel [1] [2]. The D-channel is a 16 Kb/s digital pipe between the subscriber and ISDN exchange or central office. The data link layer of the access protocol, LAPD, allows multiplexing of information types via multiple, logical data links with the elements, procedures, and frame structure of the protocol drawn from High-level Data Link Control (HDLC) [3] [4]. Multiple logical links are used to transport distinct information streams — e.g., user-to-network signaling (s-type) information and low-speed, packetized (p-type) information.

Early in our work we recognized the need for a logical link priority structure that would allow, for example, s-type information to have priority over p-type information. An important goal was that any such priority structure should not impose restrictions on low priority frame lengths — assuming, of course, that bit error rates are sufficiently low such that they are not a major factor in restricting frame lengths. A second goal was to implement the priority structure in such a way to increase the efficiency of low priority information transfer. Graceful preemption meets these goals.

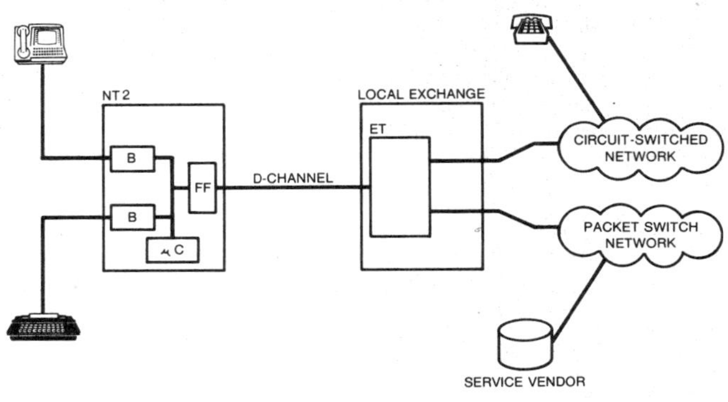

FIGURE 1

2.2 An Example

Figure 1 shows DSL access to an ISDN local exchange; only the details regarding the D-channel are illustrated. Arbitrarily chosen customer terminal equipment consists of a combined voice/data terminal and a high-resolution hardcopy device. Each share an intelligent Network Termination (NT) that implements the D-channel protocol and may or may not contain additional functions needed to control the customer terminal equipment. It consists of a Frame Formatter (FF) and micro-Computer (uC), operating in concert as a data link controller, and an individual Buffer (B) for each piece of terminal equipment. The Exchange Termination (ET) is similar in function to the NT and resides in the ISDN local exchange from which the customer can gain access to a variety of networks and services. Both the terminal and printer are assigned separate D-channel facilities for communicating with the local exchange via the ET. Each facility consists of a buffer at the ET, a D-channel Logical Link (LL) common to both the ET and NT, and a buffer at the NT. The facilities are arranged in priority such that the printer could use a logical link (LLi) that was lower in priority than the logical link used by the terminal (LLj).

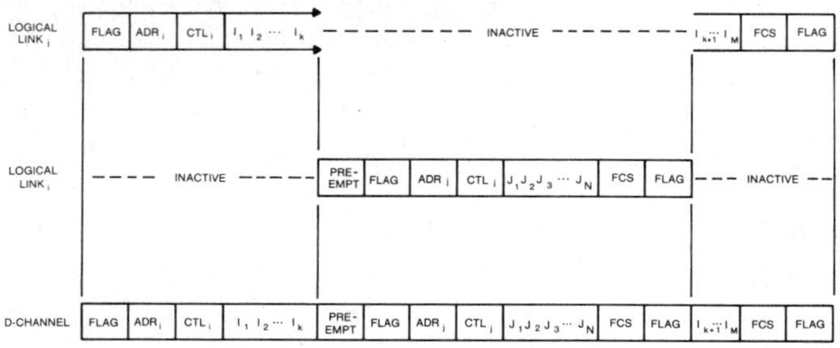

Graceful Preempion

FIGURE 2

Figure 2 illustrates the situation where the printer is receiving a lengthy frame — e.g., high-resolution image — from a service vendor via the ET. During the transmission of this frame a buffer in the ET is loaded with a message for the terminal — e.g., information associated with an incoming call. Since the ET and NT are aware of the priority relationship among the different D-channel facilities they serve, the ET recognizes that the contents of this buffer are higher in priority than the buffer currently being served and, thus, invokes graceful preemption.

Graceful preemption is affected by a cooperative effort on the part of the transmitting ET and the receiving NT. The ET begins preemption by saving the state of the logical link it is presently using (LLi) and re-initializing it's transmit state for the preempting logical link (LLj). It then transmits the PREEMPT sequence to the NT followed by the frame destined for the terminal. The ET will subsequently restore the state of LLi and continue operation from the point of preemption. The NT saves the state of LLi when it receives the PREEMPT sequence and begins searching for a FLAG. It receives the frame on LLj and restores its state to continue operation of LLi. Note that the graceful preemption operation did not disturb the ET's receive function and the NT's transmit function and was completely transparent to the operation of the terminal and printer.

This example illustrates only a single level of nesting. In practice, it is possible to have multiple, nested preemptions where the maximum depth of nesting is limited only by the number of available priority levels.

2.3 Primary Characteristics

Graceful vs. Abortive Preemption

Graceful preemption is a special case of abortive preemption in that it is non-destructive to the frame that is preempted. Reception of an ABORT causes all data received between the last FLAG and the ABORT to be discarded. Reception of a PREEMPT sequence causes the present state of the data link controller to be saved and re-initialized for reception of a new frame.

Similar to the ABORT sequence, the PREEMPT sequence is indicated by a bit pattern that is not subject to zero insertion for transparency. Thus, it is important that the bit sequence chosen for PREEMPT does not simulate FLAG, ABORT, or IDLE by its particular location in the bit stream.

The additional complexity of graceful preemption is warranted when the length of low priority frames becomes long enough to need an efficient abort mechanism.

Logical Link Priority Structure

All or a portion of the frame's address field is used as a Logical Link IDentifier (LLID) with the purpose of identifying a particular logical data link and its relative priority with respect to other logical data links. The priority structure is chosen such that the logical link priority increases as the logical link identifier increases. Therefore, logical link 0 is lowest in priority with logical link 2^N-1 being highest in priority where N is the number of address field bits used for the LLID.

At first this priority structure may appear arbitrary. However, for some HDLC-based data link protocols, including LAPD, a global address is reserved for point-to-multipoint operation. This global address value is typically all 1s in the LLID portion of the address field. If the highest numbered logical link is highest in priority, the priority structure is compatible with applications that define a global logical link and, in all probability, require that link to be highest in priority.

Permitted Points of Preemption

In theory, a frame may be preempted at the beginning of any bit interval including bit intervals associated with FLAG sequences as long as the transmitter and receiver are able to save and restore the proper state information. In practice, it simplifies things if preemption is allowed to only occur during the information portion of a frame, potentially the longest field within the frame.

Errors

An important requirement of graceful preemption is that it should not be susceptible to types of errors that require new or significantly different error recovery strategies than those already provided by the particular link access procedure of which it is a part.

Data link frames, with or without graceful preemption, are subject to bit errors in transmission. A Frame Check Sequence (FCS) is transmitted with each frame so that the receiver may detect bit errors in the frame, excluding the opening and closing FLAG sequences. Bit errors in the PREEMPT sequence — as with errors in the FLAG and ABORT sequence — will cause the frame to be unrecognizable at the receiver and require error recovery mechanisms within the link access procedure.

Procedural exceptions are errors that arise from improper execution of the protocol. An example of a procedural error is the transfer of a frame that has an invalid or undefined control field encoding, but contains a valid FCS. Graceful preemption gives rise to an additional procedural exception that results from the logical link priority structure. This exception occurs when a logical link of a particular priority is preempted by a logical link of lower priority. The response to such an exception is to discard the frame and rely on the data link protocols' error recovery strategy to recover lost or missing frames.

3. IMPLEMENTATION

As will be described, the implementation of graceful preemption that we have chosen is at the frame level of the data link layer protocol.

The line of reasoning that supports this choice is that graceful preemption is

- similar to other frame level functions, hence
- amenable to LSI implementation, and, therefore,
- can be made uniformly available in any HDLC-based protocol.

Only the basic implementation of graceful preemption will be depicted in this section. Straightforward extensions to this design can be made to provide the multi-access features described in Section 5.

The control section common to both the transmitter and receiver is referred to, but not described in detail. It consists of a simple command and status register through which the uC invokes and monitors the operation of the transmitter and receiver sections of the frame formatter.

3.1 Transmitter Description

A block diagram of the transmitter section of the frame formatter is shown in Figure 3a and its state diagram is given in Figure 3b.

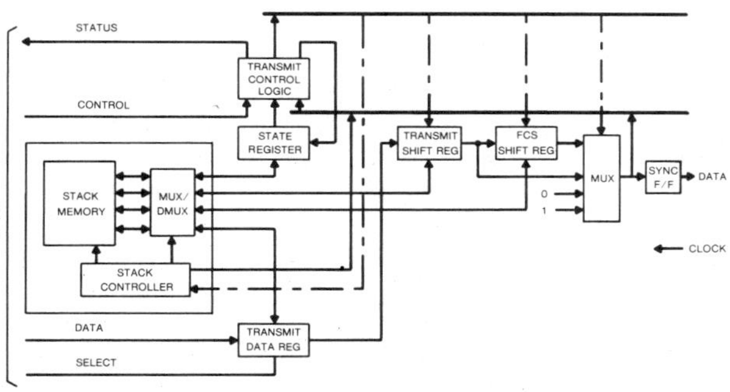

Transmitter Block Diagram
FIGURE 3a

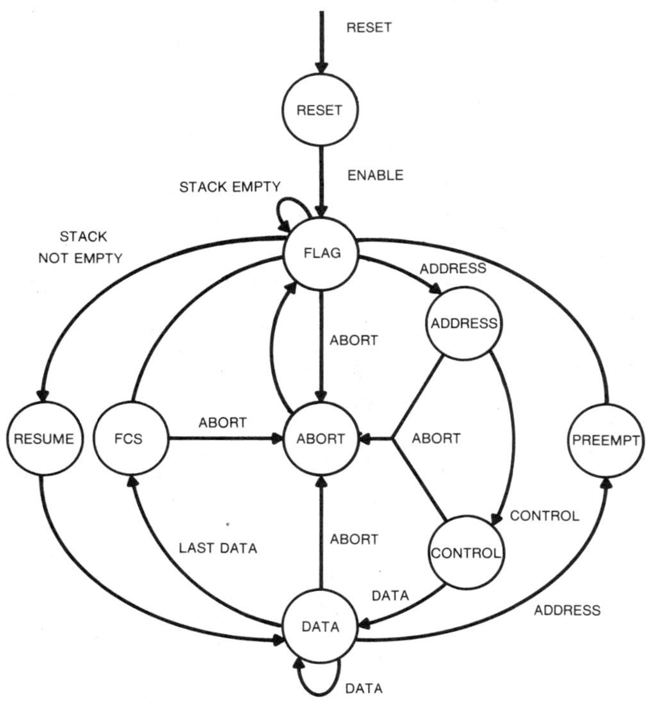

Transmitter State Diagram

FIGURE 3b

Basic Features

With but the exceptions cited in the next section, the transmitter is rather conventional in its design. It is driven by a controller consisting of a combinational logic array and a state register. When the transmit data register indicates empty, parallel data can be loaded into it where it is buffered and then transferred to the transmit shift register for serialization. The output of this shift register drives the transmitter data output via the multiplexor and sync flipflop and is also input to the FCS shift register for FCS calculation. The multiplexor allows transmit data to be sourced from the transmit shift register, FSC shift register, or constant values of 0 and 1 for FLAG, ABORT, and PREEMPT generation as well as inserting 0s into the data stream so that these sequences are not simulated by random bit sequences within the frame.

The transmitter is initialized by a reset indication from the common control section and is held in the RESET state until the transmitter is enabled when it then enters the FLAG state and continuous FLAG sequences are transmitted on the data output. As FLAGs are completed, the transmitter may enter the ADDRESS state when the first byte of data is written to the transmit data register with an "address byte" indication given to the transmitter controller by the common control section. The CONTROL state is entered as the next byte of data is loaded into the data register with a "control byte" indication given by the common control section. Subsequent loading of the data register causes the DATA state to be entered and maintained until the "last data byte" indication is received from the common control section. The last data byte is sent and the transmitter enters the FCS state, sends the FCS, enters the FLAG state, and sends the closing FLAG.

At any point in the above sequence of events, the frame in progress may be aborted by proper indication from the common control section. The transmitter then enters the ABORT state and an ABORT of 8 contiguous 1s is transmitted. The transmitter then returns to the FLAG state.

Additions for Graceful Preemption

The added feature of the data link transmitter is graceful preemption and requires the addition of a hardware last-in-first-out memory (i.e., a stack) and appropriate controller sequences.

Graceful preemption is allowed only after the transmitter has entered the DATA state. In this state an "address byte" indication causes the transmitter controller to gracefully preempt the frame currently being transmitted. The transmitter enters the PREEMPT state and will push its current state consisting of the contents of

- the transmit state register,
- the transmit data register,
- the transmit shift register, and
- the FCS shift register

onto the transmit stack. A PREEMPT sequence is transmitted followed by entry into the FLAG state. At this point the preempting frame is transmitted in the normal manner with the exception that at the close of the frame, the RESUME state is entered since the stack is not empty where the top of the stack is popped, restoring the state of the preempted frame's transmission that is then continued.

Of particular interest is the coding and generation of the PREEMPT sequence. The PREEMPT bit sequence is 11111110, 0 being the last bit transmitted. This sequence must be transmitted such that an ABORT sequence is not simulated due to 1s preceding the PREEMPT sequence in the transmitted bit stream. This is accomplished by borrowing all 1s that immediately precede the point of preemption and filling out the PREEMPT sequence with additional 1s and a 0. The transmit controller keeps a count of the number of consecutive 1s that have been transmitted as part of its state information. This count is reset whenever a true or inserted 0 is transmitted. Due to zero insertion, at most five 1s can precede a preempting frame in which case the transmit controller would fill out the PREEMPT sequence by transmitting two additional 1s and a 0. The transmitter must retransmit these five 1s when the preemption is complete since they were interpreted at the receiver as part of the PREEMPT sequence. This method of generating the preempt does not add significant overhead to the transmit controller and helps to further decrease the transmission delay of the preempting frame.

3.2 Receiver Description

A block diagram of the receive section of an HDLC frame formatter is shown in Figure 4a and its state diagram is given in Figure 4b.

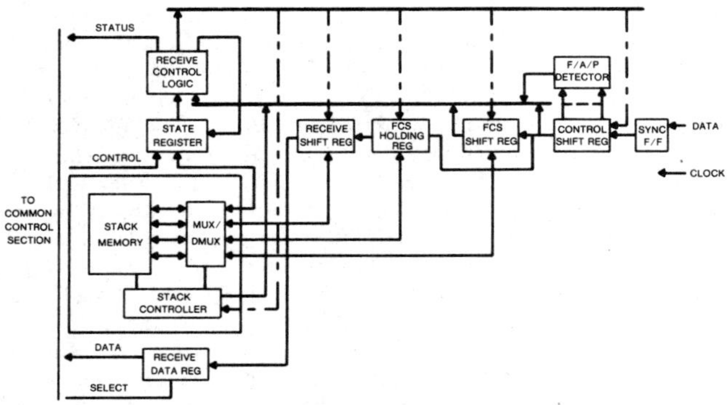

Receiver Block Diagram

FIGURE 4a

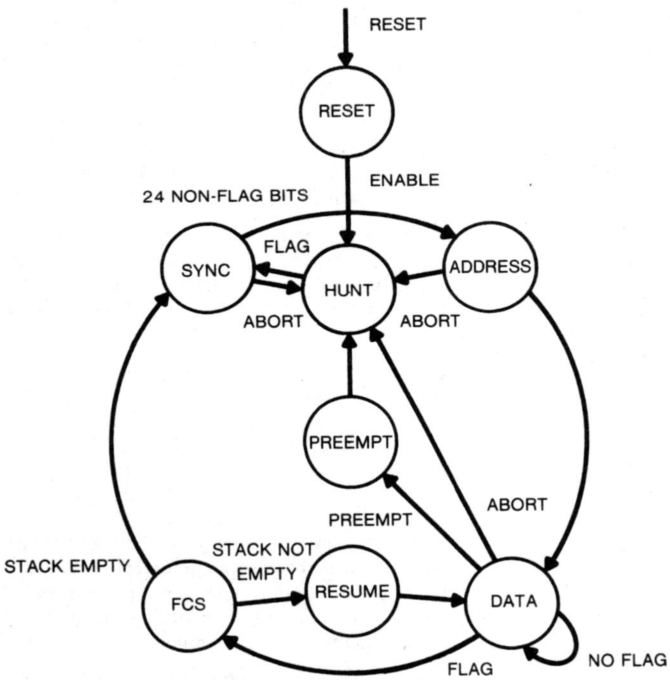

Receiver State Diagram

FIGURE 4b

Basic Features

Similar to the transmitter, the receiver is initialized by the reset input and will remain in the RESET state until the receiver is enabled. Once enabled, the receiver enters the HUNT state to search for FLAGs in the incoming data stream. When a FLAG is detected, the SYNC state is entered and will be maintained until at least 24 bits of non-FLAG data is received. If the frame is completed before 24 bits have been assembled, an invalid frame is assumed. Otherwise, the first byte of data is transferred from the receive shift register to the receive data register and the ADDRESS state is entered. The DATA state is entered for subsequently received bytes and maintained until the closing FLAG is detected. The FCS state is entered with the receiver using the 16 bits preceding the FLAG as the FCS. Detection of an ABORT in the received data stream will cause the receiver to enter the HUNT state for the purpose of recovering FLAG synchronization.

Additions for Graceful Preemption

Like the transmitter, the receiver requires only the addition of a hardware stack and appropriate controller sequences in order to implement graceful preemption.

Reception of a PREEMPT sequence causes the receiver to enter the PREEMPT state. On entering the PREEMPT state the receiver saves its state information which consists of the contents of

- the FCS shift register,
- the FCS holding register,
- the receive shift register, and
- the receive state register

on the stack and then enters the HUNT state from which the reception of the preempted frame is initiated. The RESUME state is entered at the completion of the preempting frame in order to restore the state of the previous frame.

4. SIMULATED PERFORMANCE

To gain a more quantitative understanding of the frame delay performance, a point-to-point link with two levels of priority was computer simulated. The mean frame delay for: 1) non-preemptive, 2) non-gracefully preemptive, and 3) gracefully preemptive priority was calculated for various degrees of link occupancy.

The model used was a simple one, and future studies requiring more time and resources could yield more exact results and consider a larger set of variables. For example, the use of a Poisson arrival distribution is suggested. For each graph a constant frame size is used and the time between the entry of successive frames in the transmit queue is given by:

syntax error
file gp.rp, between lines 492 and 492
t=

where

- **random** is a random variable with a uniform probability density function between 0 and 2 and has probability zero elsewhere; thus, **random** has a mean value of 1,
- **occupancy** has a value between 0 and 1,
- **frame size** is measured in bits, and
- **t** is measured in bits.

Up to 450 frames were used in the simulations and sufficient time was allowed for the last frame to complete. Frame delay is measured in bit-times and is the time between arrival in the transmit queue (an instantaneous process) and the completion of transmission. 8 bits were added to the non-gracefully preemptive frames to represent the abort character, and 6 bits were added to the gracefully preemptive frames to represent the preempt character. It is assumed that 2 bits are 'borrowed' for the average preemption; these borrowed bits are later added onto the continuation of the preempted frame.

Figures 5 to 9 present graphs of mean frame delay versus link occupancy. These plots show a smoothed representation of the data. The solid line represents non-preemptive priority, the dashed line represents non-gracefully preemptive priority, and the dotted line represents graceful preemption. Two graphs are presented for each case of frame size and proportion of high priority frames. One graph shows the delays for the low priority frames; the other graph shows the delays for the high priority frames. Note that the ordinate scale factor differs from graph to graph.

FIGURE 5

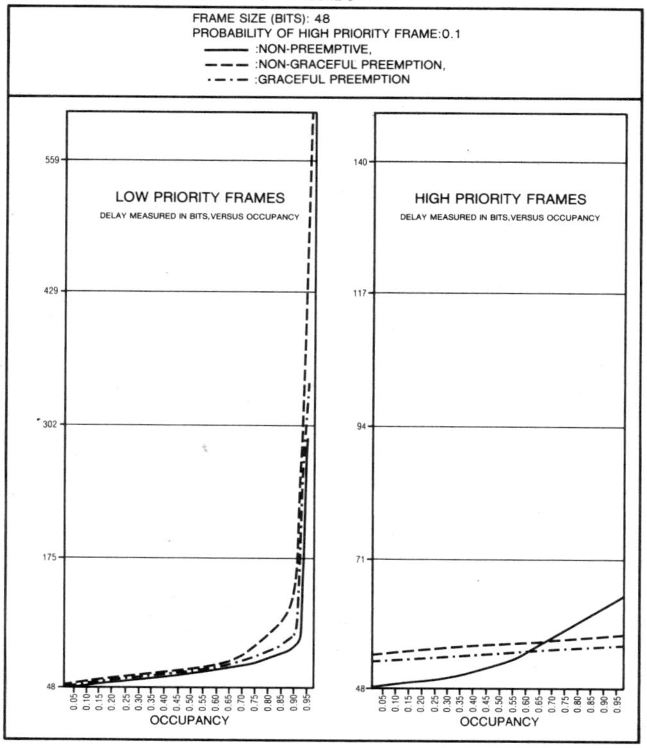

FIGURE 6

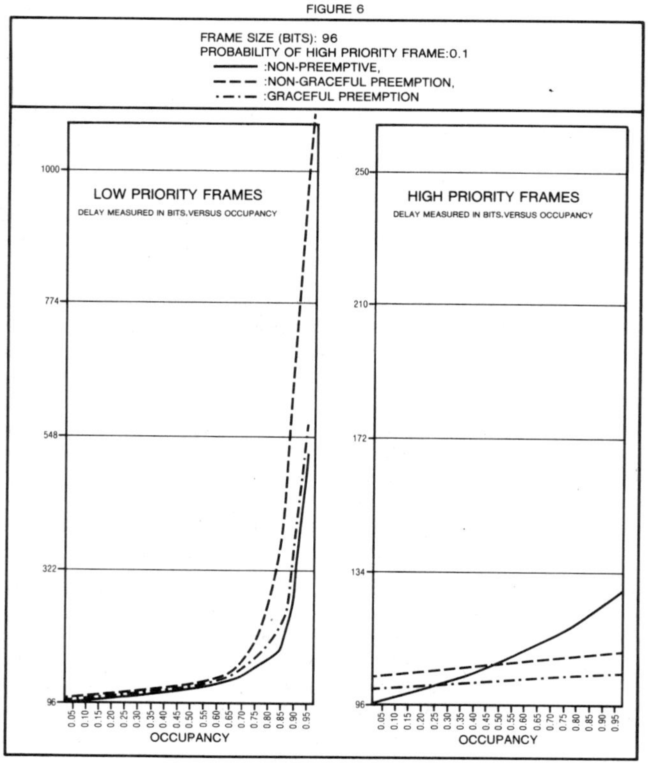

FIGURE 7

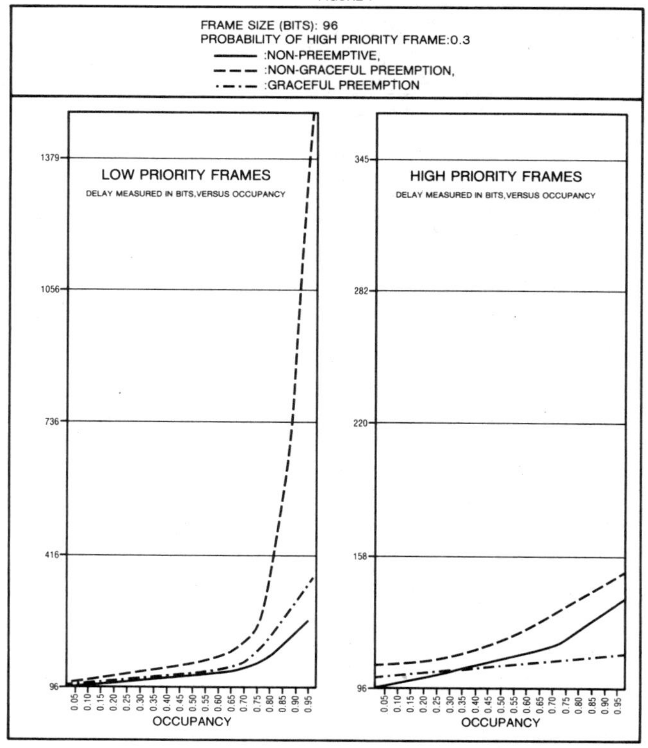

FIGURE 8

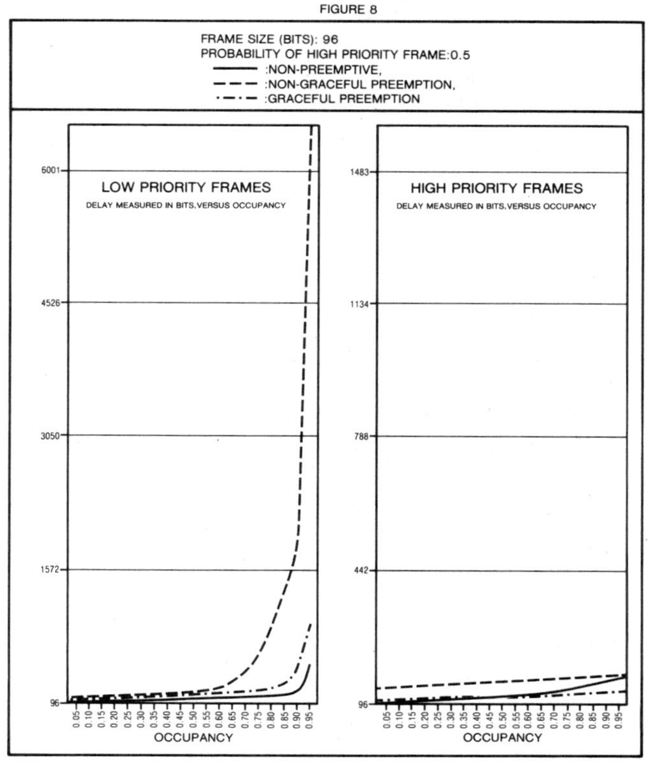

FIGURE 9

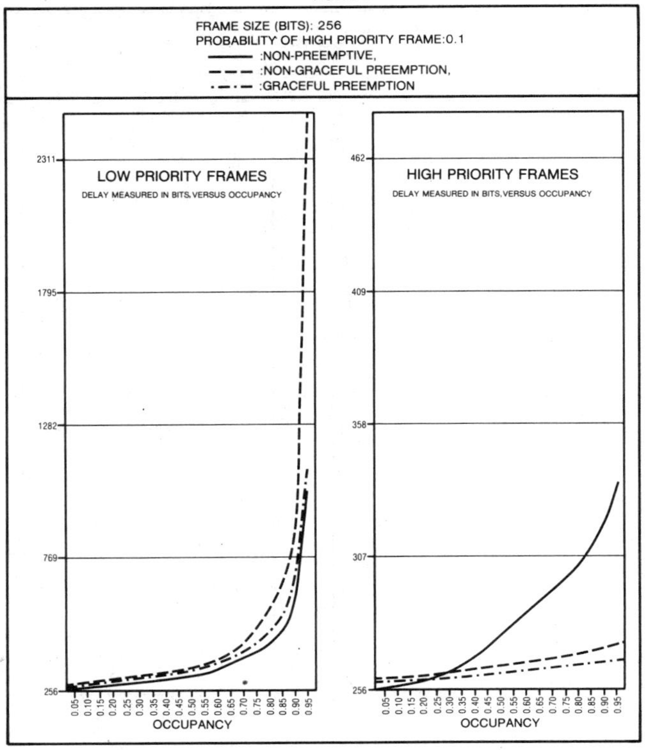

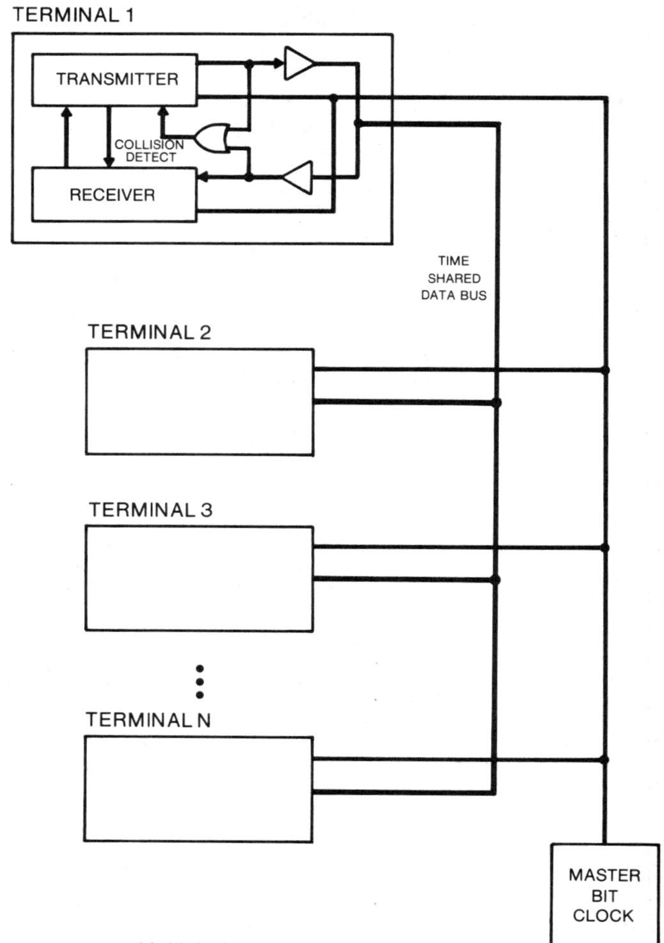

Multiple Access Bus Configuration

FIGURE 10

Examination of the graphs will confirm that:

- For occupancy levels greater than 50% graceful preemption offers the shortest high priority delays.
- For occupancy levels greater than 50% the delay of low priority frames for graceful preemption is much less than non-graceful preemption.
- Graceful preemption delays are less than or equal to non-graceful preemption delays for all levels of occupancy and both types of frames.
- All three priority mechanisms are effective ways to reduce high priority frame delay, but for large frames and occupancy greater than 50% the non-preemptive priority has significantly more high priority delay.
- For levels of link occupancy less than 50% the priority mechanisms provide little or no improvement in the mean delay of high priority frames. Future studies could examine the effect that graceful preemption has on the maximum frame delay, rather than the mean delay. It is expected that the 95th percentile of high priority frame delays would show considerable improvement at all but the lowest levels of occupancy.
- Changing the proportion of high priority messages from 10% to 50% causes a small increase in high priority delays and a large increase in low priority delays.

5. MULTIPLE ACCESS VIA GRACEFUL PREEMPTION

Graceful preemption can be extended to include not only point-to-point communication as described above, but broadcast or multi-access communication as well. The arrangement described in this section could also have ISDN application at the user-network interface where multiple terminals may be supported via a common bus [5].

The terminals in Figure 10 communicate via a time shared data bus. All terminals are synchronized by the master bit clock. It is assumed that the terminals have no information about the actions of the other terminals beyond what is received on the common bus. Graceful preemption may be an attractive alternative to existing Carrier Sense Multiple Access with Collision Detect (CSMA/CD) protocols for this configuration.

Each terminal 'listens' while it transmits and continuously monitors a signal which indicates a difference between the intended transmission and the resultant data on the shared bus. A difference indicates a collision and the terminal would back-off and wait until the frame currently being received was completed. The signals on the bus must have an electrical representation that ensures a logic '1' will win over a '0' in the event of a conflict. Alternate Mark Inversion (AMI) is a coding method which may be implemented so that a '1' voltage will have a lower impedance drive than a '0'. It is also important that the bus length and bit-rate be engineered so that all terminals receive a transmitted bit well within one bit-time.

Each terminal is assigned an address, and its priority is associated with its address. Address zero would be lowest priority. A terminal which may need to send low and high priority information could be assigned more than one address, each at an appropriate level of priority. The address field could comprise two parts: first a 4-bit source address, and second a 4-bit destination address. This could be used to provide 16 distinct levels of source priority, or the addresses could be assigned to less than 16 groups to provide for fewer levels of priority. For example address 0 to 7 could be low priority peers, and 8 to 15 could be high priority peers. In this case, if terminal 1 was currently transmitting and terminal 6 had a frame to transmit it would not preempt, however if terminal 9 had a frame to transmit it would preempt. Note that this scheme requires all terminals to maintain a current record of which source address is currently using the bus. Since the source identity is unknown to the receivers for the first few bits of a frame no preemptions may occur until the identity is determined. Simply stated, a terminal must make sure it is more important before it preempts an active transmission by another terminal.

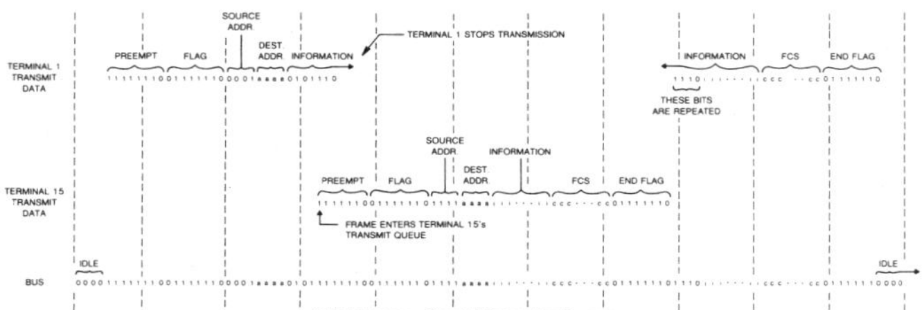

Multiple Access—Graceful Preemption Example

FIGURE 11

An example of multiple access control via graceful preemption is given in Figure 11. The idle-line state is all zeros (instead of the commonly used contiguous FLAGs sequence); this allows any terminal to override the idle state with its transmission. For the multiple access case all frames start with the preempt character. This is unlike the previously described point-to-point case where only the preempting frames start with the preempt character.

The top line of Figure 11 show the data from terminal 1 (low priority). The bottom line shows the resulting data on the bus. This example shows terminal 15 (high priority) getting a frame in its transmit queue shortly after terminal 1 has started on its information field. The second line shows the data from terminal 15; it starts with a preempt character. Note that station 15 was able to "borrow" the first bit of its preempt character from the terminal 1's information. Depending on the preceding data on the bus a preemption may borrow from 0 to 5 bits. Terminal 15 sends its frame, and when terminal 1 sees the ending flag it knows it may continue. In this example it is necessary for terminal 1 to repeat the last 4 bits it sent as it was preempted. These 4 bits were borrowed earlier.

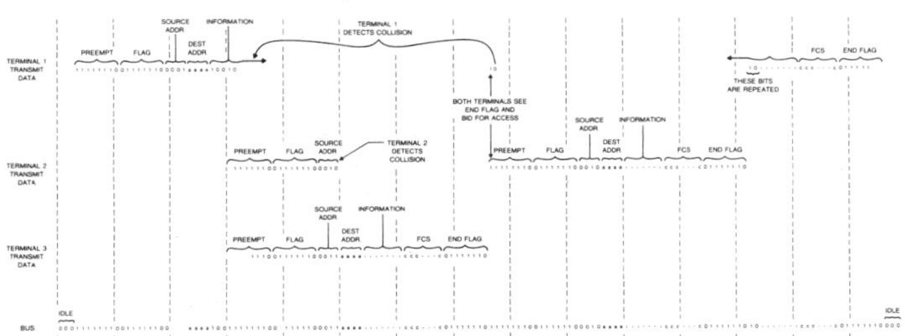

Multiple Access—Synchronization and Priority Resolution Example

FIGURE 12

A more complex example of multiple access control via graceful preemption is given in Figure 12. For this example each terminal is assigned a unique address and priority. Terminal 1 begins a transmission but is preempted by terminal 2. A few bits later terminal 3 also attempts a preemption. At this point terminal 3 could not know that another terminal had already started a preemption, but notice what happens: due to the preemptive bit borrowing both preemption attempts become bit synchronized. The synchronized flags are transmitted by both terminals with no conflicts, both terminals then send their address until a conflict occurs. By the nature of the number assignments the lower priority terminal detects the collision and backs-off until the higher priority frame completes. Terminal 3 transmits its frame and is never aware of terminal 2's attempt to gain access even though terminal 2 started 3 bits earlier. Upon completion of the frame from terminal 3, both terminals 1 and 2 believe it is their turn and transmit. Terminal 1 continues its frame by repeating the last two bits, terminal 2 starts its frame from the beginning because it recalls it lost its previous bid for access. Terminal 2 wins this time when terminal 1 detects a collision with its transmitted zero. When terminal 2 completes its frame, terminal 1 again attempts to resume its frame, this time it is successful. If this example were modified by delaying terminal 3's readyness to transmit by a few bits, then it would have noticed the access attempt by another terminal and terminal 3 would have then waited until it had determined the priority of the other terminal before preempting.

These examples show how the priority access is effectively enforced. There is always a rapid determination of who gains access. The link overhead is small and there never is a need for idle back-off waiting intervals. Thus, this method of multiple access control provides good link utilization over a wide range of occupancy and allows multiple levels of priority.

6. CONCLUSION

We have introduced graceful preemption, a powerful priority mechanism and shown an implementation which is compatible with LAPD. We have also indicated that graceful preemption may provide an attractive multiple access control method.

The process of graceful preemption can be likened to a computer interrupt. A high priority asynchronous event can interrupt the execution of a sequence of instructions, the machine state saved on a stack, the interrupt processed, and the previous state of computation restored and continued.

Graceful preemption follows a common theme: additional sophistication and complexity in the transmission terminal can improve the utilization of a communications link. Unsurpassed delay performance can be achieved for high priority frames while good low priority performance is preserved. This may allow the use of lower speed links and larger frames.

Acknowledgements

We gratefully acknowledge the patient assistance and guidance of J. A. Davis, N. J. Burzinski, and R. T. Watland in this work.

References

1. *Questions Allocated to Study Group XVIII For The Period 1981-1984*, CCITT (February 1981).

2. S. Kano, K. Kitami, H. Ohnishi, "ISDN User/Network Protocol — Overall Architecture", Proceeding of Globecom '82.

3. *HDLC — Classes of Procedures*, ISO 1501, International Standards Organization (1977).

4. *Data Communications — High-Level Data Link Control Procedures — Frame Structure*, ISO 3309, International Standards Organization (1976).

5. K. Waber, "Considerations on Customer Access to the ISDN", Proceedings of ISSLS '82.

Workshop
Multimedia Computer Mail

Chairman

F. Kou

Panelists

H.C. Forsdick
D. Deutsch
J.J. Garcia-Luna Aceves
N. Naffah
A. Poggio
J. Postel
J. White

PANEL ON MULTIMEDIA COMPUTER MAIL-- TECHNICAL ISSUES AND FUTURE STANDARDS

Moderator: Franklin F. Kuo, SRI International

Panelists: Debra P. Deutsch, Bolt Beranek and Newman, Inc.
Harry C. Forsdick, Bolt Beranek and Newman, Inc.
J.J. Garcia Luna Aceves, SRI International
Najah Naffah, INRIA Project KAYAK
Andrew Poggio, SRI International
Jonathan B. Postel, USC-Information Sciences Institute
James E. White, Xerox Corporation

ABSTRACT

A computer-based message system (CBMS) consists of computer facilities that expedite the creation, management, and nonreal time distribution of messages. These systems are increasingly being used for formal and informal communication, supporting the distribution of textual messages. However, nontext media such as voice and graphics are very important for human interaction, and are becoming more and more important in computer system applications. As a result, there is a growing need for the support of media other than text in CBMS.

Before standards for multimedia CBMS can be implemented, there are many technical issues that must be addressed. These range from the design of new mechanisms for the distribution of multimedia mail, to the design of tools needed for editing nontext media. This panel will be discussing issues encountered in the development of multimedia CBMS and an outlook for standards for multimedia computer mail.

COMMERCIAL STANDARDS FOR MULTIMEDIA COMPUTER MAIL

Debra P. Deutsch
Bolt Beranek and Newman

1. Introduction

For more than a decade, computer-based message systems (CBMS) have linked people separated by distance and time. The earliest CBMS were simple utility programs on shared mainframes. When computer networks were introduced, mail quickly became an important network service. Now commercial vendors offer a variety of CBMS services, systems, and software packages. As CBMS have grown in use, they have also grown in power. The next step forward in CBMS technology will be to add the ability to process voice and pictures along with the text that makes up today's messages. It is reasonable to expect that mulitmedia CBMS will be introduced as commercial products in coming years.

The value of a CBMS is a function of the number of users that it links. Standards for CBMS allow users of different systems to communicate with each other. Commercial standards for text-oriented CBMS are now being adopted. As multimedia CBMS come into use, it will be desirable to have standards for them, too.

2. Areas for Standardization

There are two general areas in which standards for multimedia CBMS might be developed. Standards for the system/user interface would make it easier for the users of one system to anticipate how another system will display a message, or to learn to use another system. Standards for the system/system interface allow messages originating in one CBMS to be transferred to, and processed by, another.

There are three major issues that would be dealt with by a standard for the system/user interface. The first is how the originator of a message can control or suggest how a message should appear to its recipients. A related, and particularly important problem is defining what happens when a multimedia message is to be rendered on a hardware/software configuration that cannot handle all the media in the message. For example, what happens when a message that contains voice or a facsimile image is to be displayed on a character-oriented terminal? A third area with which a system/user interface standard might deal is the particulars of the actual dialogue between the system and its user.

There are two major issues that would be covered by standards for the system/system interface. One is a transfer syntax (standard encoding) for multimedia messages, so the messages produced by one system could be interpreted by another. The other is a set of message transfer protocols, so messages could be exchanged by different systems.

From the point of view of a CBMS vendor, there is a more immediate need for standards for the system/system interface than for the system/user interface. Without a standard sytem/system interface, there is little need for a standard system/user interface, since systems could not be connected readily. While having a standard system/user interface might sell more copies of a CBMS, the economic value of a system/system interface is far more apparent. In addition, the criteria for defining a good standard for the system/user interface are much more problematic than the requirements for a system/system interface standard. Therefore, standards-development activities have concentrated on the system/system interface. The remainder of this paper deals with standards for system/system interfaces only.

3. Requirements for an Encoding Standard

There are three major design criteria for a multimedia message encoding standard. It must define representations for all types of data that may be found in a multimedia object. It must also provide structuring mechanisms sufficient to indicate the relationships that different objects have with each other as well as to represent the internal organization of the objects themselves. Finally, it must have enough power, flexibility, and extensibility to allow any kind of multimedia object to be represented.

The very nature of a multimedia message dictates that a wide variety of primitive data types be represented. These include bit-strings, necessary for facsimile, digital voice, and bitmap data, boolean and integer values for parameters, and text-strings.

It is also necesary to be able to aggregate simple objects to form more complex objects. For example, it should be possible to associate a narrative with an image. Furthermore, it must be possible to express the internal structure of each data object. For example, representing a bitmap image requires some way of indicating the aspect ratio (the number of bits in the width vs. the number of bits in the length) of the image.

While an encoding standard may define how a variety of multimedia objects are to be represented, it cannot be exhaustive and include every kind of multimedia object that might reasonably be put in a message. Instead, a good encoding standard must include mechanisms to allow new objects to be defined.

The pivotal question in the design of an encoding standard for multimedia messages is the choice between using a binary or text-based scheme. Many text-only CBMS have used text-based encoding for storing and exchanging messages. While multimedia data could be represented using text, such an approach would be costly in terms of processing and storage requirements. A binary scheme would have the advantages of efficiency and generality.

4. Requirements for a Protocol Standard

Multimedia messages have a number of distinctive characteristics. Because they may contain facsimile, digitized voice, or similar data, they can be very long. If a binary encoding scheme is used, they may contain arbitrary data. In addition, it may be desirable to make medium-conversion facilities available as part of, or ancillary to, message transfer. This is because not all users of a multimedia mail service will be able to render all the media that could be potentially included in messages.

Because a multimedia message could be very long, it is necessary that a multimedia message transfer protocol deal with errors efficiently. Also, any protocol implementation would have substantial storage capacity in order to buffer messages.

If multimedia messages are to be encoded using a binary format, their protocols must allow them to be transferred transparently. A message transfer protocol could not assume that the data consisted solely of 7-bit ASCII characters, or mark the end of a message with a special termination sequence, without significant overhead.

It is possible that a multimedia message will contain media that cannot be rendered by its recipient's user agent. One approach to this problem is not to deliver messages that a recipient cannot render. Another approach is to supply medium-conversion facilities. These facilities could be automatically invoked while a message is in transit from its originator to its recipient, or invoked by the recipient after the message has been delivered. Because media conversions can be costly and entail information loss, and because they are not strictly necessary, full medium-conversion facilities are not likely to be available to, or part of, message transfer protocols in the near future.

5. Recommendations

Multimedia message systems are still experimental. It would be premature to have a commercial standard that defined the structure and representation of multimedia objects. Because there is so little experience with multimedia objects, a full multimedia format standard would be prone to technical flaws. Such a standard could inhibit development of successful and innovative products.

On the other hand, the coming use of multimedia objects in messages should not be ignored by the people writing format standards for commercial CBMS today. It is important to make sure that these new standards are designed so they can be extended to deal with multimedia objects. If this were not the case, a future change to a multimedia standard could become very expensive.

The exact requirements for a multimedia message transfer protocol are better understood than those for representing multimedia objects. While the role of conversion facilities is still not clear, it is possible to design a protocol today. As long as the protocol can deal with large messages containing arbitrary data, it will be able to convey multimedia messages. In order to be able to abort delivery of messages that cannot be rendered by their recipients, or to automatically perform medium transformations upon those messages, it is necessary that protocol entities be able to determine which types of multimedia objects are found in a message.

Three organizations, the U.S. National Bureau of Standards (NBS), the International Telephone and Telegraph Consultative Committee (CCITT), and the International Standards Organization (ISO), are now working on message encoding and transfer protocol standards for commercial CBMS. They are taking extremely similar technical approaches in their work. Messages are encoded using a binary format. While standard representations for multimedia objects are not defined, all of the "hooks" necessary to allow vendors to create their own representations for multimedia objects are supplied. All three organizations are defining store-and-forward message transfer protocols that rely upon the session layer to provide transparent, error-free data transfer. The message transfer protocols, which are in the application layer, use checkpoints in the data stream to help recover from broken session connections. Provision is made for conversion facilities, although they are not required to be provided.

These three standard-making organizations are keeping multimedia messages in mind, but are stopping short of standardizing the representation of multimedia objects. This is a judicious strategy. Researchers and product developers will be gaining much more experience with multimedia messages in the next few years. By anticipating the requirements for transport protocol and a general message format standard while waiting to finalize a standard for the representation of multimedia objects, the writers of commercial CBMS standards will have a much better chance of creating a viable multimedia standard, compatible with the standards they are producing now.

STANDARDIZATION ISSUES IN MULTIMEDIA COMPUTER MAIL

J.J. Garcia Luna Aceves
SRI International
Menlo Park, California

Computer-Based Message Systems (CBMS) have their origins in the time-sharing computer services introduced in the 1960s. More than two decades later, many commercial CBMS exist, constituting a major tool for the flow of information in office environments. The growing use of computers in developed nations encourages their use in the transfer of information other than text--multimedia CBMS represent the next link in the chain of developments in computer mail. Standards need to be agreed upon and implemented so that future systems will not be isolated from each other.

There are three general areas where standards related to multimedia CBMS will be needed: mail distribution, message structure, and directory assistance.

Mail distribution standards will permit the transfer of "electronic envelopes" among interconnected multimedia CBMS. Such standards include: the rules for store-and-forward interhost mail exchange, and a transfer syntax (i.e., an encoding standard) to define the data types (e.g., integer, boolean, list, ASCII string) used to structure envelopes.

Message structure standards will permit the application programs--user agent (UA) in the CCITT model, user interface process (UIP) in the DARPA Internet model--of end users in separate systems to exchange machine-processable messages containing multiple media (e.g., text, voice, graphics). The standards needed in this category encompass: 1) the combination of the media into a structured message, and 2) a transfer syntax to define the data types used to structure messages. Due to the usefulness of information exchange in nonreal time, it can be envisaged that different types of application programs will be using the same interhost mail exchange services. Thus, the standards set for mail distribution should be independent of the structure of the messages themselves.

As the number of systems and users grow, it becomes more necessary to provide directory assistance to the users and processes of mail systems, so that the names and addresses of intended recipients can be found. It is not clear how directory services could be used to bridge differences among end-user facilities in heterogeneous multimedia CBMS; however, standards will be needed across national and system boundaries at least for name/address identification.

In addition to the above standardization issues, the development of user interfaces will significantly affect when commercial systems will be available and how many users will use multiple media in electronic messaging.

There has been considerable effort in the development of experimental multimedia CBMS. However, it is too early to attempt to set standards for commercial systems; while mail distribution is fairly well understood, there are many issues related to the representation and manipulation of multiple media that remain unsolved. Research programs are needed in the four aforementioned areas to understand the requirements that media other than text impose on the distribution, representation, and manipulation of electronic messages.

MULTIMEDIA COMPUTER MAIL STANDARDS VS RESEARCH

J. Postel
USC - ISI

The developing systems for multimedia computer mail show promise of providing very effective mail-style communications in the future.

By mail style I mean that the originator creates the message then sends it, and the recipient receives the message, then examines it. There may be an arbitrary delay beteen the sending and the receiving. The originator and the recipient do not have to be on the system at the same time.

There are some very important design constraints implied by the fact that the communication is mail style. The most important is that there is no opportunity for negotiation of parameters between the originatior (or his system) and the recipient (or his system).

The data in a message must conform to some set of conventions so that the receiving system can parse it. Most experimental multimedia systems use conventions that include self-identifying data types. A very large number of data types and organizational structures for the data are possible, many more than any particular mail program would implement.

One of the key issues is keeping the number of data types small so that it is likely that all the mail programs will be able to parse all the messages from all other mail programs. That is, there must be a very few conventional formats for communicating each type of medium.

The power and usefulness of a mail system is directly related to the number of people you can communicate with while using it. If different mail programs have different conventions for the format of voice data, for example, then communication using voice data is blocked, and the usefulness of the mail system is significantly limited.

Thus, if we are to have a large-scale multimedia mail system, we must have standards; not just a standard framework, but standard details and no options or private extensions.

Unfortunately, to set standards appropriately one has to know the correct answers. I claim that, in the area of multimedia computer mail, we do not know what we are doing yet.

I claim that many experiments are still required to understand how to combine the different media into messages, i.e., to find the right granularity for intermixing the different media. I claim the time and space relationship of the presentation of the different elements of a message is a critical aspect that needs much experimentation before a standard can be specified.

My overall comment is that it is far too early to be setting standards for multimedia computer mail. We need much more time to do research to find appropriate conventions.

ISSUES ENCOUNTERED IN THE DEVELOPMENT OF DIAMOND: A DISTRIBUTED MULTIMEDIA DOCUMENT SYSTEM

H.C. Forsdick
Bolt Beranek and Newman, Inc.

The Diamond Multimedia Document System is a distributed system for creating, editing, formatting, filing, transmitting, printing and archiving documents that contain text, graphics, images, and speech, as well as other objects whose presentation is performed by general-purpose application programs. Documents are used for a variety of purposes in Diamond including messages, memos, notes, and forms. Named folders are used to hold collections of documents and other folders.

Diamond is implemented on a set of distributed workstations and small server computer systems that form a cluster connected by a local area network. Document and folder presentation programs running in the user's access point (typically a workstation) interact with multiple distributed servers that provide document storage, printing, and image scanning services. Other Diamond server components perform authentication checks and inter-cluster message transport functions.

In Diamond we have considered several critical issues relating to multimedia message systems, including:

(1) Size of documents: Multimedia documents are 1 to 2 orders of magnitude larger than text documents. This has lead us to document storage disciplines that minimize replications of documents. In a distributed environment, discipline increases complexity since parts of a single document may be stored on two or more of the replicated document storage components.

(2) Presentation of messages on a variety of devices: The variety of workstations and terminals in use today leads to widely differing presentation device characteristics. Even on a single display device that supports multiple windows, the usable display space will vary. It is very important to attempt to format multimedia documents to fit the characteristics of the presentation devices in use by the reader of the document. This has wide implications regarding how information in documents is represented. In essence, the exact content and organization of a document must be recorded; however, presentation information must be expressed as relationships between the abstract components of the document.

(3) Interaction of multimedia objects: Models of documents from the print media (text, graphics and images) suggest certain ways different media interact: Line drawing boxes around text passages, arrows from features in an image to a text caption, etc. When thinking about the interactions of non-visual objects in a document, our past experiences are limiting. Research on coordinated presentation of objects in a document is a fruitful area for future work.

(4) Extensibility of object types in documents: A document should serve as an envelope for objects of a variety of media. It is possible to decouple the program that presents an object in a section of a document from the rest of the system. We have experimented with sending spread-sheet models as objects within documents. The spread-sheet program takes on the responsibility for presenting the object as part of a message. This view can be extended to include arbitrary objects and presentation programs.

MULTIMEDIA MESSAGES IN THE AGORA SYSTEM

N. Naffah and B. Mazoyer
KAYAK-INRIA

1. Introduction

The AGORA system is a distributed message system that is compatible to the initial IFIP model for CBMS.

User Agents are implemented in sophisticated workstations called the Buroviseur, and Message Transfer Agents and Directory Service Agents are implemented in special processors connected to CSMA-CD local networks, which are distributed around an X.25 public network.

Since, at the Buroviseur, the user can create mixed-mode documents containing pieces of text, graphics, facsimile images, and digitized voice, we have been facing the problem of exchanging this type of document as a message between the different entities of AGORA. One of the major issues that arose was the encoding scheme to adopt for transporting the message from one site to another.

In this presentation we will explain the suitability of the

NBS proposal that has been adopted in our system, the necessary changes to this protocol, along with some figures on our current implementation.

2. Use of the NBS Message Format for Multimedia Encoding

The main feature of the NBS proposal for a message format is the concept of "data element". Each information of a message is enclosed in a "primitive data element" that denotes the ***nature*** of this piece of information: ASCII string, bit string, integer ... Those basic components may in turn be nested into "constructor data elements" that will carry the ***meaning*** of the enclosed elements. There is no limitation on the nesting depth.

For voice and image transmission, the relevant primitive data element is, of course, "bit string". As constructor data elements, the proposal only offers a "compressed" data element, which indicates that its contents is compressed and allows the compression algorithm to be stated. There is no data element dedicated to convey voice or image information. However, this lack may be palliated in two possible ways: either defining new data elements, or using the "property-list" data element to organize the contents of existing ones.

2.1. Addition of new data elements

In the NBS proposal, provision has been made for adding new data elements: this is achieved with an "extension" data element. Thus, the proposal might be improved so as to meet the needs of multimedia message systems: "voice" and "fax" data elements could be defined.

For instance, the body of a message containing two text blocks and a facsimile image could be encoded as shown in Figure 1.

2.2. Property-list data elements

Another way of encoding multimedia messages under the NBS format is to use the property lists defined in the proposal. A "property-list" data element may be bound with every data element (primitive or constructor): in the current state of the proposal, one may use these "properties" either for stating the name to be given to a data element, or for adding comments to the contents of an element. This feature seems well suited to indicate the nature of the contents of the element: a new "property" should thus be added, which states whether the contents of the element is text, voice, graphics, facsimile, or whatever media. Using this idea, the example of Figure 1 would have the encoding shown in Figure 2.

This latter method may look clumsier, but it offers more flexibility than the first one. Indeed, the "property-list" element (and its enclosed property) may be added at any level of the syntax. Thus, in a voice message system, the whole body will be vocal, so that a voice property may be tied to the "field" data element enclosing the body.

3. Experience Acquired with the NBS Message Format

We have used the NBS proposal to develop a format suitable for the needs of the AGORA message system. The main difficulty in deriving the analyzer was to translate the proposed syntax into a proper Backus-Naur Form, which took about a month. The writing of the program itself took about two months: as a result, we obtained a 2,000-line Pascal package that includes the encoding and decoding routines.

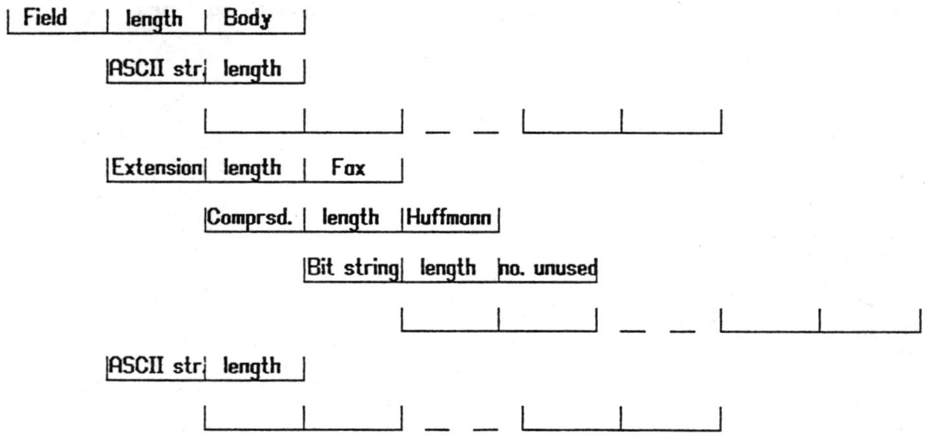

Figure 1

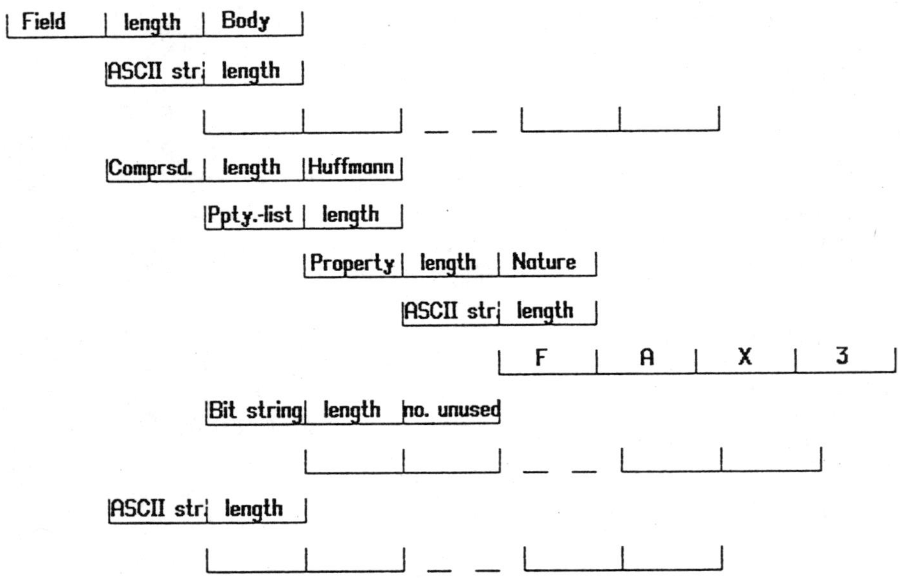

Figure 2

Workshop
Establishment Communications Systems LAN or PBXs—Which is Better?

Chairman

K. Kümmerle

Panelists

G. Hopkins
A. Braun
T. Aschenbrenner

ESTABLISHMENT COMMUNICATION SYSTEMS: LAN's OR PABX's — WHICH IS BETTER?

K. Kümmerle

IBM Zurich Research Laboratory, 8803 Rüschlikon, Switzerland

1. Background

In the sixties and early seventies, major activities in networking were focused on private and public data networks using either circuit and packet-switching technology or integrating both switching methods into a single network. In this time frame, manufacturers of main frames defined and implemented network architectures, ISO started work on the reference model of the Open-System Interconnect Architecture, and CCITT recommended the X-series of interfaces.

Local-area communication networks (LAN's) represent a comparatively new field of activity which can be viewed as an extension to data networks for making high-speed packet-switching services available to the in-house domain. Currently, much research and development work is being pursued in this field, both at universities and in industry. The term local refers to communication on the users' premises, i.e., within a building or among a cluster of buildings.

Local data and voice communication are not new. A typical example of a system widely used today for local data communication between hosts and display terminals is a star configuration where the terminals are attached to control units tightly coupled to a processor via I/O channels. The necessary terminal control functions are provided in the control unit and shared among a set of terminals. The most widely used local communication system is the Private Automatic Branch Exchange (PABX). Most PABX's installed today are optimised for real-time voice, and use analog technology.

2. Objectives and Driving Forces

2.1 Wiring

Today, we are witnessing an explosive growth of communicating devices. Many establishments forecast that the density of terminals and workstations will be approaching one per workplace by the end of this decade. Also, multisystem DP centers will proliferate, even in medium-sized or small establishments. In this environment, the system structure for local data communication outlined above becomes a serious impediment to management and growth of the system. In particular, it may lead to serious crowding of cable ducts and raceways in some buildings. Therefore, one of the problems establishment communication systems have to solve is wiring of buildings and maintenance of the wire base installed.

2.2 Technology

Unlike in the TP environment, transmission lines in the local domain do not represent an expensive commodity. Transmission systems based on twisted pairs, coaxial cable, and optical fibers continue to advance and allow data rates in the range of 1-10 Mbps throughout an office complex or factory at low cost.

Very large-scale integration (VLSI) is the key driving force:

- It allows provision of intelligent adapters to local-area networks at reasonably low cost, i.e., the cost advantage of shared-logic controllers diminishes.
- Workstations/personal computers already have and will have substantial amounts of processing capacity due to powerful microprocessors allowing the provision to the user of powerful and easy-to-use interfaces. However, it is unreasonable to expect the availability of sufficient mass storage, files, or high-quality and powerful printers, e.g., laser printers, for each workstation either for cost or space reasons.
- Digital telephone sets will have microprocessors, memory, and LCD displays to provide functions such as display of call information, time of day, elapsed time, and storage of frequently used numbers.

2.3 Economics

Economic market forces for communication and information-processing services in offices and factories are generating wide-spread interest in establishment communication systems. An example follows. In the United States, blue-collar workers have experienced a productivity gain of 30 percent since 1965, while white-collar workers have experienced a ten percent gain in the same period. This disparity will become increasingly apparent in its effect on economy as the white-collar worker grows into an increasingly larger proportion of the work force. The white-collar work force spends a considerable amount of time communicating. Ninety-five percent of the workday of a business executive is devoted to some form of communication, while secretaries spend 75 percent with it. American Bell studies indicate that middle managers and knowledge workers spent approximately 85 per cent of their workdays on some form of communication. Clearly, these data support the fact that communication systems must play a key role in improving white-collar productivity.

3. Major System Approaches

The advent of Computer-controlled Private Branch Exchanges (C-PABX), implemented in digital technology and providing standard 64 kbps PCM channels, paves the way for one approach to establishment communication systems. C-PABX's employ centralized switching with central control; the switching technology is circuit switching, and from a topological point of view, they represent star systems. Thus, with a suitably dimensioned C-PABX, both local data-switching and transmission needs of certain classes of terminals can be satisfied in addition to handling of the voice traffic. In the long run, C-PABX's may represent the interesting perspective of extending the Integrated Services Digital Networks (ISDN), currently being defined and studied for the public domain, into the local area.

System proposals not based on C-PABX's but also using centralized switches employ packet-switching technology instead of circuit switching, and therefore have the capability of handling bursty traffic. The alternative to centralized switching control is to use a distributed control structure to regulate access to the transmission system. Topologies which inherently provide broadcasting, such as busses and rings, lend themselves readily to implement distributed access control. The access-control functions are provided in adapters through which stations are attached to the network. All adapters are peer partners and there does not exist a master adapter or a master station controlling access of the others.

Within the bus and ring categories, we can distinguish according to the media access-control method. Basically, the access can be either controlled, in which case no collisions will occur, or random, which implies that collisions of transmission attempts may happen. The most widely used access-control schemes are carrier sense multiple access with collision detection (CSMA/CD) on busses and token passing on rings or busses.

In addition to topology and access method, we can classify systems according to the transmission technique. We can differentiate between baseband and broadband systems. In a baseband system, data is transmitted as electrical pulses without prior modulation of an r.f. carrier. In a broadband system, the available frequency spectrum is subdivided into different frequency bands where frequency multiplexing techniques are required to separate the bands.

4. Standardization

A variety of groups is actively involved in developing standards for local-area networks. Here, we single out ECMA (European Computer Manufacturers Association) and the IEEE Computer Society (IEEE Project 802). Historically, IEEE 802 started the standardization effort by working towards a standard for bus systems with CSMA/CD based on the work done by XEROX, Digital Equipment, and Intel. This effort broadened by additionally considering both token ring and token bus. Local-area network-standardization activities in ECMA began in 1981. In the meantime, ECMA has adapted three media control mechanisms as standards; CSMA/CD in 1982, and token ring and token bus in 1983, respectively. In Europe, ECMA was recently recommended to study PABX's as a LAN, and members started to submit proposals for a standard interface between CPU and PABX. In the U.S., three leading small computer manufacturers and four major digital PABX suppliers proposed a computer-to-PABX interface standard.

5. Objective of Workshop Session

Based on the discussion above, we can summarize and state that future establishment communication systems will have to provide the capability to interconnect a broad spectrum of systems such as departmental minicomputers, terminals, word-processing systems, personal computers, intelligent workstations, and printing devices. They will also have to support multi-media communications, i.e., data, text, fax, video, and voice.

Basically, there are two technologies emerging to satisfy these needs: local-area networks and computer-controlled private branch exchanges. The objective of the Working Session is to discuss how these technologies can meet requirements and what typical scenarios of future establishment communication systems will look like.

The subject will be discussed by

- A.R. Braun, American Bell Inc.
- T.B. Cannon, InteCom Inc.
- G. Hopkins, Ungerman-Bass, Inc.

Data Network Applications II

Chairman

A. Salazar

Interfaces and Protocol

Chairman

N. Tobol

A Function Oriented Corporate Network

P. S.-C. Wang and S. R. Kimbleton

ITT Programming, 1000 Oronoque Lane, Stratford, CT 06497

ABSTRACT

The ITT/NET is an internal corporate network built to satisfy the distributed programming requirements of ITT technology and engineering communities. This paper describes the network: its goals, its architecture, its operational environment and prototype development activities.

The various issues involved in the construction of a Corporate Network based upon diverse, existing systems and communication methods are described in detail. The architectural and implementation decisions are discussed and justified. The programming process and the methodologies adopted are presented and some conclusions are drawn as to the practicality and usefulness of formal development methods in the context of this particular project.

1.0 INTRODUCTION

ITT is, perhaps, the preeminent example of a multi-product, multi-national corporation. Managing ITT requires planning, organization, communication and control. This requires effective communications within and between sites. ITT/NET is a corporate network designed to usefully interconnect the geographically distributed hardware, programming and human resources of major ITT North American and European units.

This report is a description of the ITT/NET. It concentrates on those aspects of the network as seen by the end user, that is, network services--their selection, their functions and functional relationships and their design and implementation. Service selection is summarized in Section 2, followed by discussions of network and protocol structures (Section 3) and the programming process: specification, design, implementation and quality assurance (Section 4).

2.0 Distributed Programming Requirements and the ITT/NET

It was early recognized that an application- and service-sharing network is needed to meet the computing requirements of major ITT technical activities. In response to this need, front end processors, leased lines and telecommunications packages were installed on several IBM mainframes and a network started to evolve. However, with the growth of a major multi-national digital switch project (System 12, see [1] and [2]), problems concerning both the level of service and functional deficiencies of the network became critically important. ITT/NET is designed to solve these problems. It is a function oriented computer network designed primarily to interconnect geographically dispersed IBM mainframes, and secondarily, to connect IBM mainframes and other machines such as the DEC VAX and PDP 11. It provides the functional building blocks underlying the distributed programming environments needed during the multi-location product life cycle.

2.1 Network Services

The service selection process was guided by analysis of the technical, managerial and system support activities for the afore-mentioned System 12 project, which resulted in the following communication requirements:

R1. Access to interactive applications on remote mainframes (a Terminal Access Protocol),

R2. Access to the batch processing facilities on remote mainframes (a Distributed Job Entry service),

R3. Transfer of data between locations (a File Transfer Protocol),

R4. Development, distribution and maintainence of person-to-person computer based information among sites (an Information Transfer Protocol),

R5. Shared access to a variety of programming management and support functions such as fault report and change control systems, and

R6. Support of network monitoring, operations, management and billing.

A further requirement is that the resources and the operations of the mainframe hosts should be controlled and managed by the individual hosts without being affected, in any way, by their participation in ITT/NET.

One well-known technical solution [3] to the above requirement is to offload communications support onto a separate computer (referred to as the Network Interface Machine, or NIM, hereafter), which deals with individual hosts on behalf of the ITT/NET user. This minimizes the network's impact on the existing mainframes and, at the same time, maximizes its ability to accomodate to constant changes in network configuration (e.g., the connection of a new host to the network), and functions (e.g., the addition of a new File Transfer feature). This is the approach we have chosen to adopt.

Interfacing to IBM systems is further complicated since any impact or perturbation to existing IBM program product or application environment must be avoided if at all possible. Of the several possible approaches, Remote Job Entry (e.g., HASP [4]) emulation is probably the most popular. In this design, the network interfaces perfectly with the mainframe IBM program products and requires no change whatsoever in the mainframe's mode of operation. However, it does impose a transaction style of transport between the network (i.e., NIM) and the mainframes. This point is further discussed in Section 3 below.

2.2 Network Configuration

Each mainframe is connected to ITT/NET through the NIM, a local IBM 4300. The complete network is formed by interconnecting these NIMs through leased communication lines supplied by the various telephone authorities. The physical configuration of ITT/NET is given in Figure 1. Characteristic programming configurations for the host and the NIM are shown in Figure 2.

3.0 FUNCTIONAL ARCHITECTURE

Experiences derived from existing networks indicate clearly that the provision of user-oriented protocols such as those given above require a new protocol level to be developed. It is no longer practical to view the communication facility as a simple data pipe which can be tapped at the two ends and used for a specific application. Rather, a standard programming facility needs to be established to handle host-to-host communications. That is, in addition to the protocols listed in Section 2.1, we need a data transport mechanism, which, for ITT/NET, is called the Universal Transport Protocol (UTP), providing

R7. A program-invocable transport or end-to-end service allowing transparent data transfer among NIM applications and between NIMs and mainframes.

This collection of functions, taken together, covers the uppermost three layers (4-7) of the ISO Model for Open System Interconnection [12], and corresponds to what is commonly referred to as **High Level Protocols** (HLP).

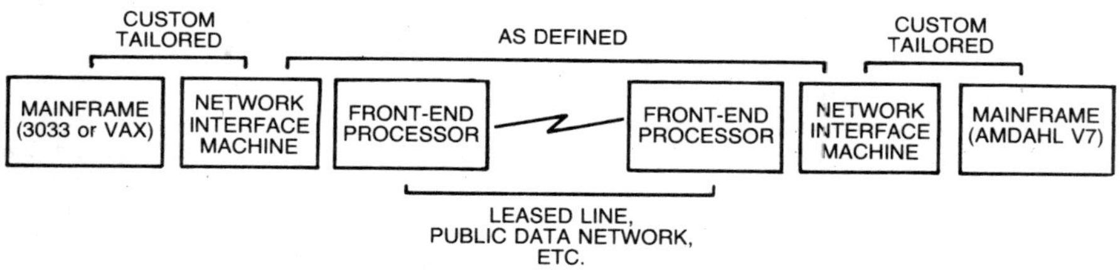

FIGURE 1. ITT/NET Network Configuration

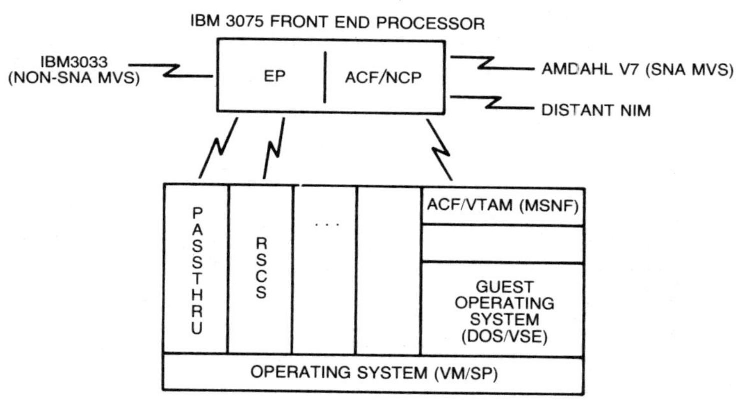

FIGURE 2. NIM PROGRAMMING CONFIGURATION

The mainframes ("hosts") are connected to NIMs, which are in turn interconnected to form a multi-domain, SNA network [5]. The NIMs handle both IBM SNA and non-SNA based hosts, e.g., IBM 370s under the MVS operating system with Virtual Telecommunications Access Method (VTAM) [6] and DEC VAX under VMS [7] with HASP emulation. This is achieved by running both SNA and non-SNA communication packages on NIM: VTAM in a guest operating system and Remote Spooling Communications Subsystem (RSCS) [8] as shown in Figure 2 below. (See [9], [10] for further details of the NIM hardware and programming configuration.)

3.1 ITT/NET Hierarchy

As the above discussion indicates, the ITT/NET protocols are organized into a hierarchy of many levels[1]: each level uses the functions of the lower level, and adds some function of its own for possible use by the next higher level.

There are four levels of interest in the ITT/NET (see Figure 3), but there may be more than one protocol within a level, representing different uses of the lower levels and different services to the upper levels. The lowest level of the hierarchy consists of vendor communication packages, which provide the basic data transmission facilities (the **communications** subnetwork). The next level specifies methods for the origin NIM application to transfer (logical) messages to a destination NIM or mainframe application. This protocol, the ITT/NET Universal Transport Protocol, is used by all higher level services (see Section 2.1) as their common **host-to-host** communication vehicle.

At the next higher level are the **building block** protocols which provide general support services (file access, remote job entry, terminal access and message transfer) for the networked environment. These are also the foundation on which the next and highest level, **multi-location development** protocols are built to serve application specific aspects of communications between remote program development support applications.

A diagrammatic illustration of this protocol hierarchy is given in Figure 3 below, together with the corresponding ISO numbers for these levels.

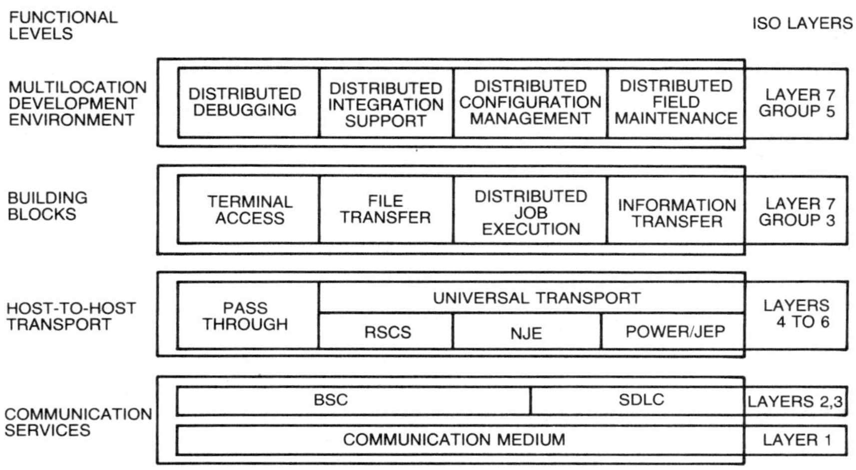

FIGURE 3. THE ITT/NET FUNTIONAL HIERARCHY

The advantages of architectural layering are well known: it promotes manageability and layer independence through functional grouping and localization. This is particularly important for the ITT/NET for the following reasons. First, it gives us the flexibility to replace level functions with equivalent ones without affecting other levels in the hierarchy. Secondly, it provides a framework upon which new protocols can be developed. Thus the two critical growth areas for ITT/NET--improvements to current protocols and construction of distributed applications--can be planned and implemented in an orderly fashion. Thirdly and most importantly, given the NIM programming base, layering not only provides functional partitioning among protocols but also forms the framework for design modularization (see Section 3.2 for further discussions).

[1] We purposefully use the term "level" instead of the ISO "layer", to emphasize the difference between our scheme and that of the Open System Architecture. In particular the numbering of our levels is entirely arbitrary although the choice of points at which to divide the levels is guided--at least in principle--by the OSI model.

3.2 Realizing the ITT/NET Hierarchy: Structural Layering

The ITT/NET protocols are implemented on an IBM machine running the VM/SP system. This operating system manages the hardware machine in such a manner that many virtual machines appear to exist.

Each user, when s/he logs onto the system, has at his/her disposal a "virtual machine" running the (single-user) conversational operating system CMS. In addition to CMS commands and utilities, users are provided the set of ITT/NET specific commands or protocols described above. These user-level (building block) protocols perform the data processing and communications functions to support the networking needs of the users as well as to provide for the creation of more sophisticated, application specific communication services (a Multi-location Development Environment).

In each user-level protocol there are three logical components (see Figure 4), each distinguished by the kinds of operations it performs:

User Support Component. USC. A component that interprets user commands, accesses user's files, and in general performs operations in direct support of the user.

Protocol Support Component. PSC. A component that performs operations needed to support the functioning of the protocol, but not directly visible to the user: buffering and file attribute--record format, record length, etc.--handling are examples of the PSC functions for file transfer protocols.

Transport Support Component. TSC. A component that transfers information from one place in the network to another by invoking and interfacing with the host access methods, such as VTAM or RSCS.

The functional layering given in Section 3.1 interact strongly with the above structural decomposition. As shown in Figure 4 the lowest level (level 1) of the ITT/NET hierarchy is composed of vendor packages such as VTAM, providing basic communication facilities. Thus this level covers the TSC-to-TSC portion of the HLP top-level structure[2].

Level 2 (UTP) erases network (SNA vs. non-SNA) boundaries to provide a "universal" transport service. The UTP packages the data from these buffers and uses Level 1 to transmit the data to the destination machine. UTP uses the SNA communication products in the NIM, in tandem with the non-SNA facilities such as RSCS networking [9]) to accomplish this. Structurally UTP is the TSC-to-PSC interface (as well as the pre- and post-processings associated with this interface, e.g., packaging of data into a form accepted by the TSC).

Top level design and test plan are formulated, and through step-wise refinement, the design is decomposed into modules and the logic and data flows that implement these modules. Also, detailed test plans are defined to validate the functional, performance and interface behaviors of the modules. The actual coding and testing (**implementation** phase) of these modules then follow, and the test results analyzed and documented.

The next phases (**limited availability, general availability** and **termination**) deals with the installation, support and withdrawal of the programs. Since our experience so far has been limited to the first four phases, we shall, in the following, confine our description of ITP programming process to this portion of the life cycle.

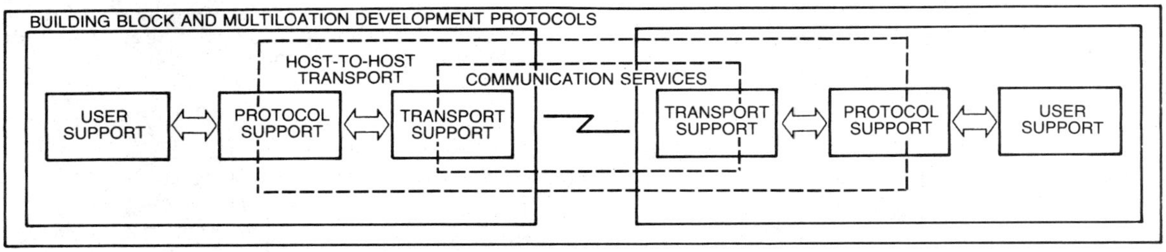

FIGURE 4. THE ITT/NET STRUCTURAL HIERARCHY

Thus, the hierarchical functional dependencies among HLPs map directly into the levels of "design layering", which, in turn, forms the basis for the top-level designs of all ITT/NET end-user protocols as will be discussed further in Section 4.

4.0 Programming Process

So far we have concentrated on our technical approach. Let us now turn to the ITT/NET programming process and describe the actual implementation of this approach. In the interest of concreteness, instead of dealing with the issue in general, we shall concentrate on one specific application, the VM/CMS implementation of the Information Transfer Protocol (ITP).

4.1 Formalized Methodology

As mentioned in Section 2, the first step we took is a System 12 communications requirements analysis. This, together with the objectives of early availability, extensibility and reliability provides the input from which the basic architectural framework (Section 3.2) and the functional specifications and the top level designs of individual protocols are derived. These activities constitute the first two phases of the programming effort - **conceptual planning** and **definition**.

The output of this phase, the functional specification, form the input to the next or, **design** phase.

4.2 An Example - the Information Transfer Protocol

As described in Sections 1 and 2, analyses of System 12 communication requirements disclosed the need of an information transfer service. That is, a function that allows a VM/CMS user to create, edit, file and distribute memos, transparently and uniformly, to other CMS and VAX/VMS users. (An MVS interface is being implemented but will not be covered here since it remains to be completed.)

The ITP definition phase starts with a feature-by-feature comparison of existing information transfer facilities and user needs, in terms of command primitives, command parameters and their execution effects. This results in the extended list of message system primitives given in Figure 5. The criteria of level of demand, implementation ease and sufficiency are then used to partition this list into three sets as shown in the Figure: a foundation or minimal set of basic services, a kernel set of essential features needed to support most near-term applications and a value-added set of desirable future enhancements.

Based upon this analysis and the goal of near-term usability, we selected the kernel set for the initial implementation and proceeded towards its top-level design.

4.2.1 The ITP System

As user interface, we selected the the IBM System Productivity Facility for VM [13][3]. This environment, and the design layering of Section 3.2, dictates that ITP operate as a reentrant SPF

[2] However, this coverage is in parts rather than as a whole: the diversity of these packages and their lack of interworkability makes it impossible to treat the ITT/NET as one single, integrated network at this level.

[3] This is the environment used for System 12 development.

\Feature Set \	Memo Preparation	Memo Delivery	Memo Storage/Retrieval	SystemWide
Foundation	allow use of existing editor(s) and formatter(s) for memo composition.	single priority level, immediate transfer to explicitly given list user-ids on recognized destination systems.	allow display and saving of incoming memos onto permanent secondary storage	no accounting, security, backup/recovery or advanced user friendly features.
Kernel	also provide embedded text entry facility within its own environment.	also provides distribution and cc: list capabilities forwarding, answering, and status querying of outgoing memo	also provides file folder capability, i.e. individual memo display and retrieval.	same as foundation
ValueAdded	in addition to kernel, also allow editing of distribution control headers during text preparation and annotation of existing memos.	in addition to kernel, provides flexible addressing, expedited and scheduled delivery, automatic acknowledgement, retry and special handling.	in addition to kernel, also allows retrieval by content and flexible display and output capabilities such as specific ordering, hardcopy and archive.	provides protection, accounting, journalling, backup/recovery and advanced human engineered interfaces.

Figure 5. Message System Services - A Categorization

procedure, in the user area of the user's CMS machine and interfaces with UTP to effect communication with distant NIMs. The programs, files and modules constituting this top level ITP are given below (in PDL notation) [14]:

```
mod ITP
   programs ITPPRI
   datasets INMEM,DRAFT,INBOX
   modules  ITPGTM,ITPSND,ITPREA,ITPINP
dom
```

where INMEM is the CMS file containing the memo to be sent or read, DRAFT and INBOX are the default "mailbox" file for storing the (newly created) outgoing and incoming memos, respectively. The program ITPPRI is the the primary processor which checks pending incoming memos, retrieves and stores them in INBOX, and decodes user commands and calls the appropriate send and read modules for processing the selected commands.

The modules ITPGTM and ITPINP are common processing routines--routines invoked by other programs rather than directly by users (i.e., from the command level).

Figure 6 is a (partial) illustration of these components and their functional relationship to SPF, UTP and the CMS file system. (The top-level design for the SEND module is given in Fig.7 for illustrative purposes. A complete description is available from [11].)

It is worthwhile to point out that at this top design level, we are primarily concerned with the functions and the functional relationships of the major ITP components (ITPPRI, ITPGTM, ITPSND and ITPREA) with each other and with the environment. Thus only the interfaces are specified fully (e.g., all possible user inputs are accounted for), whereas most of the processing details (e.g., how the memos are made up and how they are transferred to the recipients) are left unspecified.

The task of verifying the logical correctness of the design and that it satisfies the ITP service specification is approached from a formal ("verification") as well as an empirical ("testing") direction.

Formal techniques for protocol verification are still in its early development stage--so far they have only been used to verify a very limited set of "general" (i.e., applicable to all) protocol properties, and this is what we confined ourselves to[4]. In specific, we verified that ITP satisfies the following

Invariant Assertion [14], [15]:

> All valid messages sent by the user (i.e., SEND requests addressed to recipients with valid USERID and NODEIDs) are delivered to the recipient.

Details of the proof are included in the appdendix for readers' reference. The main task--the demonstration that our design meets its specification is dealt with below, using the less rigorous but far more practical method of testing.

[4] However, we did find that this exercise in mathematics invaluable in providing precision and rigor to the final design.

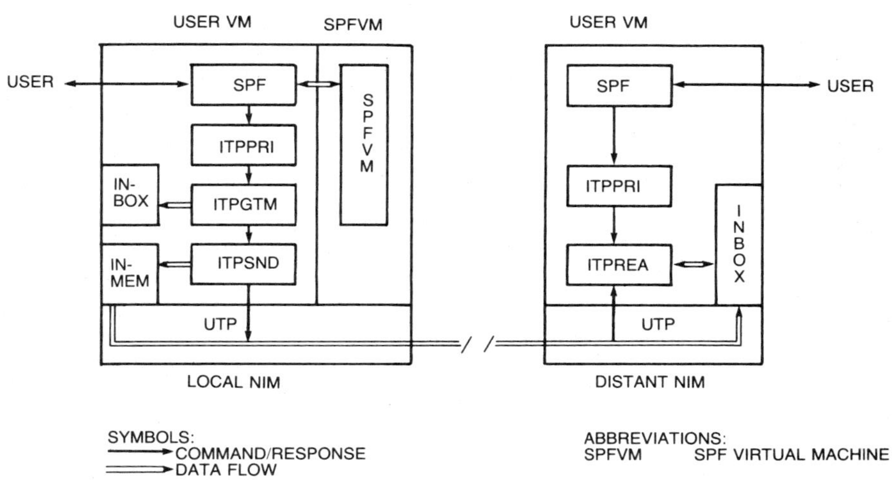

FIGURE 6. ITT COMPONENTS AND RELATIONSHIPS WITH SPF AND UTP

```
 1  proc: ITPSND(SFILE)                {ITT/NET ITP send processor      }
 2     scalar SFILE                    {fix: name of file to be sent    }
 3     sequence LIST: ADDR             {int: list of addressees         }
 4     record ADDR                     {int: addressee data structure   }
          1   USERID                   {      userid part               }
          2   NODEID                   {      nodeid part               }
 5     scalar CMD                      {int: send/edit/abort indicator  }
 6     scalar DRAFT                    {int cons: default save memo fil}

 7     do1                             {Start by making up              }
 8     .  display SEND panel           {and displaying the SEND         }
 9     .  LIST,CMD := user input       {panel to get user input.        }
10     while (user input ¬= "end")     {END PF => get out.              }
11     do2                             {Otherwise see what              }
12     .  case(CMD)                    {s/he wants.                     }
13     .  part("edit")                 {Edit?                           }
14     .  .  call SPF to edit SFILE    {call ISPLINK('EDIT',...         }
15     .  part("send")                 {Send?                           }
16     .  .  make up memo with SFILE   {make up                         }
       .  .      as body               {          memo                  }
17     .  .  send memo to each and     {                and ship        }
       .  .      everyone in LIST      {                       it off.  }
18     .  .  save SFILE in DRAFT       {--also save it somewhere.       }
19     .  part("abort")                {Abort?                          }
20     .  .  save SFILE in DRAFT       {--just save the body            }
21     .  else                         {Illegal input?                  }
22     .  .  set SEND panel msg field  {--tell user so.                 }
23     .  esac                         {                                }
24     od                              {end of dowhiledo.               }
25     return                          {Got here because user pressed   }
26  corp                               {END PF, so go back to caller.   }
```

Figure 7. Top-Level PDL Description of ITPSND

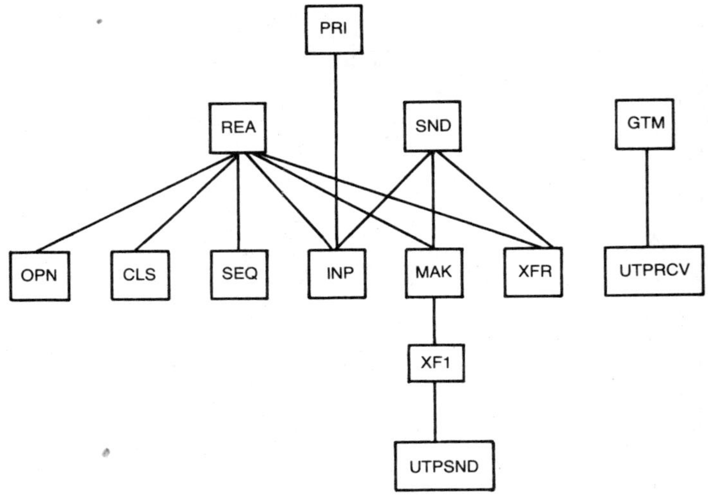

FIGURE 8. ITP MODULES AND MODULE DEPENDENCIES

4.2.2 Function Testing

Top-level test cases are devised to detect deviations of protocol behavior from that prescribed by their specification. The basic strategy is exhaustive functional testing by

1. examining the service specification,
2. finding out the logical relationship between the inputs and outputs (inputs and outputs are defined as anything that flows between ITP and its environment),
3. finding all (environment or pragmatic) constraints that these input conditions and output consequences must satisfy and from this
4. deriving all possible input/output combinations and use them as test cases, and finally
5. analyzing these cases so all input and output boundaries are covered at least once.

4.2.3 Module Organization and Module Testing

The above design (Section 4.2.1) is further expanded and reorganized until a level of detail is reached that is appropriate for module specifications. The resulting detailed design is illustrated by the following module dependency chart and the PDL expansion of Figure 8 and Figure 9 below.

Test design, at this phase, is based upon logic coverage. That is, a set of test inputs are selected and the decision table representation of the modules are formulated to check that sufficient cases are covered so that all branches and statements are covered at least once.

This is followed by the actual implementation, that is, converting the detailed design into code and the carrying-out of the tests. In the case of ITP, PL/I was used for most of the coding but since a great deal of essential VM system services (e.g., file access) are not available directly to PL/I, assembler routines were also written for the interface functions.

```
Algorithm:

 1    proc: ITPSND(SFILE)                  {ITT/NET ITP send processor      }
 2       scalar SFILE: string(FNSIZ)       {fix: name of file to be sent    }
 3       sequence LIST:ADDR                {int: list of addressees         }
 4       record ADDR                       {int: addressee data structure   }
            1   USERID:string(TKSIZ)       {      userid part               }
            2   NODEID:string(TKSIZ)       {      nodeid part               }
 5       scalar CMD:   string(1)           {int: send/edit/abort indicator  }
 6       scalar DRAFT: string(FNSIZ)       {int cons: default save memo fil}
 x.1     use SPFPANL                       {int: contains SPF panel names   }
 x.2     scalar SUBJ:  string(STRSIZ)      {int: memo subject               }
 x.3     scalar RC:    integer             {int: ret code from lwr lvl rout}
 x.4     scalar TMPMEM:string(FNSIZ)       {int cons: file for temp use     }
                                           {                                }
 7       do1                               {Start by making up              }
 8-9     .  LIST := ''                     {initial vals for input parms    }
  .1     .  SUBJ := ''                     {so we can call INP to display   }
  .2     .  CMD := ''                      {SNDPANL and get user input.     }
  .3     .  call ITPINP(SNDPANL,LIST,SUBJ,CMD,RC)
10       while (RC ¬= "end")               {END PF => get out.              }
11       do2                               {Otherwise see what              }
12       .  case(CMD)                      {s/he wants.                     }
13       .  part("edit")                   {Edit?                           }
14.      .  .  call SPF to edit SFILE      {call ISPLINK('EDIT',...         }
  .1     .  .  set SNDPANL msg field with editor return code
15       .  part("send")                   {Send?                           }
16-17    .  .  call ITPMAK(LIST,SUBJ,TMPMEM,RC)
  .1     .  .  if (bad RC)                 {Yes => use SUBJ to make up      }
  .2     .  .  then                        {a header file--TMPMEM,          }
  .3     .  .  .  set SNDPANL msg field with RC                             }
  .4     .  .  else                        {so we can append                }
  .5     .  .  .  append SFILE to TMPMEM{body to it and ship if off         }
  .6     .  .  .  call ITPXFR(LIST,TMPMEM,RC)     {to everyone in LIST.     }
  .7     .  .  .  set SNDPANL msg field with RC   {                         }
  .8     .  .  fi                          {                                }
18       .  .  save SFILE in DRAFT         {--also save the body somewhere.}
19       .  part("abort")                  {Abort?                          }
20       .  .  save SFILE in DRAFT         {--just save the body            }
21       .  else                           {Illegal input?                  }
22       .  .  set SNDPANL msg field       {--tell user so.                 }
23       .  esac                           {                                }
24       od                                {end of dowhiledo.               }
25       return                            {Got here because user pressed   }
26    corp                                 {END PF, so go back to caller.   }
```

Figure 9. Detailed PDL Description of ITPSND

This completes our description of ITP services. But before turning to the next topic, a summary of current ITP status might be of interest:

The ITT/NET Information Transfer Protocol

- Function
  - to provide an integrated set of facilities for text preparation, distribution and storage (currently supports VM-to-VM and VM-to-VAX/VMS, VM-to-VAX/UNIX transfer)
- Future Enhancements
  - other interfaces (VM-to-MVS)
  - data encryption/decryption
  - memo filing/retrieving
  - automatic answering/forwarding
  - centralized storage/archival services
- Vital Statistics
  - 2.1 KLOC PL/I (13 Modules), 1.9 KLOC 370 assembler (17 modules)
  - 12 staff months design/coding/testing
  - base version completed 08/30/81, current version 02/28/82
  - no known bugs, further stress testing required
  - installed on: three IBM 4300s at ITT Shelton and Stratford
  - level of usage: all Programming computer users
- Features
  - text preparation, storage as well as delivery in one package
  - integrated into current data processing environment
  - can handle diverse data sources
  - can be interfaced to existing document/library systems

5.0 Concluding Remarks

The ITT/NET is a high-level, application-independent framework for the construction of distributed systems and programming development tools. It eliminates the need for application-specific communication protocols and support programming. The framework consists of a network-wide communications access method (the **Universal Transport Protocol**), and a set of utilities for file and job transfering (the **File Transfer Protocol**, the **Information Transfer Protocol** and the **Distributed Job Execution** function).

Since ITT/NET is built on top of existing operating systems and communications methods, considerable care was given to the structuring of protocols to achieve this "vendor-product" independency. This paper presents the crucial decisions in the structuring of the various protocols. We hope that the architecture were formulated with caution so the decisions we made will prove to be sound architectural choices--but only time will tell.

A second focus of this paper is on the programming disciplines and practices used to realize this architecture. Emphasis was placed upon methods based upon theoretical foundations such as formal proofs and testing techniques. Our experience so far is that formal methods are indeed practical and that they contribute to improved quality in significant ways: they bring in precision and order to the programming process, and provide a standard language during each development phase for communication among users, managers, designers and implementers.

6.0 References

[1] Cox, J.E., Lawson, D.A., Denenberg, J. and Van den Brande, F. A Digital Switch for Wide Range of Application. ICC'80 Conf. Rec. (1980), 46.1.1 - 46.1.7.

[2] Lawson, D.A. A New Software Architecture for Switching Systems, IEEE Trans. Comm., vol.COM-30 (1982), 1281 - 1289.

[3] Roberts, L.G. and Wessler, B.D. Computer Network Development to Achieve Resource Sharing, AFIPS SJCC, vol.36 (1970), 543 - 549.

[4] HASP Networking PRPQ: System Programmer's Guide. Order No. SH20-1981, IBM Corporation, Data Processing Division, White Plains, NY.

[5] Systems Network Architecture General Information. (1st Ed.) Order No. GA27-3102-0, IBM Systems Development Division, Research Triangle Park, NC (1975).

[6] Advanced Communications Function for VTAM General Information: Concepts.(2nd Ed.) Order No. GC27-0463-1, IBM Corporation, Data Processing Division, White Plains, NY (1980).

[7] VAX/VMS Primer. Order No. AA-D030A-TE, Digital Equipment Corp., Software Distribution Center, Maynard, MA (1978).

[8] IBM Virtual Machine/370: Remote Spooling Communications Subsystem Networking General Information. (2nd Ed.) Order No. GH24-5004-1, IBM Corporation, Data Processing Division, White Plains, NY (1980).

[9] IBM Virtual Machine/System Product: Introduction, Order No.SC19-6200. IBM Corporation, Data Processing Division, White Plains, NY.

[10] Kimbleton, S. R. and Wang, P. S.-C., ITT/NET Communication Support for Program Development. Electrical Communication, vol.57, no.4 (1983), 320 - 325.

[11] The ITT/NET Information Transfer Protocol. Internal Documentation, ITT Programming Technology and Development, 1000 Oronoque Lane, Stratford, CT 06497 (Aug. 1981).

[12] Data Processing - Open Systems Interconnection - Basic Reference Model. International Standards Organization, Draft Proposal ISO/DP 7498 (1980).

[13] Structured Productivity Facility for VM/SP Program Reference. (1st Ed.) Order No. SC34-2047-0. IBM Corporation, Data Processing Division, White Plains, NY (1981).

[14] Linger, R.C., Mills, H.D. and Witt, B.I. Structured Programming. Addison-Wesley, Reading, MA (1979).

[15] Owicki, S.S. Specification and Verification of a Network Mail System. in "Program Construction", Lecture Notes in Computer Science, Springer-Verlag, New York, NY, vol.69 (1979), 198 - 234.

Appendix. Formal Correctness Proof for the ITT/NET ITP

In order to carry out the proof, auxiliary variables are needed to record the history of ITP memo processing: we shall use H(M1,M2,r) to denote the sequence of messages passed from module M1 to module M2 that has "r" as its recipient[5]. This enables us to restate the correctness assertion (Section 4.2.1) in terms of the history of messages passed between the user and ITP:

> For every request and every valid user u and recipient r, the assertion
>
> f=(H(u,ITP,r)=H(ITP,r,r)) holds true.

We shall proceed by first analyzing the execution sequences of ITP programs using the E-chart and trace table techniques of [14]. From the results of this analysis and the

UTP Invariant Assumption:
g=(H(ITP,UTPSND,r)=H(UTPRCV,r,r))

we then deduce, using ordinary logic, that the above assertion in fact holds.

Proof:

From the PDL descriptions of the various ITP modules (see -- Figure 7 -- and [11] we identified four separate ITP paths (labelled path 1-4) in the (loop-free version of the) E-chart as shown in Figure 10 We now proceed to look at its behavior along each path (i.e., the trace table for that path) and show that the invariant assertion holds for each case.

For brevity, the letters U and R are used to designate the message histories H(u,ITP,r) and H(ITP,r,r), respectively. Each row of the trace table expresses the current value of the data items U and R (denoted as U1, R1 for the first row, U2, R2 for the second row, etc.) in terms of their previous values. The initial histories for messages passed from the user to ITP and from ITP to the recipient are represented by H0(u,ITP,r) and H0(ITP,r,r), respectively.

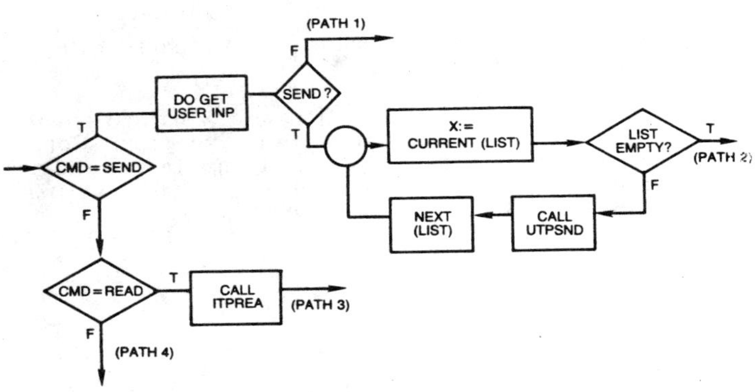

FIGURE 10. ITP EXECUTION CHART

5 The notation as well as the discussion for our proof follows closely that of Linger (Ref.[14], Chap. 6], which should be consulted for details.

function

f = (H(u,ITP,r) = H(ITP,r,r))

program (see Figure 10)

```
 1 case (CMD)
 2 part ("SEND")
 3 .  do get user input
 4 .  .  if (user input = "send")
 5 .  .  then
 6 .  .  .  do1 x := current(LIST)
 7 .  .  .  while (x ¬= empty)
 8 .  .  .  do2
 9 .  .  .  .  call UTPSND
10 .  .  .  .  next (LIST)
11 .  .  .  od
12 .  .  .  return            {path 2}
13 .  .  else
14 .  .  .  return            {path 1}
15 .  od
16 part ("READ")
17 .  call ITPREA
18 .  return                  {path 3}
19 else
20 .  return                  {path 4}
21 esac
```

proof

I. path 1 (SEND, abort)

part	condition	U(=H(u,ITP,r))	R(=H(ITP,UTPSND,r)
1	CMD=SEND	U1=H0(u,ITP,r)	R1=H0(ITP,UTPSND,r)
3-7		U2=LIST members addressed to r	R2=R1
8	abort	U3=U1	R3=R2

derivations: U3 = H0(u,ITP,r), R3 = H0(ITP,UTPSND,r)
path function: H(u,ITP,r) = H(ITP,UTPSND,r)

This together with the UTP invariants (**g**) leads directly to the intended function **f**.

II. path 2 (SEND, ¬abort)

part	condition	U(=H(u,ITP,r))	R(=H(ITP,UTPSND,r)
1	CMD=SEND	U1=H0(u,ITP,r)	R1=H0(ITP,UTPSND,r)
3-7		U2=LIST members addressed to r	R2=R1
8	¬abort	U3=U1+U2	R3=R2
11	LIST¬=empty	U4=U3	R4=R3
12		U5=U4	R5=R4+head(U2)
13		U6=U5	R6=R5
11	LIST¬=empty	U7=U6	R7=R6
12		U8=U7	R8=R7
13		U9=U8	R9=R8

derivations:
Un = ... = U3 = H0(u,ITP,r) + LIST members addressed to r
Rn = ... = R1 + head(tail(tail...(U2))) + ... + head(tail(U2)) + head(U2)
= R1 + U2 = H0(ITP,UTPSND,r) + LIST members addressed to r,
path function: H(u,ITP,r) = H(ITP,UTPSND,r).

This, in conjunction with the UTP invariance then yields the intended function f.

III. path 3 and 4 (¬SEND)

part	condition	U(=H(u,ITP,r))	R(=H(ITP,UTPSND,r)
1	¬(OPT=send)	U1=H0(u,ITP,r)	R1=H0(ITP,UTPSND,r)
20		U2=U1	R2=R1

derivations: U2 = H0(u,ITP,r), R2 = H0(ITP,UTPSND,r)
path function: H(u,ITP,r) = H(ITP,UTPSND,r)

This together with the UTP invariance (**g**) leads directly to the intended function **f**.

pass
result
pass suff

This concludes our formal proof. Note that what has been proved was the "sufficient correctness" of ITP [14], since our invariant assertion says nothing about invalid SEND requests (requests addressed to invalid USERIDs or NODEIDs).

FILING AND PRINTING SERVICES ON A LOCAL-AREA NETWORK

P. Janson, L. Svobodova and E. Maehle*

IBM Zurich Research Laboratory, 8803 Rüschlikon, Switzerland

Abstract

This paper describes the design and implementation of filing and printing services in a distributed system based on a token-ring local-area network. The main emphasis is put on the communication aspects of the client/server scenario: roles of a client and a server in a communication protocol, and the integration of communication protocols with applications.

1. Introduction

Local-area networks provide the basis for systems where human users obtain computing and data-processing services through highly autonomous personal workstations. Intelligent workstations can substantially improve the human interface, both from the point of view of function and of performance. However, intelligent workstations cannot cost-effectively provide all services available today in a large shared system. In particular, expensive hardware devices, such as high-quality printers, must remain shareable. Also, it must be possible to share software resources (information) efficiently and to communicate among users.

Shared resources must be protected and administered in an adequate way. In a centralized system, it is the responsibility of the operating system to control the use of such resources. In a distributed system, shared resources are managed by specialized machines called servers.

The general frame of our work is a distributed processing scenario based on a local-area network, where a workstation is the principal means by which a human user obtains computer services. Specifically, we concentrate on the problem of resource control and communication in the client/server model.**

Servers discussed in the literature include name servers[3,4], authentication servers[5], boot servers[4], and more specialized application-oriented servers[6]. However, the basic servers are a file server and a printer server. A file server is used both to provide information sharing, and for economical reasons. A printer server is principally a controller of a shared hardware resource.

We have designed and implemented a file server, a printer server, and a workstation-based client as the first steps towards building a distributed-system testbed for studying the client/server model. The objective of this paper is to report on the design and implementation considerations of our system.

The structure of the prototype system is described in Section 2. Section 3 focuses on the communication aspects. Section 4 discusses some implementation issues and experience. The present status of the project and the extensions planned are presented in Section 5.

2. The Prototype System

The current configuration of our prototype system is shown in Figure 1. It consists of a file server based on an IBM Series/1 minicomputer, a printer server which controls an IBM 6670 laser printer, and IBM Personal Computers as workstations. These components are connected by a token-ring local-area network.

2.1 Key Features of the Token Ring

Our local-area network is a reliable token ring developed at the IBM Zurich Laboratory[7-9]. This section summarizes the key technical properties of this network.

Physical reliability is achieved through distribution panels, from which local lobes are strung in a radial fashion to the offices (see Figure 2).

---

* Present address: University of Erlangen, Erlangen, W. Germany.

** The terms "server" and "client" are already well established in the field of distributed computer systems. For definitions, see, for example, References 1 and 2.

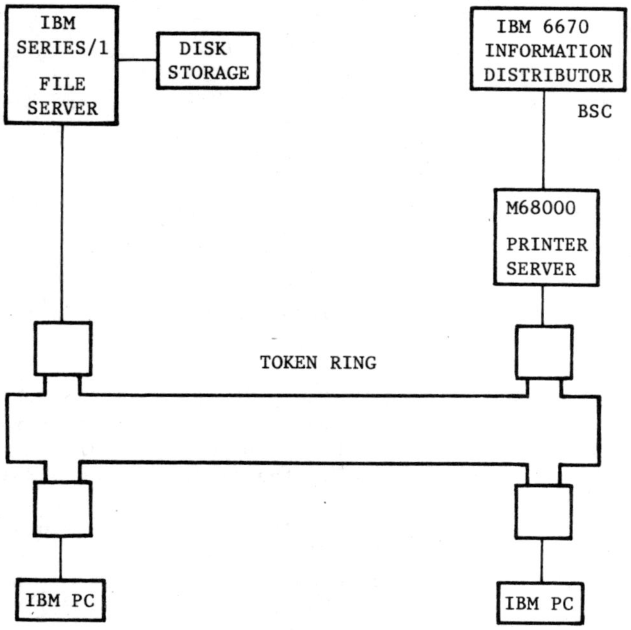

Figure 1

Prototype system.

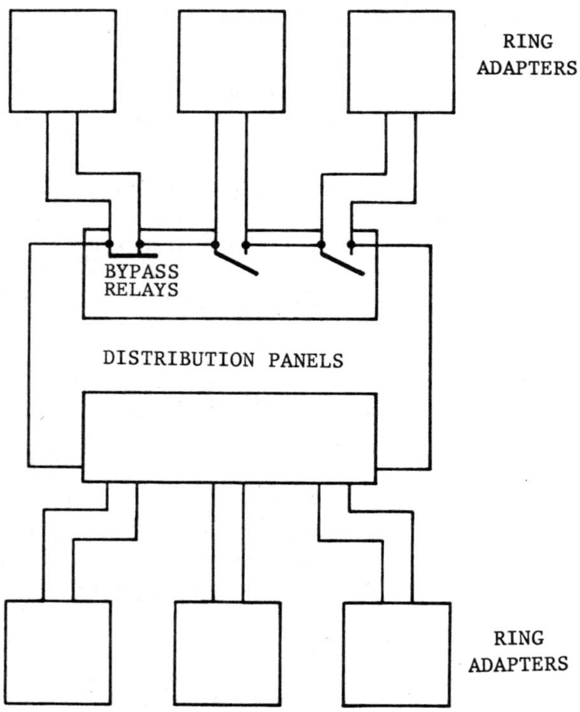

Figure 2

Ring configuration.

Bypass relays in the panels, powered from the attached stations via phantom circuits, allow inactive stations or faulty lobes and adapters to be disconnected from the ring. Distribution panels are installed at strategic points in a building to facilitate maintenance and network reconfiguration. The panels are interconnected by the main ring cable. Devices are attached to the ring via ring adapters that contain the transmission circuitry and execute the token protocol.

Robustness of the token protocol is obtained through a monitor function. The monitor function guarantees that the ring recovers from errors such as lost token (e.g., at system initialization), circulating busy token, and duplicate free tokens. The monitor function is simple enough to be provided in each ring adapter, but for reasons of efficient recovery, it is active in only one ring adapter at any one time. The passive-monitor functions activate themselves in case of an active-monitor failure. A contention-resolution mechanism enforces that only one of them wins the race and becomes the active monitor. It is important to note that the entire monitor function, including the monitor switch-over, is implemented in the adapter, and is transparent to the station attached to it.

Frames transmitted over the ring are protected by a frame check sequence. If transmission errors or station insertion/removal cause a bad frame check sequence, the frame has to be retransmitted. Frame retransmissions, however, are not managed by the ring protocol, but by logical link control or higher-level protocols.

Compared with other access methods used on local-area networks, a token ring has superior delay-throughput characteristics. It does not have the distance and speed limitations of the CSMA/CD protocol, and allows fair sharing of the transmission capacity at high load levels.

The ring provides a building block for supporting reliable distributed systems. However, no ring-specific features of the network, beyond its natural reliability, are exploited in our system design; unlike the Cambridge Distributed System[4,10], our system is independent of the actual network technology, topology, and access protocol.

2.2 File Server

Among the servers proposed and described in the literature, file servers are predominant. A file server is the most fundamental type of server in an information-processing system; it is not only needed to support application programs, but also other types of services.

The charter of a file server can be summarized as:

- provide long-term reliable storage of information, and
- support information sharing.

A survey of existing file servers[2] shows that although most of them support only a low-level model of stored data, their client interfaces are very different. Also, many of the file-server designs aim at a "universal" file server, capable of supporting the following three types of services:

- filing
- paged virtual memory
- database applications.

The designs usually emphasize very high reliability, those aimed at database applications also high concurrency. Consequently, the internal designs are very complex, but most of that complexity has nothing to do with the fact that the system is distributed. We have decided to follow a different path: develop only a simple server, and concentrate on the effects of distribution, namely, communication between clients and servers, which is the essence of the client/server paradigm. In particular, we have been studying:

- design of robust protocols
- low-cost implementations
- the role of file service in other services.

Figure 3 presents three categories of file servers in terms of three design parameters that have the most significant impact on the complexity of a file-server design. Our file server qualifies as a *simple* file server. Clients must send in and retrieve entire files. Consequently, the unit of locking is a file. Operations on individual files are atomic.

	SIMPLE FILE SERVER	UNIVERSAL FILE SERVER	DATABASE MANAGEMENT SUPPORT
UNIT OF DATA ACCESS	FILE	SEQUENTIAL SUBSET OF BYTES	RECORD
UNIT OF LOCKING	FILE	FILE	RECORD OR VARIABLE
SCOPE OF ATOMIC UPDATE	FILE	MULTIPLE FILES (MULTIPLE SERVERS)	MULTIPLE FILES (MULTIPLE SERVERS)

Figure 3

Classification of file servers.

Since we did not want to study the problems of internal file storage and management, we took an existing filing system, namely, the Tripos hierarchical file system[11] as a base. The file structure will be described in more detail in Section 4.

Figure 4 describes the client interface of the file server. The operations that pertain to files represent the minimum a file server must support. Creation of a file is implicit in the put_file operation.

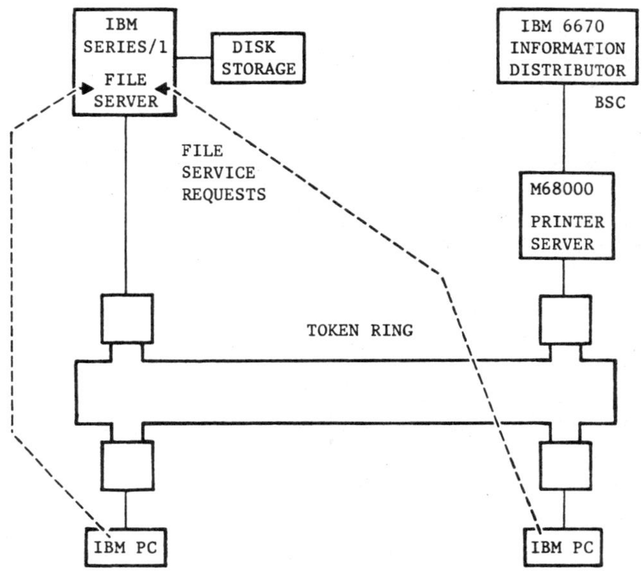

DATA STORAGE/RETRIEVAL	FILE MANAGEMENT
put_file(fn)	make_dir(dn)
get_file(fn)	list_dir(dn)
delete_file(fn)	delete_dir(dn)
	copy_file(fn1,fn2)
	move_file(fn1,fn2)

fn: path name of a file
dn: path name of a directory

Figure 4

File-server interface.

2.3 Printer Server

The printing service has two parts: the control of the actual printing device, and the spooling of files to be printed. Lampson and Sproull gave a brief description of how these two subsystems can coexist on a single machine without full multiprogramming support[12]. In our system, these two parts run on separate machines, which considerably simplifies the implementation.

What we call the printer server is the component that controls the physical printer and feeds it with data obtained from a remote spooler. A similar distribution of function was chosen in the Cambridge Distributed System. In the Cambridge system, the spooling function can be assigned to any processor in the common processor pool.[10] This increases the reliability of the printing service but monopolizes a processor in the pool. In our system, the remote spooler is a simple extension to the file server, and could run on any one or more machines running the file service.

As shown in Figure 5, a print command from a client results in the named file being copied (or sent) to a directory of the file service known as the spooler mailbox. This queueing function of the spooler does not demand any particular action on the part of the file server, which treats the mailbox as any directory in the file system. Although the dequeueing function of the spooler resides in the file service, it is completely passive: it does not make any attempt to spontaneously cause the printing of queued files. Instead, the printer server must prompt the file server to obtain the next file, if any, from the spooler mailbox; once a file has been successfully transmitted to the printer, the file service deletes it from the spooler mailbox.

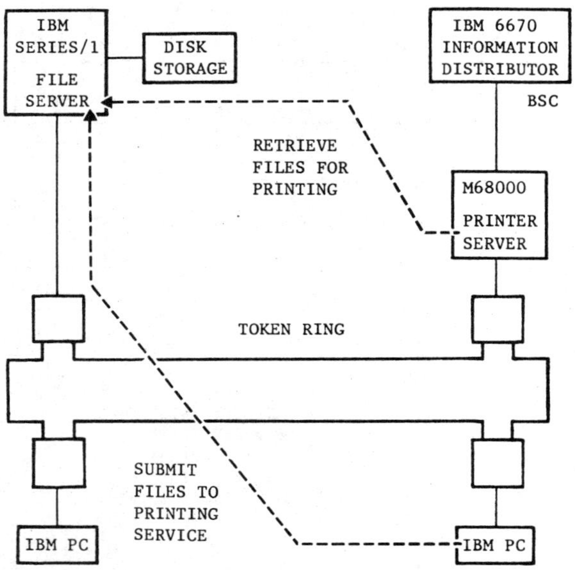

CLIENT:

print(fn) → copy(fn,spooler.mlbx.fn)

PRINTER SERVER:

next_file → get_file(spooler.mlbx.q1)
delete_file(spooler.mlbx.q1)

q1: first file in the spooler queue

Figure 5

Printing service.

In a sense, our printer server is a protocol translator. The data and control information is transmitted to the IBM 6670 laser printer one character at a time, by means of the BSC protocol. On the network side, the printer server uses a block-oriented file-transfer protocol. The printer server does not have its own secondary storage device; it controls the speed of the file transfer and performs only as much buffering as needed to keep the printer busy.

2.4 Workstations

The workstations used in our system are the IBM Personal Computers (PC) running the IBM DOS operating system. Access to the local network services from the PC is provided by the PC client, which is invoked by a special DOS command. At the invocation of this command, the PC, if currently in the stand-alone mode, inserts itself automatically into the ring, by sending appropriate control signals to its ring adapter. The PC client supports a menu-driven interface for direct use by human users.

All of the file-server commands listed in Figure 4 are supported. The put_file commands send a copy of a local file stored on a PC diskette to the file server. A file retrieved from the file server via the get_file command can either be written to a local diskette or displayed on the screen.

The PC client offers two different print commands: one for printing files stored on a local diskette, the other for printing files stored in the file server. As a result of the first command, a copy of the specified local file is shipped directly to the spooler mailbox. The second type of print command causes the file to be copied internally in the file server.

Finally, the PC client offers a simple mail service to facilitate communication with other workstations. This mail service is built on the top of the filing service. The send_mail command sends a copy of a local file to the mailbox ("mail" subdirectory) of the specified user in the file server. PC users can "inspect" (list) the contents of their mailboxes, "view" (display on the screen) individual messages without storing them locally, and "receive" individual messages by moving them to a local diskette.

3. Communication Aspects

In a ring network, frames may be lost due to:

- ring reconfiguration (station insertion or removal)
- transmission errors (bad CRC)
- no free receive buffer in the adapter of the recipient.

The first two events should be relatively rare in a local network. Research performed at our Laboratory has shown that the probability of the last event can be brought down below any target level if the network adapter is properly designed[13].

3.1 Communication Architecture

The communication architecture used in the prototype comprises six layers below the application layer. The lower two layers are based on guidelines that have been emerging lately from the local network standardization committees[14,15], while the higher layers are based on IBM's Systems Network Architecture (SNA)[16,17].

Layer 1, the bottom of the architecture, is the Physical layer. This layer implements the physical media and transmission techniques in the token ring[8].

Layer 2, Link Control (LC), according to emerging local network standards, is divided into two sub-layers: the Media Access Control (MAC) sub-layer, and the Logical Link Control (LLC). The MAC sub-layer specifies frame formatting and media-access protocols. In our prototype, the MAC sub-layer implements the token and monitor protocols outlined in Subsection 2.1.

The LLC sub-layer includes what is known as the elements of procedure according to the HDLC terminology[18]. The proposals of the local network standardization committees recommend that the LLC sub-layer support a so-called connectionless procedure, allowing the unprotected transfer of unnumbered information frames, and optionally a connected procedure, such as ABM (Asynchronous Balanced Mode), for instance[14]. We have implemented only the mandatory connectionless procedure. Thus, in our prototype, LLC supports only one information frame code point: the unnumbered one.

Layer 3, Network Control (NC), in our prototype implements simply a fan-in/fan-out function in every station. The NC layer routes frames (regarded as datagrams at this layer) from access ports to the LLC, and vice-versa.

Our protocols for the next three layers are modeled after SNA. Originally designed for master-slave environments in teleprocessing networks, SNA has evolved and undergone many enhancements, a recent and important one being support for LU 6.2 peer-to-peer communication[17]. Our experimental protocols are based on the peer-to-peer protocols for SNA's Transmission Control (TC), Data Flow Control (DFC), and Function Management (FM) layers.

The SNA TC protocols allow a client and a server to negotiate the parameters of a logical connection called a session through one (or more) two-way handshake(s). The parameters determine such factors as the maximum message size to be used throughout the session and the maximum pacing counts, i.e., the maximum number of messages that can be sent in each direction before an acknowledgement is sent back. As will be explained in the next section, our Transport Control layer also allows a client and a server to exchange information in the form of datagrams, without having to bind a session first.

The DFC layer organizes the traffic between a client and a server as a half-duplex flow of Request/Response Units (RU). Requests carry actual user data while responses carry only acknowledgement or internal network information, such as, for instance, signals controlling the flow on a session.

SNA FM, which implements presentation services as well as powerful resource and network management functions support a collection of transaction-oriented features that can be used to implement atomic and recoverable operations. Some of these features are exploited in our file server.

3.2 Client/Server Communication

Our client/server-communication model supports both datagram (single-shot) and session-based requests. A datagram request is sent in a single ring frame. A reply to a datagram request is also a datagram. A server treats each such datagram as a new request. Thus, in order to be able to use this model, not only must both the information carried by the request and the response fit into a single frame, but the operation requested must be idempotent.

Figure 6 indicates the communication model underlying the client interface of the file server. Of the datagram-based operations, only copy_file is truly idempotent. The other operation are idempotent only from the point of view of their effects on the filing system, but a duplicate request will cause an error reply from the server, since these operations cannot be repeated on a file of the same name. Thus, to be able to use this model, the client must be prepared to handle such error replies correctly. This requirement is not difficult to satisfy: since only the client can create such a duplicate by explicitly resending a request, it is also in the position to interpret correctly a potential error reply.

DATA STORAGE/RETRIEVAL	FILE MANAGEMENT
<-> put_file(fn)	• make_dir(dn)
<-> get_file(fn)	<-> list_dir(dn)
• delete_file(fn)	• delete_dir(dn)
	• copy_file(fn1,fn2)
	• move_file(fn1,fn2)

<-> session-based requests

• datagrams

Figure 6

Implementation of file-service requests.

The session-based requests all involve bulk data transfer. These requests are executed atomically with respect to communication and server failures, but it is not guaranteed that the client will be informed about the final state of a transaction; using Spector's classification of remote reference protocols, the session-based requests qualify as "only-once-type-1" remote reference[19]. A server remembers the state of a client's request only for a limited amount of time; essentially, only until the next request made on the same session, or the end of the session. To protect itself from crashed clients, the server will eventually break an inactive session, thus destroying any information that could be used to determine whether a previous request was committed. However, all of the session-based requests supported by the file server are idempotent, thus once a request has been executed atomically in the server, repeating it has no harmful effects.

3.3 File-Transfer Protocol

The file-transfer protocol consists of two parts: a session control protocol and a block-stream protocol.

The client side and the server side play different roles in each of these parts. In particular, they handle the time-out and retransmission functions very differently. The client always has the initiative; it is the driving force not only as an initiator of a request for service, but also during a file transfer. The server is passive; it responds to requests, data blocks, and prompts from a client, rejects them if they violate the protocol, but does not take any steps to get through to the client. It is the client who must be persistent, and must implement time-out and retransmission to see its requests satisfied.

Interestingly, this situation is in contrast to what is found typically in teleprocessing networks. There, an asymmetry between the user terminal and the host also exists. However, it is the host, usually called the "primary" or the "master", which carries responsibilities such as time-out and retransmission, since the terminal lacks the power to do so; in our scenario, the responsibility lies on the client side, i.e., on the side of the user's workstation in general.

In the server, time-outs are used only to prevent session resources from being tied up by non-responding clients, or clients who do not follow correctly the protocol. The time-out for a session is reset every time the server receives a frame on that session; if the time-out expires, the session is broken, the server releases the local resources allocated to that session, and any on-going file-transfer operation is aborted without side-effects for the file system. This measure protects the server from crashes of the client. However, the client could also tie up server resources uselessly by getting into a loop. Thus, the server must keep track of the number of erroneous interactions with the client, and unbind the session if the count exceeds a predefined limit.

As stated earlier, the major concern on the client's side is to ensure that the task gets done. If no server message is received prior to time-out, all client messages sent since the latest server message was received are retransmitted. These messages may be portions of a file if the client is waiting for an acknowledgement (pacing response), or it may be a pacing response to prompt the server for more data. Upon recognizing a duplicate message, the server *resends* all messages it had sent since the original of the duplicate had been received. The client *ignores* duplicates.

Thus, both the client and the server start a timer every time they start waiting for an action on the part of the other. However, the server's time-out is longer than the client's and they handle time-outs differently. Upon time-out, a client retries its latest transmission while a server aborts the session on the assumption that the client is dead.

3.4 Printing Protocol

The printing protocol has two separate parts. The first involves a transfer of the file to be printed to the spooler mailbox. As explained in Section 2, this step does not necessarily require data transfer over the network. If the file specified is stored in the file server, the file server simply copies that file to the mailbox of the spooler. When the file to be printed is in the local storage of the client, the normal file-transfer protocol described in the preceding section is used to transfer it to the spooler mailbox.

The second part of the printing protocol, controlled by the printer server, is concerned with the file transfer from the spooler to the printing device. This part is further divided into two subparts:

- transfer from the spooler to the printer server, and
- transfer from the printer server to the printing device.

Although called a "server", the printer server is in fact a *client* of the file server, or, more precisely, of the spooling service supported by the file server. The printer server polls the spooler over the network for files to be printed; in reality, it sends a special request to the file server, which is passed to the spooler function. If there is a file in the spooler mailbox at the time such a request is received, it is transferred to the printer server a block at a time; the printer server performs flow control to match the speed of the file transfer to the speed of the actual physical printer. A frame from the spooler to the printer server is passed to the printer one character at a time. A failure to communicate properly with the printing device is signalled immediately to the spooler, and aborts the file transfer. When the printer server has successfully transferred the entire file to the printer, it sends a "commit" response to the spooler; as a consequence, the file is deleted from the spooler queue. Thus, this protocol is truly an end-to-end protocol.

The printer server is persistent in trying to keep the printing service going. It tries to maintain a session with the spooler as long as the printer operates correctly. If the spooler crashes, the printer server rebinds a session at the first possible moment after the spooler has been reinitialized.

4. Implementation

The file server and the printer server were implemented in BCPL[20] under the Tripos operating system[11]. Tripos, designed at the Cambridge University (U.K.), is a portable, real-time, modular operating system for mini and microcomputers. Although very small and offering only limited memory management and user interface support, Tripos provides powerful and efficient multitasking facilities. To a great extent, Tripos is an "open" operating system in the sense of Lampson[12]. The exact configuration can be tailored to the application at hand and the hardware resources available. Tripos has proved very adequate to support non-user-programmable server machines.

The PC client was implemented in the PC Pascal under the IBM DOS operating system. DOS is a single-user single-thread operating system based on diskettes. In addition to the ISO Standard Pascal, PC Pascal provides some further support for system programming (e.g., direct access to physical memory locations) and modular design. The means for modularization is the so-called "unit", which consists of separate interface and implementation divisions. These additional features proved to be very important; they were exploited particularly in the protocol implementation.

4.1 Filing System

The Tripos file system appears as a tree of disk block lists, where each block is self-identifying and refers to its parent or brother. The disk map is never stored on the disk. Instead, every time the system is restarted, it rebuilds the disk map by inspecting the disk from the root block downward. Disk blocks not reachable from the root are considered free. If there exists only a single reference to a block, the block is considered valid. Blocks reachable from more than one place in the file-system structure are considered suspicious, and flagged.

In moving a file from one place in the hierarchical file system to another, Tripos first places a reference to that file in the target directory, then destroys the old reference, and finally updates the disk map. Thus, if the system crashes after the file has been recorded in the new place but before the old reference is destroyed, the map rebuilding procedure will flag the file header. Normally, the operator must decide which reference to drop.

The mechanism just described is used in the file server to support atomic file updates in the following way. A file-update operation is implemented by writing the new version to a time-stamped temporary file in a special directory, and then moving it in one disk write operation to the position of the old version in the tree. This disk write operation realizes the "commit" step of the update. If the system crashed immediately after the commit, it will wake up in a state where the file appears in two directories. The reference in the special directory can safely be dropped to complete the update operation. Atomicity is thus guaranteed. However, Tripos does not offer atomic stable storage as in Reference 21, so a disk failure *in the middle* of a critical disk write operation would leave the file system in an inconsistent state.

4.2 Filing and Printing Services

The Tripos/BCPL environment supports two types of concurrency mechanisms: tasks and coroutines. All tasks and coroutines execute in the same address space. Tasks communicate by sending messages; task scheduling is controlled by Tripos. A task can contain internally any number of coroutines. Coroutines are invoked in a similar fashion to procedures; their scheduling is left to the programmer. Coroutines are much less expensive than tasks in terms of the context-switching overhead.

The network protocols in the file server and the printer server were implemented with efficiency as a key objective, at the cost of sacrificing some of the architectural modularity of the protocols; some of the layers that are clearly distinct in our architectural model, are implemented in the same software module. The principal ways towards low cost communication are minimizing the overhead of context switching, and eliminating data copying between protocol layers. Thus, we concentrated on eliminating task switching along the path of each individual request. Also, whenever possible, we use coroutines rather than tasks to represent concurrent activities. Finally, data sent or received by a client or server are never copied within the communication subsystem; we use buffer windowing similar to Reference 22.

Figures 7 and 8 show the internal structure of the file server and the printer server, respectively.

Since the printer server is dedicated to a single function and contains only a single session at a time, all of the protocol levels have been compressed to a single task that manages all the necessary resources. The data received from the ring are never copied within the printer server: they are passed in the same buffer all the way to the BSC handler and from there directly to the printer.

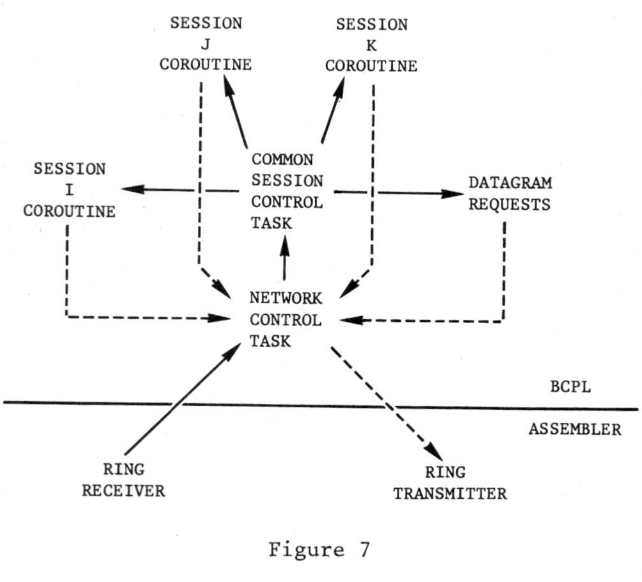

Figure 7

File-server structure.

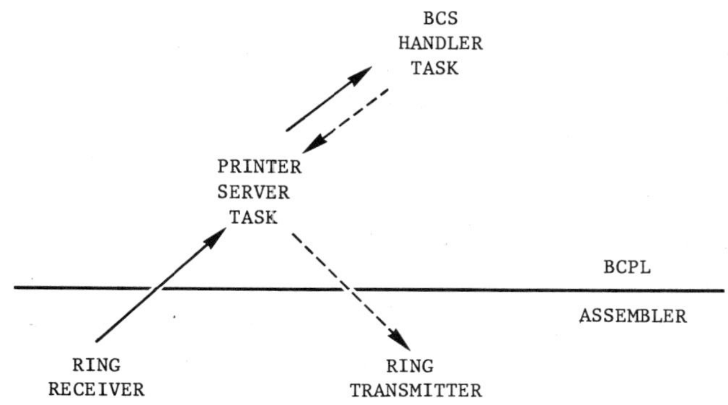

Figure 8

Printer-server structure.

In the file server, the only copy operation is to or from the file-server application itself out of or into disk cache buffers. This operation cannot be avoided unless the ring frame size is coupled direct to the size of disk records, a constraint that clearly cannot hold for all disks, and is therefore unacceptable.

Since we envisioned putting other servers, for example, a name server, on the same hardware as the file server, the communication control was split into two tasks. One task executes the NC protocol, routing frames to and from other tasks representing clients and servers. All of the requests for file services are directed to the file-server task. Within this task, individual session transactions are represented by coroutines. Any session ready to receive data must pass a sufficient number of empty buffers to NC. In addition, the file-server task allocates and passes to NC several empty buffers for datagram requests. All these buffers are interchangeable. NC manages them as a pool, since at the time it receives a frame from the network, it cannot know for which entity it is intended. When it receives a frame for an entity that has no more buffers in the pool, it does not pass the frame to it, but frees the buffer immediately.

4.3 PC Client

One important precondition in the implementation of the PC client was the fact that the current DOS and PC Pascal do not support concurrent processes. Consequently, the entire client is implemented as a sequential Pascal program. This solution is adequate for accessing of network services, due to the passive role of the server in our client/server protocol. Since all actions are always initiated by the client, the client does not have to be prepared to deal with messages asynchronous to its current activities.

Since a workstation is a more "general-purpose" machine than the servers, it is important to facilitate easy modifications and support of different types of communication. Thus, in the implementation of the PC client, we put more emphasis on well-structured, modular code than on performance. Each network layer is implemented as a separate PC Pascal unit; an additional unit is used to control the ring insertion and removal of the PC ring adapter.

4.4 Experience

The servers as implemented today are very small. The file- server code takes 17 kwords of primary memory (16-bit words), out of which 8 kwords are used up by the communication protocols and ring drivers. The communication portion of the printer server represents 4 k of 32-bit words.

Tripos tasks and coroutines proved to be well suited to support the parallelism inherent in real-time communication software, but we should have liked better facilities for managing static storage accessible to multiple concurrent activities (tasks or coroutines). The main shortcomings of BCPL are the lack of typing and the very primitive data structures.

Although the file server and printer server do not share any code, having the same programming environment and tools on both of the machines proved to be very helpful. Specifically, the common model of concurrent activities and the corresponding discipline of synchronization and communication provided a good base for discussing the implementations of the protocols, and simplified the debugging.

The PC client uses 25 kwords (16-bit words) of primary memory, including about 10 kwords of the Pascal runtime support. Among the high-level languages available on the PC, Pascal seemed best suited for our purpose. However, while it is good for producing well-structured and modular code, the lack of concurrency mechanisms made the implementation of the network protocols on the PC more difficult than in the servers.

5. Conclusions

The file server, printer server and PC clients described in this paper are operational.

As stated in the Introduction, our goal is to study the client/server model of distributed computing. From this point of view, the major aspects are the distribution of function, and the communication protocols. We chose to have the printer spooler function implemented as an extension of the file service; the printer server is essentially a protocol translator, which extends the network error and flow control up to the application, that is, to the IBM 6670 controller. The file server provides standard filing services, but at the communication level, the server is driven by the clients.

Our current implementation of the communication protocols is tailored to the function of a particular machine. In both the file server and the printer server, the local resource management is tied closely with the communication control. The passive role of a server in the client/server protocol allowed us to implement the PC client as a sequential Pascal program.

Acknowledgements

Several people contributed to making the system operational. We wish to express our gratitude especially to P. Zafiropulo, who designed and implemented the BSC handler for the printer server, and K. Moritzen, who implemented the user interface of the PC client. Special thanks are due to K. Kuemmerle for his careful reviews and valuable criticism of the paper.

References

[1] Mitchell, J.G., "File servers for local area networks," Lecture Notes, Course on Local Area Networks, University of Kent, Canterbury, England, March 1982, pp. 83-114.

[2] Svobodova, L., "File servers for network-based distributed systems," Technical Report RZ1187 IBM Zurich Research Laboratory, Rüschlikon, Switzerland, November, 1982.

[3] Abraham, S.M., and Dalal, Y.K., "Techniques for decentralized management of distributed systems", *Proc. IEEE COMPCON,* Spring 1980, pp. 430-437.

[4] Needham, R.M., and Herbert, A.J., *The Cambridge distributed computing system,* Addison-Wesley, 1982.

[5] Needham, R.M., and Schroeder, M.D., "Using encryption for authentication in large networks of computers," *Commun. ACM,* Vol. 21, No. 12, December 1978, pp. 993-999.

[6] Birrell, A., Levin, R., Needham, R., Schroeder, M., "Grapevine: An exercise in distributed computing", *Commun. ACM 25,* Vol. 4 (April 1982), pp. 260-273.

[7] Bux, W., Closs, F., Janson, P., Kümmerle, K., and Müller, H.R., "A reliable token-ring system for local-area networks," *Proc. NTC '81,* New Orleans, Louisiana, November 1981, pp. A2.2.1-A2.2.6.

[8] Bux, W., Closs, F., Janson, P., Kümmerle, K., Müller, H.R., and Rothauser, E.H., "A local-area communication network based on a reliable token-ring system," *Proc. Int. Symp. Local Computer Networks*, Florence, Italy, April 1982, pp. 69-82.

[9] Müller, H.R., Keller, H., Meyr, H., "Transmission in a synchronous token ring," *Int. Symp. Local Computer Networks*, Florence, Italy, April 1982, pp. 125-147.

[10] Needham, R.M., "System aspects of the Cambridge ring," *Proc. 7th ACM Symp. on Operating Systems Principles*, Asilomar, California, December 1979, pp. 82-85.

[11] Richards, M., Aylward, A.R., Bond, P., Evans, R.D., and Knight, B.J., "TRIPOS: A portable operating system for minicomputers", *Software Practice and Experience*, Vol. 9, No. 7, July 1979, pp. 513-526.

[12] Lampson, B.W., and Sproull, R.F., "An open operating system for a single-user machine," *Proc. 7th ACM Symp. on Operating Systems Principles*, Asilomar, California, December 1979, pp. 98-105.

[13] Wong, J.W., and Bux, W., "Analytic modeling of an adapter to local area networks", *Proc. GLOBECOM82 Conf.*, IEEE, Piscataway, NJ, pp. 527-532, 1982.

[14] "IEEE 802 local network standard: Draft C", IEEE, May 1982.

[15] "Final draft, ECMA standard on local area networks (token ring)", ECMA Working Paper, December 1982.

[16] Sundstrom, R.J. and Schulz, G.D., "SNA's first six years: 1974-1980," *Proc. Fifth Int. Conf. Computer Communication*, Atlanta, Georgia, October 1980, pp. 578-585.

[17] Gray, J.P., "SNA operating system services to support distributed processing", *Proc. '82 IEEE Int. Large Scale Systems Symp.*, Virginia Beach, VA, October 1982, pp. 161-165.

[18] "HDLC frame structure", "HDLC elements of procedure", and "HDLC balanced classes of procedure", Standards ISO-3309, ISO-4335, and ISO-6256.

[19] Spector, A.Z., "Performing remote operations efficiently on a local computer network," *Commun. ACM*, Vol. 25, April 1982, pp. 246-260.

[20] Richards, M., Strevens-Whitby, C., *BCPL -- the language and its compiler*, Cambridge University Press, 1980.

[21] Lampson, B.W., and Sturgis, H.E., "Crash recovery in a distributed data storage system," XEROX Palo Alto Research Center, Calif., April 1979 (to be published in *Commun. ACM)*.

[22] Dion, J., "Reliable storage in a local network," Tech. Rep. No. 16, University of Cambridge, Computer Laboratory, Cambridge, England, February 1981 (Ph.D. thesis).

Resource Management in a Distributed System

Mark Yudkin

Cambridge University Computer Laboratory,
Corn Exchange Street, Cambridge CB2 3QG, England.

Abstract

In the Cambridge Distributed System, developed at the Computer Laboratory, Cambridge, terminals, machines and peripherals are separated by a ring network. A problem that arises is the establishment and control of suitable connexions between the individual components, so that users may use machines, machines may use peripherals or other machines, etc. in a secure manner.

This paper describes an experimental mechanism used to control the connexions and provide security in our particular system. The solution is not restricted to the Cambridge ring, although a different architecture may suggest alternative solutions more suited to its specific features. Some possibilities are discussed.

1. Introduction

The Cambridge Distributed System [5] provides a large number of services running permanently at fixed addresses ("static services": those which run on dedicated machines) carrying out particular functions, such as printing, tape handling, authentication, logging and giving the time. There are also a set of machines, known collectively as the Processor Bank; ownership of whose members is uncommitted. They may be allocated to users when required to perform whatever service the user desires. Control of machines in the processor bank is performed through the use of a set of services known as the Ancillae[1] which enable the temporary owner of a machine to exercise at least the same degree of control over that machine as if its control panel were physically accessible to its owner.

----

1 Ancilla - Latin: housemaid

There is a separate Ancilla for each type of processor and the Ancillae provide a uniform interface for all processors.

Any service may use other services, subject to authentication issues. There are also a small number of services without dedicated machines, and when appropriate tools for managing these become readily available the number of such services is likely to increase. It is the secure management of these so-called "dynamic services" which is of interest here; management being defined as controlling the creation and destruction of services. The mechanism needs to be able to handle both dynamic and static services uniformly and transparently: users ought not to be able to tell the difference, except perhaps for timing effects.

We wish to provide a system allowing services of any complexity to be created and layered on top of other services. Security dictates that only those authorized to use a service may do so; allowing mutual cooperation of suspicious services means that keys representing users or services cannot be passed from one to the other, for fear of their being abused.

2. Authentication

Objects (users, machines, services etc.) are represented in the Cambridge Distributed System by their possessing an entry in an Active Name Table. This holds their name, authority, access key and control key, each represented by random 64-bit unique identifiers. The access key is the proof that the owner is the object whose identity is name, where authority is the agency which caused the entry to be created. The control key is required for the entry to be deleted or modified. Further details may be found in [4] or [5].

In our system, however, one object may not wish to apply to a service by passing the objects own access key because it does not trust the service sufficiently. What we do is to interpose a trusted service (called the Manciple[1]) one of whose functions is to perform the relevant authentication (of the client) on behalf of the service. If successful, the Manciple will issue a key allowing access to the service.

Thus a service, upon being created, will issue an allowance (a 64-bit well-known permanent unique identifier); objects suitably authorized will obtain a capability (a 64-bit random number encoding the allowance, his name and certain access rights). Presentation of this capability to the service enables the object to obtain the service with no security compromise. The service can find out who its client is but not that client's access key. This capability is separate from the address, since the address at which a service may be obtained is generally fixed in a "static" service. This is different from Tanenbaum and Mullender's Amoeba [7]. One advantage is that the initial contact address is not subject to negotiation between the allocation system and the newly created service.

In practice, services may offer many different classes of service, depending upon its client's qualifications. For example, one user's access to a filing system generally differs from other users'. In addition, systems programmers generally have greater access to system files, and represent a different class of user. In the authentication system on the Cambridge Distributed System there is the notion of a privilege, being represented by an Active Name Table entry with the authority "PRIV". Objects may claim those privileges to which they are entitled by applying to a Privilege Manager.

In our system, services represent their different classes of service by different allowances. Upon creation, a service issues a list of allowances; associated with each will be a non-empty set of privileges, all of which must be held by the client before that particular allowance may be claimed. (In fact, the allowance list will probably be issued by the service's Secretary: this is discussed further in section 3). The list of allowances is ordered so that if allowance A appears before allowance B, then the set of privileges associated with A is not a subset of the set of privileges associated with B. Furthermore no two (distinct) allowances in a list have identical sets of privileges. These conditions are sufficient to ensure that the list of allowances can be ordered and that the list is finite, given a finite number of privileges. In practice allowance lists tend to be small.

---

1 Manciple - (sb.) an officer who buys provisions for a college.
More obvious terms (like "resource manager") evoke different pre-determined connotations in different environments.

An operation called refinement is used to issue an allowance to a client. A client's access key may be associated with a number of privileges, making it a simple matter to determine if a client has a particular privilege. Refinement works by scanning the list of allowances in order, checking each allowance in turn to see if the client is entitled to that allowance (that the client holds all of the associated privileges), stopping as soon as a suitable allowance is found.

Since services may be layered on top of other services, one might think that possession of a capability implies possession of the capabilities for all subservices. However, users of a service must not be allowed full access to the subservices. (Imagine the chaos that could arise if users of a large time-sharing operating system were given the same access to the disk drives as the operating system.) Possession of a capabilty by a service does not imply possesssion of that capability by its clients. It is worth comparing this with the analogous case of protected procedures in capability computers such as CAP [8] or Hydra/C.mmp [9].

To protect against failures, capabilities have an associated timeout, and must be refreshed at regular intervals. If a capability times out, the reference count associated with the service is decremented. Upon reaching zero, the reference counts for all subservices are decremented and the service can be reclaimed. This is because there may be many capabilities in existence for a service. If a subservice is revoked, so are all services layered on top of it. Since services appear to be layered as a tree structure - a spanning tree of the dependency graph, there can be no cycles.

3. The Manciple and Service Secretaries

At the centre of the resource management system is the Manciple, which looks after all requests for services. The Manciple takes very little action to fulfil requests, it simply forwards requests to other services (known as Service Secretaries) whose purpose is to provide the particular service when required. By causing all requests to be channelled through the Manciple, the authentication issues may be easily handled.

Service Secretaries must be provided for each "generic" service type and these implement all policy issues related to the provision of the service. It is also their job to know how to manufacture the services they manage and to provide the allowance lists. There is only ever one notional instance of a Service Secretary in existence at any time and it must keep its state over failures (the Manciple provides a suitable stable storage facility for Service Secretaries). Distributing a Service Secretary over several machines is analogous to distributing the database associated with a Secretary.

In the following, items in square brackets ([]'s) are optional, items which may have 0 or more occurences are followed by an asterisk (*). The reply will contain a return code, which is zero if successful, when the additional information shown will be present, otherwise it should be interpreted as an error code.

3.1 Manciple Interfaces

The Manciple provides the following interfaces for clients:

```
service   (service name, caller's access key,
            [caller's control key], caller's name,
            caller's authority, attributes*, [rights],
            privileges*, [uninterpreted bit string])
          -> (service address, capability)

refresh   (capability, timeout) -> ()

finish    (capability) -> ()

allowPass (capability, other's access key,
            other's control key, other's name,
            other's authority, [rights])
          -> (new capability for other)

refine    (capability, [rights], like privileges*,
            hate privileges*)
          -> (new capability)

amplify   (capability, [rights], like privileges*,
            hate privileges*)
          -> (new capability)

identify  (capability)
          -> (service name, service address,
            service secretary's name, owner's name,
            owner's authority)
```

There are four rights associated with a capability: passable, amplifiable, public and unconfined. Passable and amplifiable determine whether or not pass and amplify is allowed; public allows a service the user's access key (and control key if given); unconfined is discussed briefly in section 4. Those operations which return capabilities (allowPass, refine and amplify) will AND together the rights of the original capability with the rights given.

The **service** interface enables the user to obtain a service by quoting its name. He gives the Manciple his authentication information, together with a list of privileges he could hold but may not presently have (the Manciple will check such a claim with the Privilege Manager). For each service there will be a list of attributes he may require: these are clearly service specific. Like all names, they are permanent unique 64-bit identifiers. The uninterpreted bit string may contain further information about the required service; in any case the Manciple simply passes it to the Service Secretary for the service, uninterpreted (see later).

The **refresh** interface implements a dead-man's handle. Because it is difficult to determine if a remote service has died, we require that the owner regularly refresh its capability. In practice, owners generally hand the capability to the service for it to refresh. The timeout is some reasonable value, typically a few minutes. Should the capability time out the owner or service is deemed to have lost interest (or died) (with noone debugging it). When all capabilities associated with a service have timed out or been deleted (see finish below), the resources associated with a service may be forceably reclaimed.

The **finish** interface allows a service or its owner to indicate that the owner of the given capability has finished with the service. The resources associated with the service may be reclaimed when all outstanding capabilities for the service have been deleted or have timed out.

The **allowPass** interface provides the holder of a capability the ability of making a new capability for another user. It requires the holder (H) to provide the authentication information for the other user (X). The operation will fail if the capability does not have the passable right. The new capability will be for user X, and the **verify** interface (see below) will return X's name rather than H's. If H wishes to pass a capability to user X, and they are suspicious of each other, then they should arrange for the action to be performed by a service which they both trust (H passes the capability to the mutually trusted service while X passes his authentication information to it).

The **refine** interface enables the allowance list from which the capability was derived to be refined again, starting at the allowance corresponding to the given capability.

The **amplify** interface enables the allowance list to be refined again starting at the top, but stopping no later than the given capability. The operation will fail if the capability does not have the amplify right.

The **identify** interface is not actually necessary, since all the information it provides can be determined at the time it was issued. Nevertheless it can be useful to be able to determine the information at a later stage.

The Manciple provides the following interfaces for services or their Secretaries:

```
verify    (capability, service's access key,
            service's name, service's authority)
          -> (allowance, user's name)

check     (capability, service's access key,
            service's name, service's authority) -> ()
```

```
retrieve  (service secretary's access key,
           service secretary's control key,
           service secretary's name,
           service secretary's authority,
           service secretary's address, allowance)
        -> (service address, service's access key,
           allowance list, subservice's capability *,
           [uninterpreted bit string]) *

revoke    (capability, service's access key,
           service's name, service's authority) -> ()
```

The **verify** interface is provided to allow a service to check that a capability is valid and has not been revoked (see below). It returns the allowance that generated it, together with the owner's name.

The **check** interface is like the **verify** interface above, but returns no additional information.

The **retrieve** interface allows a Service Secretary to retrieve information it previously deposited with the Manciple. This implements state saving stable memory for the Service Secretary. The major item is the uninterpreted bit string, which is the uninterpreted bit string returned by the **instance** request (to be discussed). If allowance is omitted the result is a list of the information normally provided, containing all information previously deposited.

The **revoke** interface enables a service or its Secretary to revoke a capability. This means that any attempt to verify or check it will fail, as will refresh, allowPass, refine, amplify and identify. If the capability is omitted, all capabilities for the given service are revoked.

3.2 Service Secretary Interfaces

The Service Secretary looks, to the Manciple and the rest of the system, like a service. It differs in that its "Service Secretary" is the Manciple, and its only users are the Manciple and the services it provides. Requests from its services include that service's access key for authentication (a service can hardly be suspicious of its Secretary), and requests from the Manciple include the Service Secretary's access key. Since the Service Secretary's access key is known only to itself, the Manciple (which will not disclose it) and the authentication system, it is adequate proof; no capabilities are needed.

Service Secretaries provide the following interfaces for the Manciple:

```
instance (service name,
          service secretary's access key,
          attributes *, [rights],
          [uninterpreted bit string])
      -> (service address, service's access key,
          service's control key,
          service's authority, (allowance,
          associated privilege set) *,
          subservice's capability *,
          [uninterpreted bit string])

finished (service's access key,
          service secretary's access key,
          allowance) -> ()
```

The **instance** interface enables the Manciple to obtain a service from its secretary. The service name parameter is superfluous, but enables the service secretary to detect errors in the service - Service Secretary mapping. The attributes list, rights and uninterpreted bit string are those which were passed in to the Manciple's **service** interface. The Service Secretary will create a service instance (possibly calling the Manciple's service interface for required subservices). The result will be the service's address and authentication information (its name is known by the Manciple - it was part of the request), together with the allowance list and capabilities for all subservices used in creating the service. The uninterpreted bit string contains state information which the Secretary wants kept stably. It can be retrieved by the **retrieve** entry (see above).

The **finished** interface instructs the Service Secretary to clean up after the service instance, as it is no longer required. The Service Secretary does not need to advise subservices used in making the service, as the Manciple does that.

There are no standard interfaces Service Secretaries must provide for their services; any interfaces which are provided are at the discretion of the author of a service and are private.

4. Other Possibilities

The mechanism used is that chosen for the Cambridge Ring. It is obviously possible to use the same mechanism on other local area networks. However some features of the Cambridge Ring have affected the design. The Cambridge Ring has no broadcast mode. The ring interfaces for many of the processor bank machines contain small awkward micro-processors which are unsuitable for anything but trivial ring connexions. The ring is assumed to provides secure point-to-point transmission: transmissions cannot be compromised or observed by any processor (without physically altering the ring hardware).

If the ring interfaces contained more powerful processors, much of the allocation and authentication system could be put into the interfaces. Because the interfaces run fixed, unchangeable programs, we have user protected memory to use (as with many operating systems) for holding classified information. Therefore access keys could be held in the interface's memory, and the capability mechanism introduced here for dealing with mutual suspicion would be largely unnecessary. This is now comparable to a machine with a capability architecture, such as CAP [8] or

Hydra/C.mmp [9], where each domain is a remote service. The Manciple would have only to handle the book-keeping. Services running in the host machine would refresh the access key by sending refresh messages to the host's interface, which would perform the refreshing across the ring. This however makes it very hard to maintain and enhance the system and is probably unsatisfactory for these reasons alone.

If the ring were to have a broadcast mode, the book-keeping facilities of the Manciple could be supplemented by broadcasting messages to every machine to find out what it was doing. The ring interfaces would always be able to answer such enquiries by remembering what was loaded (loading requests go directly to it); failure to provoke any reply indicating failure of the node. The stable memory requirement of the Manciple could be removed.

The total system could therefore comprise a map between generic service types and their Secretaries, and a number of Service Secretaries which upon creation insert their addresses into the map. The presence of a unique instance of a Service Secretary is ensured using the same mechanism as is used in a local area network in which any station can become the monitor. A booting service would also be provided to boot Services Secretaries and services, although this could be removed if the interfaces were capable of fulfilling booting requests directly. Taken to the extreme, interfaces could implement the entire allocation scheme.

Another issue is the data confinement problem. Although it is clear that the partial confinement problem cannot be solved without specialized architectures for each processor on the network [1,2,3], it is possible to solve the total confinement problem of preventing a single user service from accessing services other than those explicitly allowed by its client. In this way data can be kept confined to a specified set of services, which is sufficient for some classes of problem. In particular those services which do not require other (suspicious) services can be prevented from disclosing any information sent to them. This requires the notion of transmission keys which need to be handled by the interfaces; interfaces refuse to transmit a block unless presented with a valid transmission key for the particular transmission by the host. Further details will not be given here.

If the network could not provide secure end-to-end transmission, some form of end-to-end encryption, such as the Needham and Schroeder protocols [6] could be used.

Of these ideas, only data confinement has been implemented, and this cannot be enforced by every processor in our environment.

5. Performance Measurement and Conclusion

The Manciple has been implemented on the Cambridge Ring and together with a couple of Service Secretaries is capable of providing a "Tripos" operating system or dialect running on LSI4 or 68000 microprocessors. A simple user interface is provided for the convenience of users. Some performance measurements have been taken, performance being measured mainly as the time taken to provide the required service. These will be summarized here.

In general the mechanism works satisfactorily. To reduce the number of physical machines needed, the Manciple and Service Secretaries live on the same machine, although their only communication is through the ring. The system has been demonstrated with the Manciple and Service Secretaries running on separate machines.

The dominant factor in performance is the time taken to load a machine. With a 10MHz packet ring containing 3 packets (allowing use of every fourth) of 38 bits (16 data bits), plus a 1 bit (minimum) inter-packet gap, maximum point-to-point bandwidth is 1Mbit/sec. Booting a machine involves the data travelling around the ring twice: once from the fileserver to the Ancilla and once from the Ancilla to the machine. Ignoring protocol and processing overheads, loading 64Kbytes takes 1 second. In practice there are delays introduced by processing in the fileserver and Ancilla, reading the disk, ring contention, etc. and the actual loading time is about 3 - 5 seconds (depending upon load).

Access to the file server is the main bottleneck. Thus the decision to have the Manciple provide the Service Secretaries' stable storage, whilst a little unclean, appears to have been correct compared with the alternative of having each use the file server directly. The Manciple backs up its state using the file server. The cost of non-loading ring transmissions, authentication checking and processing in the Manciple and Service Secretaries appear negligible by comparison. There are occasional delays seen when the fileserver is loaded, since the Manciple will not verify or check a capability before the associated state has been saved: it gives a retryable error code.

It seems likely that a considerable gain in performance could be achieved by pre-manufacturing commonly used services during idle moments. Should a different service be required no harm has been done. The Manciple would have to be responsible for record keeping, and either it, or another service could be responsible for predicting future demand, balancing the numbers of services and other decision making. It would be useful for Service Secretaries to provide an interface of the form: "If a service instance had been requested, would it have been provided?" This interface is designed to provide a hint only; its purpose is to allow a possible balance between services to be determined rapidly, although not perfectly. An affirmative answer will continue to be correct at least until the Manciple makes a service request (assuming no hardware failures). Pre-manufacturing has not been implemented in the current system.

References

1. D.E. Denning
   A Lattice Model of Secure Information Flow
   Comm. ACM 19/5 (May 1976) pp 236-243

2. D.E. Denning & P.J. Denning
   Certification of Programs for Secure Information Flow
   Comm. ACM 20/7 (July 1977) pp 504-513

3. J.S. Fenton
   Information Protection Systems
   Ph.D. Thesis, University of Cambridge 1973

4. C.G. Girling:
   Authentication in Project Universe
   Proceedings 6th International Conference on Computer Communication pp 395-400

5. R.M. Needham & A.J. Herbert:
   The Cambridge Distributed Computer System
   Addison Wesley Publishing Company 1982

6. R.M. Needham & M.D. Schroeder
   Using Encryption for Authentication in Large Computer Networks
   Comm. ACM 21/12 (Dec 1978) pp 993-999

7. A.S. Tanenbaum & S.J. Mullender
   An Overview of the Amoeba Distributed Operating System
   ACM Operating Systems Review July 1981 pp 51-64

8. M.V.Wilkes & R.M. Needham
   The Cambridge CAP Computer and its Operating System
   North Holland 1979

9. W.A. Wulf, R. Levin & S.P. Harbison
   Hydra/C.mmp: An Experimental Computer System
   McGraw Hill 1981

Interfaces and Protocol

Chairman

N. Tobol

Interfaces Between Protocol Layers on a Multiprocessor System

Wilfredo A. Colon-Castro
Deborah A. Kirkman

American Bell
Holmdel, New Jersey 07733

A multi-layer, X.25 based protocol has been implemented on a multiprocessor system. The higher layer protocol resides in the system processor while the lower level protocol (X.25 levels 2 and 3) runs on a peripheral processor. This paper focuses on the boundary between the system and peripheral processors. It discusses how flow control is done, how control information is passed across the boundary, and the synchronization problems that arose. In addition, it describes effects on performance resulting from splitting the protocol across the two processors.

1. Introduction

This paper describes aspects of a protocol layer[1] interface that is implemented on a multi-processor system. The performance constraints of the system precluded putting all of the protocol on a single processor. Instead, software was partitioned between a 16 bit system processor and an 8 bit peripheral processor. Because processors run independently of each other, the partition creates information flow problems. On the system processor, an operating system imposes even further constraints on passing information across this boundary.

1.1 Requirements

The purpose of this protocol implementation or subsystem is to provide communications services over virtual circuits in a star network (refer to Figure 1). User programs on the system processor require the high-level services of formal connection and disconnection, and a guarantee of message delivery and message order. This paper discusses the architecture of the protocol subsystem in the terminal nodes. Due to differences in hardware and software environments, the architecture of the protocol subsystem in the central node is significantly different.

In addition, there is a fixed set of user pairs--thus there is no need for dynamic allocation of virtual circuits. Instead, circuits are allocated statically, with a particular circuit being assigned to a pair of users.

1.2 Hardware Architecture

The X.25[2] [3] [4] protocol subsystem executes in a multi-micro processor environment (refer to Figure 2).

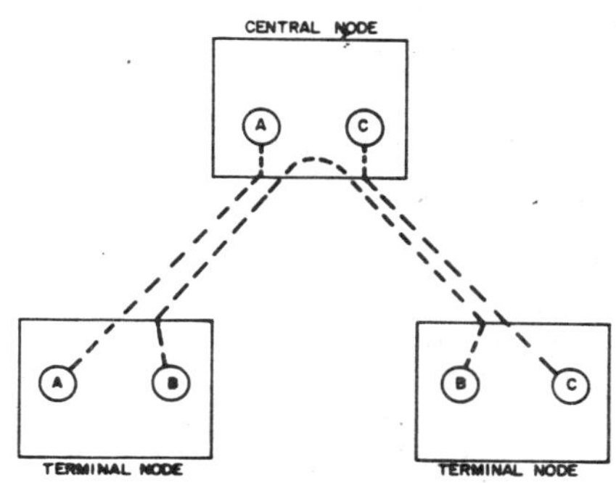

Figure 1. Network **Topology**

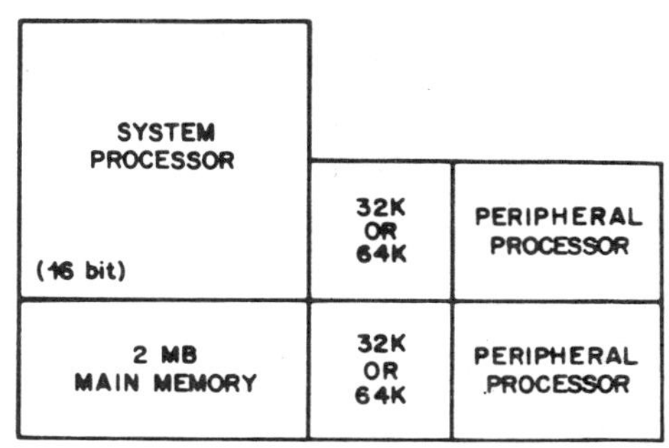

Figure 2. System Configuration

The system processor is an 8 megahertz (MHz), 16 bit general purpose microprocessor with access to two million bytes of random access memory (RAM) plus the local memories of the peripheral processors. Each peripheral processor is an 8 bit micro-computer with 32 or 64 thousand bytes (KB) of RAM. Specifically, the peripheral processor used by the protocol subsystem is equipped with 64KB of RAM, a 4 MHz general purpose microprocessor, a counter-timer chip, and a universal synchronous-asynchronous receiver-transmitter (USART) chip.

The system and peripheral processors communicate on a master-slave basis. The system processor is always the master and requests service by writing to a dedicated area of the peripheral processor's local memory. A peripheral processor, although unable to affect main memory, can interrupt the system processor to get service for requests it places in a second dedicated area of its local memory. The system processor performs all data moves between main and peripheral processor memory.

1.3 Software Environment

Programs on the system processor do not have access to the details of the hardware architecture but instead run under a multi-tasking, time-shared operating system. One service provided by the operating system is a driver that manages communications between software on the system and peripheral processors.

System processor software uses the driver to access the peripheral processor as a device with several entry ways or sub-channels. The only operations programs can perform on these sub-channels are *open* (initialize and make available for data transfer), *close* (terminate data transfer and make idle), *read* (receive data), and *write* (send data). Another operating system function related to the driver is a data notification service. With this, software running on the system processor can arrange to receive a notification whenever data is available on a sub-channel opened by the software.

In contrast, there is no operating system on the peripheral processors. The software on each of these processors is tailored to one specific task and is written to directly control the processor which is executing it.

All code for the protocol is written in C,[5] a structured high-level language. This language provides a rich set of control constructs (refer to Figure 3) and a rich set of data types such as signed and unsigned integers, bit fields, pointers, arrays, and records or structures. C is well suited for microprocessor work because it produces compact, efficient object code.

```
if (condition) {statement(s)} else {statement(s)}

while (condition) {statement(s)}

switch (expression) {
        case value-i: statement(s); break;
        case value-j: statement(s); break;
        ...
        case value-n: statement(s); break}

function(param-1, ..., param-n);
```

Figure 3. Sample C control constructs

Programs for the system processor are written entirely in C. For the peripheral processor, C code provides adequate performance while maintaining high levels of readability and maintainability. In the peripheral processor only some microprocessor specific assembly language is used for subroutines that must deal directly with the hardware and/or meet stringent real-time constraints.

2. Boundary Solutions

2.1 Software Partitioning

The first design decision was to determine the physical location of all software modules. The three main objectives were:

1. to offload the system processor as much as possible;

2. to avoid overloading the peripheral processor; and

3. to minimize the complexity of the interprocessor interface.

After consulting with other implementors of the Link and Network layers,[6] [7] it was decided that the peripheral processor could support both layers. The higher-level protocol,[1] which must interface to user processes on the system processor, was placed in a process running under the operating system. This system structure works well because of the complexity of the higher level protocol and the application interface.[2] However, about half of the higher level protocol code was dedicated to interfacing to the user applications and the lower levels. Much of this extra code could have been avoided if there had been enough processing power in the peripheral processor.

2.2 The Interface Structure

Due to the needs of the user pairs, virtual circuits are assigned a (static) one-to-one mapping to sub-channels on the peripheral processor (refer to Figure 4).

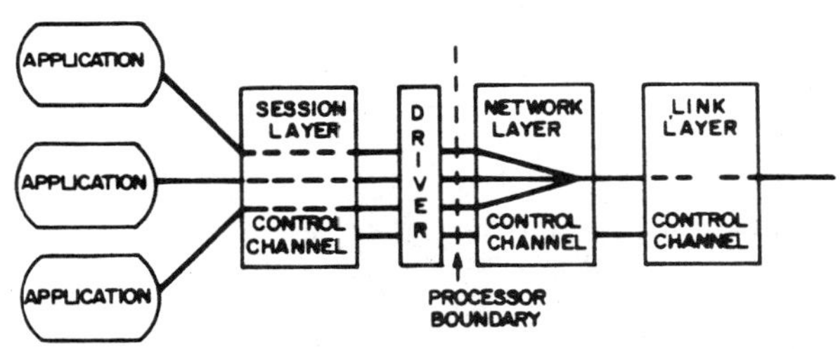

Figure 4. Structure of the Interface

Thus the higher level protocol can instruct the Network layer[8] to transmit data on a particular virtual circuit by writing to its assigned sub-channel; it can likewise receive data on a virtual circuit by reading its assigned sub-channel.

---

1. This is the BX.25 Session Layer. "Session Layer" and "higher level protocol" are treated interchangeably, as well as the term "lower level protocols" with the Link and Network layers.

2. The higher level protocol takes 37KB of executable object code plus 45KB for buffer space. The lower levels take 19.5KB of executable object code and use the remainder of the 64KB of memory for buffer space.

In addition to these sub-channels, one sub-channel is reserved for control transactions between the two separated layers. For example, this channel is used by the high-level software to instruct the network layer to reset a virtual circuit. This sub-channel, called the "control channel", is also used by the peripheral software to pass diagnostics, notifications, acknowledgements, and statistics to the higher layer.

The operating system device driver performs the message packetization and assembly required by the network layer. To the higher level protocol, the driver appears to deal with contiguous messages. Thus when data is passed to the network layer over a sub-channel, it is broken up automatically into fixed length (128 bytes) packets with additional space for protocol headers and internal information. When data is passed upwards to the high level protocol, the operating system constructs a contiguous message from network layer packets.

Data notifications from all sub-channels are concentrated into one operating system message queue (refer to Figure 5).

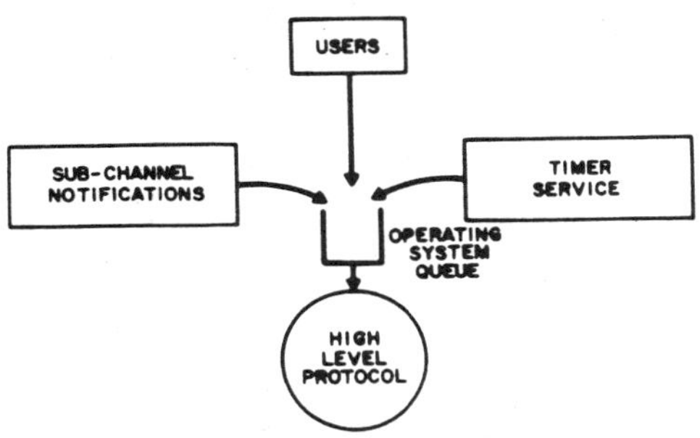

Figure 5. Operating System Enqueueing

This is the same queue used by applications interacting with the high level protocol and by the service process that provides timing information for it. The high level protocol polls this queue with a system call that returns the highest priority message in the queue. If the queue is empty it waits for work to do. This method of receiving transactions provides an automatic scheduling for the high level protocol.

2.3 Flow Control and Synchronization across Processor Boundaries

The separation of control and data information provides intrinsic flow control between processors. The high level protocol does not have to read data from sub-channels. It may choose to ignore a data notification, for example, if its own buffer space is full. If the Network layer runs low on buffer space, it can then invoke peer flow control. Control information is always available through the control sub-channel even if a data sub-channel is flow controlled.

Separate paths, however, create synchronization problems. There is no guarantee that, for example, an indication of a reset procedure on a virtual circuit will reach the session layer before an indication that more data has arrived on the same virtual circuit. This condition was remedied by assigning a higher priority to control over data notifications.

Additional handshaking is needed when the X.25 network layer detects missing or out of order data.[3] The network layer re-establishes synchronization through the reset and restart procedures. A reset forces a particular virtual circuit to a known state, and may result in lost data. A restart is roughly equivalent to a reset on each virtual circuit of the network layer, and again may result in lost data. The higher level protocol can retransmit lost data; it does not discard a message until the network layer indicates that the last packet of the message has been acknowledged. During a reset procedure the high level protocol is blocked from writing to the affected sub-channel until it acknowledges that it has received a reset indication from the network layer. This blocking prevents the high level protocol from inadvertently transmitting messages out of sequence in the case that it attempts to transmit before receiving a reset indication. After acknowledging the reset indication the session layer can retransmit all unacknowledged messages and any new messages it has to transmit since the reset.

3. Where the Boundary Becomes a RoadBlock...

3.1 Compilers and Code Creation

Software for both processors is written in C. Thus many C features, such as data structures, could be shared by the modules running on each side of the processor boundary.

One problem came from the structure padding that is done by the compilers. Padding is not consistent between the compiler used for the system processor and the one for the peripheral processor. As a result, the data structures shared by both modules have to be explicitly padded so that the alignment of members does not change.

3.2 Interface Shortcomings

To send a message, the higher level protocol must execute the following steps:

1. Write the message to the data sub-channel,
2. Receive a data notification from the message service about the control channel, and
3. Read the message acknowledgement from the control channel.

This is a total of three system calls per message plus internal processing.

3. This can occur when the retransmission and error recovery procedures of the link layer are unable to correct a problem.

To receive a message, the higher level protocol must:

1. Receive a data notification from the message service about the data sub-channel, and

2. Read the message from the data sub-channel.

Although this interface is fully asynchronous, the higher level protocol spends more of its processing time executing system calls than processing protocol data. Ideally, only three system calls would be needed, one to write data to the sub-channel, one to read data from the sub-channel, and one to read acknowledgments from the control channel.

3.3 Driver Shortcomings

The protocol between the device driver and the peripheral processor software created very inefficient transactions. Each operation by the system software, (eg, a write request), requires two transactions, one to allocate buffers in the peripheral and one to write data into the buffers.

In addition, transactions across the driver interface occur sequentially. Each side must wait for the current transaction to be acknowledged before initiating the next transaction. This driver/peripheral interface creates a synchronous coupling when most other operations on the two processors are asynchronous.

3.4 Performance

The performance characteristics of the interface were studied by exercising it at three levels (refer to Figure 6):

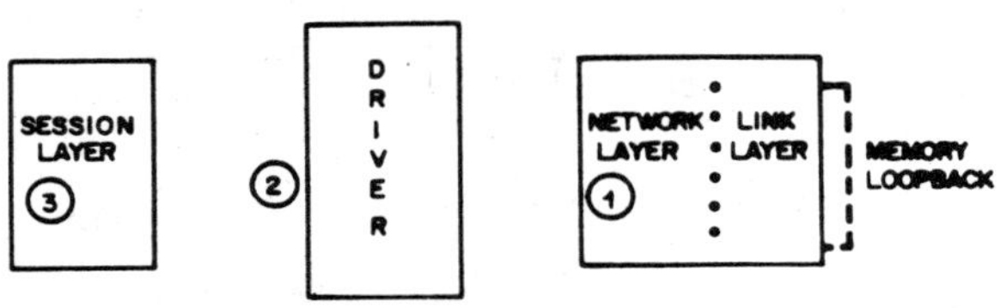

Figure 6. Levels of Exercise for Performance Studies

1. at the peripheral processor level with no device driver interaction,

2. at the device driver level with no higher level protocol interaction,

3. at the higher level protocol with no application interaction.

For these studies, the hardware interface to the communications link was bypassed by an in-memory loopback.[4] This eliminates the major bottleneck in the peripheral processor.

First, the peripheral processor code was altered so that it generates its own data instead of receiving it via the driver. Under this circumstance, the peripheral processor (running the network and link layers), achieves a total throughput of 82.3K bits/sec.[5]

Next, the peripheral processor and the device driver were exercised by a program that did no higher level protocol processing. Control data was ignored and the data notification service was not used. The message size used is 128 bytes. These conditions made the driver the bottleneck of the system. Total throughput for this case is 24K bits/sec.

Finally, the full higher protocol was used to exercise the driver and peripheral processor. Messages sent by the higher protocol, also 128 bytes long, were generated internally to eliminate the application interface. This setup includes processing of the data notifications and control data. With this additional processing, throughput drops to 10.2K bits/sec.

More measurements were made without bypassing the communications link.[6] Figure 7 shows peripheral processor throughput versus line speed when it was driven •, internally (ie, without the device driver), and ■, by the device driver, but without higher protocol or control channel processing.[9] At the higher bit rates the throughput does not increase linearly because the peripheral processor can not keep up with the instantaneous volume of data. Using the device driver always results in lower throughput. At the higher bit rates the device driver approaches its maximum throughput very quickly. At the lower bit rates the difference results from the synchronization mechanism between the higher layer and the network layer. Once the window of the network layer is full it must wait for acknowledgements from its peer to resume transmission. Its peer, however, must wait for the device driver to read each message before acknowledging. This added delay limits throughput.

---

4. This is roughly equivalent to an infinite bandwidth link that consumes no processor time.

5. Thoughput was measured as the total data transmitted and received per second over full duplex data paths.

6. Multiply throughput values from the graph by four (4) to compare with results bypassing the physical link. The source of the data for the graph was a series of tests using two full duplex links (lines) simultaneously.

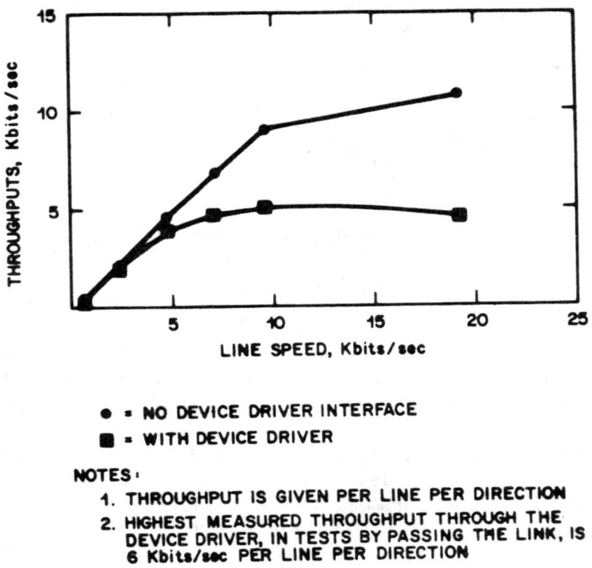

Figure 7. Throughput versus Line Speed

4. Conclusions

This implementation is designed for a system that does not have enough resources for executing it in either the system or peripheral processor. The resulting interface creates separate data and non-data channels that invite race conditions. The driver has an inherent limitation as to how many requests it can satisfy. Further, the structure of the interface makes heavy use of system calls, three for every message transmitted and two for every message received. This makes the boundary between processors the bottleneck of the subsystem.

On the positive side, the placement of the layers balances the utilization of processors and provides good flow control and asynchronous operation. The implementation forced at least one protocol boundary to be totally transaction oriented due to the unfriendly interactions with a device driver. The high level protocol, residing on the system processor, provides services that lower layers cannot provide to users and insulates them from low-level failures. Even a failure of the peripheral processor is insulated from users since the high-level protocol acts as a central interface to the services of the lower layers on the peripheral processor. Further, as protocols become more complicated, either module at this boundary can be changed without change in the other.

References

1. International Standards Organization, "Reference Model of Open Systems Architecture" Document ISO/TC97/SC16/N227, June 1979.

2. Bell Laboratories, "OSN Communications Protocol Specification BX.25" Issue 3, June 1982.

3. M.S. Sloman, "X.25 explained" *Computer Communications* Vol. 1 no. 6, December 1978.

4. "CCITT Recommendation X.25" Rev. 1980 (Yellow Book).

5. Kernighan & Ritchie, "The C Programming Language" Prentice-Hall, Inc. 1978.

6. S.G. Chady, G.W. Lankford, D.E. Woolf, "A Multiprocessor Approach to New Microprocessor Applications" *Proceedings of the 1980 Bell Laboratories / Western Electric Microprocessor Symposium.*

7. F.M. Burg, "Design Considerations for Using the X.25 Packet Layer in Data Terminal Equipment" *Proceedings IEEE INFOCOM* April 1983.

8. F.M. Burg, "Standardizing the User Side of the X.25 Interface" *Computer Communications* Vol. 5 no. 5, October 1982.

9. Comparable results for a different implementation were reached by L. Leske and D. Grothe, "Software Tailors Z80-based System to Interface Demands of X.25 Network" *Electronics* June 30, 1982.

5. Acknowledgements

We would like to thank some of the many people who have contributed to this project; John Morris and Phil Wisoff, who were involved in the initial design, John Hutchinson, for fixing "the last bugs" in the high level protocol; G.W. Lankford, for his consultation and help in estimating code sizes, Harry Moore and Fred Burg for their protocol expertise, and finally, Andy Salazar, for his inspiration and support during the project and while producing this paper.

PRIORITIZING PACKET TRANSMISSION IN LOCAL MULTIACCESS NETWORKS

Lionel M. Ni*

Department of Computer Science
Michigan State University
East Lansing, MI 48824

Xianji Li

Department of Computer Science
Hunan University
Hunan, P.R.C.

Abstract: Carrier sense multiple access with collision detection (CSMA/CD) protocols have been extensively studied and developed for local area networks. In CSMA/CD protocols, all messages are treated equally in competing for the communication channel. Thus, important or time-critical messages may be severely delayed. In this paper, a new CSMA/CD protocol with message-based priority functions is proposed. A priority code comparison period is needed to determine the highest priority class that can compete for the comunication channel. A contention period based on CSMA/CD scheme is then followed. Both nonpreemptive discipline and preemptive discipline are discussed. In each discipline, both the single mode and the batch mode are considered and compared. The overhead in implementing the proposed protocol, either for a few or for a large number of priority classes, is shown to be minimal. In general, a preemptive single mode scheme provides a better performance. The requirements of hierarchical independence of performance and fairness are satisfied.

1. INTRODUCTION

Carrier Sense Multiple Access with Collision Detection (CSMA/CD) protocols have been extensively studied and developed for local area networks. The most successful design for a protocol of this kind is the Ethernet [MeBo76]. In CSMA/CD protocols all messages are treated equally in competing for the communication channel. As the channel throughput approaches the channel capacity, the average packet delay will be rapidly increaseed. Thus, some important or time-critical messages may be severely delayed.

---

* This research was supported in part by the U.S. Engineering Foundation under grant RI-A-82-11 and in part by the U.S. National Science Foundation under grant ECS-83-04967.

Prioritizing the handling of various data and control messages is important for network performance. Defining more than one distinct priority level for packets is useful in decreasing the queueing delay for important packets and to ensure that the most critical network functions are not delayed. For example, to balance the load of various computers in a local network, control messages which carry the current load information of host computers must be transmitted with the highest priority; otherwise, the current load information could be outdated when received [Nilm82]. Many other applications, such as sensor data, process control, interactive applications, etc., are all time-critical. A prioritized CSMA/CD (PCSMA/CD) protocol is indeed necessary.

Only a few PCSMA/CD protocols have been proposed in the past. Two kinds of priority functions have been adopted. A station-based priority function was proposed by Franta and Bilodau [FrBi80]. This scheme assigns different rescheduling delays to different stations. Message-based priority functions provide a more dynamic approach to be assigned to messages rather than stations. In fact, station-based priority functions can be considered as special cases of message-based priority functions. In this study, a message-based priority function is considered.

The central scene in implementing a message-based priority function is the strategy used in the assessment of the current highest priority class among all stations. Two message-based priority functions have been proposed and have shown that priority function can reduce packet delay significantly for those urgent packets. Iida et al. use various lengths of preamble signals to indicate different priority levels of messages [IIYO80]. The higher the priority class is, the longer the preamble will be. The preamble length of the i-th priority class is linearly proportional to the priority level i. Thus, the overhead caused by implementing such a preamble priority scheme is increased linearly as the number of priority classes increases.

The second message-based priority function was proposed by Tobagi [Toba82]. A priority-reservation scheme is implemented. Each priority class is assigned with a fixed reservation slot.

The lower the priority class is, the later the slot will be gained. Thus, the overhead caused by reservation becomes significant as the number of classes increases, particularly, if low priority messages are major components of the traffic in the network.

Rom and Tobagi [RoTa81] have indicated four requirements in designing prioritized schemes: 1) hierarchical independence of performance; 2) fairness; 3) robustness; and 4) low overhead. However, some of these requirements are often contradictory goals, for example, fairness and low overhead. Thus, we should try to find trade-offs between them. Here fairness is defined for packets within each priority class. An ideal fairness should be defined in a global FCFS basis. However, with distributed control in CSMA/CD protocols, this ideal goal cannot be achieved. In this study, in addition to provide equal opportunity to contend for the channel, fairness can be partially improved.

This paper proposes a message-based priority scheme for CSMA/CD protocols, namely, the p-code comparison scheme. The incurred overhead, either for a few classes or for a large number of classes, in implementing this scheme is smaller than in the other two schemes. In the following sections the p-code comparison scheme will be discussed in detail. Then this scheme is compared with the priority-reservation scheme. Two kinds of protocol operation modes, the single mode and batch mode, are investigated under the p-code-comparison scheme. For each scheme, both nonpreemptive discipline and preemptive discipline are discussed. The proposed protocol is verified by simulation experiments.

2. Definition of Prioritized CSMA/CD Protocols

In CSMA/CD protocols, a single communication channel is shared by all stations based on a distributed random access strategy. A collision is detected as soon as it occurs. The communication channel has three different states: idle, contention, and transmission [Tane81]. To implement priority functions in the CSMA/CD protocol, an extra state, the p-code comparison state, is added. Two operation modes are considered in this study. In the single mode operation, the channel will enter the comparison state after successfully having transmitted one packet. In the batch mode operation, a group of packets with the same priority class will be transmitted before entering the next comparison period. The state transition diagram for both modes are depicted in Figure 1.

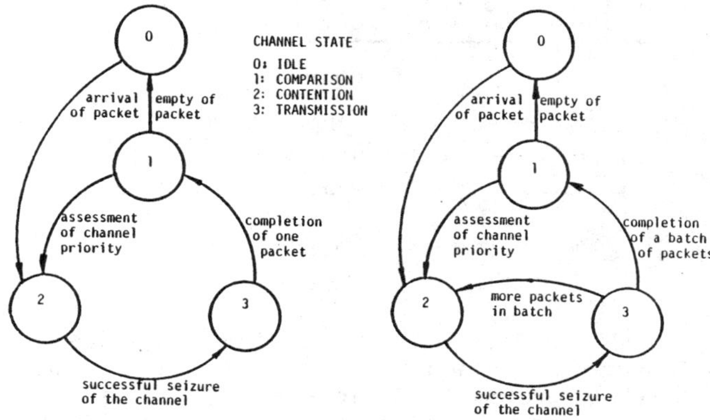

(a) Single Mode (b) Batch Mode

Figure 1. The state transition diagram of prioritized CSMA/CD (PCSMA/CD) protocols

The channel can be in one of the four states mentioned above: idle, comparison, contention, and transmission. During the comparison state, the highest packet priority class will be identified among those ready-to-go packets in all stations. Only those stations having the highest priority packets will compete for the channel and the channel enters the contention state. Collision and idle may occur alternatively and repeatedly in the contention state. Once a station acquires the channel, the channel enters the transmission state and that station will transmit one packet. In the single mode operation, the channel will then enter the comparison state. In the batch mode, all packets with the highest priority registered in the comparison state will contend for the channel until all of them have been successfully transmitted. Thus, the channel will enter the contention state again if there are more packets; otherwise, it will enter the comparison state. If no station is ready in the comparison state or all stations are quiet, the channel is in the idle state. Since the beginning of the comparison period is synchronized by the end of a successful transmission, any packet arrival in the idle state will cause the channel to change state from idle to contention instead of comparison.

The major difference between our scheme and others lies in the strategy used during the p-code comparison period. The p-code comparison determines the current highest priority class among all ready-to-go packets. Before the comparison algorithm is described, the following necessary assumptions and definitions have to be made.

Each station in the network is able to monitor the channel and to detect three kinds of events over the channel: (1) "idle" - no transmission; (2) "success" - successful transmission; and (3) "collision" - two or more transmissions. Figure 2 shows a diagram representing different events over a channel. With the carrier sensing and collision detection capabilities, this assumption can be implemented as indicated in [DeIX82]. Two time epochs, EOC (end of carrier) and EOB (end of batch), are defined to indicate the beginning of a new priority comparison period for single and batch modes, respectively. Details of EOC and EOB will be described in later sections. The end-to-end propagation delay is denoted by T. A comparison slot takes a round-trip end-to-end propagation delay, which is equal to 2T, and a carrier sensing time.

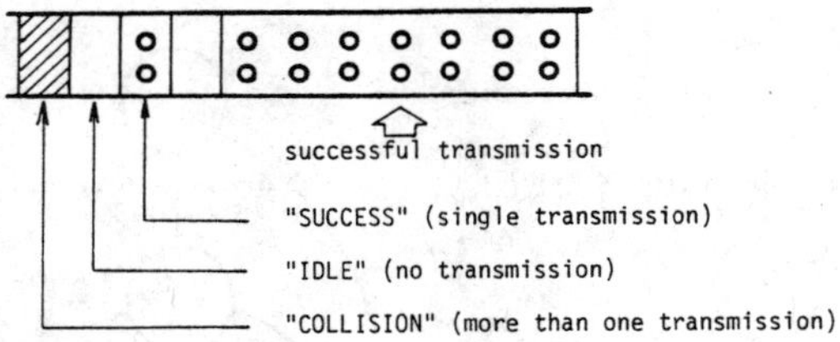

Figure 2. Three kinds of events over the channel

Each station in the system maintains a waiting queue in which all arriving packets are ordered according to their priority classes. If more than two packets have the same class, they are ordered according to their arrival times. The priority code of each station is always the priority class of the packet in the front of the waiting queue.

The current highest priority class is also named channel priority. The channel priority may be changed in each p-code comparison period. Once the channel priority is determined in the comparison period, all packets residing in the waiting queue of each station with the same priority as the channel priority must be registered and will be referred to as registered packets. A station is called a contending station if it has at least one registered packet in its waiting queue.

Let $N=2^n-1$ be the maximum number of priority classes. Each priority class can be represented as an n-bit binary p-code $p=(p_{n-1}, \ldots, p_0)$, where p_i is either 0 or 1 and $p>0$. Class-N is the highest priority and class-1 is the lowest priority. Note that $p=0$ is reserved for indicating that the system is in the idle state. During the comparison period, each comparison slot will complete the comparison of one binary bit starting from the most significant bit of the p-code of all stations. The basic idea behind the p-code comparison scheme is that during the comparison period, only higher priority classes will survive and lower priority classes will be aborted. The number of comparison slots required depends on the priority class and the event occurring in each slot. In the worst case, n comparison slots are needed. In the best case, one slot may be sufficient.

When the time epoch EOC (or EOB) is detected, the p-code comparison algorithm, which is executed by each station, operates as follows.

(1) For all bits of the p-code except the last bit p_0.

If the bit is 1, a "1" is sent to the channel and event is detected. If the event is "success," then the comparison is truncated and the packet starts to be transmitted; otherwise, the next bit is tried in the next slot.

If the bit is 0, then nothing is done and the event is detected. If the event is "idle," then the next next bit is tried in the next slot; otherwise, the transmission of p-code is aborted and the next EOC (or EOB) is waited for.

(2) For the last bit p_0.

If the bit is 1, then the comparison period is truncated and the packet starts to be transmitted.

If the bit is 0, then nothing is done and the event is detected. If the event is "idle," then the packet starts to be transmitted; otherwise, the next EOC (or EOB) is waited for.

A flowchart description of the algorithm is shown in Fig.3. Any station may abort itself if it is aware that there is at least a higher priority class station in competition. For example, if there is a bit 0 at a comparison slot and it detects that the event over the channel is not idle, this means that at least one other station has a higher priority. Thus, it must be aborted. On the other hand, if a station sends a "1" and detects an event of "success," then it is the only station with the highest priority and gets the channel. If an event of "collison" is detected, this means that more than one station has the same or higher priority. Thus, they have to try the next comparison slot. For the last bit, if it is a 1, then there is no need to send that "1," because it must be the highest priority station.

For an n-bit priority code, at most 2^n-1 priority classes can be assigned. If only 2^{n-1} different classes are needed, the priority code still needs n bits. But the size of the comparison period can be reduced to one comparison slot

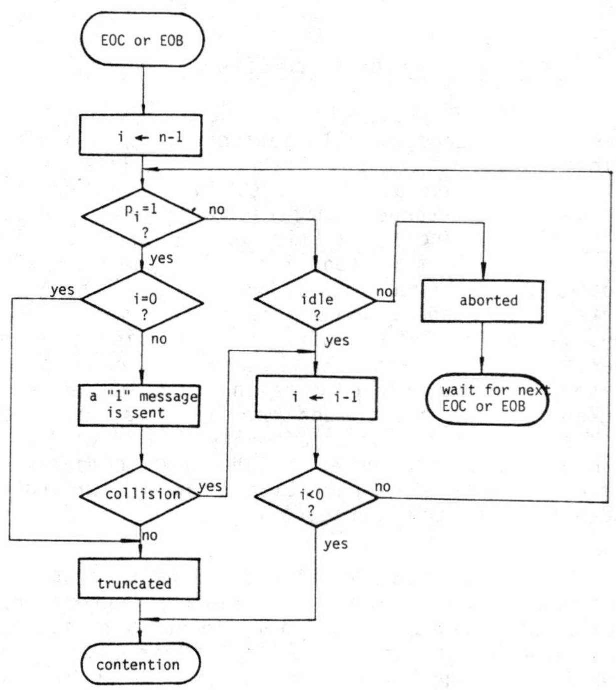

Figure 3. Flowchart description of the p-code comparison scheme

for the highest priority class, $N=2^{n-1}=(100...0)$. In this case, if the event of the first comparison slot is not idle, then the channel immediately enters the contention period and only stations with the urgent packets can compete for the channel. Thus, the priority resolution scheme further favors the urgent packets by reducing the comparison overhead. In the following discussions and simulation experiments, 4 bits of p-code (n=4) and 8 (N=8) different priority classes are assumed unless otherwise specified.

After the comparison period, contending stations will enter the contention period. Two scheduling disciplines are considered: nonpreemptive discipline and preemptive discipline. In each discipline, both single mode and batch mode are possible. First the nonpreemptive discipline is described in which the current transmitting packet cannot be preempted by newly generated higher priority packets.

A. Nonpreemptive discipline

(1) Nonpreemptive single mode. As mentioned in previous sections, all contending stations will contend for the channel in the contention period. Once a station successfully seizes the channel, a packet can be transmitted in the transmission period. When the transmission is over, the end of carrier (EOC) marks the time epoch of the next p-code comparison period. Figure 4 gives an example of the channel activity in this mode.

In the example of Fig. 4, let K_i represent the number of stations with priority class i, i= 1,2,...,8. For ease of explanation, each station has only one packet with the same priority as the station priority. At the beginning, two stations are ready to transmit and the priority for both of them is 4. Four slots are needed in the p-code comparison period (PCP) in which three of them are idle and the second slot has a collision. In the contention period, one of them will seize the channel. The channel then enters the transmission period. Note that in the contention period, the channel is in the collison state or in the idle state (due to rescheduling delay), alternatively. Suppose that in the contention period, a station has a newly generated packet with priority level 6 as marked in Fig.4. Based on the nonpreemptive discipline, this station with a newly generated higher priority packet will keep silent. Once the packet has been successfully transmitted, the EOC signals another PCP. Now one station has priority 4 and another station has priority 6. In the PCP, only three slots are necessary. The state of the first slot is idle because both $p_3=0$. The state of the second slot is collision because both $p_2=1$. The state of the third slot is success because only the station with priority 6 puts a "1" in that slot. Thus, the station with priority 4 is aborted and the PCP is truncated. In this case, the contention period can be skipped and the packet with priority 6 can be successfully transmitted. At the third EOC, only one station is ready to transmit with priority 4. In this case, two slots are needed and a packet of class 4 is finally transmitted.

(2) Nonpreemptive batch mode. In the batch mode, all registered packets must be transmitted before the channel enters the next PCP. For this purpose, one continuation slot must immediately follow every successful transmission packet. Every station has to put a "1" in the continuation slot if it has more registered packets to transmit. Thus, if the slot is not idle, the state returns to the contention period from the transmission period; otherwise, an empty continuation slot marks a time epoch, end of batch (EOB), which indicates the beginning of a new PCP. Figures 5 and 6 demonstrate the flowchart description and an example of the nonpreemptive batch mode.

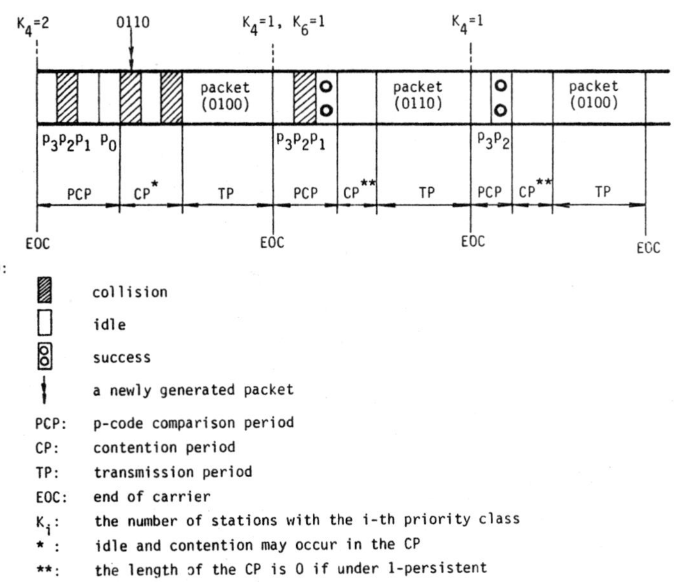

Figure 4. An example of channel activity of the nonpreemptive single mode PCSMA/CD

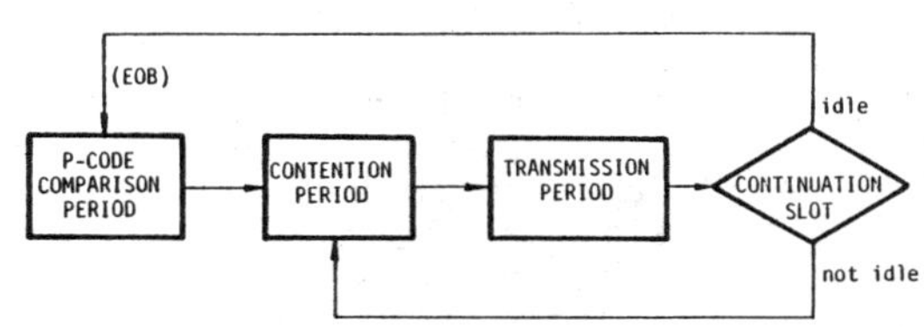

Figure 5. Flowchart description of the nonpreemptive batch mode PCSMA/CD

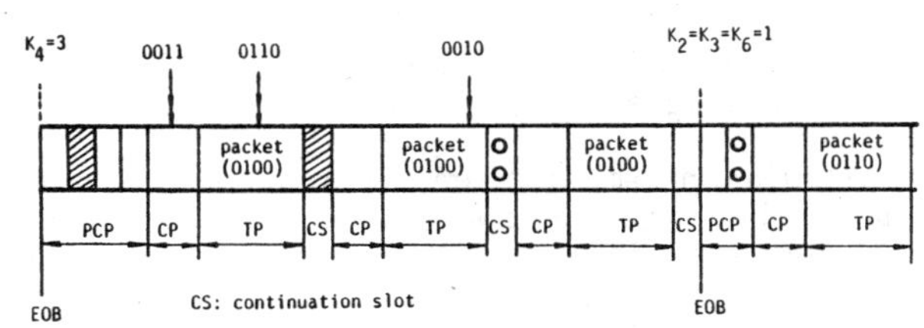

Figure 6. An example of channel activity of the nonpreemptive batch mode PCSMA/CD

The concept of registered packets can partially improve the fairness because registered packets have arrived at a past time interval. New arrivals will not be registered until the next PCP. In this sense, partial fairness can be achieved according to packet arrival time intervals. In the above discussions, the EOC or EOB time epoch indicates the beginning of a new PCP. If no reservation has been made in the PCP, the channel will enter the idle state. The EOC or EOB can appear again only after a successful transmission is made using the conventional CSMA/CD mechanism.

B. Preemptive discipline

The major disadvantage of nonpreemptive discipline is that it cannot satisfy the first design requirement: hierarchical independence of performance. In other words, under nonpreemptive discipline, increasing loads from lower priority classes may degrade the performance of higher priority classes. This is true especially in the nonpreemptive batch mode, in which a higher priority packet arriving after the PCP has to wait until the whole batch of lower priority packets have completed their transmissions. A station is referred to as a preempting station if it has a newly generated packet with a higher priority than the channel priority.

In Tobagi's scheme [Toba82], a newly generated packet may preempt an ongoing transmission, i.e., in a transmission period of a lower priority level. In this case, the channel utilization is further decreased due to wasted transmission. Although this scheme may be useful in a military environment, preemption of ongoing transmissions will not be considered in this study.

(1) Preemptive single mode. Since preemption is not allowed in the transmission period, preemption can only occur at idle times of the contention period. In the contention period, the preempting station will keep on sensing the channel. If the channel is idle, it will start to transmit. If a collision is detected, the preempting station involved in the collision will wait until the next PCP (one try); otherwise, a successful transmission will indicate a EOC and the channel will enter a new PCP. The collision may be caused by preempting stations or by contending stations or a mix of them. However, there is no way to distinguish these types of collisions. The preempting stations can try only once; otherwise, different higher levels of preempting stations may contend for the channel without knowing the priority of each other. In the latter case, the channel will become a nonprioritized CSMA/CD protocol among those contending and preempting stations.

Allowing preemption in the contention period can partially improve the channel utilization by decreasing the idle time due to rescheduling delay. Note that a contending station may also become a preempting station. In this case, the higher priority packet will be transmitted instead. An example of the preemptive single mode is illustrated in Figure 7.

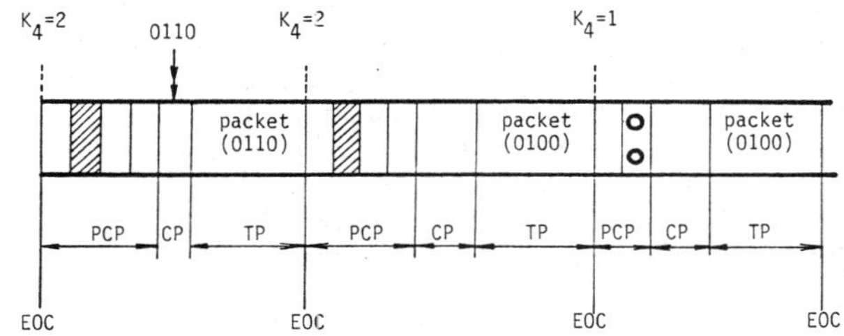

Figure 7. An example of channel activity of the preemptive single mode PCSMA/CD

(2) Preemptive batch mode. In the batch mode, preemption is allowed in the contention period as it is in the preemptive single mode. Furthermore, a preemption slot is added between the transmission period and the continuation slot. A preempting station will put a "1" in the next preemtion slot. Three possible events may occur in the preemption slot:

(a) If the event is "success," it means that only a single preempting station made a reservation. The preempting station may transmit the packet immediately and the channel will be in the transmission period. At the end of transmission, another preemption slot is reserved as usual.

(b) If the event is "collision," it means that more than one preempting station attempts to transmit. The channel changes its state to PCP immediately.

(c) If the event is "idle," the next slot will be the continuation slot as in the normal case.

If a preempting station detects a collision in the contention period during its first try, that station will wait for the next preemption slot to make a reservation. A flowchart description and an example of the preemptive batch mode are illustrated in Figures 8 and 9, respectively.

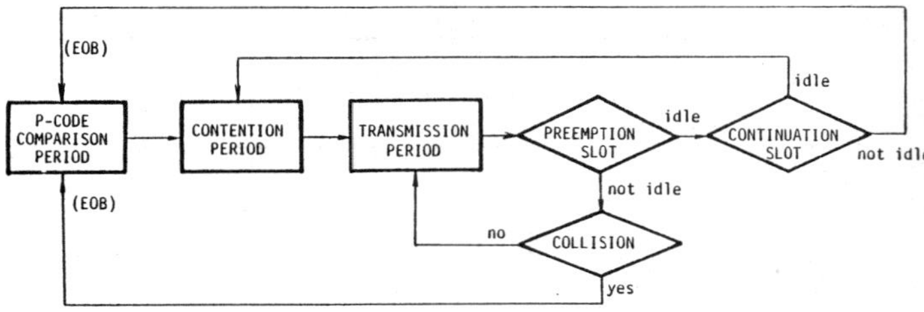

Figure 8. Flowchart description of the preemptive batch mode PCSMA/CD

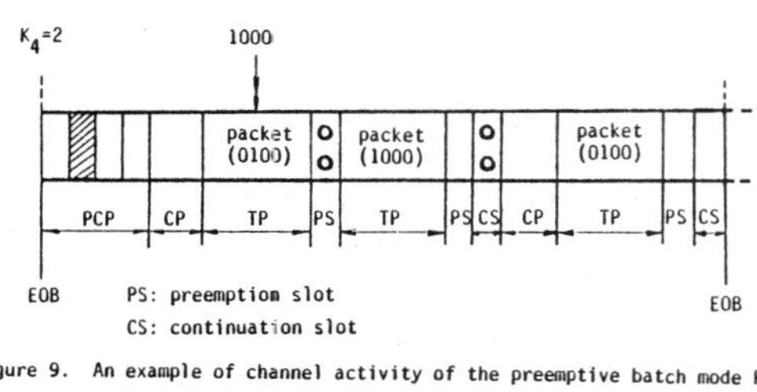

Figure 9. An example of channel activity of the preemptive batch mode PCSMA/CD

3. Simulation Results and Performance Analysis

A series of simulation experiments have been conducted to measure and compare the performance of various prioritized CSMA/CD protocols. Details of the simulation experiments can be found in [LiNi83]. In this section, the focus is on numerical results pertaining to the priority functions and the effect of various system parameters on its performance. In the simulation study, the end-to-end propagation delay, T, is used as the basic time unit. Other notations used in the illustrating figures are listed below:

- N: the number of priority classes
- D: average packet delay of all packets
- D[i]: average packet delay of packets with priority i, i=1,2,...,N
- V[i]: variance of packets with priority class i
- L: one packet length (unit: T)
- S: throughput or the number of packets completed per L ($S \leq 1$)
- S[i]: thruput of packets with priority class i
- PC: p-code comparison scheme
- PR: priority reservation scheme
- NS: nonpreemptive single mode
- NB: nonpreemptive batch mode
- PS: preemptive single mode
- PB: preemptive batch mode

The simulation experiments of this study are based on the following workload distributions and system parameters: 1) the packet generation is exponentially distributed for all priority classes; 2) the packet is uniformly distributed among different priority classes; 3) the number of stations is 5; 4) the channel bandwidth is 1 Mbps; 5) the end-to-end propagation delay, T, is 5 usec; and 6) the packet length is fixed with 500 bits or L=100T.

A. Throughput-Delay Characteristics

The throughput-delay characteristics, D[i] vs. S, of the nonpreemptive single mode protocol is shown in Fig. 10 for 8 different priority classes. Different priority classes exhibit different delay characteristics. The higher the priority is, the smaller the delay will be as was expected. The delay versus the total system throughput, D vs. S, is also indicated by the dash line. As the system throughput approaches the channel capacity, the packet with urgent information has to suffer an intolerable delay in a nonprioritized CSMA/CD protocol as revealed by the dash line. However, with the prioritized CSMA/CD protocol, those important packets with a higher priority can still be transmitted with much less delay in such a heavy-load situation. Obviously, the gain is paid by increasing the delay of lower priority packets. Throughput-delay characteristics for other operation modes has a similar relative performance.

B. Effect of Different Priority Assessment Schemes

The priority reservation scheme proposed by Tobagi [Toba82] is compared with the proposed

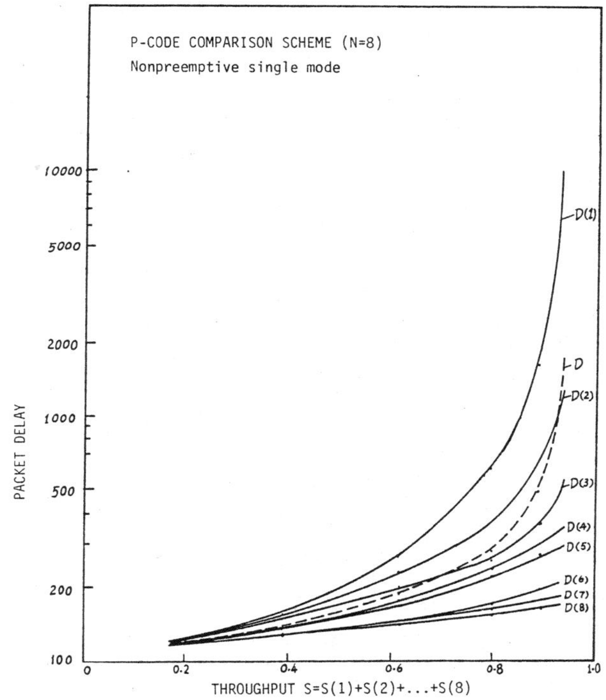

Figure 10. Throughput-delay characteristics for the nonpreemptive single mode PCSMA/CD

p-code comparison scheme by observing their throughput-delay characteristics. Figures 11 and 12 show the throughput-delay curves with respect to two different priority assessment schemes for N=4 and 8, respectively, where both of them assume a nonpreemptive single mode after the comparison period. From these figures, the following two conclusions are made: 1) the p-code comparison scheme provides a lower overhead than that of the priority reservation scheme and 2) the larger the number of classes is, the better the advantage will be.

The difference between these two comparison schemes is mainly due to the different number of comparison slots (or reservation slots) required to identify the highest priority class. Let O_{pc} and O_{pr} represent, respectively, the number of comparison slots required for p-code comparison scheme and priority reservation scheme. In the worst case, we have

$$O_{pc} = n = \lceil \log_2(N+1) \rceil \quad \text{for } i=1,2,\ldots,N$$

$$O_{pr} = (N+1-i) \quad \text{for } i=1,2,\ldots,N$$

For lower priority classes in a system with a large number of priority classes, i.e., $i \ll N$, we have

$$O_{pc} / O_{pr} = \lceil \log_2 N \rceil / N \quad \text{for } i \ll N$$

In this case, the p-code comparison scheme takes a lower overhead. More precisely, the p-code comparison scheme is better if the priority class i is within the following range:

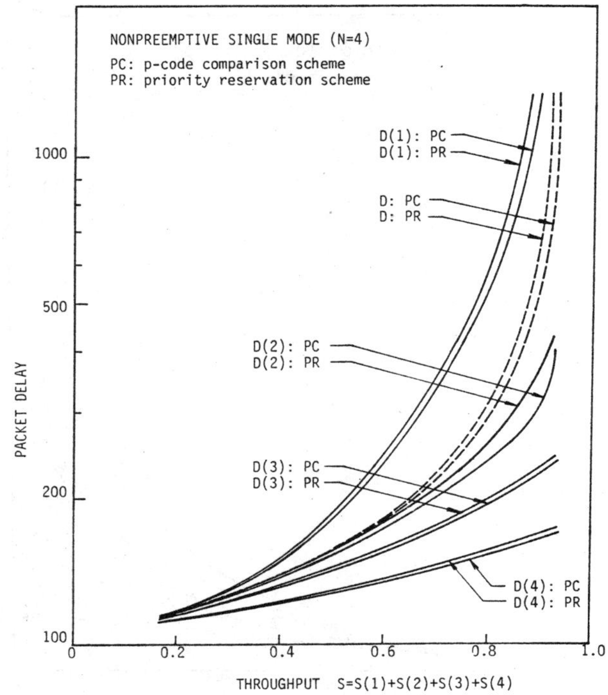

Figure 11. Sensitivity of packet delay to two priority assessment methods in nonpreemptive single mode PCSMA/CD with N=4.

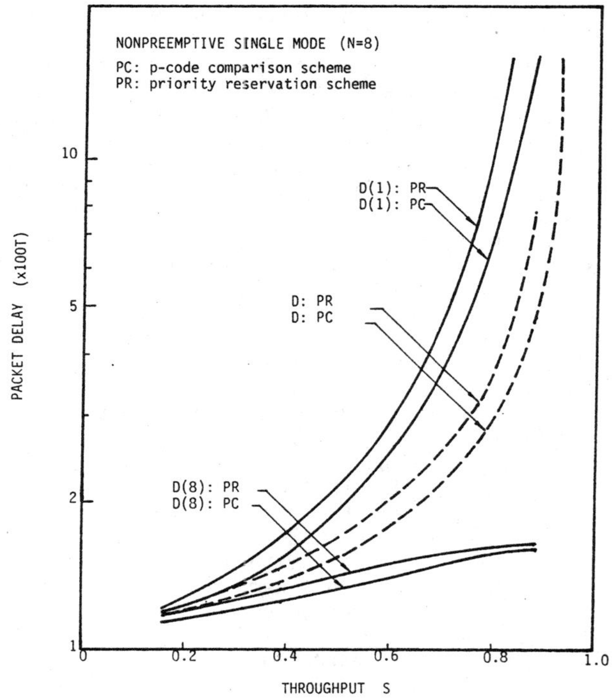

Figure 12. Sensitivity of packet delay to two priority assessment methods in nonpreemptive single mode PCSMA/CD with N=8.

$$1 \leq i \leq N + 1 - \lceil \log_2(N+1) \rceil$$

If i is not within the above range, the priority reservation scheme may perform better. However, this drawback can be alleviated by the truncation capability provided in the p-code comparison scheme. In the priority reservation scheme, the overhead for each priority class is fixed as shown above. But in the p-code comparison scheme, the overhead may vary depending on the event in the comparison slot. The number of comparison slots may be truncated if a success event is detected. The truncation capability favors, particularly, higher priority classes. Table 1 lists the various possible overheads of each priority class caused by implementing two different comparison schemes for N=2, 4, and 8, respectively. In the case of N=8, the p-code comparison scheme may take more slots than that of the priority reservation scheme when i=7 and i=6. But on the average, the overhead is decreased.

C. Effect of Preemption on the Performance

The drawback of nonpreemptive discipline is in its dependence on the performance of different priority classes. In the batch mode, the interval between two consecutive p-code comparison periods is larger than that of the single mode. Thus, the probability of the number of newly generated higher priority packets is greater, especially at the heavy-load condition. This implies that the higher priority packets have to wait a longer time because of the transmission of lower priority packets, which violates the design requirements of hierarchical independence.

Figures 13 and 14 show the effect of preemption on the performance for the cases of single mode and batch mode, respectively. In both figures, the throughput-delay curve of two extreme priority classes, D[1] and D[8], is displayed. The objective of preemption is to prevent lower priority packets from blocking higher priority packets. In both operation modes, the delay of the higher priority classes is further decreased at the expense of increasing the delay of lower priority classes. In the batch

Table 1. The number of overhead slots required of two priority assessment schemes

N = 8

priority classes (p-code)	priority reservation scheme	p-code comparison scheme
8 - (1000)	1	1
7 - (0111)	2	2,3
6 - (0110)	3	2,3,4
5 - (0101)	4	2,3
4 - (0100)	5	2,3,4
3 - (0011)	6	3
2 - (0010)	7	3,4
1 - (0001)	8	3

N = 4

priority classes (p-code)	priority reservation scheme	p-code comparison scheme
4 - (100)	1	1
3 - (011)	2	2
2 - (010)	3	2,3
1 - (001)	4	4

N = 2

priority classes (p-code)	priority reservation scheme	p-code comparison scheme
2 - (10)	1	1
1 - (01)	2	1

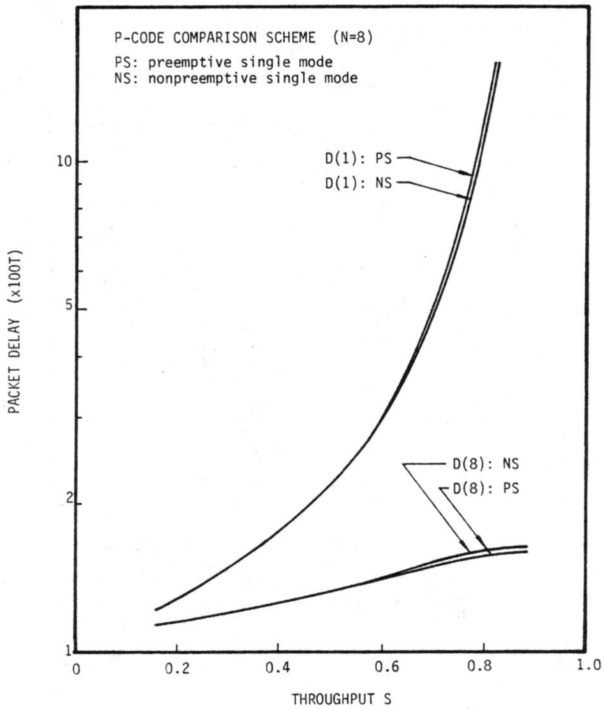

Figure 13. Throughput-delay characteristics for nonpreemptive single mode and preemptive single mode PCSMA/CD with N=8.

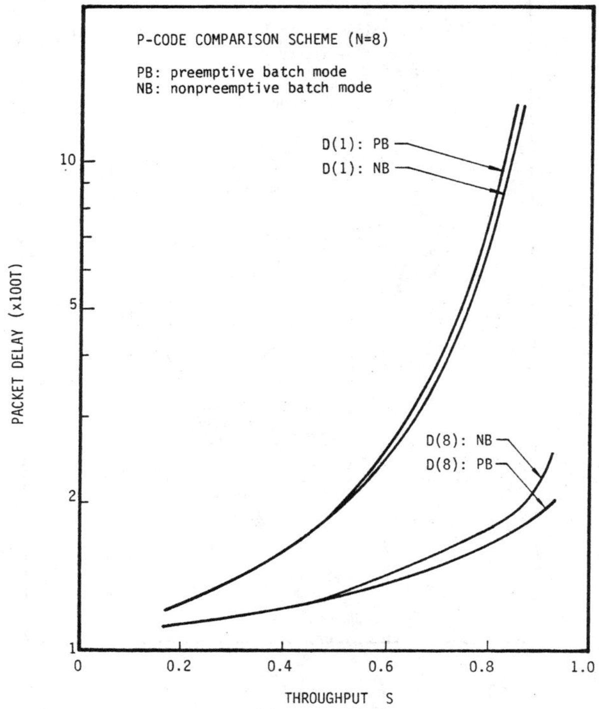

Figure 14. Throughput-delay characteristics for nonpreemptive batch mode and preemptive batch mode PCSMA/CD with N=8.

mode, performance improvement is more significant than in single mode. This is because an extra preemption slot reserved at the end of each successful transmission allows another preemption opportunity. The average channel utilization is also improved by adding the capability of preemption because the channel idle time due to rescheduling delay is partially eliminated by higher priority classes. Note that the extra preemption slot may be eliminated if the channel priority equals the highest priority class, N.

The design requirements of hierarchical independence is further reinforced by adding the capability of preemption. Figures 15 and 16 display the relationship between the variance of the delay to the system throughput in the nonpreemptive batch mode (NB), nonpreemptive single mode (NS), preemptive batch mode (PB), and preemptive single mode (PS) PCSMA/CD for the highest priority level and the lowest priority level, respectively. As revealed in Fig. 15, the delay of the highest priority packets becomes increasingly worse for the batch mode when the offered load increases. The improvement of performance and fairness is shown by the decreasing of the variance of the delay. In general, the preemptive discipline provides a smaller variance. But the difference is insignificant in the single mode for the highest priority packets and will be explained in the next section. In Fig. 16, the variance of the delay of the nonpreemptive discipline is slighly lower than that of the preemptive discipline for the lowest priority class. In the preemptive discipline, the lower priority packets are likely to be preempted, and thus the variance of the delay is increased.

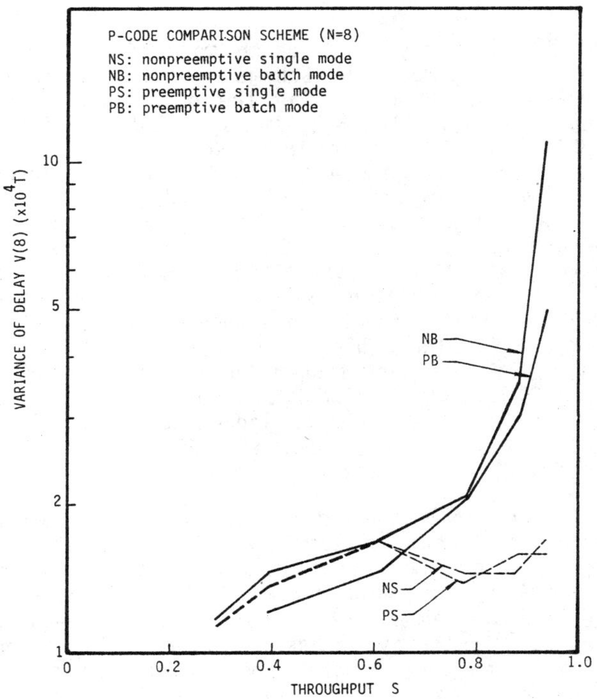

Figure 15. Variance of packet delay, V[8], for nonpreemptive single mode, nonpreemptive batch mode, preemptive single mode, and preemptive batch mode PCSMA/CD with N=8.

D. Comparison of Single Mode and Batch Mode

Figure 17 illustrates throughput-delay characteristics for the preemptive single mode

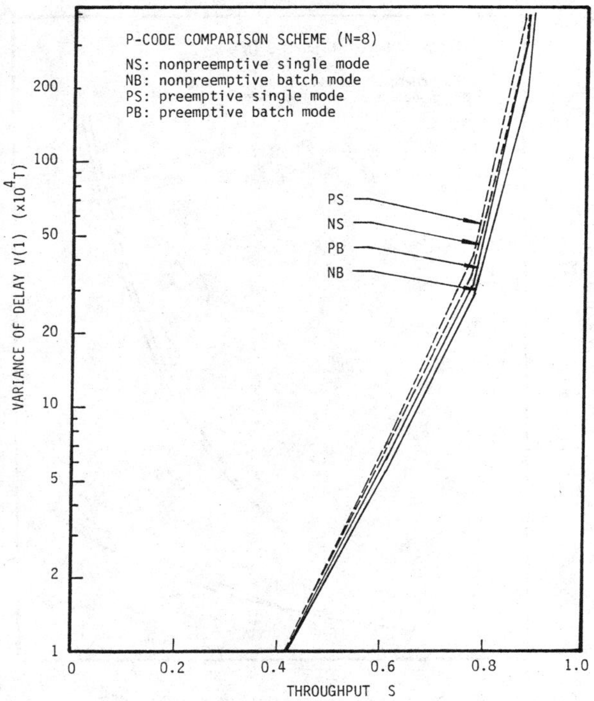

Figure 16. Variance of packet delay, V[1], for nonpreemptive single mode, nonpreemptive batch mode, preemptive single mode, and preemptive batch mode PCSMA/CD with N=8.

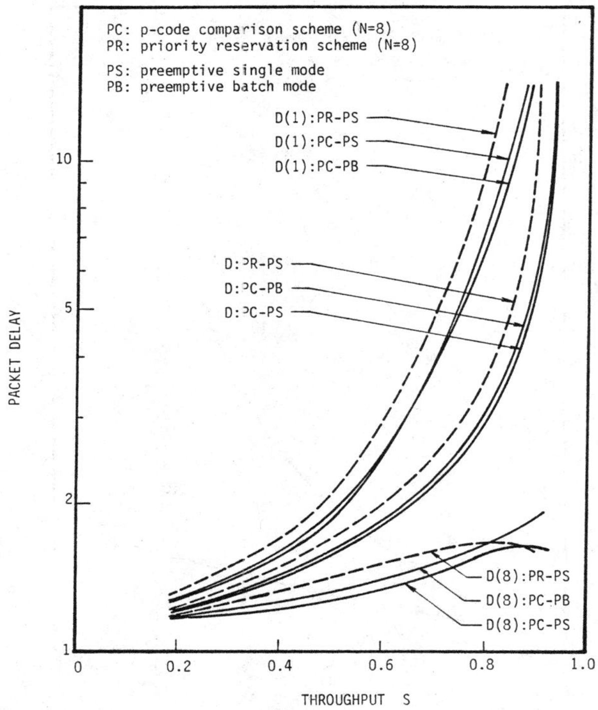

Figure 17. Throughput-delay characteristics for preemptive batch mode and preemptive single mode PCSMA/CD using p-code comparison scheme and preemptive single mode using priority reservation scheme with N=8.

(PC-PS) and preemptive batch mode (PC-PB) using the p-code comparison scheme and the preemptive single mode (PR-PS) using the priority reservation scheme (in [Toba82], it is called a semi-preemptive discipline) in the case of N=8. For the sake of clarity, instead of a family of 8 curves, only two extreme cases, D[1] and D[8], as well as the case of the average delay, D, are shown. The performance of the PC-PS PCSMA/CD protocol is better than that of the PR-PS PCSMA/CD. When the offered load is high (S>0.8), the performance of PR-PS PCSMA/CD is better than that of PC-PB PCSMA/CD for those high priority classes, D[6] to D[8]. The average system delay, D, in PC-PS PCSMA/CD and PC-PB PCSMA/CD is always better than that in PR-PS PCSMA/CD as indicated by dashlines. Now, the difference between PC-PS and PC-PB schemes will be compared.

In general, the batch mode reduces the occurrence of comparison periods at the expense of providing one more continuation slot at the end of each transmission period. Let c[i] represent the average number of comparison slots required for the priority class i, where $1 \le c \le n$ and $1 \le i \le N$. In the single mode, the number of overhead slots is b[i]c[i] if b[i] packets are transmitted. In the preemptive batch mode, the number of overhead slots will be 2b[i]+c[i] because one continuation slot and one preemption slot are added. The success of the preemptive batch mode relies on b[i] and c[i] being large enough such that

b[i]c[i] > (2b[i]+c[i])   for i=1,2,...,N

For lower priority classes, c is usually close to n and the batch size b is usually greater than 1 at heavy load. The reason for the latter case is the blocking of lower priority classes; thus, more lower priority packets are waiting in the queue. For a uniform distribution of priority classes, we have $b[i] \ge b[i+1]$. Thus the batch mode provides a better performance for the lower priority classes as shown in Fig.17 at heavy-load condition. In the light-load condition, the batch size b is very likely to be 1. In this case, the single mode is always better than the batch mode. However, in the light-load condition, the channel is idle for most of the time. The performance difference, thus, is insignificant as shown in Fig. 17. Figure 17 is based on the uniform distribution of priority classes. If most of the packets are lower priority classes, such as the geometric distribution, the batch mode will show a better improvement.

For the highest priority class, c[N]=1, the above criterion is never satisfied. For other higher priority classes, c is somewhere between 1 and n depending on the offered load. The simulation results show that the delay of priority classes greater than 3 in batch mode is slightly longer than in single mode. This is caused by a smaller value of b for these higher priority classes. Another interesting property is that the delay of the highest priority class will decrease a little bit when the channel approaches the maximum throughput as shown in Fig. 17 under the single mode operation. At such very heavy-load condition, the channel is totally dominated by the highest priority packets. The situation in which the highest priority packet is waiting for the completion of a lower priority packet will never occur because the lower priority packets have no chance to get the channel. However, this fact does not appear in the batch mode. In preemptive batch mode, a higher priority packet may be transmitted immediately if it is the only one made reservation in the preemption slot. When the channel throughput further increases, the probability that more than one station wants to make reservation in the preemption slot is high. In this case, the channel has to enter the comparison period and, of course, the delay will be increased for those higher priority packets.

The advantage of the batch mode is its higher degree of fairness. In CSMA/CD protocols, a new arrival may be transmitted earlier than an old packet. Furthermore, it is possible to have an indefinite wait during a heavy load if a packet fails to get the channel in every try, although the probability of this situation is extremely slight. The same situation may also occur in the single mode. However, in the batch mode only registered packets can be transmitted. Even the new arrival which has the same priority as the channel priority cannot be registered until the next comparison period. In this sense, an indefinite wait within the same priority class can be eliminated. An indefinite wait by lower priority classes of packets is still possible if higher priority classes of packets keep on holding the channel.

The degree of fairness of the batch mode over single mode is shown in Fig. 16 which displays the variance of the packet delay of the lowest priority class. For the lowest priority class, only a slight improvement is shown when the offered load is high. For the highest priority class, the average batch size is very small. Thus, the fairness is not improved by implementing the batch mode. Furthermore, the extra overhead in implementing the batch mode makes the variance of the delay even worse as demonstrated in Fig. 15. The design trade-offs between fairness and overhead have to be determined. If the unfairness of those small lower priority packets can be ignored, the preemptive single mode PCSMA/CD does show a better performance than others.

In the preemptive batch mode, the performance is degraded mainly due to the two extra slots, continuation and preemption. When the channel priority is the same as the highest priority class, N, the extra preemption slot can be eliminated. During the p-code comparison period, when an event of "success" is detected, this implies that there is only one contending station. Therefore, the continuation slot can be eliminated. The performance of the preemptive batch mode can be improved by providing more intelligence in the hardware protocol design.

Another way to alleviate the deficiency of the batch mode at the higher priority classes is to allow mixed mode operation by providing more intelligence in the protocol. In the mixed mode, if the channel priority after the comparison period has been determined to be higher than a certain threshold, then the channel enters the single mode; otherwise, the channel will enter the batch mode. The performance improvement of the mixed mode is still under study and will be reported later.

4. Conclusions

This paper is concerned with the problem of prioritizing packet transmission in carrier sense multiaccess local communication systems. A message-based priority function is implemented by adding a p-code comparison period to the original CSMA/CD protocol. Different design alternatives including single mode, batch mode, preemptive discipline, and nonpreemptive discipline have been carefully investigated and compared. A preemptive single mode PCSMA/CD protocol displays its superiority above other protocols.

The additional overhead caused by the introduction of the priority scheme was discussed. The overhead is also shown to be minimal compared to other schemes. In addition to low overhead, the proposed prioritized CSMA/CD protocol also satisfies the requirements of fairness, hierarchical independence of performance, and robustness.

REFERENCES

[DeIX82] DEC, Intel Co. and Xerox Co., The Ethernet, A Local Area Network Data Link Layer and Physical Layer Specification, Version 2.0, 1982.

[FrBi80] Franta. W.R. and Bilodeau, M.B., "Analysis of a prioritized CSMA protocol based on staggered delays," ACTA Information 13, 1980, pp.299-329.

[IIYO80] Iida, I., Ishizuka, M., Yasuda, Y. and Onoe, M., "Random access packet switched local computer network with priority function," in Proc. Nat. Telecommun. Conf., December 1980, pp.37.4.1-37.4.6.

[LiNi83] Li, X. and Ni, L.M., "A simulation model of prioritized CSMA/CD protocols," in Proc. of the IASTED Int'l Sym., Applied Simulation and Modelling (ASM'83), May 1983.

[MeBo76] Metcalfe, R.M. and Boggs, D.R., "Ethernet: Distributed packet switching for local computer networks," Comm. ACM, 19:7, July 1976, pp.395-404.

[NiIm82] Ni, L.M., "A distributed load balancing algorithm for point-to-point local computer networks," Proc. of the COMPCON 82 Fall, September 1982, pp.116-123.

[RoTo81] Rom, R. and Tobagi, F.A., "Messaged-based priority functions in local multiaccess communication systems," Computer Networks, 1981, pp273-286.

[Tane81] Tanenbaum, A.S., Computer Networks, Prentice-Hall, Inc., 1981.

[Toba82] Tobagi, F.A., "Carrier sense multiple access with message-based priority functions," IEEE Trans. on Communications, Vol.COM-30, January 1982, pp.185-200.

PERFORMANCE POTENTIAL OF COMMUNICATIONS INTERFACE PROCESSORS

by C.M. Woodside

Department of Systems and Computer Engineering
Carleton University, Ottawa, Canada

Abstract

Interface processors are being developed in hardware and firmware for communications protocols at higher and higher levels (HDLC, X.25, Ethernet ...), for smaller and smaller host systems. How far this process will go depends on the driving factors of increased performance and simpler implementation of the systems which use the protocols. A simplified performance model with parameters, which encompasses a large part of all systems using communications, is used to find those parameter combinations offering various degrees of performance improvement. The results can be used to approximately distinguish those cases which will provide the market for performance improvement via higher-level interface processors.

1. Introduction

Hardware and firmware interface processors for communications are being made for higher and higher levels of protocol (HDLC, X.25, Ethernet [1] ...) and for smaller and smaller host systems, down to microcomputer-based workstations and intelligent terminals. Interface processors are chip-level, board-level or computer-level subsystems which are installed for three reasons:

- to simplify and speed up the implementation of protocols in systems,
- to exploit the fact that the physical-level interface board may have space to spare,
- to improve the overall system performance, by offloading the host.

This paper examines the performance issue. If a certain amount of protocol processing on the host (x_C seconds/message) can be moved to an interface processor (where it takes x_F seconds/message), what is the effect on system throughput, including all the other processing? This question is answered with a simplified basic model with a user-server workload pattern and a minimum number of parameters, in Section 2. The user-server pattern of distributed processing is the most widespread, including for example tasks running on large hosts making requests for remote data, or workstations on a local network using a file server, name-server, etc. Models for several more general patterns of distributed processing are reduced to equivalent versions of the basic model in Section 3. Section 4 discusses the benefits of the added interface processor. The Conclusions also discusses the use of the model for optimal allocation of protocol functions.

Performance analysis using queueing models, sometimes quite large and elaborate, has become a well-developed subject (e.g. Reiser [2], Schwartz [3]). Elaborate models are justified by their fidelity to the details of operation, and their accuracy of prediction. The models of this paper have rather been made as small as possible, with the aim of simplifying the discussion of interface processor performance. Some important system cases are not covered; they are summarized at the end of Section 3.

2. Case 1: The Basic Model

The basic model represents a user-server workload in which N application tasks, running in a single workstation P, cycle through five steps, as follows.

Step	Mean Duration (sec)
1. Processing on P	x_P
2. Communictions protocol processing, either on P:	$x_C = cx_P$
or on F:	$x_F = bx_P$
3. Remote service delay (transmission and server)	$x_R = ax_P$
4. Protocol processing, as step 2	x_C or x_F
5. Processing as step 1.	x_P

If the processing times of send and receive are different, the average is used; this has no effect on the model solution. The steps make up a computation unit, and the throughput in computation units/sec. is λ_0 without F, or λ with F. We will determine and the throughput ratio (λ/λ_0) as functions of N, a, b, c, using the queueing models shown in Figure 2(b).

The network and the remote servers are assumed to be substantially unaffected by the workstation parameters either because a large part of their load is from other sources, or because they are not heavily loaded. Each task begins a new cycle as soon as it completes the last. For solution purposes processing steps 1, 2, 4, 5 will be assumed to have exponentially distributed execution times.

The model without F in Figure 2(b) is a standard M/M/1//N queueing model (see for example Kleinrock [4], section 3.8) with the solution

$$\lambda_0 = \frac{1}{x_p(1+c)}\left\{1-\left[\sum_{k=0}^{N}\left(\frac{1+c}{a}^k\right)\frac{N!}{(N-k)!}\right]^{-1}\right\} \quad (2.1)$$

With the interface processor F, a standard queueing network solution algorithm such as mean value analysis [5] will determine λ. In the notation for the algorithm let the subscript Z denote the devices P, F and R in turn.

Define

T_Z = mean time per computation unit spent at device Z

y_Z = execution steps at Z, per computation unit

$\lambda^{(N)}$= throughput for a system with N tasks

$n_Z^{(N)}$ = mean number of tasks waiting for a using device Z, in a system with N tasks.

The mean value analysis algorithm is as follows:

Step 1. Initialize N=1, $y_P=y_F=2$, $y_R=1$, $n_Z^{(0)} = 0$ for Z=P,F and R, and $T_R = x_R$.

Step 2. $T_Z = y_Z x_Z (1+n_Z^{(N-1)})$ for Z = P,F

Step 3. $\lambda^{(N)} = N/(T_P + T_F + T_R)$

Step 4. $n_Z^{(N)} = \lambda^{(N)} T_Z$ for Z = P,F, and R.

Step 5. Stop when the desired N is reached, else increment N by 1 and repeat from Step 2.

Some asymptotic results for large and small values of a and N have been assembled in Table 1. They result from elementary queueing consideration of simplified cases.

The number of parameters is reduced by one by normalizing x_P to unity, so $x_R=a$, $x_F=b$, $x_C=c$. The value of $\lambda(N,a,b,c)$ found this way can be used for other values of x_P by time-scaling, to give the throughput $(x_P)^{-1}\lambda(N,a,b,c)$. The ratio (λ/λ_0) is unaffected by the scaling and depends only on (N,a,b,c).

An example with c=0.2 and a=0.5 was solved, giving the values of (λ/λ_0) plotted in Figure 3 for values of N in the interval [1,10] and of b in the interval [0,2]. Figure 3 suggests that, to make λ/λ_0 large,

- larger N is better,

- b must not be too large, although b/c may exceed unity, meaning that F may be slower than P.

Solutions for other values of a and c show (as expected) that a large value of "a" reduces the range of N and b that give throughput improvement, and a large value of c enlarges the same range of values.

Table 1: Asymptotic Throughput Results

Condition	Asymptotic Result	
a=0	$\lambda_0 = 1/[2x_p(1+c)]$	(exact)
	$\lambda = (1-b^N)/[2x_p(1-b^{N+1})]$	(exact)
	$(\lambda/\lambda_0) = (1+c)(1-b^N)/(1-b^{N+1})$	(exact)
N=1	$\lambda_0 = 1/[x_p(2+a+2c)]$	(exact)
	$\lambda = 1/[x_p(2+a+2b)]$	(exact)
	$(\lambda/\lambda_0) = (2+a+2c)/(2+a+2b)$	(exact)
$N \to \infty$	$\lambda_0 = 1/[2x_p(1+c)]$	(exact)
$N\to\infty$, b small	$\lambda = 1/[2x_p]$	(limit as $b\to o$)
	$(\lambda/\lambda_0) = (1+c)$	(")
$N\to\infty$, b large	$\lambda = 1/[2x_F]$	(limit as $b\to o$)
	$(\lambda/\lambda_0) = (1+c)/b$	(")

Modelling a Real System

Poh, Stoneburner and Wood reported in [6] on a experiment comparing the performance of two different minicomputer front-end processors, linking a Honeywell H6000 host running a message-generating task to the Arpanet. Configuration A had host processing ($x_P$sec) and the network protocol NCP (x'_C sec) on the host, and further interface processing (x_{FA}sec) on a front-end processor. Configuration B had the same "host processing" on the host, and a different interface processor with both NCP (x'_F sec) and the same further processing (x'_{FB} sec, corresponding to x_{FA}). They called the configurations WIN and NFE respectively. The comparison is slightly different from our previous discussion because both configurations have front-end processors, but it does have a discrete protocol function (NCP) moved from the host to the front-end, which is our primary concern. The three-resources model described above applies to both cases, with parameters for A being $x_{PA} = x_P + x'_C$; x_{FA}; and $x_{RA} = x_R$ and the parameter for B being $x_{PB} = x_P$; $x_{FB} = x'_F + x'_{FB}$; and $x_{RB} = x_R$ sec.

The host processing times were found from the interference between communications processing and a CPU-intensive background benchmark (their Tables I, II and III), as $x_P = 0.030$ sec, and $x'_C = 0.039$ sec. Thus, moving the NCP protocol processing to F reduced host processing from 69 to 30 milliseconds per message, in their trials.

The interface processing was not fully reported, but was inferred from the saturation throughput with no load (their Table III). From some experimenting with the model it seems that saturation must have occurred in the front end, so to give the measured throughputs $\lambda_A = 2.62$, $\lambda_B = 4.42$, the values must be roughly $x_{FA}=0.190$, $x_{FB}=0.113$. However, a separate set of delay measurements in Tables IX and X, which agree well with x_{PA}, x_{PB} and x_{FB}, suggest that x_{FA} is less than 0.190. After some experimentation, x_{FA} was taken as 0.160 sec and x_R as 0.035 sec. Configuration B had flow control with a window size of 5 messages, which resulted in five messages being outstanding most of the time during the tests. This situation was modelled by five equivalent tasks instead of one, each with one message outstanding at a time.

The agreement of the models with the data is displayed for each configuration, with one and four connections - configuration B being modelled with five subtasks for each connection. The throughputs are:

Configuration	Connections	Throughputs Measurements	Throughputs Model
A	1	2.03/sec.	2.03/sec.
A	4	(1)2.62	3.05
B	1	(2)2.87	2.90
B	4	(1)4.42	4.41

Notes: (1) Row one of Table III, center of the range given, allowing for 7290 bits/message.

(2) From delay figures in Table IV, showing 5 messages in (4x56+1518) msec, $\lambda_B = 5/(1.742) = 2.87$

This agreement seems very reasonable. It may be concluded that the simple basic model can be applied to real data, with caution. The matter of flow control and of multiple messages outstanding is taken up in the next section, in Case 3.

3. Other Workload Patterns

The following four variations on the basic workload pattern have been reduced to equivalent basic models of the form discussed in Section 2 for Case 1.

Case 2: Variable Number of Active Tasks

User interaction time between computation units, or other reasons, may cause a task to enter a dormant state D as shown in Figure 4, with probability d and for mean time x_D. Then the number of active tasks varies with time. For solution purposes however, D and R can be amalgamated by increasing x_R by dx_D which is the mean dormant time per computation unit; this gives the basic model again. The same approach will model a random idle time when a user takes a break, or when processing is undertaken at an attached device (provided the device is used by only one task or is lightly loaded).

A second cause of variation of N is a rush-hour pattern, in which N varies with the time of day. Then it is more natural to fix N at the largest value and study it as a worst case.

Case 3: Multiple Messages per Computation Unit

There are two key parameters,

m = messages sent and received per computation unit

f = average number of messages (and associated processing steps) active at one time, for one task.

and there may be three different subcases as follows.

Case 3(a): If the computation unit is a concatenation of subunits as illustrated in Figure 5(a), (each with the Case-1 execution pattern), then each subunit is equivalent to a unit in Case 1 with subunit execution times x_P, x_C and x_F. Let λ' be the solution to this Case 1 problem; then $\lambda=\lambda'/m$.

Case 3(b): For more general send-receive patterns (such as that illustrated in Figure 5(b)) the same kind of subunits are overlapped in time. The workstation performs just as if it had a larger number of active tasks - let us call them subtasks - each of which can execute one computation subunit at a time. This is equivalent to a Case-1 model with N' tasks, with;

$$N' = pN \quad (p > 1)$$

p can be chosen as the largest number of messages in parallel that can occur in practice. Whatever p is chosen, a dormant state D is added as in Case 2, to account for periods when a task has less than p messages outstanding. The dormant period has d=1 and x_D is determined to give the correct average number f of active subtasks. The mean number of dormant subtasks is (from f) $N' - fN = (p-f)N$, while by Little's result it is λx_D, so

$$x_D = (p-f)N/\lambda \tag{3.1}$$

This value for x_D can be determined iteratively, solving the model using x_D (beginning with $x_D = 0$) and determining a new x_D from (3.1). For large x_R it has the limit $x_D \approx x_R((p/f) - 1)$.

Case 3(c): Flow control is an important aspect of network performance, which places a limit of f_{max} on the outstanding messages. This gives Case 3(b), with $p=f_{max}$. If one task may be communicating on several separate flow-controlled connections then p is the sum of the limits.

Case 4: In cases 1-3 there is some kind of message received for each one sent, even if only an acknowledgement. If this is not so, then "virtual messages" requiring zero processing time are inserted to balance the send and receive activity in each computation unit, and the appropriate earlier case is used. There are two parameters:

p = the resulting mean messages per computation unit, including "virtual messages"

e = the resulting fraction of messages which ae "virtual"

Once p and e are determined, Case 3(b) can be applied, using execution times x_P, x_F, x_C, x_R reduced by the factor $(1-e)$. The mean value solution will only be approximate, because the distributions ae no longer exponential. In some circumstances p and e may be measured directly as:

$$p = \text{mean of max } [\tilde{p}_s, \tilde{p}_r]$$

$$e = (\text{mean of } |\tilde{p}_s - \tilde{p}_r|)/p$$

where $\tilde{p}_s$ = messages sent per computation unit (mean = p_r)

$\tilde{p}_r$ = messages received (mean = p_r)

Suitable assumptions also give models for p and e - two examples will be described. First, suppose $\tilde{p}_s = 1$ or 2, with probability q for the value 1, and $\tilde{p}_s$ and $\tilde{p}_r$ are independent. Then a simple enumeration of the four possibilities gives $p = 2 - qq'$, $e = q + q' - 2qq'$. Alternatively, suppose $\tilde{p}_s$ and $\tilde{p}_r$ are geometrically distributed and independent. This gives a Markovian model which yields (see Appendix):

$$p = [(1+p_r)(1+p_s)]/[p_r+p_s+p_rp_s]+e \qquad (3.2)$$

$$e = [p_r+p_s+2p_rp_s]/[p_rp_s(p_r+p_s)]$$

<u>Case 5</u>: It is now possible to remove the limitation of the user-server workload pattern, and to consider a more general pattern of cooperating tasks with communiction among peers (Figure 6). Consider first an analogy to the basic case, with send and receive alternating in all tasks. The computation unit has two parts. In the first part a task executes a processing step and then suspends itself to send a message:

Step 1. Process at P (x_p sec.)

Step 2. Protocol process at P or F (x_C or s_F sec.)

Step 3. Transmission (x_R sec.)

In the second part the <u>receiving task</u> in another workstation continues the unit:

Step 4. Protocol process, as 2

Step 5. Process, as 1.

If the cooperating workloads are <u>symmetrical</u> we need to model only one station, as before, and let steps 4 and 5 be executed on it. This corresponds exactly to a loop-back test on a workstation, except that the network delay s_R takes its operational value. But this is just the model of Case 1, with x_R now reduced to represent only the one-way network delay. All the generalizations of Cases 2-4 may now be applied, to reduce other general cooperative workload patterns to Case 1.

Some important workload cases do not reduce to our Case 1. An example is a background workload running on the workstations, not using the network; it requires a more elaborate model with a second class of task running only on P. Also, if there are other workstation devices, which may limit performance, they must be represented explicitly in the model.

<u>The Performance Impact of an Interface Processor</u>

The basic model of Section 2 will now be examined to further characterize the function $(\lambda/\lambda_0) = g(N,a,b,c,)$. In particular we ask, for a given c and N, and improvement level k, what (a,b) values give:

$$(\lambda/\lambda_0) > (1+k) \qquad (4.1)$$

For the asymptotic cases in Table 1, the conditions corresponding to (4.1) are given in Table 2. Notice that if $N=1$ the contours of (λ/λ_0) in the (a,b) plane are straight lines; Figure 7(a) shows the contours for $c=0.2$ and $N=1$.

Table 2: Asymptotic Contours $(\lambda/\lambda_0) = 1+k$

Condition	Asymptotic Contour
$a = 0$	$kb^{N+1} - (1+c)b^N + (c-k) = 0$ (4.2)
small a, small b	$a \simeq 2N(c-k)/k$ (contours become roughly perpendicular to a axis)
$N = 1$	$ak + 2b(1+k) = 2(c-k)$
$N \to \infty$, b large	(limit) $b = (1+c)/(1+k)$
$N \to \infty$, a small	$b \simeq (1+c)/(1+k)$ (contours become roughly perpendicular to b axis)
$b = 0$	$\frac{[1 - g(1/a)]}{[1 - g(1+c)/a)]} = \frac{(1+k)}{(1+c)}$ where $g(w) = \left[\sum_{k=0}^{N} w^k N!/(N-k)!\right]^{-1}$ (solve numerically)

In general, it is necessary to compute values of (λ/λ_0) to find the contours which bound the regions satisfying (4.1). Figure 7(b) shows an example for c=0.2, and N=6.

Notice that

- the region for any k is much bigger for N=6 than for N=1 (compare Figures 7(a) and 7(b)).

- there is a critical "a" (approximately a=N for large N) above which no improvement is possible.

- a straight line joining the intercepts of each contour would be a moderately good approximation, although it errs on the optimistic side.

The intercepts are a* and b*; b* is given by result (4.2) in Table 2 with (λ/λ_0) replaced by (1+k), and solved for b, and a* is found by solving as usual with b=0, interpolating over a to obtain the desired (λ/λ_0).

Conclusions

The basic model gives the interaction of four important factors in determining the performance advantage of an interface processor. Some unpromising-looking combinations, for example with the interface processor somewhat slower then the host in doing protocol processing, are shown to perform quite well.

The optimal allocation of layer functions in a layered protocol scheme (like the Ethernet protocols, or the OSI basic reference model [7] can be determined by a search process using the basic model of this paper. Although the model is approximate, it is closer to the real issue of optimization (i.e., performance) than the communication-minimization approach of Stone [8] or Haessig and Jenny [9].

Acknowledgements

This research was supported by the Natural Sciences and Engineering Research Council of Canada under its Strategic Grants Program for Computers and Communications.

References

[1] H.J. Hindin, "Dual-chip sets for vital link for Ethernet local-network scheme", Electronics, Oct. 6, 1982, pp.89-91.

[2] M. Reiser, "Performance evaluation of data communication systems", Proc. IEEE, vol. 70, pp. 171-196, 1982.

[3] M. Schwartz, Computer Communication Network Design and Analysis, Prentice-Hall, 1977.

[4] L. Kleinrock, Queuing Systems, v I", Wiley, 1975.

[5] M. Reiser, S.S. Lavenberg, "Mean-value analysis of closed multichain queueing networks", J.A.C.M., vol. 27, pp. 313-322, 1980.

[6] S. Poh, P.D. Stoneburner, D.C. Wood, "A performance study of a network front end", Proc. Sixth Data Communications Symposium, pp. 126-136, Nov. 1979, IEEE Catalog 79CH1405-0 CSCB/C.

[7] International Standards Organization, Data Processing - Open Systems Interconnection - Basic Reference Model, Draft Proposal ISO/DP7498, 1980.

[8] H.S. Stone, S.H. Bokhari, "Control of Distributed Processes", Computer, July 1978, pp. 97-106.

[9] K. Haessig, C.J. Jenny, "Partitioning and Allocating Computational Objects in Distributed Computing Systems", Information Processing 80, North-Holland, 1980, pp. 593-598.

Appendix to Section 3 (Case 4)

The process by which the number of send and receive operations are generated can in this case (geometric $\tilde{p}_s$, $\tilde{p}_r$) be modelled by two independent discrete Markov chains, which stay in state 1 with probability q_s or q_r to generate another message, or make a transition to state 0 to stop. This joint process with 4 states is illustrated in Figure 8. A little thought shows that p is the mean number of steps needed to reach (0,0) from (1,1), while e is the total mean number of steps spent in (0,1) and (1,0), along the way. The results (3.2) are then found using the intermediate results:

- $p_s = (1-q_s)^{-1}$, $p_r = (1-q_r)^{-1}$, so $q_s = 1-p_s^{-1}$ and $q_r = 1-p_r^{-1}$;
- mean time in (0,0) = $(1 - q_s q_r)$;
- probability of going to (0,0) via (1,0) is $(1-q_s)/(2-q_r-q_s)$;
- mean time at (1,0) in that case is $(1-q_s)^{-1}$;
- probability of going to (0,0) via (0,1) is $(1- q_r)/(2-q_r-q_s)$;
- mean time at (0,1) in that case is $(1-q_r)^{-1}$.

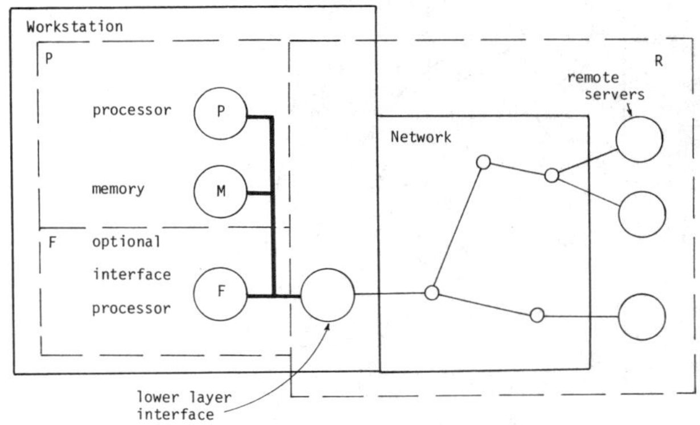

Figure 1(a) Workstation/Network structure in the Basic Model, Partitioned into Resources P, F, and R.

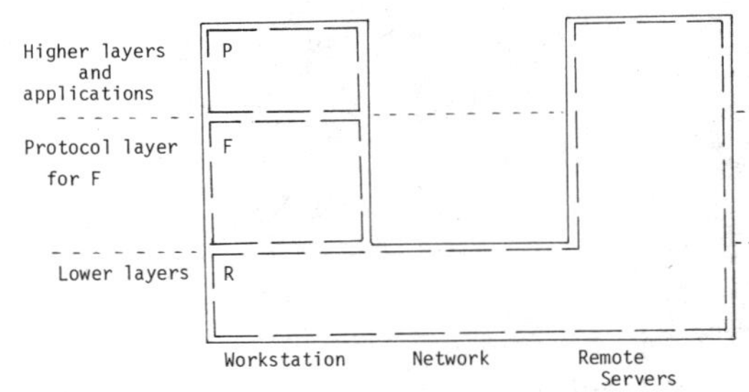

Figure 1(b) Protocol Layers Executed by P, F, and R (Basic Case).

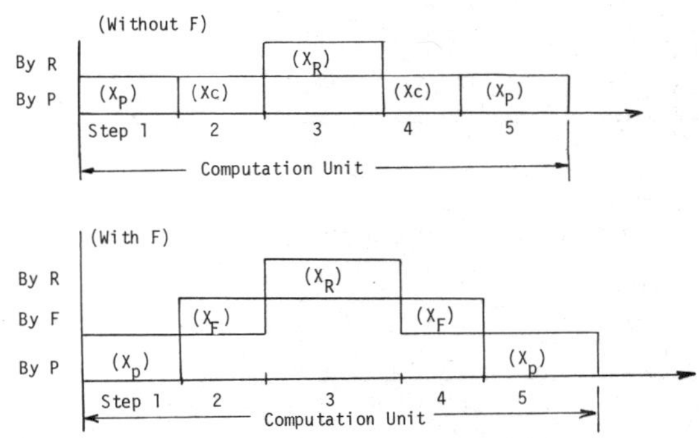

Figure 2(a) The Time Structure of a Computation Unit in the Case 1 Model. Step 2 is the Protocol processing.

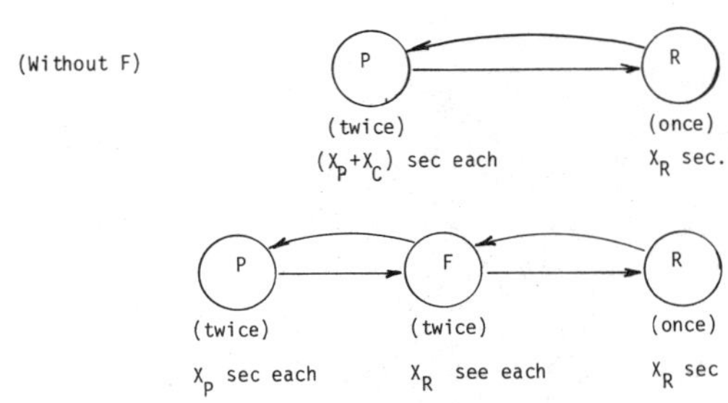

Figure 2(b) Queueing Models for Case 1

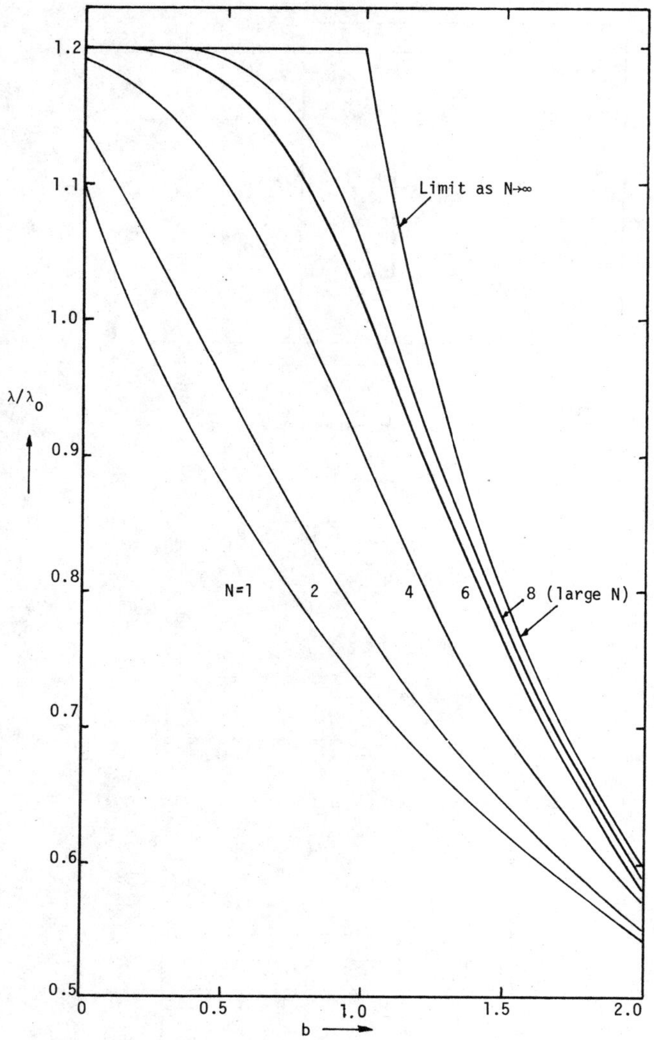

Figure 3 Performance Improvement Ratio (λ/λ_o) versus b, for c=0.2, a=0.5, and various N.

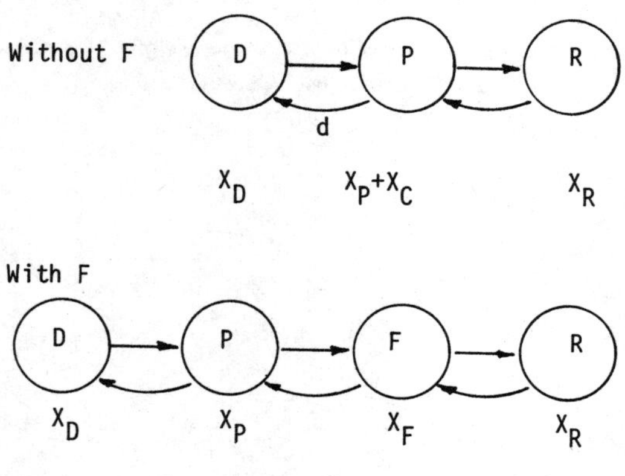

Figure 4 An Additional Dormant State (Case 2)

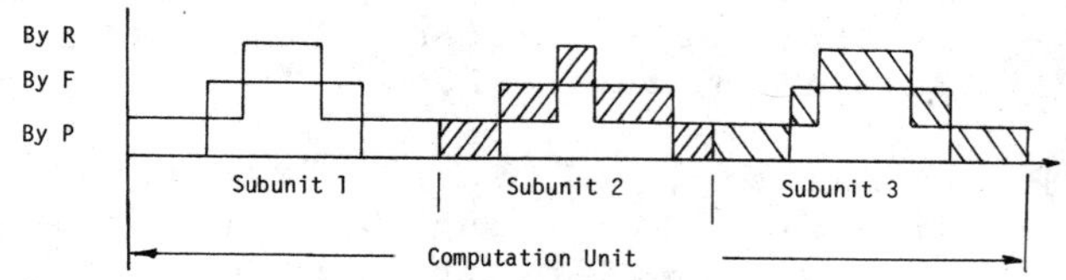

Figure 5(a) Multiple Messages: Concatenation of Simple Subunits

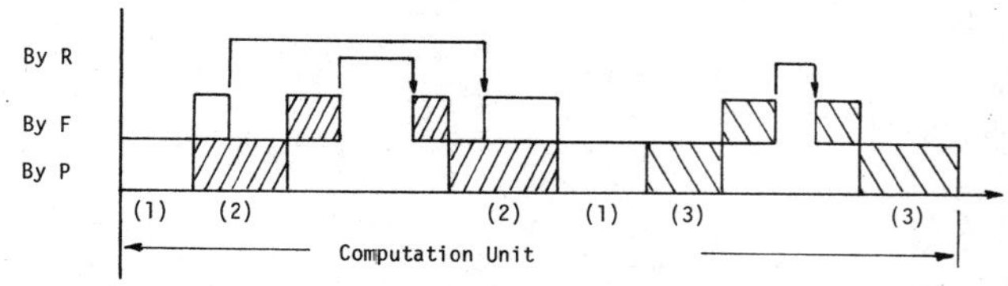

Figure 5(b) Multiple Messages: General Pattern

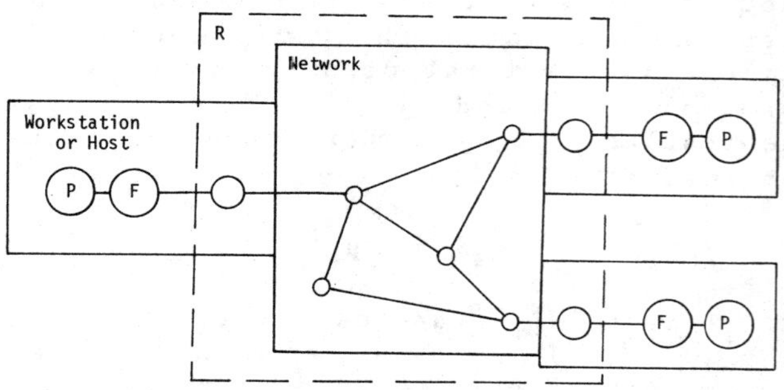

Figure 6. Communication among Peers (Case 5)

(R represents only the lower protocol layers)

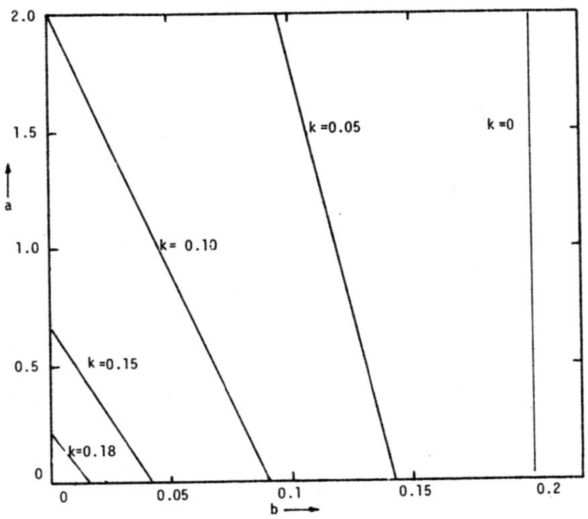

Figure 7(a) Contours of Performance Improvement with the Interface Processor, for N=1, c=0.2 (Values of a and b giving $(\lambda/\lambda_o) = (1+k)$)

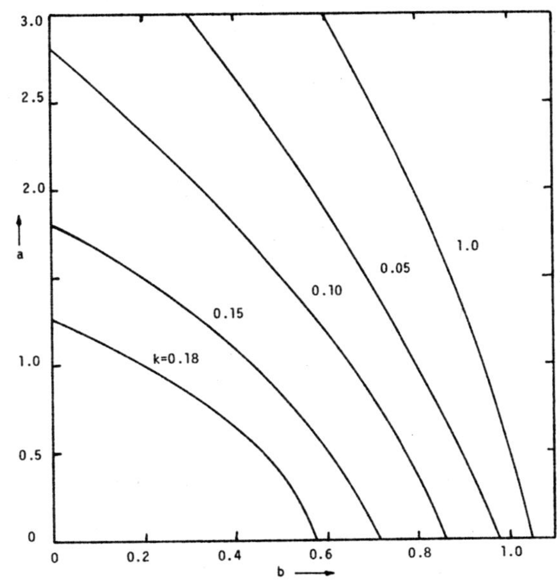

Figure 7(b) Contours of Performance Improvement with the Interface Processor, for N=6 c=0.2 (Values of a and b giving $(\lambda/\lambda o)=(1+k)$)

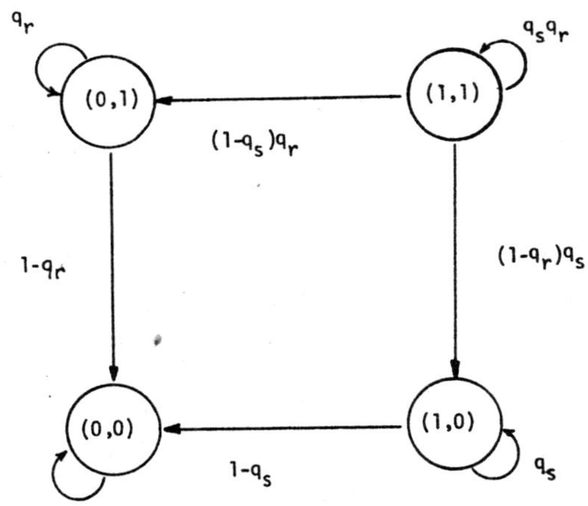

Figure 8 Markov Chain Model for the Appendix

Late Paper

OPTICAL STORAGE OF PAGE IMAGES AND PICTORIAL DATA -
OPPORTUNITIES AND NEEDED ADVANCES IN INFORMATION RETRIEVAL

William R. Nugent
Jessica R. Harding

Automated Systems Office
Library of Congress

ABSTRACT

We describe two current development projects at the Library of Congress using high-density optical storage, both of which require more advanced and improved computer-based information retrieval methodologies than existing bibliographic retrieval systems. A much greater emphasis will be placed on the information content of the articles rather than on the broad subject categories in general use for computer retrieval citations to book materials. Needed approaches include the linking of selected external reference sources and the extraction of character-encoded index information from the page images by OCR techniques. Our position is that extremely high density storage of articles in a single subject area requires a finer resolution in the retrieval system accessing the material. A single side of a 12-inch digital optical disk, for example, can hold 15 years of the Journal of the ACM.

1.0 THE DIGITAL OPTICAL DISK PROJECT

1.1 Text Materials to be Stored as Digitized Images

The Library of Congress has embarked upon a pilot project using digital optical disk to store the digitized images of one million pages of text over a two-year period and provide rapid access, display and printing of those images to seven work stations located in the three buildings of the Library.

High-use current periodicals will be given initial emphasis and will include journals in science, technology, and business; newspapers in German, Portuguese, Japanese, Thai, French, and Hebrew; government documents such as the Budget of the United States and the Congressional Record; United States Agriculture Decisions and Social Security Rulings from 1960-1975; maps, atlases, and microfilm, selected manuscript collections and music. Currently, these periodicals are in such demand that copies are not always available due to the large number of requests.

At the document preparation station, printed library materials will be entered into the Library Of Congress Information System (LOCIS) database with the document number corresponding to the Library retrieval number. A machine-readable batch index sheet will be generated as the leading page of each identifiable record. Documents are then batched and sent to the input station where they will be scanned and digitized at 300 lines per inch resolution, by a high speed scanner. During this scanning process, the machine-readable batch index sheet is also read, and this indexing information is sent to the Library of Congress indexing data file. The resulting images are temporarily stored on a digital magnetic buffer where the images are inspected for quality and proper sequence. The data on the magnetic disk is then transferred onto digital optical disk. The 12-inch disk to be used has a storage capacity of 10^{10} bits which is equivalent to about 20,000 book pages, 12,500 periodical pages, or typically two to three years of a weekly news magazine.

The Library's central computer system will support user searching via access points in the Library's existing information retrieval system (LOCIS) and will interface with the image storage system to provide access to the text of the articles by means of document control numbers. After the first page is displayed on the CRT, the user will be able to page through the article, using commands similar to existing LOCIS commands which allow similar movement within the bibliographic search files. The user will have the option to command an offline batch printer to print those pages that he wishes to receive in hard copy form.

1.2 Text Access Methods to be Applied

There are three text access methods which will be experimented with in the pilot project. The first two methods represent the two extremes in terms of utility and cost for the majority of the high use periodical materials which will be stored on the system and for which no existing search tools are available on the Library's computer system. The third method is for the small fraction of this material for which the Library's Congressional Research Service has already provided computer search tools in connection with its Citation file, a data base of citations to current material relating to public policy, among which are citations and brief abstracts of articles in some high-use periodicals.

The first method, which we call the "Bound Volume" approach, is the digital optical disk equivalent to the usual library practice of collecting a year's output of a periodical and binding the issues together into a single physical volume, which volume becomes the item accessed and used by the reader. To use the previous example of the Journal of the ACM, a researcher searching the computer literature would use external reference guides such as H.W. Wilson's Applied Science and Technology Index, literature citations he had noted, personal recollection, or knowledge that a development of interest occurred in a particular year and was reported upon in JACM. In a conventional library he would then request a particular year of JACM, and a bound volume of issues published that year would be delivered to his reader's desk. Upon delivery, he would have available all of the access tools which were a normal part of that bound volume: successive tables of contents with article titles, authors, and corresponding page numbers; possibly an annual index of titles, authors, and in some less likely cases, arrangements by subject area or by permuted title terms, also with issue and page number pointers. In some cases, a succession of illustrated cover pictures with text highlighting feature articles or special topics would also be present and useful.

The digital optical disk equivalent to this approach represents the least cost method in terms of human data preparation work of manual indexing, abstracting or adding information other than that on the printed pages. Only periodical identification, issue and article identification and page number data need be keyed entries in character encoded form.

If a disk having 15 years of the Journal of the ACM were available, its primary point of access would be the journal name and year. This information would be the primary method of selecting a particular disk and confining the page-images accessed to those corresponding to one year of the 15-year collection of the example. Once this had been established, the reader could be given a selection menu to view the annual index if present, successive table of contents, successive covers, successive first pages of articles, unconstrained successive page-images, or a page-image corresponding to a particular page number of the original document. Minimum extra information is added and other than some minor conveniences of direct page access and the avoidance of handling the generally large and heavy bound volumes, the user would be performing the same operations which he would apply to a physical volume of bound issues. But while a significant savings in library shelf space is obtained, this approach offers no essential advantage or disadvantage to the user of such information over that of using the physical bound volume.

The second method, which we call the "index and abstract" approach, requires a costly intellectual-labor-intensive effort whereby a person familiar with the subject areas covered by the periodical reads the articles and enters index terms and a brief abstract into the computer, and as in the previous case, keys it to the periodical to which it refers, and additionally to the appropriate page numbers of the article. While this produces a quality access tool to the articles on the digital optical disk, its cost exceeds that of scanning and storing the page images of the article.

The third approach is used when a pre-existing search tool exists on the central computer system, as may be the case for some recent articles on public policy such as those indexed and abstracted by LC's Congressional Research Service and searchable on the Library's central computer. In this case, the minimum-required information of the "bound volume" approach is created and a simple flag is placed in the display screen to indicate that a particular article is available on digital optical disk and this flag is made to point to a corresponding disk address.

1.3 Problems With Existing Text Access Methods and Approaches to Improvement

Most library-oriented information retrieval systems emphasize access to books rather than articles in periodicals and tend to follow conventions of cataloging based on long-established traditions of physical card catalogs. Such traditions tend to limit subject access since each additional subject term used required an additional catalog card.

With an entirely electronic system, there are several new approaches of promise which will be examined during the course of this pilot project. One is the linking of the character-encoded reference guides to periodical literature, now becoming available from publishers, to the corresponding printed guides. A second method is computer-based automatic indexing methods which would process the full text of the digitized page images after performing optical character recognition of the page images. The provision of the full text of articles rather than merely bibliographic citations to them is a major improvement by itself, but the automatic extraction of index and abstract information from this same full text is the most needed future improvement.

2.0 THE ANALOG VIDEODISC PROJECT

2.1 Pictorial Materials to be Stored as Video Images

In addition to storing digitally scanned images of printed pages, another aspect of the pilot project is to convert more than 40,000 images from paper print motion pictures, motion picture stills, prints, photographs and posters, and audio tapes to five laser videodiscs. An additional non-image component of this project is the recording of musical concerts on digital and laser-based audio Compact Discs. Some of the items under consideration to be filmed and incorporated into the videodisc are:

o 4,000 Cabinet of American Illustration drawings, cartoons, cover designs, sketches for posters and illustrations for magazines, novels and children's books that were executed chiefly between 1880 and 1910 representing approximately 200 artists.

o 4,000 ink, watercolor, gouache, pencil and crayon by American artists of political and humorous cartoons published in American newspapers and magazines from 1860 to the present.

o 600 glass lantern slides and approximately 250 black and white photo prints from nitrate negatives.

o Almost 30,000 glass negatives of the Detroit Publishing Company of views and scenes of the United States, copies of negatives, reproductions and paintings.

o 58 large format copyright deposit color photoprints made by adding color lithographically to black and white negatives.

o 5 albums of Detroit Publishing Company mounted photoprints of views of the United States and two foreign countries.

o 1,687 Farm Security Administration and Office of War Information color slides and transparencies of the United States and Puerto Rico capturing Depression-era America, ca. 1939-1943, which are presently in cold storage to preserve them.

o 2,250 photoprints of the Middle East presented to the Library by Abdul-Hamid II of views and scenes of the Ottoman Empire, ca. 1893.

o 2,500 architectural drawings in varied media of the Architectural Drawings Collection.

o 4,000 political posters from 1965 to 1980, many in Chinese arranged by country.

o Two television videotape productions.

o 91,000 motion picture stills.

While preservation is the primary objective of this part of the pilot project, the videodiscs of the non-text collections will provide simultaneous advantages in on-line reference retrieval allowing researchers to survey a large quantity of material without the frequent handling necessitated by manual searches. Because of the fragility of some of the items, such as large posters, glass slides, nitrate film and photographic negatives, they are not now generally accessible to researchers.

2.2 Image Access Methods to be Applied

The Library will investigate the use of the disk in conjunction with a computer-generated captioning method. In this system, the caption identifying the image would be typed into a terminal connected to a microcomputer and stored on a "Mini-Wini", a small magnetic disk using the fixed (e.g., non-removable Winchester disk technology and storing up to 20 megabytes of data.)

Although a data base using an enhanced Library of Congress cataloging format (MARC) is desired it is intended that a separate and abbreviated data base will be established. The user will consult a printed index, determine the pictorial items he wishes to view, key in the pertinent title, creator and date information, and the images of the selected items will appear on the screen for viewing.

One advantage of this configuration of establishing a data base separate from the videodisc is that the information can be updated or changed at any time. Descriptions of the items displayed will be electronically overlaid on the videodisc images.

2.3 Problems With Existing Image Access Methods and Approaches to Improvement

Libraries, by their nature, have tended to emphasize book materials and the cataloging practices common to book materials for all objects in their collections. Just as a chapter gains its importance by being part of a book, so too a particular photograph or a particular work of art has tended to be subjugated to the collection of which it is a part, in terms of cataloging or indexing. Also following book practice, the form, size, and medium of pictorial items has tended to dominate description of content. Effective image retrieval, however, requires identification of and access by the things in the picture. In defense of these historical practices, however, it has not been cost-feasible and is not now cost-feasible to apply the same effort level to the cataloging and indexing of a single pictorial item that is applied to a book of much larger content.

One near term improvement would involve the use of free form descriptions of content, much like those in the catalogs of commercial art galleries and art auction houses, with computer-based content analysis of the full text descriptions. In the longer term, however, it appears that image recognition methods based upon artificial intelligence and scene analysis will become necessary to distinguish the items in a two-dimensional image and their salient characteristics. This is a very broad and pressing problem which is not at all particular to libraries. There are now increasing volumes of digitized images being beamed down from satellites which must still be manually examined, classified and indexed by human photo-interpreters. We believe that the automated processing of image information is the greatest challenge of the next decade.

3.0 A RETRIEVAL SCENARIO FOR THE LATE 1980's

An important beginning is being made by the Library of Congress' pilot project which we believe is the precursor of a major change in information retrieval systems. By placing primary information items themselves on computer-accessible media, rather than merely references to these information items, a central information retrieval system is potentially made feasible which is both comprehensive and medium-independent. A future researcher should be able to operate a single multi-function terminal and retrieve all items relevant to his topic of interest, independently of the medium that houses these items. Retrieved items would include the full text of relevant monographs, reports and journal articles; relevant pictorial material including photographs, works of art, maps, and motion picture and television documentaries; and the sound of related music, lectures and speeches.

In earlier years, the lack of effective information storage devices was the barrier to such comprehensive information retrieval systems. Today the storage devices exist and the software systems to orchestrate these multiple devices are the only missing links. It is one object of the Library of Congress' pilot project in optical storage to create some of the early links needed.

4.0 REFERENCES

1. Betz, Elizabeth W., Graphic Materials: Rules for Describing Original Items and Historical Collections, Library of Congress, Washington, D.C., 1982, 155p.

2. Betz, Elizabeth W., Subject Headings Used in the Library of Congress Prints and Photographs Division, (Preliminary Edition), Library of Congress, Washington, D.C. April 1980, 479p.

3. Goldstein, Charles M., "Optical Disk Technology and Information," Science, February 12, 1982, pp. 862-869.

4. Nugent, William R., "Application of Digital Optical Disks in Library Preservation and Reference," Proceedings, 1983 National Computer Conference, Anaheim, California, May 16-19, 1983, AFIPS Press, pp. 771-775.

5. Nugent, William R., "Optical Disk Technology," Minutes of the One Hundredth Meeting Association of Research Libraries, Scottsdale, Arizona, May 1972, pp. 62-83.

6. Nugent, William R. and Harding, Jessica R., "Advances in Videodisc Technology for Public Access to Non-Print Collections" to be published Proceedings, First Annual Conference of American Library Association Library and Information Technology Association LITA), September 17-21, 1983.

7. Mole, Dennis, "The Videodisc as a Pilot Project of the Public Archives of Canada," Videodisc/Videotex, Volume 1, Number 3, Summer 1981, pp. 154-161.

8. "Museum of Fine Arts, Boston, Selections From the Permanent Collection," Videodisc Projects Directory, Videodisc/Videotex, Volume 2, Number 1, Winter 1982, pp. 57-58.

Author Index

77 044